ARCHAEOLOGICAL RESOURCE MANAGEMENT IN THE UK

Archaeological Resource Management in the UK
An Introduction

Edited by JOHN HUNTER
and IAN RALSTON

SUTTON PUBLISHING

INSTITUTE OF FIELD ARCHAEOLOGISTS

First published in the United Kingdom in 1993 by
Sutton Publishing Ltd
Phoenix Mill · Thrupp · Stroud · Gloucestershire · GL5 2BU

Paperback edition first published in 1997

Reprinted in 2001

British Library Cataloguing in Publication Data
A catalogue record for this book is available from the British Library

ISBN 0 7509 1607 9

To Margaret and Sandra

Typeset in Times 10/11 point
Typesetting and origination by
Alan Sutton Publishing Ltd
Printed and bound in Great Britain by
J.H. Haynes & Co. Ltd, Sparkford.

CONTENTS

PREFACE

In the twenty-two chapters of this book, we have asked our colleagues to try to draw together diverse aspects of the structure, outlook and operation of archaeology in the UK at the present time, and in some instances to consider its relevance to modern society. We felt, on the basis of archaeology's transformation during the last two decades, that there was need for stock to be taken and an overview given. The contexts of British archaeological practice have altered radically since the late 1970s: changes in planning controls, heritage legislation, land-use practices and social awareness have drawn the archaeologist into important new professional arenas affecting the whole of archaeology's broad spectrum, from legislation to tourism, from churches to underwater sites, as well as in the processes by which archaeological sites and landscapes are selected for examination, academic study, preservation and public interpretation. Nowhere, it seemed, had these changes been monitored, listed and commented upon in any detail in a single volume.

Both of us have also been directly concerned with the teaching of cultural resource management at our respective universities. One of the problems has always been in trying to assemble not only the strands of the subject itself, but also the published sources. There are a few glossy books that deal with the broader generalities, but little that charts the development of the individual components that make up the whole. Such information survives in our files as short papers from journals, pamphlets, leaflets, government circulars and advice notes, unreadable statutes and newspaper cuttings, now mostly inaccessible or obscure and almost invariably out of print. This book will, in part, serve as a permanent replacement for such collections.

To some extent this is also a history of public archaeology. Our present students entered this life in the mid-1970s when archaeology was shrill with the voices of rescue archaeology and implications surveys; and when hundreds of people were prepared to work at a moment's notice for next to nothing. But today the students' first encounter with the subject belongs to an age of contractors, curators, tendering, mitigation strategies and Planning Policy Guidance Note 16. This book also recounts why practices have changed.

The chapters and extensive bibliography do not constitute a textbook *per se* of archaeological resource management. Rather we hope to have provided a handbook that will be of use to students and colleagues both in the archaeological and heritage worlds. We trust, too, that the book will serve as a *vade mecum* to the increasing range of professionals in neighbouring subjects – e.g. planning, development, environmental assessment, engineering and recreation – for whom contact with field archaeology in one of its new guises has become a more or less regular occurrence.

The title includes, as far as we are aware, a new coining in the phrase 'archaeological resource management', an amalgam of two phrases currently used as definitions: cultural resource management, and archaeological heritage management. The former is a linguistic immigrant from North America already used to describe the content of courses at a number of UK universities and to identify one of the 'Areas of Competence' for Membership of the Institute of Field Archaeologists. It is thus reasonably embedded in English as a challenger to archaeological heritage management, again used in the title of university courses (IFA 1992) and in publications (Cleere 1989). In trying to find a form of words that fairly reflected the contents of this book, we were keen to avoid misrepresentation, whether by commission or omission. Thus 'archaeological' seemed preferable to 'cultural' as a description of the material covered. Furthermore, at a time of increasing recognition of the erosion of the archaeological record, we considered it more appropriate to focus attention on the significance of archaeological remains as 'resources' rather than as 'heritage'.

This book is the first to carry the joint imprint of the Institute of Field Archaeologists, an organization now a decade old that links archaeologists working in different sectors of British archaeology (central and local government, education, the private sector and charitable trusts, as well as the self-employed). The IFA now serves as the most important forum in the UK for the development of archaeological practice and professionalism. Although not its sole function, external pressures, especially politically inspired changes, have ensured that concern with the practice of archaeology has been central to the IFA's deliberations during its first ten years. We are grateful to the IFA's councillors in session 1991–92 for allowing us to persuade them to devote some of the IFA's modest financial resources to underwriting the production of this collection of essays, which seek to take stock of the transitions and to provide a guide to the new terrain.

Although most of our authors are IFA members, the contents of this book represent the authors' personal opinions and must not be taken either as an official IFA perspective (except in the case of direct citation of its documentation) or as that of their employers. It will rapidly become clear to the reader that the management of archaeological resources is a subject undergoing rapid evolution in which professional attitudes, ethical positions, and consideration of the relationships between theory and practice are all actively debated. We have attempted to exercise editorial control as lightly as possible in the matter of allowing place for different opinions, so that we hope that something of the competing flavours of, and tensions within, contemporary archaeological resource management are apparent.

We are grateful to our contributors, all of whom produced copy to a very tight timetable – many of them exactly on schedule. Our thanks also go to Ann Hamlin, DoE (Northern Ireland), for her assistance with our contribution; David Breeze, Historic Scotland, for advice on terminology; Bill Finlayson, Manager, CFA, University of Edinburgh, for making seemingly countless incompatible disks readable; and to Mark Pollard, University of Bradford, for access to facilities that much simplified final editing. Rupert Harding of Alan Sutton Publishing Ltd guided our relations with the publisher expertly.

Finally Ellie, Natalie, Edward, Tom, Tom and Ben deserve the apologies of two fathers who were just a little preoccupied over Christmas 1992.

John Hunter and Ian Ralston
Bradford, January 1993

THE CONTRIBUTORS

David Baker, Conservation and Archaeology Officer, Bedfordshire County Council, Bedford (Chapter 10)

Robert Bewley, Head of National Mapping Programme, Royal Commission on the Historical Monuments of England, Swindon (Chapter 18)

Carl Bianco, Cathedrals Officer, The Cathedrals Fabric Commission, London (Chapter 9)

David Breeze, Chief Inspector of Ancient Monuments, Historic Scotland, Edinburgh (Chapter 5)

Henry Cleere, World Heritage Co-ordinator, International Council on Monuments and Sites, Paris (Chapter 11)

Simon Collcutt, Managing director of an independent archaeological consultancy practice (Chapter 15)

Timothy Darvill, British Property Federation Professor of Property Development and Archaeology, Bournemouth University (Chapter 16)

Antony Firth, Researcher, Faculty of Law, Southampton University (Chapter 7)

Peter Fowler, Professor of Archaeology, University of Newcastle upon Tyne (Chapter 1)

David Fraser, Principal Inspector of Ancient Monuments, English Heritage, London (Chapter 3)

Chris Gaffney, Partner of Geophysical Surveys of Bradford (Chapter 18)

John Gater, Partner of Geophysical Surveys of Bradford (Chapter 18)

Jane Grenville, Lecturer in Archaeology, University of York (Chapter 12)

Ann Hamlin, Principal Inspector of Historic Monuments, Environmental Services, Department of the Environment (Northern Ireland), Belfast (Chapter 4 and Appendix to Part Two)

Catherine Hills, Lecturer in Archaeology, University of Cambridge (Chapter 19)

Ian Hodder, Reader in Archaeology, University of Cambridge (Chapter 2)

John Hunter, Senior Lecturer in Archaeology, University of Bradford (Chapter 4)

Andrew Lawson, Unit Director of the Trust for Wessex Archaeology Ltd, Salisbury (Chapter 14)

Ian Longworth, Keeper, Department of Prehistoric and Romano-British Antiquities, British Museum, London (Chapter 6)

Lesley Macinnes, Principal Inspector of Ancient Monuments, Historic Scotland, Edinburgh (Chapter 22)

Mike Parker Pearson, Lecturer in Archaeology, University of Sheffield (Chapter 20)

Susan Pearce, Professor of Museum Studies, University of Leicester (Chapter 21)

Ian Ralston, Senior Lecturer in Archaeology, University of Edinburgh (Chapter 4)

Ian Shepherd, Regional Archaeologist, Grampian Regional Council, Aberdeen (Chapter 10)

Bill Startin, Principal Inspector of Ancient Monuments, English Heritage, London (Chapter 17)

Roger Suddards, Chairman, Hammond Suddards Research Ltd, Bradford; Commissioner, English Heritage (Chapter 8)

Roger Thomas, Inspector of Ancient Monuments, English Heritage, London (Chapter 13)

CHAPTER 1

ARCHAEOLOGY IN A MATRIX

Peter Fowler

INTRODUCTION

Archaeology itself may be about the past; archaeological resource management (ARM), by definition, is in the present (Cleere 1989). Furthermore, it is based on an assumption that there will be a future, indeed that the future will require a past. 'Surely,' pleaded Colin Renfrew at the Cambridge Interpretive Archaeologies conference in September 1991, 'we can at least all agree that the past happened?' I doubt it. In the First World's age of multiple everything, not least of eclectic personal consumption, a concept of the past is probably twitching its mortal last; post-modernity rules and pasts proliferate (Harvey 1989; Kolb 1990; Boyne and Rattansi 1990).

Such a vision is a long way from the traditions of historicity, the corridors of absolutism, in which archaeology has developed (Daniel 1975). Archaeologists found things; some found out things. They loaded their things into museums; curators put some on display and told those who chose to come what had been found out about those things, for example, that they were made of bronze and, interpretatively, that they were 'Chalcolithic'. Very helpful, big deal. Sometimes both archaeologists and curators boldly went further and asserted the meaning of some objects, for example, 'this bronze dagger belongs to the "Wessex culture"', overlooking the fact that such a 'culture' is entirely a 20th-century concept that certainly did not 'happen' three-and-a-half thousand years ago (cf. Hodder 1989). A conceptual label became a museum label, but perhaps few were the wiser. Nevertheless, to a very marked degree this is the public perception of archaeology in which the subject remains largely trapped, especially as material for media consumption. 'We need a story; archaeologists are far too cautious – and they disagree with one another so, even though we go to the experts, we cannot get a strong story-line' (a clear message of a session I chaired during the Archeos film and video festival at the British Museum in November 1992).

Here is a first issue, an exemplar of the conundrum whether archaeology should be only what it is academically or what its publics want. Should archaeologists agree not to disagree in public, denying an essence of their discipline – intellectual debate – as a price of market acceptability? In this case, of course, and by analogy much more widely, the problem is that the accretional, linear model of scientific, academic-based progress in our acquisition of what was delusorily thought to be knowledge (Bowler 1989) fragmented from the 1960s onwards, that is, from the start of the working lifetimes of those who, like the writer, are now the subject's seniors merely through the passage of time (the only criterion used here for a word defined by the *Oxford English Dictionary* as 'more advanced in age'). This fragmentation is seen in almost every facet of the subject: its rationale, scope, objectives, organization and personnel (Shanks and Tilley 1987b) but, curiously perhaps, not its methodologies, which have homogenized as they have expanded (cf. Renfrew and Bahn 1991).

The fragmentation has been driven by three pressures: intra-archaeological, intellectual and sociological. It is a moot point whether the first is a product of the last two or an independent response to archaeologists' and archaeology's needs. The three essentially prevail still and provide the matrix within which the discipline operates as an intellectually vibrant interface of Arts and Science, and from which its pragmatic offspring, ARM, like the prince in a fairy tale, ventures forth to do good. There is absolutely no point in or to ARM unless it does exactly that; but of course 'good', like princes and the beautiful maidens they inevitably acquire, is a relative concept, ethically and sociologically adjustable, shifting with intangibles like mood, taste, and the very sands of time that are the matter of archaeology (Green 1984).

The intellectual frameworks of archaeology itself, from which management procedures stem, are discussed in Chapter 2; the database that is manipulated within those frame-works, sometimes to management as distinct from research ends, is discussed in Chapter 3 and the organizational structure of archaeology in the UK by the editors in Chapter 4. The specifically archaeological theoretical parameters, databases and organizational structure exist, however, within a larger matrix. This – intellectual, social, economic and political – becomes particularly evident in a number of issues – hotspots, as it were – where pastness interfaces with present, where the present comes face to face with various aspects of its pasts (Lowenthal 1985; Wright 1985).

This is the phenomenon briefly explored here, with particular reference to ARM. November 1992 happened to illustrate numerous facets of the phenomenon, especially in the form of public issues, in a concentrated and, to an extent, synchronous and juxtaposed way. The month (though any would have done as well) is, then, taken as metaphor of the present, using two incidents as case studies to raise some contemporary issues affecting archaeological resource management in the UK, with backward glances to the situation twenty and more years ago.

PRESENT ISSUES: NOVEMBER 1992

The Windsor Castle fire

A fire at Windsor Castle proved particularly germane. The news of it was immediately shocking; transmitting that news by live television was visually dramatic. So too were the newspaper air photographs of the burnt-out shell – though they also showed how small a part of the whole complex had actually been affected. Simultaneously, and almost before the embers had cooled, the story as news changed into seriously debated public controversy about three issues: safety precautions and conservation in historic buildings; the power of heritage to trigger strong reactions, in this case of a basic constitutional issue; and the old chestnut, re-emerging in a public debate that William Morris would have recognized, about whether to restore or build anew – that is, pastiche or creativity, replication or innovation, exact replacement for the sake of visual continuity or historical continuity by replacing the old with the new. All three issues are central to archaeological management.

The first was predictable, for after every fire the question has to be asked: 'How did it start?' often with the rider 'Whose fault was it?' Here, the fact that both anti-fire electrical and art-conservation works were in progress in the area where and when the fire began added point to the questions. The official enquiry report, less than two pages of it, in fact pointed to a combination of these two types of work as creating the circumstances in which the fire started, though the details need not detain us further.

The relevance here is that since ARM often involves both site works and artefact con-servation, those who would manage archaeology have clear general, and specific statutory, responsibilities over such potential hazards as fire, health and safety, just as does any other manager in the 'real world'. Just because such work begins from academic assumptions or is pursued for research or aesthetic reasons is totally beside the point; intellectual elitism or scholarly 'ivory towerism' are no excuse for managerial ignorance or carelessness in such matters. The point may be laboured and it is certainly well known to, and accepted by, professional archaeological managers. But it is stressed prominently in this essay both for its own importance and to counteract any starry-eyed romanticism about the practice of late 20th-century archaeology. Such may exist among a public accustomed to soft-focus televisual archaeo-ventures and in particular among would-be archaeological careerists weaned on laughably exciting but professionally unacceptable images of Indiana Jones-type archaeology.

The consequences of the Windsor Castle fire also took off, after but a few hours of commiseration for the royal family, in two other, different directions: constitutional and financial. These were sparked, let us remember, by nothing more than a fire that did not actually destroy an irreplaceable art collection in a gutted though small part of a castle; but it was a royal castle. From this flowed an iconographic dimension: Windsor as emblematic of Englishness – rather than merely a particularly interesting castle originating in the Norman period – and, above all, of royalty itself. When, within twenty-four hours of the fire, the Secretary of State for the Heritage promised not just complete restoration but that the Government, that is, the taxpayer, would pay the full cost, unofficially estimated at £60 million, a full-scale, acrimonious public debate began. This was not about responsibility for the fire, not about the cost of restoration itself, but about the very constitutional nature of the UK. Whether the country becomes a republic, or settles down with a modified Crown, again need not detain us, though the power of a heritage incident to trigger such basic issues is hardly likely to be assuaged by the Government's declaration a few days later of the Queen's offer to pay taxes.

The story has a double relevance here. It is particularly apposite if, as other chapters in this book claim, archaeology would embrace, in addition to its abandoned sites and empty ruins, standing buildings like people's homes (Chapter 8) and cathedrals (Chapter 9) (which can also burn, e.g. York Minster). Managers of that archaeology should never underestimate its power to contain, and therefore release, strong emotions. Particularly is that so when the resource in question, perhaps through its history but more probably through associations acquired irrespective of its scientific value, has crossed a magic line, transmuting itself from being merely archaeological to emerge as 'heritage' (Hewison 1987; Fowler 1992). People may be indifferently content to leave archaeology to archaeologists, but heritage belongs to them. One of the most difficult judgements for an archaeological manager to make is whether his or her charge has enjoyed that transformation; and often the manager will not know until, for any one of a whole host of reasons, a particular site suddenly comes into the public gaze.

Prudhoe Castle, for example, was quietly slumbering along on the banks of the Tyne as it has done for decades, indeed centuries since its heyday as a Percy stronghold, offending no-one nowadays nor apparently particularly loved. Then an apparently simple management decision to remove some trees around it – nothing to do with its archaeological integrity or historic interest – provoked a violent, vitriolic public reaction. People liked the trees; they were their trees, part of their view, part of their scenery when they took the dog for a walk. So the twofold message here is that while, of course, management of an archaeological resource has to be archaeologically correct, the decision itself and its implementation have to occur within some sort of public parameter: pastness, at least in the UK, performs now in the present, not just for its own sake or that of its practitioners. In that sense, ARM is not only political but is on a par with other issues like national education and health, sensitive to and debated by the public interest (Gathercole and Lowenthal 1990).

3

The third issue arising from the Windsor blaze concerned the nature of restoration, a matter that could arise at any monument. It was particularly prominent as the smoke cleared from the photogenic new ruin, graphically juxtaposed beside record photographs of its former magnificence. Another management practicality: record that for which you are responsible. The Royal Commission on the Historical Monuments of England (RCHME) had prepared a photographic archive of Windsor Castle some years previously. No sooner had the Secretary of State made his announcement about the method of payment for restoration than his automatic assumption about restoration was itself queried.

The very public questioning homed in on two facets: first, should the present generation slavishly restore when the essence of Windsor Castle was that the historically interesting and iconographic monument that it had come to be by 1992 was a compound of many 'new' buildings and rebuildings over nearly a thousand years? And, secondly, as a somewhat bemused public learnt in the days following the fire, given that much of the structure that had been destroyed was not 'old' but a 19th-century gothic fantasy of what Victorians thought 'medieval' should have been, were we right, in principle and pragmatically, to pour millions of pounds of taxpayers' money into re-faking a fake? 'We know that Windsor Castle is not all it seems. Its present romantic profile reflects work done at the time of King William IV. Some have seized on the fact that this is not a genuine medieval castle but a Regency fake to argue that it is fatuous to spend so much time and effort restoring a fake' (Mellor 1992). Further, as the Royal Institution of British Architects was quick to point out, would it not be more appropriate to the spirit of the monument and of our times to seize the opportunity by designing a suite of late 20th-century buildings to add to the structural compote comprising the thousand-year-old castle?

Every archaeological manager is likely to face the issues embedded in this public controversy. Even without a fire or other disaster, the management of buildings, ruins, even earthworks, requires minimally their maintenance, probably their enhancement, and sometimes, not least for public presentation, their rebuilding in one form or another. The official, traditional British response has always been 'consolidate as found' (Apted *et al.* 1977; Thompson 1981). To consolidate, the minimalist approach, or to rebuild, restore, replicate, renovate, reinstate, replace, recreate – all such, and more, are nuances of response involving management decisions, often as much not to take a particular step as to do something that will change the site or building in question. The fact, little-appreciated, is that 'heritage' is not unchanging; the very fact that any item has been identified as such means that it is paradoxically bound to change as a direct result of its selection and the consequential need to 'keep' it. A consequence is that the appearance of a heritage item, and sometimes its actual nature, is not fixed but the product of such decisions. ARM is therefore to some extent creative and, even when consciously neutral, almost bound to be so. Characteristically such issues arise over interiors. The National Trusts, for example, continually face dilemmas with their buildings, ranging from great country houses like Castle Ward, Northern Ireland, where there was much angst over the restoration of the entrance hall's Germolene-coloured wall surfaces, to single-room homes like the birthplace of George Stephenson, Wylam, Northumberland; and often the issue is not just whether to restore or not, but what to restore to? Stephenson's home, for example, has recently been subtly changed from a vaguely 19th-century ambience to a specifically late 18th-century interior; restoration after the genuinely disastrous fire at Hampton Court, another royal residence, has seized the opportunity to replace a former stylistic mishmash in the state apartments, not as it was before the fire, but 'to their condition at the time they were built by King William III' (Mellor 1992).

Such decisions are not, however, confined to the seeming recherché dimensions of architectural authenticity and interior decoration; they are as much present out of doors too. They lie behind such creations as the Butser Ancient Farm, the building of a 'genuine', new gateway into the Roman fort at South Shields, the less obvious restoration-cum-reconstruction of the 5,000-year old west end of the Stonehenge cursus by the National Trust, and the current modelling of an 'Anglo-Saxon landscape' overlooking the River Tyne near the monastic church of the Venerable Bede at Jarrow. They continue in the even more subtle contexts of conservation management of the form of the Uffington White Horse and the nose of the Cerne Abbas Giant.

The Windsor Castle fire, then, raises some important issues immediately and pragmatically. These issues are about practical site management, conservation of fabric and objects, the emotive power of heritage, especially as a trigger for the expression of public concern, and the ethics and practice of various restorative strategies. Of course such issues must be publicly discussed, but someone has to take decision about them for actions to proceed. Even to leave the gutted buildings just as they are – which will not happen – would require as positive a decision as that which will be taken from among the options. We can be equally certain that, whatever that decision is, it will be both controversial and very publicly debated.

Generalizing from this particular, here is the nub for contemporary ARM. The issues are not new, for cultural conservationists have been struggling with them since conscious preservation began to be thought about in the 17th century, but it simply has to be accepted (and preferably welcomed) that nowadays debate about them will be public and decisions about them will be controversial. This applies whether the resource (a landscape, building, site or object) is at the top of the heritage hierarchy – national, royal, big, old and a major tourist attraction (and it might even be scientifically significant too) – or whether it is an anonymous bump in, or a mundane object from, a local field. It will mean something to someone; someone will 'own' it. It is bound to possess a public interest, or a potential for one; if it does not, then its mishandling through failure to recognize that interest will ensure that it quickly acquires one. This encapsulates the single biggest difference in terms of ARM between the 1960s and the 1990s: the public interest. Woe betide the archaeological manager who ignores, is ignorant of or, worse, despises, that interest; for with it go what individual members of our society, and those speaking for that society collectively, now regard as their 'rights'. Real or imagined, it matters not; such rights, and the means to express concern about them, exist.

ENGLISH HERITAGE AND ENGLAND'S HERITAGE

English Heritage (EH) held a press conference on 26 October 1992; its consequences dominated November archaeologically. The purpose was apparently to launch its Strategy for the Future (English Heritage 1992a). If its purpose was actually to stir up a heritage hornets' nest, then it was superbly successful; there has not been so cerebral or prolonged a public debate outside archaeological circles about archaeology in my lifetime, even at the height of the Rescue campaign twenty and more years ago. If, on the other hand, its purpose was to promote, justify, explain, gain support for and start implementing what were described in the accompanying press release as 'Powerful plans', the occasion was an abysmal failure. It provoked (indeed, because of a leak three days earlier, it was also preceded by) a universally hostile reaction that, *inter alia*, brought into question the very existence of the organization and the fitness for office of its chairman. There must be lessons here for the archaeological manager: what went wrong, or right, depending on the point of view?

Quality and intensity of public and media reaction apart, the significant feature here was that the publicity was entirely media led; it was not archaeologically inspired or stimulated, nor did it have to be. The 'seniors' (above), and many others involved in archaeological management, locally as well as nationally, merely responded to a stream of enquiries from television, radio and newspaper persons; and politicians, colleagues and neighbours. The first point is, therefore, that archaeological managers nowadays have to be adept at handling the media as well as performing for it; rather more discriminatingly, they must also be able to judge when to push and when merely to follow a public bandwagon that is careering along under its own momentum.

More fundamentally, they must so position themselves that they are actually in touch with their constituency; they must have some awareness of what their publics think, are likely to think, and how they will probably react. While EH manifestly had a fairly sharp idea of what it was proposing to do, like many other organizations it clearly had no idea at all of how its proposals would be seen by those regarding themselves as having a stake in the same field, paradoxically people and organizations predisposed to see EH, at one and the same time, as both their leader and their servant. Worse, it conveyed an impression that it cared even less. Consequently, especially as it emerged that no consultation had taken place with outside interests (or even peer-respected senior professionals), the message projected was 'We know; you don't', and alienation was assured.

Dictatorship, however well-intentioned, is seldom a recipe for success and never when, as was clear in this case, its prescriptions flow from unawareness; it is predictably a recipe for disaster in heritage matters and in the sort of society that now inhabits England. Archaeological managers should not attempt it; however tedious the time spent in consultation, it is time that has to be so spent. Nor is this specific to archaeology: ask any manager dealing with people. You have to carry people with you, and especially when they pay the manager and already 'own' that which their manager manages. Unfortunately, EH gave the impression that it thought it alone owned that which it managed, and it seemingly confused the needs of English Heritage with those of England's heritage.

The second point is the significance of the media phenomenon itself. It would certainly not have manifested itself, as a long-running (by media standards), national expression of real interest and concern, twenty years ago; in fact, at the time of the Rescue 'archaeology in crisis' campaign, it did not, at least not without a lot of help. Triggered by a different incident in 1992, with EH seen to be parsimonious with both its cerebration and explanation, the media were in fact making the same point as one of the vibes from the Windsor Castle fire: pastness is now public property; interest in and concern for it are now matters of public debate; archaeological and heritage managers must now, therefore, discharge their responsibilities not only with an eye to the public interest but very much in the public domain. Archaeological managers are being watched, and are publicly accountable not just for what they do but for why they do it.

We can look to a string of individual incidents, usually involving excavations and/or discoveries of treasure, as a cause of this change – such as London's Mithraic temple, the 1950s Stonehenge excavations and Atkinson's Silbury Hill work, through to the more recent Rose Theatre episode and various metal-detector treasures. To my mind, however, the shift in public perception is the result of trends rather than events: the slow, cumulative drip, drip effect of realistic television and radio programmes, of countless lectures by the small army of adult education missionaries that annually takes to the rural byways and the further reaches of the Northern Line, and of the increasingly concerted effort by organizations to take archaeology to people locally through a diversity of mechanisms like open days on excavations, special evenings at museums and the designation of heritage trails. It is called education in the best sense of that word (Binks *et al.* 1988; cf. Stone and Mackenzie 1990; Chapter 20).

Such education is not entirely altruistic, perhaps, for its strong motivation comes from conviction, but the result is beneficial to the tutor, the participator and the subject. Of course, other, non-archaeological, trends in British society have also contributed to the shift, perhaps even created the conditions in which it has been able to happen, but for the archaeological manager the important point is that it has happened. He or she is therefore in a very different situation now compared to that in which this writer started, an enviable but somewhat irresponsible one in which the only due was to the highest academic standards of the subject and my employing organization, with virtually the only expression of public interest along the lines of 'Fancy anyone paying you to do that'. As many have found before and since then, it was the hard graft of extramural teaching that taught me about another, legitimate and more pressing public interest. It seems to me that such person-to-person contact is an essential of archaeological management, for nowadays it has to consist not just of what the manager thinks but of what his or her constituency thinks. Which brings us back to the EH press conference and its sequel.

The occasion for the conference was primarily to announce the plan for EH, acting as the heritage executive of the state, to dispose of part of the patrimony. The part was a long list of monuments and archaeological sites constituting a significant portion of the portfolio of 'Guardianship Monuments', or 'Properties in Care' looked after directly by EH, a portfolio built up over more than a century since the first Ancient Monuments Act in 1882. That the impression was initially given of privatization, of even selling some of the monuments, did not help the course of rational discussion. In any case, however, the relevant point here is that, whatever the merits of the plan, its publication immediately illustrated a wide schism between what the managers, EH, thought was reasonable and what its constituency thought. Part of the reason for this was that no justification, other than pragmatism deeply tinged with marketplace economics, was provided to buttress a plan that actually involved fine matters of theory and professional knowledge, but far more significant was the misjudgement evident in the failure to anticipate public and professional concern. The problem was aggravated by the chairman of EH's dismissal of the latter as 'arrogance', apparently for questioning the decision by pointing out that there was rather more to the matter than mere institutional convenience, that is, that academic and philosophical issues were involved, notably in judging the significance of monuments; and, more seriously, of his admission that the scale and force of the former was 'surprising'. The good archaeological resource manager should not be caught out on either score.

A MATRIX: THEORY, PRACTICE AND SOCIETY

The furore over EH's initiative can be variously explained. One attractive theory sees it as touching a raw nerve in the public psyche, sensitized at a time of considerable political and economic uncertainty and great sociological change. Ancient monuments, it can be argued, were and are seen by many people as some of the few fixed points in personal landscapes, things that are old, revered, visitable and touchable, and things too that not only 'belong' to the people in a general sense but that also give people a sense of belonging to a place, a community. In a time of post-modernist mood, when so much bespeaks attitudes of 'take anything and anything goes', a deeply conservative reaction of clinging to some elements of the known is to be both expected and respected. Historic buildings and archaeological sites clearly have a role to play here, as psycho-sociological placebos maybe, but personally and probably communally significant nevertheless. While their management with that in mind may well be a whole dimension away from the practicalities of choosing which mortar to use for wall repairs or where to site the public conveniences, it represents a deeper, more subtle aspect of the manager's task easily overlooked in the hassle of day-to-day tasks and the adrenalin-inducing occasions of TV interview and press conference.

The working archaeological resource manager will also run up against preconceptions, leading to definitions by others, of what his or her task is. The EH episode incidentally illustrated this with the EH chairman's ill-informed surprise that part of the resource in his care consisted of 'only bumps in fields' (M. Wainwright 1992). That he thereby dismissed a major part of the patrimony – the earthwork evidence of former land use that constitutes such a vital element in one of the UK's great glories, its historic landscapes – unconsciously exemplified the fact that 'the heritage' is a fairly tightly circumscribed notion even in well-educated circles. This was all too well illustrated in the debates on the National Heritage Bill in 1982–3 and in the First Report of the House of Commons Environment Committee (HMSO 1987; cf. Fowler 1987). The archaeological manager's view of the scope of his or her responsibility, extending to 'bumps in fields' and their equivalents, could well run up against those limits, leading to agonizing appraisal of whether precedence lies with professional or lay perception of the nature and significance of the resource.

Professionally there can be only one answer: the professional judgement based on academic criteria. But the distinction clearly to be drawn in such clashes is that between the archaeological view on the one hand and the political/financial/legal on the other. Colleagues, probably superiors, in the latter fields may well have to take a final decision, perhaps against the professional advice of the archaeologist; or the senior archaeological manager, with responsibilities wider than his or her purely archaeological ones, may have to do so accordingly. In the latter case, then obviously the senior manager, albeit an archaeologist at heart, will have to take the correct decision in the light of the other aspects of the situation. Nevertheless, that cannot involve, for example, knowingly destroying 'bumps in fields' merely because they are such; that sort of action is only acceptable if it has been established, for example, that the 'bumps' are only a fragment of, say, common, late and insignificant ridge-and-furrow and not a fragment of rare, early and highly significant ridge-and-furrow.

'The best' may be the concept at stake here, but criteria for defining it are essential; the quality of 'bestness' is not self-evident. Significance is all and, while allowance has to be made for cognitive values of the sort mentioned above, a resource without academic value is ultimately difficult to defend. Rather more difficult in a way, however, is the challenge confronting a manager who is, or perhaps was initially, also an archaeologist. He or she will know the need for long-term policies to be based on good data and intellectual fibre, but at the same time he or she will also know that success depends empirically on persuading others. In practice, it is not sufficient merely to know that one's view is archaeologically correct. Powers of persuasion, in committee, with local councillors, with bureaucrats, with non-archaeological peers, are additionally required, adding to the requisites of a good archaeological manager. But there is nothing different in that compared to any other managerial role.

Many pasts other than the archaeological one exist, however, and, picking their way through the available assortment, a lot of people, in all sorts of ways, now want to have access to some of them (Chippindale et al. 1990; Devereux 1991). Whatever their wishes, and whatever their own interpretations – and obviously many of them will be far from the core of archaeological 'correctness' – that which is desired is closely related to actual sites, the resource at the heart of the archaeological manager's role. Paradoxically, nevertheless, much that the latter would regard as within his or her remit would not be seen by others as archaeological. This applies, for example, to buildings, townscapes, countryside and landscapes. The countryside in particular is generally not seen as artefactual; rather others see it as natural, a divide represented in England by the tripartite bureaucracy of the Countryside Commission, English Nature and English Heritage (though the first two are subsumed in new, single agencies in Scotland and Wales). The archaeological manager must perforce spend much time in denying limitations of his or her remit to single sites and material underground and his or her activities to excavating, while watching for opportunities to point out to others the archaeological implications of their proposals and activities.

In professional circles the point is now generally taken that land management and land-use change in particular have an archaeological potential, for enhancement as much as in avoiding damage (Chapter 22), but while an archaeological search is now commonly built into numerous professional processes such as Town and Country Planning, Environmental Assessment and designing a new trunk road or motorway, it is still relatively rare for the archaeological factor to be taken into account in normal land management unless some development is in mind. Exceptions would include the admirably holistic management approach of the National Trust and, increasingly, of the National Parks.

They, however, have responsibilities to allow, even encourage, access by the public, and not far down that road lies the whole question of tourism, interpretation, the 'visitor experience', the ambivalences of what has been coined as 'heritat', and what might be termed the 'heritage economy' (Tabata *et al.* 1992; Boniface and Fowler 1993). Willingly or otherwise, the archaeological resource manager is an active participant in this. His or her decisions might, for example, not create the best revenue-producing honey-pot site required by the financial targets of the relevant organization; decisions about opening and closing times, or about the route of a tourist trail, could well not serve the commercial needs of coach-tour operators. In such a situation, now common, the manager of the past is very much bound up with the needs of the present, yet constrained by the long-term needs of the resource. The question is clearly what, in the last resort, is ARM about? The matrix in which it occurs and operates should indicate at least part of the answer.

Techniques of preservation have changed over the years and are now, for example, much more scientific in several senses of that word; they are presumably more effective in prolonging the life of the resource. That has for long been one of the objectives of management: only the means of achieving it has altered. The single most significant change compared with twenty-five years ago is simply one of numbers: the resource to be managed is vastly increased and the size of its audience is now of a different order. Much management is therefore reactive, trying to cope in particular with a greater and apparently never-ending stream of visitors. To remark on the fact is not, however, to explain it.

Any explanation is bound to be controversial but essentially one possible model of ARM's rise and rise needs to operate at only two levels. At an obvious level, ARM is necessary to counter and meet the needs of large numbers of people with increased leisure, expendable cash, fantastically improved mobility, better education and higher expectations of their personal quality of life. Such a well-known explanation might cover the great majority of visitors. But another level of explanation is necessary: after all, for many now enjoying improved standards of living, history was the dullest of subjects at school and they do not need to spend their hard-gained freedom, of time as much as money, in visiting one or more aspects of 'pastness'. Obviously one can talk about nostalgia as a major component of this other level, but that can hardly apply in terms of direct memory to anything earlier than about 1910. Where the pitch has been deliberately made at this angle in theme parks and museums, immediately pre-First World War seems to be the going time at the moment (presumably it will move forward in time, though somehow the 1920s and 1930s do not convey quite the allure of the Edwardian era; but cf. Frayling 1992). Nostalgia for anything earlier is a cultural product, fantasy maybe, as for a former if timeless Arcadia.

Rather would my model seek to involve that oddest of human attributes, curiosity, motivated by a perhaps altogether too idealistic belief in each individual's need for his or her own 'quest'. This may well take the form of some sort of pilgrimage, not necessarily religious in any formal sense, but nevertheless a journey, sometimes intellectual or emotional rather than only physical, to visit a time or place of personal significance. But, more generally perhaps, behind the holiday or weekend desire for a good day out, with opportunities to eat well and shop needlessly, lies, I believe, an unconscious wish simply to find out, not just a quest to discover what the past or a place was like but equally how these archaeologists and historians know what they say they know (cf. Layton 1989b; Shennan 1989).

If something like this be so, then performance as much as product is a key to successful presentation by those charged with responsibilities for the past in contemporary society; especially when we note that, if tourism really is to become a major prop of the world's economy, ARM will in future not merely be operating in an increasingly complex local society. It will also be performing for a whole series of overlapping cross-sections of the world's diverse societies merging, as tourists and probably more deeply, into a homogeneous culture (Featherstone 1990; Boniface and Fowler 1993). In what is currently an intensely insular, chauvinistic attitude towards its heritage among the peoples of the UK, the global, multiracial, multicultural dimension of ARM in an economically driven tourist culture may well prove to be the crucial development before the new generation of archaeological managers themselves become 'seniors'. The dynamics of the matrix will, in any case, ensure that archaeological resource management is unlikely to stultify in the foreseeable future.

CHAPTER 2

CHANGING CONFIGURATIONS: THE RELATIONSHIPS BETWEEN THEORY AND PRACTICE

Ian Hodder

Archaeology embodies a tension between theory and practice. On the one hand, the practice of digging demands a down-to-earth logic. On the other hand, archaeology more than most other disciplines depends on theoretical imagination in order to breathe life into dry-as-dust traces. Throughout its history archaeology has tended to deal with this tension by being circumspect about theory and by devoting itself to a common-sense view. Archaeologists have clung to the 'facts' themselves and have eschewed the dangers of unsubstantiated theorizing. It was Colt Hoare's opinion in 1812 (1812: 7) that we should 'speak from facts not theory'. In 1888, in discussing the evil of biasing the collection of archaeological evidence according to current theories, Pitt Rivers (preface to Vol II) suggested that 'when fulness and accuracy are made the chief subject of study, this evil is in a great measure avoided'. In 1954 Hawkes described a ladder of inference that doomed most reliable interpretation to the lower rungs of the ladder: technology and economy. In 1982 Philip Barker argued that we must be careful 'to keep the interpretation separate from the evidence on which it is based' (1982: 26). Archaeology came for many people to be synonymous with the collection of information, minimally interpreted through the application of common sense. As a result it was recently possible for Champion (1991: 151) to write: 'I know of no general attempt to assess the relevance of recent theoretical debates to the practice of field archaeology; all too often they seem to be regarded as irrelevant, while work in the field continues in a determinedly empirical and unselfcritical manner'. Champion catalogues the evidence for the minimal impact of theory on practice as evident in abstracts and journals (1991: 144–51).

Contrary to the consensus view that theory and practice have little impact on each other, I want to argue in this chapter that if looked at over the long-term development of archaeology, links between theory, field archaeology and heritage management can be identified. Certainly these links always involve tensions rather than holistic integration, but there is much evidence for some form of dialectical interaction, for a unity of opposites.

THE RISE OF AN EMPIRICIST SCIENCE

Most, if not all, societies have bodies of knowledge about their origins and historical development, whether in the form of myth, legend, oral history, written history or material evidence. In many, if not most, societies the past remains alive and connected to the present. Meanings and spirits inhabit monuments, and ancient villages affect the lives of people in contemporary society (e.g. Condori 1989).

If all societies have pasts, few have archaeology. The rise of archaeology is associated with developed countries and the Enlightenment. Few societies indulge in methodical excavation of their ancient monuments. Indeed, such excavation would often be seen as sacrilege to a past that continues to live and act in the world.

In Western societies some trace of such an attitude can still be observed in sensitivities concerning the excavation of Christian and recent human remains (Chapter 20). But for the most part, the past has become for us 'another country' as Lowenthal (1985) has so cogently argued. It is only because the past has become disconnected from us that we can dig it up in a systematic and disinterested way.

Archaeology as it is understood in the West, then, is only possible when the past is dead. Archaeology is associated, by definition, with the distanced eye. It involves stripping the past of its subjective import and looking at it with a new objective gaze. It is associated with the rise of the Enlightenment attitude and with the rise of science. For example, archaeology as a science played a role in the battle against mythical and religious ideas about human origins and in the controversy concerning the work of Darwin. Despite some recent claims to the contrary, archaeologists have always claimed to be scientific. In 1651 Bacon had written that 'too great a reverence for Antiquity is prejudicial to the advancement of science'. In the very first volume of *Archaeologia*, published by the Society of Antiquaries in 1770, the growth of antiquarian research was linked to the general rise of the 'sciences, and an opposition was made between narratives embellished poetically and the 'regular and elaborate inquiry into every ancient record and proof' described by Bacon.

The main historical moment at which archaeology as a science emerged to confront traditional belief was in the late 19th century as archaeology became institutionalized in public hands and the first Ancient Monuments Protection Act (1882) was passed (Cleere 1984). As Clark noted later, British archaeology had to reach a certain level of accuracy and discipline before it could be perceived as worthy of public funds (1934: 414). For Clark it was of the utmost significance that the first government appointee to the post of Inspector of Ancient Monuments under the 1882 legislation was the first scientific archaeologist – General Pitt Rivers. Chapman (1989) has shown the importance of links to scientists in the development of Pitt Rivers's work. Clark (1934) noted that earlier archaeologists were acting in an arbitrary, privileged manner when they devastated monuments. The past, removed from private to public hands, would no longer legitimate traditional privilege and personal authority. The objective scientific attitude, in which personal bias was limited, allowed the state to exert its power for the conservation of a national heritage for the good of all. Pitt Rivers's methodical excavation and detailed recording, his emphases on typologies, specialist reports and specialist jargon must all be set within the wider context of the rise of an objective scientific attitude tied to the rise of an impersonal state archaeological apparatus.

Although Pitt Rivers did develop complex theories about the progress and degeneration of archaeological types (1874), his main impact was on the growth of archaeology as objective description within an empiricist theory of science.

Despite the strictures of Collingwood (1939, 1946) on the importance of theory-led field research and despite the wide impact of the synthetic and theoretical writing of Childe (e.g. 1927, 1949), throughout the first half of the 20th century the empiricist stance, wary of theory, remained dominant. According to the empiricist conception of science the facts are self-evident. What is important is the detailed, objective description of data. Indeed, the main theoreticians of the period, such as Childe and Collingwood, were not renowned as field archaeologists. Rather, the experience of Collingwood's application of theory in the excavations at the site of King Arthur's Round Table (1938) served to demonstrate the dangers of meddling in theory. A blinkered hypothesis-testing procedure had produced circles of prehistoric post pits that were later shown to be nothing more than animal burrows (Bersu 1940a).

The common-sense, empiricist view also proved to be successful as techniques became more sophisticated. Bersu's (1940b) extensive excavation at Little Woodbury or J.G.D. Clark's (1952) integration of environmental and economic evidence gradually led to the use of more rigorous and more sophisticated scientific methods. The application of the first computer-based methods in the 1960s (Hodson *et al.* 1966; Doran and Hodson 1975) led to the wider use of standardized coding and typological systems.

But as scientific techniques extended their influence into archaeological practices at all levels, some of the underlying tensions became increasingly evident. For example, according to the empiricist view, emphasis was placed on the detailed description of data rather than on theoretical construction. And yet it increasingly became clear that archaeological types, for example, are not self-evident. Different people tend to code the same data differently and produce different typological schemes (e.g. Doran and Hodson 1975). As noted at the beginning of this chapter, archaeology is dependent on theory and it became increasingly difficult to ignore this theoretical dimension. Perhaps a more significant factor in the reaction against empiricism was that the steady collection of data did not seem, by itself, to be leading to major advances in knowledge. We might be able to submerge the data in descriptive terms and labels that we have invented (such as Ebbsfleet and Mortlake pottery styles, or Transepted Gallery-Grave) but what did it all amount to? One of the first arguments of New Archaeologists such as David Clarke and Lewis Binford in the 1960s and early 1970s was that knowledge did not progress simply as a result of the collection of data but as a result of theoretical development.

ARCHAEOLOGY AS A RESOURCE

I wish to argue that during the 1960s, 1970s and early 1980s archaeology came to be seen as a resource in two quite different but related ways. On the one hand, within the New Archaeology (a term used to describe the new directions taken in archaeology in the 1960s and early 1970s), archaeological data came to be seen as a resource for the testing of hypotheses about general propositions. On the other hand, with the rise of the Rescue movement archaeological data came to be seen as a cultural resource to be saved and preserved. But in both cases the notion of a 'resource' created a utilitarian view of the past as passive material. The self-aware theorizing did not lead to an active and creative use of material archives.

Hypothesis-testing and model-building

One of the main contributions of the New Archaeology was the overturning of a sceptical and common-sense approach to theory. As part of the discipline's loss of innocence during this period, a wider range of interpretations of the past became possible, fuelled by ideas from anthropology, ethnoarchaeology and experimental archaeology. In particular, a systems approach to social and economic processes was adopted as the main plank of the new programme, often couched in a neo-evolutionary framework. There was a particular interest in the adaptive aspects of ranking and exchange, especially regarding ceremonial monuments, cemeteries and settlement patterns (e.g. Renfrew 1973; Renfrew and Shennan 1982; Chapman *et al.* 1981). In terms of practice, these sets of theories underscored the importance of settlement survey and sampling, and the attempt to understand social and economic variation within the site as a systemic whole perhaps encouraged the shift from Wheeler's box trenches to area excavation, although this shift can also be explained as a response to continuous urban excavation and large-scale gravel extraction, as we shall see below. The theoretical commitment to adaptive, ecological explanation was translated into Site Catchment Analysis (Higgs 1972) and into the introduction of a range of intensive data recovery methods from seed machines to water sieving.

In 1973 Clarke was able to define several types and levels of theory. He identified various aspects of an overall general theory for archaeology that consisted of metaphysical, epistemological and logical theories. More practical aspects of the general theory were described as predepositional and depositional, postdepositional, retrieval, analytical and interpretive theory. During the 1970s, site-formation processes became a major area of concern, leading to a more critical approach to site interpretation (Schiffer 1976; Bradley and Fulford 1980; Fisher 1985) and assisting archaeology through the development of depositional and postdepositional theories.

Perhaps the greatest debt owed to New Archaeology by field archaeology is in the introduction of rigorous sampling strategies. At last a literature became available (e.g. Cherry *et al.* 1978) that could be referred to in constructing regional or on-site strategies. The various types of systematic or probabilistic sampling have now become standard practice, even in rescue contexts.

In fact it can be argued that New Archaeology did involve a close link with field practice precisely because its main contribution was in the realm of method rather than theory. As later debate has shown, while the New Archaeology saw great gains in the application of a wide range of scientific techniques, the range of theories was relatively narrow.

On the other hand, the commitment to a positivist, hypothesis-testing framework encouraged archaeologists to begin to divorce theory from practice and to link this divorce to the institutional separation between universities and most field units. Self-conscious theoretical argument increasingly came to be the domain of academics and students, debated at annual Theoretical Archaeology Group conferences. The New Archaeology also exacerbated the split between research and rescue by promoting issues geared to research projects, such as problem orientation, hypothesis formation, sampling in order to test propositions, and careful detailed collection of data. All these concerns may often have appeared as luxuries not affordable in early rescue contexts.

It is clear that the view of the data as a passive resource led to a downgrading of practice within theoretical and academic debate. The commitment to hypothesis-testing led to a separation of theory from practice, and the overall emphasis on cross-cultural generalization led to a limited concern with particular data sets and historical contexts.

The rescue of information

At the same time, the theoretically downgraded field arm of archaeology was undergoing rapid expansion and becoming self-consciously professional. Jones (1984), for example, describes the massive increase in rescue excavation expenditure and the growth in local authority spending on archaeology in the 1970s. Much of this expansion took place in the context of the rise of urban units and in relation to large-scale continuous excavation at sites such as Winchester. There was a concomitant revolution in archaeological methods, especially the recording of complicated and deeply stratified excavations. Philip Barker's work at Wroxeter showed that large-scale open-area excavation combined with meticulous examination of the bottom of the plough soil could identify even 5th- and 6th-century buildings. Large-scale gravel extraction led to yet further refinement of cleaning, sampling and recording techniques on rural sites.

In the area of urban archaeology, this new scale of work served to demonstrate that archaeologists need not remain handmaidens to historians – they could uncover different and independent evidence, of value in its own right. In other areas too the independence of field archaeology came to be strengthened. For example, the speed and scale of the new work necessitated the streamlining and standardization of recording procedures and the wider use of computer technology. This concern with the efficient recovery of information concerning cultural, economic and ecological materials may often have shared techniques with non-rescue research. But as the field profession became more specialized and professional, its expertise came to be more separate from theoretical debate.

The independence of the field profession, with its own discourse and disciplinary structures, was possible because the field profession, while also seeing archaeological data as a resource, looked at that resource in a different way. The banner under which large parts of the archaeological community served read 'save information about the past before it is destroyed'. The preservation of information was justification in itself, and there was little need to engage in theoretical discussion about how the data might be interpreted. So once again a utilitarian view overshadowed attempts to link theory and data, and much of the data came to rest uninterpreted and often unpublished in archives and museums (Chapter 19).

In any case, the distinction between research and rescue archaeology began to be broken down as the amounts of time, staff and money devoted to major rescue projects outstripped research projects and as the range of questions asked in some rescue contexts expanded and became more sophisticated. Rescue archaeology came to be where the most advanced research could be carried out. But such research was rarely linked to larger-scale theoretical issues (however, see e.g. Pryor 1985).

By the late 1970s and early 1980s tensions that had remained latent were becoming apparent. What was the point of the massive build-up of undigested information? Who was the past being saved for in this way? Why was the theory of the New Archaeology and the philosophy that it had espoused so out of date? Why did hypothesis-testing not seem to work in practice? The notion of archaeological data as a resource seemed limited in increasingly obvious ways.

ARCHAEOLOGY AS INTERPRETATION

In the 1980s the institutional separation of theoretical discussion in British archaeology in the face of the specialization and proliferation of sub-groups and acronyms in practical areas led to further introspection and rarification of theory. Theory became ever more divorced from practice. There were three trends in the theoretical debate. From the late 1970s the work on precapitalist societies by the French school of neo-Marxists had an increasing impact in archaeology, for example in the writings of Friedman and Rowlands (1977; Rowlands 1980) and Bradley (1984). One practical impact was on some museum displays (Clarke *et al.* 1985). More recently Wallerstein's core–periphery concepts have led to renewed interest in long-distance exchange, especially in prestige goods (Rowlands *et al.* 1987; Champion 1989).

A second theoretical trend concerned various approaches to the idea that material culture is meaningfully constituted, and to the problems of interpretation. One approach has moved from structuralism and the model of language to a consideration of the problems of 'reading' material culture as one might read a text (Hodder 1982, 1986, 1987; Tilley 1990). This direction of research emphasizes the multiple meanings given by different people in the past and present to the same material objects. The multiplicity of material meanings can be taken in the direction of extreme relativism and the construction of the past in the present (Shanks and Tilley 1987a, 1987b). A strong influence here has been post-structuralism (Baker and Thomas 1990; Bapty and Yates 1990). Alternatively, a hermeneutic approach can be espoused in which interpretation makes relationships between past and present and so informs both (Hodder 1992). According to this latter view the past is not simply constructed in the present because our interpretations have to adapt to the patterned material remains – archaeologists work in a spiral of interpretation, trying to grasp theory and data into a coherent whole. A rather different direction that can lead to a similar end-point derives from a consideration of material culture as ideology (e.g. Miller and Tilley 1984). Here the concern has increasingly been to consider the ideologies related to different and subordinate interest groups in society (Miller *et al.* 1989), and to explore the role of material culture meanings in relation to gender relations (Gibbs 1987; Gero and Conkey 1990). The meanings associated with the use of space in monuments (e.g. Thomas 1990) and across the landscape (Barrett *et al.* 1991) have proved to be of particular interest. The notion of structured deposition encapsulates the idea that discard patterns on monuments and settlements might be organized in socially meaningful ways (Richards and Thomas 1984; Hill 1989). This latter work does influence the understanding of the pits and ditches with which most archaeologists work and undermines a common-sense approach. We cannot take discard patterning as self-evident since some 'other' or ritual meaning may have been involved. And we cannot simply impose universal objective notions of discard but have to interpret discard practices within a particular social and cultural framework of meaning.

A third direction in the theoretical archaeology of the 1980s included feminist archaeology and was influenced by the post-structuralist debate, but it had a more general commitment to the critique of the relations of power in which archaeology was carried out and written. This argument, derived from various German schools of social philosophy (e.g. Shanks and Tilley 1987; Hodder 1986), remained abstract. But in contrast to the other two theoretical directions, critical archaeology contributed more fully to practical considerations. For example, many critically aware archaeologists took an active part in the controversy over the Southampton 1986 World Archaeological Congress (Ucko 1987). Feminist issues have become recognized in all areas of archaeological practice. The writing of archaeology has come under critical scrutiny as part of a changing discourse of power geared to different sets of interests (Tilley 1989; Hodder 1989).

While much of the theoretical debate under these three headings remained obtuse and abstract, I have mentioned some ways in which theory did have implications for practice. But equally there were areas of practice that gradually have begun to forge a more open approach to theory. For example, the increasing prevalence of scientific techniques in all areas of archaeological practice threatened to amass unused information that only an engagement with theoretical debate could hope to unlock. Similarly, attempts have been made (e.g. by English Heritage) to situate at least some rescue archaeology within a research agenda. In addition, theoretical moves were encouraged by the realization that the hypothesis-testing procedure of which New Archaeologists had been so enamoured turned out not to be a good way of describing what archaeologists do in practice on any kind of site, whether rescue or research (e.g. see the criticisms of Barker 1982). During excavation, unexpected lines of enquiry are opened up and any rigid adherence to the testing of initial hypotheses would involve ignoring evidence that may be relevant to the question in hand or that might be of interest to other archaeologists. In fieldwork, the questions are always changing and new lines of argument become available. In both rescue and research contexts a good excavator is not a rigid hypothesis-tester. Hermeneutics is a much better description of what archaeologists actually do than is positivism.

Although some interaction between post-processual theory and practice can be identified, for the most part theory and practice went their separate ways in the 1980s and early 1990s. But during this period both came to be influenced by similar conditions that affected them in similar directions. Within the theoretical debate disquiet began to be felt at the gap that was widening between theory and the practitioners of the subject (e.g. Baker and Thomas 1990). I have already described the theoretical move towards interpretation rather than universal causal explanation. But such a move, especially when allied to critical perspectives, raised the questions: 'Whose point of view are we interpreting and who are we interpreting for? Should we not be concerned with wider and subordinate perspectives?' Within archaeology more generally, there was an increasing concern to make the past more widely and equally access-ible to all social groups. This move was linked to the increasing commercialization of heritage. Archaeology and museums came to be part of the post-modern age. The concern was to make the past more active, to involve it in interpretations to which many people would have access, to set sites in a landscape as part of amenity provision.

The rise of the notions of heritage that so came to dominate the 1980s and of the heritage industry, a term that Fowler (1992: xv) feels he may have been the first to use in 1985, encapsulates a tension within the way the past is used in contemporary society. On the one hand, the terms have come to be associated with commerce and enterprise, with shallowness, façade and image-addiction (Hodder 1992: 276–80). There are a number of characteristics of archaeology that make it attractive as a source of images in this post-modern world and that make it commercially exploitable. For example, when we see and touch archaeological objects, they bring us close to a long-distant past. Such objects are ripe for exploitation in terms of time travel and cultural 'tourism', sometimes associated with reproduction and re-enactment. And the past that is visited in this way can be a popu-lar and accessible past not restricted to the documents and palaces of past elites but including the everyday lives of past women and men. In addition, archaeology produces material objects that can easily be turned into commodities and sold in the marketplace, either literally as reproductions and souvenirs or figuratively as interpretations that are 'packaged' using the latest media gimmicks. The effect of these processes is often to pro-duce a fragmented past that is disconnected from context and in which histories or prehis-tories do not mean anything other than nostalgia, fun, thrill, excitement.

On the other hand, the term heritage derives from the notion of inheritance – of a mean-ingful connection between the past and the present, of a past that matters. In several areas of contemporary life the past is being used to make a connection with the present, to tell a story about ourselves. Certainly symbols of the past are used to create senses of unity, nationalism and regionalism. But at the individual and local level too, people use local history and genealogy in order to create a more immediate sense of place.

Archaeologists are beginning to be aware of, for example, black history and women's perspectives. Archaeology is important in this regard because its very materiality allows groups to ground their claims in a certain objectivity. In a very material sense archaeology gets in the way of mass commercial development and often provides a focus for local protest about the destruction of environments and places that hold meaning for people.

One of the reasons heritage saw a boom in the 1980s (Hewison 1987; Merriman 1991) was that the past came to play a role both in a commercial, disconnected, meaningless present and in a desire for connection and meaning. The debate over preservation provides an example of this tension. The dominant authorities and institutions in archaeology and heritage have espoused preservation, even preservation from the destructive archaeological trowel. Such an attitude fits well within earlier notions of the past as dead, locked away, closed off from inter-pretation, unable to play an active role in contemporary society. Beyond preservation there is a series of options that leads to a more active view (Fowler 1992; Chapter 1).

Conservation requires management of the past. Restoration is predicated on an attempt to replace the past as far as possible 'as it was', and more interpretation is inevitably involved. Reconstruction implies still further interpretation. Re-creation includes the active reliving of the past, attempting to turn 'then' into 'now'. Moving along this sequence from preservation to conservation to restoration to reconstruction to re-creation, we see a shift from the official to the marginal and towards a more popular, active, inter-preted, living past. Archaeological practices today, at all levels, involve making decisions about where to be situated along this continuum.

I have so far mainly described developments in theory and heritage practice that express the new interpretive emphasis. It is perhaps too early to be clear of the impact on field archaeology itself. One implication is that archaeologists are increasingly aware of the need to produce reports of their work for a wide variety of audiences from developers and planners to a wider public and schoolchildren. The traditional academic report has often come to play a less central role. There is also an increasing debate about archives: how can these be made more accessible and more used? And should the production of archaeological records, in whatever form, be standardized, an attitude that derives from an objectivist view of the world. But how much interpretation is already contained within terms such as pit, wall, ditch, Neolithic? Can terminologies ever be neutral and should we not examine the social construction not only of formal categories but of all archaeological knowledge?

There is an increasing concern with such critical questions within field practice, and an increasing concern to interpret the data contextually within its own terms, by comparison among different data sets rather than through the imposition of external schemes (e.g. Barrett and Kinnes 1988; Barrett 1987; Hill 1989).

CONCLUSION

I have tried to show that theory and various types of archaeological practice seem related in their historical development despite the fact that institutionally they were often separated and despite the fact that each seemed to follow its own line of development. What is the unity that held the opposites together? To some degree they needed each other, depended on each other and reacted against each other. For example, institutional separation meant that each area had to carve out its own distinctive expertise.

Thus few field units came to be lodged in universities and the discipline's professional body came not to be the Institute of Archaeologists (cf. the Institutes of British Geographers or Town Planners) but of Field Archaeologists. Thus each domain developed its own sub-disciplinary discourse, independent of the others. It is perhaps true to say today that few university departments of archaeology, while teaching field techniques, can teach them at the level required by the field units. And similarly few professional practitioners have the resources to keep abreast of the latest theoretical debates.

With all this diversification and specialization, the reason that theory and practice developed in tandem at all is largely that both were responding to similar pressures in society at large. In particular, the expansion of archaeology and the destruction of the landscape in the postwar decades, the expansion of the universities and of government provision for archaeology all led to an optimistic and positive outlook in the 1960s and 1970s in which a wide range of the latest scientific techniques were harnessed for diverse archaeological uses. Thus, both theory and practice saw advances in procedures, increasing systematization and a greater use of aspects of science.

But in the 1980s and 1990s, theory and practice came to be contextualized in a postmodern world in which subordinate voices were being revalued, in which the interpretation of the past came to be part of the enterprise culture. Ever since the rise of archaeology as a discipline, the past had been conceived as inert, to be observed and described at a distance. But now for the first time the public demand that had always been there to some degree came to the fore. The past had to be made alive, to be interpreted, to be made accessible, whether that meant Disneyland sensationalism or the television series *Down to Earth* (Chapter 19). Both pure theory and pure empirical practice have come under threat. Theory has undermined the notion of neutral practice, and the practical demand for interpretation in the real world has lessened the relevance of elite theoretical abstraction. Today, both practice and theory need each other in order for the past to be alive, to play an active role in the present.

CHAPTER 3

THE BRITISH ARCHAEOLOGICAL DATABASE

David Fraser

TOWARDS A DEFINITION

Any attempt to describe the British archaeological database must begin by recognizing that there has not been a single successful attempt to compile a set of archaeological information that is complete and consistent. There is no such entity as the British archaeological database: rather, archaeologists have to manage with a complex set of overlapping collections of information gathered by different individuals and organizations at different times for different purposes. There have been some attempts to achieve complete coverage to some consistent standard for some geographical areas, and there have been some attempts to draw together information from various sources to improve accessibility, but there is no single British source of archaeological information. Enquiries of the sort 'How many 13th-century pele towers are there in Britain?' and 'Provide a list of all henge monuments in modern urban areas' can only be answered by consulting a large number of individual records in disparate locations, and there is no guarantee of uniform information quality. The single major source of discontinuity is the division of Britain into England, Wales and Scotland: with the exception of the three Royal Commissions, which have made largely successful attempts to ensure that their records are consistently compiled, there is no single organization that has a duty or objective to compile and maintain the British archaeological database.

But this rather pessimistic statement ignores the pragmatic fact that there is a wealth of excellent archaeological data in Britain used daily by several thousand professional archaeologists and many more interested, and no less competent, unpaid archaeologists. Indeed, once it is recognized that archaeological data is messy, ill defined and constantly being refined, then the nature of the existing systems become easier to understand, and their power to inform is better placed in context.

INCLUSIONS AND EXCLUSIONS

A definition of the existing British archaeological database is best attempted by referring to inclusions and exclusions. Every component record in the database includes locationally referenced descriptions of sites and monuments. These descriptions cover human activity from the earliest Palaeolithic period to the present day. Inclusion in an archaeological record generally implies that the human activity has ceased or has survived beyond its normal time span. 'Sites' and 'monuments' are interpreted very widely, and there is a tendency to include rather than exclude information if there is an easily available source.

Nevertheless, some types of information are generally excluded. Descriptions of historic buildings are usually seen as the remit of other record systems, as are descriptions of natural history, and non-human biological items. There is a commonly held view that information concerning archaeology, architectural history, natural history and biology is all part of the same fuzzily defined resource management database, but beyond a few locally based attempts, there has been no serious effort to define or construct such a record.

One class of data with an uneasy relationship with the archaeological database is that concerning collections of artefacts, commonly held in museums. There is a vast and productive enterprise devoted to cataloguing and describing the contents of museums, and many collections contain objects and information of central importance to field archaeologists. A county planning department might hold a record of the place where a gold torc was found, while the county museum might maintain a catalogue entry giving much detail of the same torc, displayed in its galleries. Even if each record contains a cross-reference to the other, the basic divide between field archaeology and museum archaeology is maintained, and there is little formal uniformity between the records.

A second class of data sitting uneasily on the margins of the archaeological database can be broadly defined as countryside heritage: ancient woodlands, flora-rich grasslands, medieval land divisions, and landscape features of all sorts that owe their origins to human management at some period in the past. Few archaeologists would deny that such information is properly part of the archaeological database but there have been few successful efforts to integrate it completely. When faced with the directing of scarce resources in the construction and maintenance of databases, archaeologists perceive that other matters are more central to their concerns than countryside features.

THE CONSTRUCTION OF THE DATABASE

The archaeological database has been constructed in two basic ways. The first method is by systematic field observation, where trained field archaeologists have walked selected areas of the land of Britain and have compiled consistent records of all archaeological entities they have observed. The outstanding example of this endeavour is the work of the field surveyors of the Ordnance Survey (OS), whose remit was to provide data concerning visible archaeological sites for display and publication on topographic maps. The second method is by documentary trawl of published information of all kinds, including academic reports, journals of learned societies, and many kinds of ephemeral literature. The outstanding and enduring example of this work is that carried out by the recorders of the OS and the three Royal Commissions.

The fundamental unit of recording in the archaeological database is not uniform. In essence, there are three different methods: by land parcel, by event and by archaeological entity (IAM 1984). The land-parcel method creates a new record for each piece of defined land, such as an agricultural field, or an urban block, or the land owned by a single person, or simply the land enclosed within a line drawn on a map or plan. Everything of archaeological interest within that land parcel is attributed to the record. The prime example of a land-parcel record is the schedule of ancient monuments where each entry is defined by a verbal description and a plan showing an area of land within a drawn line.

Another method of defining a record in an archaeological database is by event. These may include major excavations, minor field investigations, the finding of an artefact, the observation of structures during building work, or simply the taking of an aerial photograph. Examples of such event-based records include the *Excavations Index* compiled by the Royal Commission on the Historical Monuments of England (RCHME), and the catalogues of aerial photographs compiled by many organizations. Characteristically, event-based records include little interpretation of the information they contain.

The third method of defining a record is by archaeological entity. In such records, the unit of recording is a distinct feature or structure that is well understood and has a comprehensive definition (even if that definition is the subject of intense academic debate). Examples are 'henge', 'hillfort', 'moated site', 'castle', and 'smelt-mill'. The spatial extent of such records may not be clearly defined, and may overlap with other entities, but the record refers to a concept that is part of the common archaeological vocabulary. One attempt to provide a dictionary for this is the *Thesaurus of Archaeological Site Types* jointly published by the English government organizations (RCHME and English Heritage 1992).

In reality most components of the archaeological database contain records that are defined by all three methods: by land parcel, event and entity. This is a result of pragmatism: few records have the resources to interpret fully the information they receive (especially if this requires a field visit) and so it is accessed in the format in which it arrives. The common thread in all three methods is locational referencing: every record is tied to a specific place. Sometimes the place is very accurately defined down to a unique exact point or area, and sometimes the place is more vaguely described, as within a field, or within a certain distance of a known point, or even within a parish. But the vast majority of records in the British archaeological database are referenced in some way to a location: this will make the database a prime candidate in the future for the application of Geographic Information Systems (GIS).

THE COMPONENTS OF THE ARCHAEOLOGICAL DATABASE

The Record of Scheduled Monuments

The Ancient Monuments Protection Act of 1882 was the first public and legal recognition of the need for what would now be called an archaeological database. The legislation incorporated a schedule of monuments throughout Great Britain and Ireland (Chapter 5), which forms the basis for the current schedule of ancient monuments. After successive revisions, the statutory authority for the schedule now resides in Section 1 of the Ancient Monuments and Archaeological Areas Act 1979 (AMAA Act).

In addition, Section 2 of this legislation requires the publication of the schedule, a duty fulfilled by the responsible organizations in the form of county or region-based lists showing the location and name of each monument in the schedule (e.g. SDD 1989; DoE 1988).

These published lists of scheduled monuments are only an extract from a comprehensive archaeological database – the Record of Scheduled Monuments (RSM) – curated by Historic Scotland, English Heritage and Cadw. The number of entries is relatively small, with about 4,500 for Scotland, 2,700 for Wales, and about 13,000 for England, although the number of protected monuments and hence entries will rise considerably in the next decade. On the other hand, the amount of information contained in each entry is extensive and constantly updated by means of regular visits by field monument wardens, reflecting the national importance of this select, protected group of monuments. The RSM does not generally hold original archive material, but will contain references to the records held by the Royal Commissions, Sites and Monuments Records (SMRs) and other records.

Taking the English RSM as an example, each scheduled monument entry includes sub-records for different archaeological entities, or 'items', and contains data in four categories:

a. Location and identification
- Scheduled Monument title
- archaeological item title(s)
- Scheduled Monument grid reference
- archaeological item grid reference(s)
- county
- district
- parish
- height above Ordnance Datum

b. Descriptive
  - Scheduled Monument description
  - confirmation of boundary of protected area
  - Scheduled Monument assessment of importance
  - archaeological item description
  - archaeological item assessment of importance
  - monument class
  - period
  - components
  - history of events
  - sources

c. Management
  - Scheduled Monument management statement
  - area of protected site
  - other designations on site
  - other designations around site
  - current land use
  - form
  - condition
  - stability
  - vulnerability

d. Administration
  - file reference
  - administrative history
  - owner(s)
  - occupier(s)
  - other interested parties
  - record compilation date

In addition, the three component parts of the RSM include a map record capable of defining the exact extent of each Scheduled Monument, and subsidiary records of legal, administrative and conservation action.

The Royal Commissions

Britain has three organizations with the duty of compiling a national archaeological record. All three were originally granted Royal Warrants by Edward VII in 1908. In order of seniority, and using the shortened versions of their titles currently favoured, they are:

The Royal Commission on the Ancient and Historical Monuments of Scotland (RCAHMS)

The Royal Commission on the Ancient and Historical Monuments of Wales (RCAHMW)

The Royal Commission on the Historical Monuments of England (RCHME)

Each (until the revision of their Royal Warrants in 1992) had a similar remit: 'to make an inventory of the ancient and historical monuments and constructions connected with or illustrative of the contemporary culture, civilisation and conditions of life of the people from the earliest times, and to specify those which seem most worthy of preservation.'

Since 1908 this remit has been interpreted in several ways. For the greater part of the century, the Royal Commissions concentrated on the publication of volumes, known as *Inventories*, based on detailed field survey carried out by their own investigators. *Inventories* are normally county-based, each volume containing descriptions of several hundred monuments, and are well illustrated with drawings and photographs of the highest quality. Perhaps a third of the land area of Britain has been covered by *Inventories*, beginning with the old counties of Berwickshire in 1909, Hertfordshire in 1910, and Montgomery in 1911. Where an *Inventory* entry exists for a particular site or monument, it will reflect the highest standards of scholarship prevailing at the time of publication. For example, the Scottish Royal Commission has recently published the seventh and last volume in the *Inventory* of the former county of Argyll (RCAHMS 1992): the seven volumes are a remarkable distillation of knowledge completely fulfilling the objectives of the original Warrant.

In recent years, the Royal Commissions have recognized that publication to *Inventory* standard is too slow, given currently available resources, to meet modern archaeological needs. Each has attempted a contemporary restatement of its objectives, with the English Royal Commission's reading: 'to compile, and assess, curate and make available the national record of England's ancient monuments and historic buildings for the use of individuals and bodies concerned with understanding, interpreting and managing the historic environment' (RCHME 1992a). These restatements have been formalized in the issue of new Royal Warrants and the Commissions have adopted a variety of strategies to reflect the changed context of their work. The Scottish Royal Commission embarked in the 1980s on a series of rapid identification surveys, carrying out more selective and less intensive fieldwork, and publishing lists of sites and monuments in outline detail (e.g. Lamb 1982). It has also published more synthetic accounts with detailed information held in a central archive (e.g. RCAHMS 1990). The English Royal Commission has given much attention to studies of selected topics limited in scope and area such as the textile mills of Yorkshire (RCHME 1992b) and the earthworks of Bokerley Dyke (RCHME 1991).

All three Royal Commissions have also recognized that the modern archaeological database is not the sum total of published volumes but rather a continually evolving, constantly updated, mechanically accessible collection of information from a variety of disparate sources, not all of which can be equally validated. A constituent part of each National Monuments Record (NMR) is an archaeological database containing more than the material published in *Inventories*. Indeed, 'the Archaeological Database, and the Architectural Register together with the Collections of photographs, drawings and manuscripts now provide the Inventory . . . first envisaged' (Murray 1992: 210).

The (English) National Archaeological Record (based in London and Southampton) holds records of about 150,000 sites, more than 25,000 photographs of archaeological interest dating from the 1860s onwards, the (English) National Excavations Index, the English archives of the former OS Archaeology Division, and reports, drawings, and photographs compiled by RCHME and other fieldworkers. The (English) National Library of Air Photographs in Swindon contains 300,000 oblique and 3,500,000 vertical air photographs providing a complete record of the landscape since the beginning of the Second World War.

The National Monuments Record of Scotland (based in Edinburgh) contains records of some 70,000 archaeological sites, more than 700,000 drawings, and more than 650,000 photographs. It incorporates the Scottish archives of the former OS Archaeology Division and archives relating to excavations.

The National Monuments Record for Wales (based in Aberystwyth) has a total number of records approaching 80,000, although this includes historic buildings, monuments of all periods and other entities excluded from the totals mentioned above for England and Scotland. As in the other NMRs, the Welsh record contains the Welsh archives of the former OS Archaeology Division and excavation archives. It also includes 700,000 terrestrial and air photographs, 30,000 drawings and plans, and 30,000 large-scale maps.

The curators of each of the three national archaeological records have been forced to tackle the difficult question of whether their record is the record or simply an index to the record housed in many different places. In England an agreement between RCHME and the Association of County Archaeological Officers (ACAO) suggests that the National Archaeological Record 'will serve as the index to the contents of the often more detailed locally based [Sites and Monuments] records' (Aberg and Leech 1992: 168). In Scotland the National Monuments Record for Scotland is seen as 'the most comprehensive record available for archaeological monuments in Scotland' (Murray 1992: 210). In many ways this question is only relevant in the context of local and central government politics: the national archaeological records are both the best single accessible source of national data, and an index to many other local databases, including county-based sites and monuments records.

Sites and Monuments Records (SMRs)

A comparative newcomer to the British archaeological database is the network of locally based SMRs. The early history of this network has been summarized by Burrow (1984b; see also Chapter 10): in response to a growing need for accurate archaeological information to be fed into the planning system, from the 1970s onwards local authorities invested in the staff and resources required to compile and maintain a database for their own administrative area. In England the movement received considerable political and financial support from the Inspectorate of Ancient Monuments. In early years there was scant recognition of SMRs but their authority and usefulness is now enshrined in the English and Welsh General Development Order (Statutory Instrument No. 1813, 1988) – an adjunct to the formal planning system and the Town and Country Planning Acts – and in formal planning advice published in England (DoE 1990a) and Scotland (SOEnD 1992a and 1992b). Since 1990 the three Royal Commissions have been given the role of sponsoring and enhancing the development of SMRs.

A structural weakness of SMRs is that they are dependent upon the continued existence of their parent authorities, and local government is in a continual state of review. However, experience to date (notably the abolition of the English metropolitan counties) suggests that the SMRs are sufficiently robust, with sufficient political support, to survive the reorganization of local government. In England and Wales the ACAO, and in Scotland the Association of Regional and Island Archaeologists (ARIA) ensure that the SMRs operate together for their mutual benefit and improvement.

In England there are forty-six county-based SMRs. The majority have a county council as their parent organization. Six former metropolitan counties (Tyne and Wear, Merseyside, Greater Manchester, West Yorkshire, South Yorkshire and the West Midlands) have SMRs monitored by formal or informal joint committees of district or borough councils: these are based in a variety of institutions. The SMR for Greater London is curated by the London Region of English Heritage's Conservation Group. Of the SMRs housed in county councils, the most common location is the department responsible for planning or economic development, but a significant proportion are housed in other departments. One final anomaly is the SMR for Lancashire, curated by Lancaster University, but receiving some funding from Lancastrian local authorities.

A survey in 1984 (IAM 1984: 33) showed that the sum total of records then accessed to all forty-six SMRs was 302,000, with the largest number of records being in Devon (21,000) and

Cornwall (24,000). Since 1984, the number of accessed records has only increased by a small proportion, but the depth and accuracy of the information in each has been continuously reviewed.

The organization of SMRs in Wales reflects the general organization of archaeology in the Principality. Four archaeological trusts (for Gwynedd, Clwyd and Powys, Dyfed, and Glamorgan and Gwent) curate SMRs for their respective areas, and an SMR is maintained in the planning department of Clwyd County Council. The Welsh SMRs contain well over 60,000 records in total.

In Scotland, SMRs are curated by regional and island authorities. Seven of the nine regional and two of the three island councils have well-developed SMRs. As with England, most are located in departments of planning and development. The areas that currently do not have an SMR are Tayside and Lothian Regions and the Western Isles. A study carried out in 1991 suggested that the total number of records in those regions and island areas with SMRs was about 72,000 (Murray, pers. comm.). The Scottish Royal Commission continues to play a part in the development and enhancement of these records.

The single overwhelming strength of the network of SMRs is, paradoxically, the same as the weakness alluded to earlier: they are locally based. Most SMRs are accessible to all working archaeologists in the county or region, and the SMR staff are well placed to take note of new discoveries, newly found sources of material and threats of all kinds to archaeological resources. Perhaps most significant of all, SMR staff are the best source of information on the gaps and shortcomings of their own records, since a number of years of constant use of a relatively small database encourages familiarity with the archaeological resource in a way that is no longer possible for a single individual to acquire (because of the sheer quantity of data) with a national record.

Other components of the database

There are many other organizations that might claim to constitute important parts of the British archaeological database. These include the *Victoria History of the Counties of England* (VCH) which has published many valuable volumes on the early history and archaeology of selected counties, mostly broken down into parish surveys. They also include the many museums that maintain and curate locational records as part of their duty to maintain contextual information relating to their physical holdings. There are also books, pamphlets, articles, unpublished archives, research documents with limited circulation, and the unspoken thoughts and theories of thousands of archaeological workers – all are indisputably part of the database. But none are primary records in the way the RSM, the NMR, and the SMRs have become: ideally the three major components of the database will contain references or indexes to every other source of archaeological information.

USERS OF THE ARCHAEOLOGICAL DATABASE

In one sense, most users of the British archaeological database never consult the database themselves: the public dissemination of information on archaeology is carried out by means of television and radio programmes, newspaper and magazine articles, classroom teaching, talks, lectures and exhibitions (Chapter 19). All these media rely heavily on the distillation of information that has been processed and accessed into the various components of the archaeological database, and subsequently retrieved, interpreted, and synthesized into comprehensible and interesting packages. Even the most populist pamphlet for the visitor to Hadrian's Wall relies on a mosaic of facts and ideas about the

Roman occupation of Britain, the Roman army, and the native population that has been built up over the last century as a result of archaeological and historical research based on information contained in the common archaeological database.

More immediate users of the database fall into three categories: conservationists, researchers and educationalists. These categories are not distinct, and all three may be represented in the same individual at a single time. Nevertheless, they do articulate three distinct reasons for using the database. 'Conservationists', in the broadest sense and including planning archaeologists, are concerned with land management, with protecting the archaeological resource from being depleted or destroyed, and in steering land managers towards constructive and positive exploitation of the archaeological past. 'Researchers', including excavators, are more concerned with constructing images of the past and interpreting the remains of past human activity in a way that is understandable and attractive or interesting to modern people. 'Educationalists' are responsible for translating and transmitting these constructed images to a wide audience. All three categories of user have a common desire to see the archaeological database maintained and expanded, and they speak with a common voice in seeking to protect the database from being reduced or dismembered.

Conservationists

The conservationist users of the archaeological database include inspectors of ancient monuments employed by government heritage bodies, county and regional archaeologists employed by local authority development and planning departments, archaeological officers employed by major land-hungry organizations supplying goods, power, entertainment and transport, and archaeological consultants employed by a wide variety of clients assessing the heritage implications of their operations. The objective of all these users is to collect and interpret the available archaeological information to assist several government ministers, local planning committees, other statutory and non-statutory bodies, and organizations concerned with the investment of money. All of these decision-makers need to make informed and rational decisions about the future of the land for which they are responsible, and will frequently be required to balance archaeological considerations against a host of other social and economic factors.

Conservationists have become, without any question, the heaviest users of the archaeological database in the last decade or so, with many specific enquiries of short duration and many complex enquiries requiring deep interrogation of the database. This pattern is substantiated by the fact that local planning authorities have become heavy investors in the database, with county (and regional and island) SMRs being the rapidly expanding component of the database. SMRs are the most frequently consulted, by a wide margin, of all of the publicly accessible records. A survey by Lang in 1989 (Lang 1992: 175) suggested that strict planning-related enquiries accounted for more than 70 % of all enquiries to SMRs. On the whole, the Royal Commission databases have failed to capture this large growth of conservation-related endeavour: many archaeologists would like to see the power and accessibility of the NMRs being harnessed to assist in the achievement of conservation objectives.

Example 1: archaeological management of a local authority estate
Cambridgeshire County Council is the owner of some thirty farm estates in the county. As a responsible land manager it commissioned a report on each of these estates with a view to planning the future management of its land to the highest standards of archaeological conservation. The published report (Malim 1990) contains detailed management prescriptions for each estate and for each of the archaeological monuments on that estate. The primary archaeological record source was the Cambridgeshire SMR, with additional infor-

mation being provided by the nine volumes of the VCH, two volumes of the RCHME's *Inventory* of the county, and other published sources (Malim 1990: 18).

Example 2: an environmental assessment of a proposed landfill disposal site

In accordance with the planning regulations governing large-scale development proposals, Wimpey Waste Management Ltd prepared an Environmental Statement (Aspinwall and Company 1991) in support of their application to Cheshire County Council to develop a new landfill waste disposal facility at Risley, near Warrington in Cheshire. One of the ten technical reports in a very lengthy statement was commissioned from the Lancaster University Archaeological Unit. This report focused on the importance of the buried archaeology and standing buildings at Old Abbey Farm, a small medieval moated settlement. Following limited excavation and survey, the report assessed the relative importance of the moated settlement by comparing it (using a simple quantitative scoring system developed by English Heritage's Monuments Protection Programme) with all other known moated settlements recorded in the Cheshire SMR. The report concluded that 'Cheshire possesses a large number of moated sites, many of them in better condition and with more historic importance and greater amenity or re-use potential than Old Abbey Farm' (Aspinwall and Company 1991: vol. 1, 58).

Example 3: a local development plan

Every local authority in Britain is required to produce one or more development plans to provide guidance in the reaching of decisions under the planning legislation. Since the archaeological consequences of proposed development are a material consideration, many plans (and a great variety of formal and informal planning guidance produced by local authorities) contain policies that depend on an appreciation of the archaeological database. As one example, the Local Plan for Newbury, Berkshire (NDC 1990) refers to the SMR maintained by Berkshire County Council. It identifies four broad areas where it is most likely that development will have archaeological implications: the Saxon and medieval centres of six historic towns, the alluvium-covered bottoms of four river valleys, the Berkshire Downs, and two civil war battle sites. The plan then sets out three policies designed to mitigate the effects of any development proposals on the archaeological heritage of the district.

Researchers

Archaeological researchers are those users of the database who most closely correspond to the popular view of the field archaeologist. Typical researchers might include university and college lecturers, undergraduate and postgraduate students, excavators and surveyors exploring the context of their field projects, and post-excavation assistants searching for comparable sites.

Example 4: the palaeoenvironment and archaeology of a tidal estuary

As part of a wider research project into the Romano-British reclamation of the wetlands of the Severn estuary, Allen and Fulford (1990) examined in detail the documentary and archaeological sources for the third-century AD reclamation of the parish of Longney in Gloucestershire. Much of their data comes from the artefactual material garnered from field survey, but they acknowledge two important record sources: the SMR curated by Gloucestershire County Council, and unpublished material held by the VCH of Gloucestershire in the Gloucester Record Office.

Example 5: a regional study of a specific class of monument
The Neolithic chambered cairns of Scotland have long been the subject of detailed research
by Miss Audrey Henshall into their physical structure and their contents. In recent years this
has taken the form of regional surveys accompanied by analytical discussion. For example,
her jointly published work on the chambered cairns of Orkney (Davidson and Henshall 1989)
gives a detailed inventory of eighty sites in Orkney, and describes their present appearance,
all modern archaeological activity, and all the recovered artefacts. In their acknowledgements, the primary locational archive quoted by Davidson and Henshall is the National
Monuments Record of Scotland (NMRS). Throughout the inventory there are frequent
references to the NMRS and to the surveys carried out by Dr Raymond Lamb, the Orkney
Archaeologist who curates the SMR for the islands.

For many researchers the archaeological database is only the starting point of their work
and they frequently contribute more, in the long term, than they extract from it. In terms
of magnitude of use, researchers are probably the least significant users, but their
enquiries are rarely short or simple and usually require complex interrogation of the database. For this reason, researchers are among the most skilful and experienced of users.

Educationalists

Educational users of the archaeological database cover the full spectrum of formal education from the nursery school to higher and further education, and also take in the expanding array of informal education which shades into leisure and recreation. Typical users
might be the primary school teacher preparing for a visit of his class to a local guardianship monument, the extramural lecturer delivering a course on the Roman antiquities of
her local region, and the tourist guide responsible for showing coachloads of visitors
around heritage attractions.

An important tool for all educationalists (and, indeed, for conservationists and
researchers) are the OS maps which portray archaeological sites: the Royal Commissions
provide information to the OS to update continually all OS maps. In most cases, educationalists' use of the archaeological database results in a verbal presentation to a limited
audience, so the examples below of published or widely distributed material are not perhaps typical.

Example 6: a popular guide to the heritage of a region
In recent years two new authoritative series of regional guides to archaeological monuments and buildings have emerged: *Exploring Scotland's Heritage*, published by the
Scottish Royal Commission in eight volumes; and *Exploring England's Heritage*, to be
published in eleven volumes in association with English Heritage. Each volume, covering
a small number of counties or regions, contains general essays on selected topics, and a
short description of a hundred or more of the best archaeological sites. The intent of both
series is well expressed by Professor Barry Cunliffe in his introduction to the English
series. England, he writes, is 'a beautiful, gentle country full of fascinating corners,
breathtaking sights – an eclectic mix of insurpassable [*sic*] quality. All you need is someone with vision to show you how to start looking' (Weaver 1992: vii). Each volume relies
on the personal knowledge of the distinguished archaeologist author, as well as formal
access to the archaeological database. For example, the volume for Grampian (Shepherd
1986) was written by Grampian's regional archaeologist, who acknowledges the assistance of the staff of RCAHMS, his own department, and several smaller archives.

Example 7: a teachers' guide to a Roman villa

Lullingstone Roman Villa, near Eynsford in Kent, is a property in the care of English Heritage. To assist the enjoyment and educational value of school visits, the Education Service of English Heritage has published a handbook for teachers (Watson 1991). It describes the site, suggests activities for children, and provides much information for teachers on Lullingstone, life on a Romano-British estate, and the exercise of archaeology in general. Although there are no direct references or acknowledgements to any compon-ent of the primary archaeological database, the list of resources for teachers (Watson 1991: 37) includes publications specific to Lullingstone, publications on Roman Britain and Roman archaeology ranging from general guides to very specific topics, and other resources such as videos and museums to visit. Each of these resources rely for their fun-damental information on the archaeological database.

Educationalists are the broadest and most disparate set of users, and include many individ-uals who may only ever make a small number of enquiries of the database. Despite this, among their number are the most influential of users and several SMRs have deliberately set out to court this sector, anticipating an increase in its importance in the future.

CONCLUSIONS

Lang (1992: 177) identifies five current issues facing SMRs that are equally relevant for the wider archaeological database: these are enhancing the scope of the database, integra-tion with related databases, technical developments in computing, including the develop-ment of time-series analysis procedures (tracking the progressive changes in the record and the site to which it refers), and funding of the database. These are issues that will con-tinue to occupy archaeologists over the next decade and into the future.

This brief description of the British archaeological database allows two more general conclusions to be drawn. The first is that the components of the database contain a vast amount of archaeological information collected over the last century by many archaeolo-gists for different purposes. That information is now used for many other purposes and there is no necessary correlation between the source of information and the use to which it is now being put. Unevenness in the quality of data collection is recognized to be a prob-lem, but information is constantly being updated and validated as needs are perceived and as resources are made available to fulfil those needs.

The second inescapable conclusion is that the dynamic nature of all archaeological records requires every record to be professionally curated. A record needs staff trained professionally in field survey and documentary research, experienced in the technical aspects of maintaining a computerized database, and competent in the art of structuring and answering partly formed inquiries. Without such staff, the record becomes a weighty megalith, impressive in its unrealized potential for enhancing knowledge, but dumb and very capable of being completely misinterpreted.

ACKNOWLEDGEMENTS

I am grateful to those with whom I have discussed the contents of this chapter and those who have provided information: Ian Ralston, Diana Murray, Ian Shepherd, Donnie Mackay, Hilary Malaws, Bill Startin, Henry Owen-John and Neil Lang. The archaeological profession is indebted to all cur-ators, past and present, of the various components of the archaeological database.

CHAPTER 4

THE STRUCTURE OF BRITISH ARCHAEOLOGY

John Hunter and Ian Ralston
with contributions by Ann Hamlin

INTRODUCTION

Even a cursory investigation of the development of field archaeology in the UK over the last half century immediately highlights its underdeveloped structure in any formal sense. Structure infers an organized framework of functions administered by an overall authority. Archaeology exhibits none of this, except in Northern Ireland (below); instead it shows piecemeal, if quantum, evolution during the decades 1970–90 in which central government, local government, learned societies, universities, amenity groups and individuals responded in large measure autonomously to an unprecedented set of changes threatening the archaeological environment.

In the beginning, if such a phrase can be used to mark a point in the 1960s that might epitomize the old order of archaeology's public function, professional, applied field archaeology was essentially practised by the small archaeological staffs of state or quasi-state bodies backed by long-established statute or Royal Warrant. Elsewhere, the keyword was research – essentially museological, seasonal and performed by those who were either interested enough or could afford to participate. Thereafter, and with increasing impetus throughout the 1970s and 1980s, this arrangement was progressively changed in response to a set of unprecedented demands posed by the quickening pace of the impact of modern development on the archaeological resource, and the increasing recognition that the latter was finite. The emergence of archaeological units, trusts, county archaeologists and indeed many university departments stems from this period. They belong to the era of so-called rescue archaeology (Rahtz 1974b; Jones 1984; Owen-John 1986; Barker 1987), which witnessed changes in the dynamics of archaeology, in funding and in legislation, and which widened the professionalization of archaeological practice. This reorientation brought into focus, for many more archaeologists than had previously deemed this a central concern, the need for basic philosophies of heritage management.

Rescue archaeology spawned responses at all levels: it created an ad hoc, ungainly, evolving structure that largely compounded earlier geographical inequalities in archaeological attention and resources, despite contrary advice (CBA 1974). The rapid expansion of rescue work, although widely welcomed, also resulted in disparate and inconsistent policy control. The acquisition of resources was heavily dependent on the public purse, and was thus modified by governmental initiatives, notably those that saw many young unemployed engaged on archaeological work-experience schemes. These developments were acceptable to the archaeological community not because they were especially effective, but in considerable measure because they witnessed an exponential leap in the financial support available for field archaeology. Further, the number of separate agencies underwriting this work multiplied: retrospectively, the system must have appeared to many impossible to alter – a *fait accompli* of historical accident ('Gildas' 1988).

The rescue boom was not however a unitary phenomenon. It underwent progressive modifications resulting from external influences and internal re-evaluation. It has, nevertheless, bequeathed an important legacy to archaeology today (Mytum and Waugh 1987; Spoerry 1992a). Efforts to formalize the disparate structure inherited from the rescue phase have produced a proliferation of committees and liaison bodies: some progress has been made, in attempts to audit the relevant resources (Hart 1987), for example. The need for rationalization, including the disbursement of the restricted research funding available to British field archaeology, has also borne fruit in the establishment of the Forum for Co-ordination in the Funding of Archaeology.

Alongside the growth of new archaeological organizations during this period, the long-established state-funded services involved in field archaeology have also been progressively modified.

CENTRAL GOVERNMENT

State involvement with field antiquities can be traced back to Henry VIII, whose dissolution of monastic holdings led to the Office of the King's Works taking on responsibility for the care of redundant ecclesiastical buildings as well as outmoded royal strongholds. A fundamental change in emphasis in state involvement with historic and archaeological remains had to wait until late Victorian times. The passing of the first Ancient Monuments legislation during Gladstone's administration in 1882 was accompanied by the creation of the position of Inspector of Ancient Monuments, held by Pitt Rivers, the first of a distinguished series of early antiquarians holding that, and equivalent posts in other parts of the UK.

The appropriate government office, originally housed within the Ministry of Public Building and Works, was eventually subsumed, in England, within the Department of the Environment in 1969. Much of its present function developed there as a response to the rapid changes of the 1970s. Policy and funding were implemented via a body of inspectors answerable to the Ancient Monuments Board; it was charged with regional responsibilities for both rescue archaeology and relevant areas of statutory preservation. In England, the inspectorate was assisted by area advisory committees composed of local academics, fieldworkers, senior archaeological personalities and participating local authorities, although this devolved advisory structure was not paralleled elsewhere. These and other 'quango' committees were abolished as a result of changes emanating from government since 1979.

Statutory powers were increased by the passing of the Ancient Monuments and Archaeological Areas Act 1979 (AMAA Act 1979, see Chapter 5). Additional funding enabled the establishment of a mobile Central Excavation Unit (Anon 1986), the functions of which have been modified in recent years (see Chapter 14), and the development of a strong central laboratory facility in London to cover conservation, analytical, palaeoenvironmental and geophysical demands. Despite the addition of regional contract laboratories, post-excavation resources of these types remained wholly overloaded (DoE 1978).

The whole facility was nominally removed from civil service status in 1983 by the creation of the Historic Buildings and Monuments Commission (HBMC, popularly known as English Heritage). HBMC combined the functions of the Ancient Monuments Board and the Historic Buildings Council in a 'super-quango' deliberately established at arm's length from government; the intention was to optimize on a degree of funding flexibility and operational versatility unavailable to a civil service department. A parallel although slightly later change saw the creation of Cadw in Wales. In Scotland the appropriate government department remained until late in the decade largely uninfluenced by the quasi-governmental English model; the name was changed, however, to Historic Scotland.

The activities and the funding policy of English Heritage (EH) are best reflected in its annual reports (e.g. HBMC 1989), and in a discussion paper (English Heritage n.d.) which presented a snapshot of financial distribution on a regional, period and priority basis throughout England and Wales (see Chapter 13). Included within the typical budget are allowances for education (in accord with EH's role of public dissemination), for basic survey cover (as a portion of the overall state funding of this key activity) as well as for excavation. A substantial part of the budget continues to be earmarked for publication, of both backlog and current fieldwork funded by central government. Publication problems resulting from rescue archaeology were identified and partly resolved in an Ancient Monuments Board report (DoE 1975a), with sequels (e.g. Cunliffe 1982). The most recent publication proposal is that of a consortium of organizations led by the Society of Antiquaries (1992): the group's proposal, an attempt to answer the publication problems posed by increased developer funding (see Chapter 19), met with widespread opposition in its initial, draft form.

The introduction of new planning directives in 1990 (see Chapter 10) effectively altered the status of English Heritage from major national funding agency and policy co-ordinator to that of a lesser funding agent (as the 'polluter pays' philosophy is extended into field archaeology), but with proactive archaeological potential; it provided, too, an advisory capability, for example with respect to project management (English Heritage 1991b) and policy guidelines (English Heritage 1991a). The same environment of developer funding also caused greater autonomy among units (below): degrees of privatization occurred (see Chapter 14) that even spread to components of the central facility. Thus Historic Scotland's Central Excavation Unit – Archaeological Operations and Conservation Ltd (AOC) – is now part of the private sector.

The national agencies of England, Wales and Scotland, whether loosely or rigidly attached to central government, share particular responsibilities, both for the day-to-day curation of archaeological resources (English Heritage 1991d; Historic Scotland 1991) as well as for 'the Estate' (that is, those monuments and their surroundings in state care). The principal legislative framework for their activities is that furnished by the AMAA Act 1979; for Northern Ireland see below.

In terms of oversight of legislation affecting ancient monuments and field archaeological resources, the government departments holding the principal responsibilities are the Department of the Environment, the Welsh and Scottish Offices, and the Department of the Environment (Northern Ireland). The recently created Department of National Heritage has now also taken on some responsibilities, for example, with regard to the potential impact of the convention on archaeological protection (CoE 1992) signed in Malta in early 1992. Its contribution is largely unassessed but its initial responsibilities, despite its title, seem to be limited to England. In England and Wales, despite the creation of English Heritage and Cadw, respectively, the statutory responsibility for monuments remains vested with the respective Secretaries of State. The system continues to function through the inspectorate; the processes of scheduling Ancient Monuments (and the enhancement scheme in England – the Monuments Protection Programme (Darvill *et al.* 1987) and the maintenance of Guardianship sites is a statutory function of government irrespective of the vehicle through which it operates (Davies 1985).

SURVEY AND RECORD AT NATIONAL LEVEL

In the first decade of this century, and partly as a result of sustained extra-parliamentary pressure, the Royal Commissions on Ancient and Historical Monuments were created by Royal Warrant with the unenviable remit of preparing an inventory of the 'culture, civilisation and conditions of the life of the people . . . from earliest times and to specify those which seem most worthy of preservation'. The Warrants have since been redefined and were reissued in 1992, taking into account gradual changes in practice and scope (Chapter 3). The Commissions were, and remain, centrally funded, but are not part of the civil service. Policy and decisions are ratified by commissioners appointed by the Crown and implemented by skilled investigators.

In all cases (except in Northern Ireland, below) the Warrant was implemented primarily by county-based survey of both upstanding as well as buried remains at a level of detail and a pace which, while permitting the display of very considerable scholarship, became incompatible with the changing requirements of field survey during the 1970s. The production of lavish and expensive *Inventory* volumes, necessarily at a slow pace, was increasingly acknowledged as difficult to justify in the rescue environment. The need to implement a more basic level of survey cover, but more extensive in area terms, was perceived as urgent; the Commissions were able to take an advisory role in this reorientation.

The significance of non-intensive National Monuments Records (NMRs), held by the respective Commissions, develops from this period, as does diversification into thematic publications and more popular works, drawing on the Commissions' survey activities. It is, however, the development of NMR facilities, including aerial photographic resources (Chapters 3 and 18), that most reflects the changing needs of modern field archaeology. These include the provision of a database for Sites and Monuments Records (SMRs) and evaluation needs, and of central archive repositories for the outcomes of increasing amounts of fieldwork.

During this period the Royal Commissions were also obliged to absorb the work of the Archaeological Division of the Ordnance Survey (below). The Commissions were largely unaffected by the changes that altered, for example, English Heritage's relationships with central government in the early 1980s. Since 1992, the Commissions have additionally taken over responsibility for making inventories of sites within territorial waters (Chapter 7), reflecting further rationalization in governmental procedures.

Another strand of considerable importance in the quantification and depiction of Britain's field archaeological resources came through the recording of field antiquities by the Ordnance Survey (OS), the state's official cartographic agency. Much archaeological data was collected in the mid-Victorian detailed survey of the UK; that which did not appear of the published version of the maps was incorporated in the OS *Name Books*, those for England unfortunately having been a casualty of the bombing of Southampton during the Second World War (Davidson 1986).

After the First World War, the OS appointed its first archaeological officer, O.G.S. Crawford in 1920, a post which was subsequently expanded to become a branch and latterly a division of the OS, prior to its demise when the Serpell Committee thought fit to pass central responsibility for archaeological survey entirely to the Royal Commissions. Pride of place must however be accorded here to the OS's field archaeological surveyors; the OS remains the sole body to have attempted field survey of Britain's field archaeological resources on a nationwide basis. The records assembled by the OS field surveyors, in card form, now underpin both the NMRs, constituent parts of the Royal Commissions (see above), and intensive SMRs assembled at local authority level (see below and Chapter 10).

LOCAL GOVERNMENT

During the 1970s and 1980s local authorities, encouraged by central government, did much to improve the curation of the archaeological resource. Outwith their museum services, the employment of archaeologists by local authorities was rare until the early

1970s; thereafter, with Department of the Environment encouragement, many county and metropolitan councils in England established intensive SMRs for their areas, appointing the additional specialist staff necessary to achieve this. The exercise was primarily intended to create a database of archaeological remains to serve decision-making within the context of local planning; it additionally provided a strong curatorial facet as forward-planning strategies developed (see Chapter 10). The compilation of the database often took the form of implications surveys, an overview of which (Heighway 1972) pointed to the particular severity of the threat within ancient towns. It is ironic that the existing museum service, although locally funded and often with a resident core of archaeologically trained personnel, and analytical, conservation and other facilities, played little formal part in the development of this national archaeological structure. Latterly, however, storage and archiving requirements, among other factors, have caused this to be reassessed (Museums Association 1989; Lewis 1989; Chapter 21).

In many instances, archaeologists (often located on the staffs of planning departments) were complemented by the establishment of field teams, with the capacity to undertake rescue excavations, to conduct programmes of survey and fieldwalking, and also, in some instances, to undertake educational work. By the end of the 1970s this regional network, although weighted heavily towards the south and southeast of England, was consolidated by the presence of county archaeologists in nearly all county planning departments in England, and in the new regional areas of Wales (where the creation of multi-function archaeological trusts was the norm: see below), but somewhat less densely in Scotland (Beresford Dew 1977; Spoerry 1992b). Variability in the speed of compilation and the level of detail incorporated in regional SMRs reflected the uneven distribution of financial and manpower resources – factors that the Royal Commission's *Survey of Surveys* (RCHME 1978) and subsequent work by English Heritage (IAM 1984) did much to emphasize.

The impetus of this development of archaeological provision at the local level was considerable. Sustained and effective pressure orchestrated by the pressure group RESCUE (below), underpinned by the results of intensive fieldwork ahead of motorway and building construction, demonstrated that the threats to finite and irreplaceable archaeological resources were many and severe. The work of influential small groups like the Rescue Archaeology Group in Wales (Owen-John 1986) demonstrated that high-quality fieldwork, including excavation, was achievable over prolonged field seasons employing small teams of professional archaeologists, a radical departure from previous practices. The pace of redevelopment in the cores of historic towns, and the scale, wealth and complexity of archaeological deposits (most especially perhaps in York and London, but demonstrated most effectively to a surprised public in Deansgate, Manchester), equally demanded an archaeological response not equatable with the rhythms of previous archaeological fieldwork, in most cases limited to relatively short field seasons when staff of other archaeological organizations, notably universities, were either available or at liberty to take on such responsibilities.

The Department of the Environment's strategy at that time was thus to build up a system of territorially based multi-county units, loosely reflecting the Council for British Archaeology's regional structure. This operated with an admixture of funding drawn from central and local government sources, although a small level of developer funding had begun to appear in the input figures by 1974. In some instances it became increasingly possible to obtain voluntary financial support from developers (Hobley 1987; Anon 1989); in London in particular a substantial, integrated archaeological service was created. More recently the obligation for pre-development assessments to consider the treatment of cultural heritage as a necessary component of working costs (below) has led to further reorientation, but before this became government policy, UK government spending on rescue archaeology rose spectacularly in line with increasing fieldwork needs and rising standards of practice (Beresford Dew 1977; Chapter 14). Additional funding also became available locally from various Manpower Services Commission programmes – training schemes that artificially boosted the available fieldwork resource from the public purse. Many excavations, especially those in urban environments of which Perth is a notable example, became possible as a result. Such projects lasted until the second half of the 1980s, when changes in the ground rules for such schemes radically diminished the scope for using them in the furtherance of archaeological work (Drake and Fahy 1987; Mellor 1986, 1988).

The pattern that developed in Wales and Scotland was somewhat different. In Wales (CBA Wales 1988; Owen-John 1986), a number of multi-function regional trusts, not directly integrated with the local authorities, but often consulted on planning-related matters, was established. Contrastingly, the employment of archaeologists within local authority planning departments (Manley 1987) has remained rare, such that the units generally fulfil both curatorial and contracting roles. In Scotland, the decentralization of the control of archaeological resources developed much more slowly (Chapter 10). State support for rapid survey was initially made available to the Society of Antiquaries of Scotland, but was subsequently reallocated to the Scottish Royal Commission, which has since received further financial inputs from the Scottish Office specifically for strategic survey in relation to afforestable lands. Certain regional and island authorities employ archaeologists (in no case more than two), essentially in the first instance to compile SMRs and to advise on planning matters. On the urban front, the City of Aberdeen, exceptionally, developed a small integrated archaeological service. By contrast, the Perth-based but territorially wide-ranging Scottish Trust for Urban Archaeology was again set up initially under the aegis of the Society of Antiquaries of Scotland, but with a heavy reliance on Scottish Office funding at the outset.

ARCHAEOLOGICAL UNITS AND TRUSTS

Archaeological organizations, usually designed as field units, emerged throughout the 1970s and became consolidated and to some extent fossilized during the cutbacks in public spending in the 1980s. By the end of that decade, many such organizations responded to the new scope of planning controls (notably the Environmental Assessment Regulations from 1988). Subsequently, the role of the development control function of the planning system in curating archaeological resources was formalized in policy guidance to local authorities (DoE 1990a; Welsh Office 1991; SOEnD 1992a, 1992b). Resources for archaeological work were increasingly obtained from a wider range of private clients (Chapter 14), the majority being commercial developers. In acting thus as contractors to the corporate sector, a number of units, particularly those still based within local government, saw potential conflicts arising with their existing area-based curatorial roles (Chapter 16). The greater diversity of funding sources, and ongoing relations with client organizations, also enabled certain units to develop a remit geographically wider than their territory as originally defined by local or central government spending patterns. New units, outwith the local authority ambit, and thus not bound by such territorial conventions, also came into being. The impact of this change, the demise of terrritoriality, was to introduce new stresses within the archaeological community as competitive tendering (CT) for fieldwork projects, previously allocated on a territorial basis, arose (Chapters 15 and 16).

Although the evolution of units has been remarkably rapid, it still reflects the piecemeal fashion in which organizations emerged in a variety of different administrative guises, in local authority departments, as independent charitable trusts or, latterly, in universities and as private companies. Most large ancient towns, and especially those in the south of England, have their own resident units. Of these, Carlisle, Oxford, York, Canterbury, Lincoln, London, Gloucester, Southampton and Winchester are among the foremost examples. Several of these centres received greater legal protection with the full implementation of provisions in the 1979 AMAA Act (Chapter 5). The protection of the cores of historic towns, made possible by Section II of the 1979 Act, was never employed outside England, and this provision is now under review. At Winchester, however, the archaeological group was uniquely proactive – a research unit undertaking urban excavations at an unprecedented and unrepeated scale. The group was later supplemented by a separate urban rescue unit. Few of these units however tackle projects outside their home urban centres.

The location of units and trusts was to a large extent dependent on the activities of individuals and pressure groups within the relevant areas. Success depended on a number of factors, not least of which were local authority sympathy (expressed in part financially) and public co-operation. Sociologically, the most responsive areas were predominantly the wealthier middle-class regions of the south of England; less successful were parts of northern England, southwest England and most of Scotland. Restrictions in public funding in the early 1980s effectively fossilized the creation of units at that point in the evolution of regional archaeological presence (Beresford Dew 1977: 5).

The present picture largely reflects that position although there is a fundamental difference: in their origins most units were heavily funded from local authority resources; as a result their operational remits were strictly contained within local authority boundaries (Chapter 14). Thus the concept of territoriality was born; not only did this have immense implications when competitive tendering emerged in the late 1980s, but a further concomitant was that many areas of the country were either inadequately resourced or not covered at all.

The original concept of the multi-county unit, as promoted in England, would have permitted a more even distribution of archaeological services, each unit being provided with back-up facilities, a career structure for its staff and a means through which policy could have been directed centrally (Chapter 13). Instead an inequitable system emerged: policy-making was largely vested at the local level, and considerable inconsistencies in practices and approaches arose from one area to the next. Some units were specific to ancient towns (for example, York), some to metropolitan authorities (for example, Greater Manchester), some to whole counties (for example, West Yorkshire) and a small number to multi-county areas (for example, Wessex). The nature of their funding lay substantially within the confines of rescue work, and especially excavation. Research objectives played a lesser role, although these could be combined, albeit crudely, with threat-oriented work. Only in places like Wessex could a more rigorous academic approach be implemented, for example, on a thematic basis (Ellison 1981), because the larger geographical canvas allowed research objectives such as the development of urban infrastructure, the scope of trade or the impact of religion to be pursued within the rescue opportunities at the regional level.

The structure of individual units varies, but usually embraces in-house both excavation and post-excavation staff. The management is headed by a director, himself or herself an archaeologist, often aided by an administrator. The organization may additionally contain conservation, photographic and other post-excavation facilities. Larger units also undertake educational work: an early but useful organizational model, including this role, was proposed for London (Biddle and Hudson 1973: 41–6). Later, and in tandem with the move towards a measure of independence from central and local government financial support, many units adopted more sophisticated management systems, marketing ploys and costing strategies in keeping with the commercial environment in which they now find themselves (see Chapters 14 and 15).

These developments occurred in tandem with the emergence of archaeological consultants, the latest group to be spawned by the demands of the commercial world (Chapter 15). Most units also acted in this role, but the new, wider system of operation gave scope for individuals and small groups to set up in private practice. Such consultants are obliged to tender for work in evaluating or assessing the archaeological implications of the development schemes proposed by government departments, agencies and companies. Other specialist units, concentrating for example on aerial photography or geophysical survey, are generally sub-contracted to other archaeological units. The practice of field archaeology thus finds itself in the front line of commercial and contractual operations (Chapter 16); and thus, to an extent previously unparalleled, exposed to direct involvement in planning enquiries and litigious operations. A number of the larger construction or engineering companies, for example Gifford and Partners, employ their own in-house archaeological expertise, a move now spreading to planning consultancies and landscape architects. At the time of writing, however, most such organizations seek archaeological inputs from archaeological units and consultancies. Very few predominantly archaeological units claim to have the expertise to take on the full scope of, for example, environmental assessments.

ARCHAEOLOGICAL MANAGEMENT IN NORTHERN IRELAND

The organization of archaeology in Northern Ireland is so different from that in the rest of the UK that brief separate treatment is appropriate. The differences arise from a different historical development and different legislation (see Appendix to Part Two, p. 134). Responsibility for State Care monuments goes back to the disestablishment of the Church of Ireland in 1869. The 1920s and 1930s saw the addition of powers to protect by scheduling, to control archaeological excavation by licensing, and to administer the law relating to archaeological finds. To these responsibilities were added others in 1950 with the establishment of the Archaeological Survey of Northern Ireland within the Ministry of Finance. The two staff members were appointed to carry out archaeological and architectural survey on the pattern of the Great Britain Commissions, though without a Royal Warrant. During the 1960s and especially the 1970s the number of staff increased and much effort was directed to rescue excavation, as elsewhere in the UK, as well as protection, record-building and continuing survey.

The present range of work is therefore very wide (Hamlin 1989; DoE (NI) 1990). State Care monuments numbering 176 are conserved, maintained and presented. There are just over 1,000 scheduled monuments and in 1992 the first three field monument wardens were appointed. An SMR was built up during the 1970s, as elsewhere in the UK, and now, with information on about 13,000 sites, it provides the basis of the protection work through monitoring all land-use applications potentially affecting monuments. Only one survey volume has been published – *An Archaeological Survey of County Down* (MoF 1966) – but two further county surveys are in preparation, on Armagh and Fermanagh, and the basic identification survey of all six counties is due to be completed in 1995. Architectural and industrial survey are largely taken up with recording threatened buildings.

Excavation work has concentrated on threatened sites, chance discoveries, and investigation before conservation work. The book *Pieces of the Past* (Hamlin and Lynn 1988) illustrates the way in which research themes have been pursued through rescue opportunities, for example rath-mounds of the Early Christian period. There was no Manpower Services Commission funding in Northern Ireland, and though some job creation labour was used for historic monuments work it did not contribute significantly to excavation. There has recently been some development of contract archaeology, though not on the Great Britain scale, and there is little developer funding. Planning Policy Guidance Note

16 (PPG 16, DoE 1990a) has already been referred to in several Northern Ireland planning appeals and a Northern Ireland planning and archaeology document is under discussion. The commercial pressures of the 1980s have had far less impact in Northern Ireland than in Great Britain, but there are particular pressures at present from regeneration and similar enhancement schemes in historic settlements, funded in part by the International Fund for Ireland and the European Community Regional Development Fund .

In October 1992 the Northern Ireland Monuments and Buildings Record was opened to the public. This can be seen as the Northern Ireland equivalent of the (non-intensive) National Monuments Records, with its constituent parts (Sites and Monuments, Industrial Heritage, Architectural and Gardens) being the intensive records, all housed in one location. During 1993 a start will be made on compiling an inventory of sites in territorial waters (see Chapter 7), and this is combined with the curatorial role: under an agency agreement with the Department of National Heritage, the Department of the Environment for Northern Ireland is responsible for administering the Protection of Wrecks Act (1973). Under the 1971 Historic Monuments Act (NI) (see Appendix, p. 134) it is also responsible for administering the law relating to archaeological finds and pursuing breaches of the law, for example, unlicensed searching for archaeological material with a metal detector. Finally, there is a wide range of public relations and educational work, including co-operation with schools, contributions to exhibitions, organization of events, production of popular publications, and talks.

Northern Ireland thus has a centralized, integrated archaeological service that combines the functions of many central, regional and county bodies in Great Britain, and this service is part of a highly centralized structure of administration in Northern Ireland. The historic monuments and buildings work is carried out within the Environment Service, a grouping created within the Department of the Environment for Northern Ireland in 1990 to bring together responsibility for countryside and wildlife, environmental protection (see Chapter 22), and historic monuments and buildings. DoE (NI) is also responsible for planning, housing, transport, roads and water. There is no county tier of local government. In 1973 the six counties were abolished as administrative units, so Northern Ireland saw none of the archaeological developments at local authority level which were such a feature of England in the 1970s. The 27 district and borough councils have very limited powers. Some do run local museums, in which a few archaeologists are employed, but there are no local authority archaeologists and no county units or SMRs.

To a certain extent the Northern Ireland provision may seem to resemble the 1960s Great Britain position already characterized as 'applied field archaeology practised by the small archaeological staff of state . . . bodies' (above), and in scale it may seem to resemble a large English county. Yet it covers a far wider range of functions than any single body in Great Britain, combining protecting and recording, acting as both curator and contractor. In the particular circumstances of Northern Ireland, with 80 % of the land under agriculture, a population of 1.5 million, and no site more than about two hours' drive from Belfast, this integrated organization makes for a very effective operation, each aspect of the work contributing to the others, resulting in cross-fertilization and multiplication. The work is firmly based on the philosophy of stewardship, and the protection and best management of the inherited resource for present and future generations.

NON-GOVERNMENT AND VOLUNTARY ORGANIZATIONS

Since the 18th century (but more particularly from the reign of Victoria), the creation of learned and/or amenity societies has been a major factor in the development of British field archaeology, and in the dissemination of information and opinion. The senior organization is the Society of Antiquaries of London, established in 1707. The 19th century saw this complemented by further national societies, such as the Royal Archaeological Institute, as well as by a range of county-based organizations. Of the latter, the Society of Antiquaries of Newcastle upon Tyne (1813) is the oldest (Jobey 1990). Some of these are exclusively archaeological in their interests, but many also embrace local history and/or natural history. The county organizations normally have between 500 and 1,500 members, publish journals (and in some instances monograph series), and may have amassed libraries and archives of importance, as is the case notably with the Yorkshire Archaeological Society. Some also run museums. The largest of these 'broad-canvas' societies in membership terms is the Society of Antiquaries of Scotland, with some 2,800 members (in 1990).

The principal characteristic of many of the societies formed in this century has been balkanization, either in terms of geographical scope or of period interests. In the latter category, the earliest foundation (1911) is the Society for the Promotion of Roman Studies, with some 3,200 members (1990) the biggest in the UK, although its interests are Empire-wide and not exclusively British. The Prehistoric Society was formed in 1935, by a takeover of the East Anglian society and the widening (in this instance to world-scale) of its geographical scope. Other national societies with period-based or more specific remits were established between the mid-1950s and the mid-1970s: medieval, nautical (again international in scope), post-medieval, and industrial. Many of these have developed policy statements on the need for support for research (and its prioritization) or legislative changes required to safeguard the archaeological resource (as in the case of the Nautical Archaeology Society) within their domains (Chippindale and Gibbins 1990; CBA 1988a, 1988b). Others have developed as institutions that have attracted considerable academic respect, for example the Cambridge Committee for Aerial Photography, whose archives now constitute one of the main national photographic databases.

Since the Second World War, and more especially between the mid-1950s and the early-1980s, a large number of smaller, local groups has been established. Indeed, the median date for the establishment of all archaeological societies (over 150) listed in a recent *Current Archaeology* survey is about 1960 (Selkirk 1990). With typical memberships of between 50 and 200, these groups are a product of the popularization of archaeology in the post-war period, and in many instances of the perceptions of threats to the archaeological resource at the local scale: such groups normally lay stress on active fieldworking amongst their interests. This may be conducted in their own right, or in collaboration with locally based professional archaeologists. This relationship is placed under some stress by the changing nature of the organization and funding of much field archaeological endeavour, as noted above and elsewhere in this volume (Chapter 20).

In Northern Ireland, while there is widespread general good will towards monuments, and a major case like the Navan Fort Public Inquiry in 1985 can attract intense interest, amateur archaeology is underdeveloped compared with Great Britain. There has been a huge growth in local history societies since the 1970s and there is an active Federation for Ulster Local Studies. These societies often number archaeology among their interests, but their activities rarely extend to practical archaeology.

Archaeology was traditionally viewed as an amateur pastime whose manpower resources were co-ordinated by the Council for British Archaeology (CBA), established in 1944 as the successor to the Congress of Archaeological Societies, with a regional network. The CBA's activities were based mainly on active local fieldwork (usually in England), with regular meetings of groups interested in a wide range of relevant topics. The CBA has responded to the demands of modern archaeology with a committee structure representing areas such as scientific applications and policy, the countryside, urban affairs, churches and education; membership of these is drawn from the professional, academic and voluntary sectors with an active publication outlet to match. The CBA is unique in representing all elements of British archaeology; in Scotland its sister organization, the Council for Scottish Archaeology, takes a similar role (Proudfoot 1986).

Independent and funded substantially by annual grants from the British Academy, the CBA is of established reputation and respected opinion; its policy recommendations have been widely implemented. In the case of churches and cathedrals, for example, where redevelopment has significant archaeological implications and where different legal restraints apply from those in the secular world (see Chapter 9), the CBA instigated a network of archaeological consultants within the Anglican diocesan framework, in effect creating a specialist tier of archaeological activity and/or advice within the national structure. Arrangements for archaeological input can now be found in other national or regional organizations, for example, within the National Trusts (Thackray and Hearn 1985; Smith 1986), the National Parks (White and Iles 1991; Cleere 1991), the successors to the Nature Conservancy Council and the Forestry Commission (Forestry Commission 1991; Chapter 22) as well as within former utilities in the gas and water industries.

Also active in identifying the awareness and expansion of archaeology was RESCUE, the Trust for British Archaeology, set up in 1971 as a pressure group without the establishment or restrictions of public funding. Much of the initial, and inevitably reactive, response by concerned archaeologists and their public supporters to the recognition of the threat to archaeological resources can be attributed to RESCUE's voice and to the tireless efforts of those who worked within it (Rahtz 1974b; Jones 1984; Barker 1987). The organization was also highly important in the generation of increased government funds and in the creation of archaeological units. RESCUE's independent contribution, although diminished by the changing focus of archaeological practice since the 1980s, nevertheless remains relevant (Spoerry 1992b).

Most recent, however, has been the emergence and growth of groups representing the divergent but related interests of different professional sectors. These include the Association of Museum Archaeologists (AMA), the Standing Conference of Archaeological Unit Managers (SCAUM) and the Standing Conference of University Professors and Heads of Archaeology (SCUPHA). The foregoing are all UK-wide; the local authority sector is covered by the Association of County Archaeological Officers (ACAO), their District equivalent (ADAO), and in Scotland, the Association of Regional and Islands Archaeologists (ARIA). All provide the voice and opinion of specialist professional interests within the overall framework.

The most broadly based professional organization is the Institute of Field Archaeologists (IFA), which received Board of Trade approval in the early 1980s. There are also two professional associations covering all of Ireland: the Irish Association of Professional Archaeologists (IAPA) and the Organization of Irish Archaeologists (OIA), the latter originating with a group of archaeologists outside permanent established posts.

More than any other indicator, the emergence of the IFA marks the arrival of archaeology in the professional world. The functions of the IFA embrace the establishment of working standards, the development of codes of practice, the provision of training and the dissemination of information, as well as the implementation of a disciplinary framework for the profession. Membership is by proven competence and ability at a number of levels: member, associate, practitioner and affiliate. Members are validated according to their training, competence and experience within specific fields: excavation, survey, aerial archaeology, environmental archaeology, finds study, recording and analysis of standing buildings, cultural resource management, underwater archaeology, and research and development. The designation of a member with specified 'areas of competence' (AOC) is thus a reflection of peer judgment by other archaeologists within the IFA, and is also an indication to associated professionals such as architects, engineers and surveyors with whom the archaeologist may be working of his or her particular expertise. The IFA also has a number of committees attending to a range of issues such as professional standards, contractual practices, disciplinary matters, equal opportunities and career development and training.

THE EDUCATION SECTOR

During the post-war period, the provision of archaeological teaching in the universities expanded rapidly in relation to the exposure of the discipline in the remainder of the higher education sector. Joint- or combined-honours archaeology courses (typically with Classics, History or English) blossomed into single-honours courses (Tindall and McDonnell 1979) and by the early 1980s, around half of the UK's (then) fifty universities had archaeologists on their teaching staff, usually within specifically designated archaeology departments; their total number was approximately 200 (Austin 1987). The teaching of the subject in most departments was (and remains) avowedly directed at the liberal arts, with few departments placing emphasis on vocational aspects of the discipline. Provision for science-based teaching at more than a basic level was restricted to relatively few departments. Although most departments include the archaeology of the British Isles within their focus, geographical and temporal coverage outwith the British Isles varies widely (Binns and Gardiner 1990 for summary). Many single- and joint-honours archaeology graduates pursue careers other than in field archaeology: in some cases this is a deliberate choice, but in others this is a product of the limited career opportunities in the sector (Joyce *et al.* 1987).

There was some, albeit ambiguous, evidence that numbers of applicants for the discipline had reached a plateau by the mid-1980s; attempts at University Grants Committee (UGC) *dirigisme*, coupled with externally induced financial pressures, provoked a crisis at this time. Partly as a result, a number of universities have now ceased teaching archaeology at undergraduate level: Leeds, St Andrews, Lancaster and Aberdeen. Some movement of staff between institutions also occurred during that decade, but other institutions, more favourably financed, have been able to add new courses (for example, Oxford). Bournemouth Polytechnic's (now University's) innovative undergraduate heritage and practical archaeology syllabuses should also be mentioned here.

Developments during the decade included the establishment of an umbrella organization, the Standing Committee of University Professors and Heads of Archaeology (SCUPHA), to represent the discipline in its dealings with institutions and the successors to the UGC. With the IFA, this body has agreed a core syllabus for undergraduate degrees in archaeology, which, while including vocational aspects, remains broadly within the liberal tradition.

More recent government-inspired changes in higher education have seen deliberate increases in student numbers. This expansion has led to a calculated squeezing of the unit of resource; in a movement towards greater efficiency many institutions have modularized their courses, enabling students to be more selective in tailoring the syllabus they follow.

Another major change during this period has been the rapid development of intermediate-level postgraduate courses, aimed either at specific aspects of the discipline (ranging from scientific and computer applications through cultural resource management) or as conversion courses for those wishing to enter archaeology from a related disciplinary background. A listing of these is available in the IFA's *Directory of Educational Opportunities* (IFA 1992).

Opportunities for research are restricted by the availability of financial support. Major sources include the vote to the Science-Based Archaeology Committee (SBAC) of the

Science and Engineering Research Council (Pollard 1989, 1990), as well as funding from the British Academy and both the Scottish and Northern Ireland Education Departments. SBAC funds both innovative application of techniques as well as pure scientific development on a competitive basis; funded support for more routine applications of proven methods is harder to obtain. The Co-operative Awards in Science and Engineering (CASE) award scheme offers opportunities for collaborative work between universities and external organizations, including archaeological units. The Natural Environment Research Council has not normally considered archaeology to lie within its remit, although some of the research it funds has been undertaken jointly with university departments of archaeology. The Economic and Social Science Research Council has never considered archaeology to be within its domain although a number of university archaeology departments are in social science faculties. Nor does it form any part of the remit of these bodies to address geographical imbalances in research-based activity within the UK. In general, funding from central government sources for postgraduate vocational training in archaeological resource management is unobtainable, and most of the intermediate-level postgraduate courses that have emerged in recent years thus tend not to highlight their vocational relevance. The overview of funding for archaeological research is best addressed in the *Hart Report* (SERC 1985).

The UGC (Arts) Sub-Committee review of archaeology departments (UGC 1989) posed a number of threats to the status quo: in keeping with government policy, differential funding was proposed in favour of a handful of more scientifically based departments, the prospect of rationalization was raised, and the concept of 'centres of excellence' aired. The eventual outcome was a dilution of the original proposals, but a small number of staff did move and the Universities Funding Council (UFC) implemented a system of differential funding to universities according to perceived levels of science teaching within their schools of archaeology. The UGC Sub-Committee also expressed the view that departments should be concerned with regional reviews of the academic priorities for archaeological research. Opportunities for this role to develop have been restricted, partly because many university teachers are not primarily concerned with the archaeology of their institution's immediate hinterland and partly because the funding and organizational structure of field archaeology has increasingly resulted in the development of area-based strategies becoming the preserve of archaeologists in local authority employment. Additionally, the limited availability of funding for non-threat-oriented field research within Britain has fuelled the tendency for university-based British archaeologists to work abroad, and thus to train their students overseas.

Although the university system plays no formal part in any state or regional archaeological structure, the growth in professionalism, and other contemporary pressures, have led to staff of university departments taking a much greater involvement in external activities. This may be limited to the devising of sampling programmes and the processing of scientific analyses of a wide variety of kinds for external clients, making use of capacity in departmental laboratory or other specialist provisions, or it may extend to the establishment of archaeological units set up to undertake contract work, initially at least on a territorial basis. Among the longer-established of such undertakings are the London Institute of Archaeology (Drewett 1987) and Birmingham University Field Archaeology Units, the former concentrating its work within the UK in Sussex. As with local authority and private sector units, much of the work of these teams consists of short-term evaluation and other fieldwork generated by developments such as the Environmental Assessment Regulations 1988, PPG 16 (DoE 1990a; Welsh Office 1991) and the Department of Transport's Trunk Roads Programme (Friell 1991), although certain institutions have targeted more specialist markets, such as forensic applications of archaeological practice.

CONCLUSIONS

Compared even with a decade ago, the number and variety of organizations employing archaeologists has grown considerably. In many ways, the range of employment positions of archaeologists is comparable to those of architects and planners; most are vulnerable to the same economic cycles of expansion and contraction in employment.

It is sometimes easy to forget within this new professionalism that the justification for professional archaeology is to safeguard resources for future generations, and to examine those that cannot be preserved according to the best prevailing academic standards. There must remain considerable doubt as to whether the still-disparate structure currently functioning is entirely appropriate to this end. The imposition of the concept of 'the polluter pays' has generated many practical innovations in the field, in desk-based and laboratory research, and in improvements in managerial practices, as practising archaeologists come into more formal contacts with a wide range of professionals in other domains.

There are, however, fundamental issues affecting archaeological practice that risk being left aside by these changing currents. Among these lie the scope for designing academic research strategies to broaden the understanding of the archaeological environment (as opposed simply to identifying and recovering more data), and the establishment of consistent policies for heritage management. This dilemma is not new: archaeology's past, present, and – no doubt – its future, will continue to be inhibited by the legacy of its historical structure.

CHAPTER 5

ANCIENT MONUMENTS LEGISLATION

David J. Breeze

INTRODUCTION

The Ancient Monuments Protection Act of 1882 was the first conservation measure passed by the British Parliament. It came over 200 years after the first conservation measure in Europe, which was undertaken by Sweden in 1660 (for the history of legislation see Kennet 1972; Boulting 1976; Thompson 1977: 58–74; MacIvor and Fawcett 1983; Cleere 1989; Ross 1991). The 1882 legislation protected 26 ancient monuments in England, 3 in Wales, 21 in Scotland and 18 in Ireland. These monuments were named in a Schedule or list appended to the Act and thus was born the term 'scheduling'. The 1882 Act has been succeeded by a further eight relating to the protection of ancient monuments (for Northern Ireland see Appendix, p. 134): the current primary legislation is the Ancient Monuments and Archaeological Areas Act 1979 (AMAA Act 1979). Archaeological and historical sites and landscapes are also protected, in a general way, in other legislation, and also through formal agreements with a variety of bodies concerned with the management of different aspects of the countryside.

The AMAA Act 1979 refers to the Secretary of State throughout as the person empowered under the Act. This should now (1992) be taken to refer to the Secretary of State for the National Heritage in England, the Secretary of State for Scotland and the Secretary of State for Wales. In Scotland, the Secretary of State's duties are undertaken by Historic Scotland (HS) and in Wales by Cadw: Welsh Historic Monuments. In England several activities under the AMAA Act 1979, for example, scheduling, the granting of Scheduled Monument Consent and the designation of areas of archaeological importance, are undertaken by the Department of National Heritage (DNH) with the advice of English Heritage (EH). The aims, objectives and functions of the three state bodies – EH, HS and Cadw – are detailed in their *Corporate Plans*, which are published annually.

THE ANCIENT MONUMENTS AND ARCHAEOLOGICAL AREAS ACT 1979

Scheduling

The AMAA Act 1979 states that the Secretary of State 'shall compile and maintain . . . a schedule of monuments' which 'may . . . include . . . any monument which appears to him to be of national importance', on land or in UK territorial waters, so long as it is not 'occupied as a dwelling house by any person other than a . . . caretaker' and is not 'used for ecclesiastical purposes'; monuments may be added to the list or excluded from the Schedule of Monuments or any entry in the Schedule relating to a monument may be amended (Sections 1 (1), (3), (4), (5); 53, 61 (8)).

The Act defines a monument as:

> (a) any building, structure or work, whether above or below the surface of the land, and any cave or excavation;

(b) any site comprising the remains of any such building, structure or work or of any cave or excavation; and

(c) any site comprising, or comprising the remains of, any vehicle, vessel, aircraft or other moveable structure or part thereof which neither constitutes nor forms part of any work which is a monument as defined within paragraph (a) above;

and any machinery attached to a monument shall be regarded as part of the monument if it could not be detached without being dismantled. (Section 61 (7))

In effect only items that can be removed readily by hand are beyond the protection of scheduling, though this is yet to be tested in the courts. In general, items listed in paragraph (c) are rarely protected through scheduling (see Chapter 7 for the protection of wrecks; and the Protection of Military Remains Act 1986, the purpose of which is 'to secure the protection from unauthorised interference of the remains of military aircraft and vessels that have crashed, sunk or been stranded').

A distinction is also drawn in the Act between a monument, as described above, and an ancient monument, which is defined as 'any Scheduled Monument; and any other monument which in the opinion of the Secretary of State is of public interest by reason of the historic, architectural, traditional, artistic or archaeological interest attaching to it' (Section 61 (12)).

The criteria for judging national importance in England and Wales are published in the relevant *Planning Policy Guidance: Archaeology and Planning* (PPG 16 (England) Annex 4 and PPG 16 (Wales) Annex 3). The eight unranked criteria, which are indicative rather than definitive, are:

Survival/Condition: the survival of the monument's archaeological potential both above and below ground is a crucial consideration and needs to be assessed in relation to its present condition and surviving features.

Period: it is important to consider for preservation all types of monuments that characterise a category or period.

Rarity: there are some monument categories which in some periods are so scarce that all of them which still retain any archaeological potential should be preserved. In general, however, a selection must be made which portrays the typical and commonplace as well as the rare. For this, account should be taken of all aspects of the distribution of a particular class of monument not only in the broad national context but also in its region.

Fragility/Vulnerability: highly important archaeological evidence from some field monuments can be destroyed by a single ploughing or unsympathetic treatment; these monuments would particularly benefit from the statutory protection which scheduling confers. There are also standing structures of particular form or complexity where again their value could be severely reduced by neglect or careless treatment and which are well suited to protection by this legislation even though they may also be listed historic buildings.

Diversity: some monuments have a combination of high quality features – others are chosen for a single important attribute.

Documentation: the significance of a monument may be given greater weight by the existence of records of previous investigation or, in the case of more recent monuments, by the support of contemporary written records.

Group Value: the value of a single monument (such as a field system) is greatly enhanced by association with a group of related contemporary monuments (such as a settlement and cemetery) or with monuments of other periods. In the case of some groups it is preferable to protect the whole including the associated and adjacent land rather than to protect isolated monuments within the group.

Potential: on occasion the nature of the evidence cannot be precisely specified but it is possible to document reasons for anticipating probable existence and importance and so demonstrate the justification for scheduling. This is usually confined to sites rather than upstanding monuments.

The Ancient Monuments Board for Scotland (AMBS 1983, Section 28) offered advice as a guide towards the scheduling of monuments in Scotland:

A monument is of national importance if, in the view of informed opinion, it contributes or appears likely to contribute significantly to the understanding of the past. Such significance may be assessed from individual or group qualities, and may include structural or decorative features, or value as an archaeological source.

In addition, the Board offered the following advice as a working definition:

For a monument to be regarded as being of national importance it is necessary and sufficient –

first, that it belongs or pertains to a group or subject of study which has acknowledged importance in terms of archaeology, architectural history or history; and

second, that it can be recognised as being part of the national consciousness or as retaining the structural, decorative or field characteristics of its kind to a marked degree, or as offering or being likely to offer a significant archaeological resource within a group or subject of study of acknowledged importance.

In England DNH schedules monuments on advice from EH, whereas in Scotland the authority to schedule lies with HS, and in Wales, Cadw. There is no appeal against a decision to schedule a monument (apart from through the process of judicial review), and the law offers no provision for the payment of compensation. Although it is not a statutory requirement, owners of monuments are normally advised of the intention to schedule in advance of its implementation and time is thus available for discussion about the proposal and its implications. Scheduled sites are registered as a charge in the local land registry in England and Wales; and recorded at the Register of Sasines in Scotland. The National Monuments Record (NMR) and local authorities, including the Sites and Monuments Records (SMRs), are also notified. Lists of Scheduled Monuments are regularly published, on a county basis in England and Wales and on a national basis in Scotland.

In 1986 EH commenced the Monuments Protection Programme (MPP – see Chapter 17) designed to review and evaluate existing information about sites of archaeological and historical interest so that those of national importance could be identified and scheduled (Darvill et al. 1987: 393). Cadw has also begun an exercise to evaluate all known archaeological remains in Wales and identify those that may be suitable for scheduling. In Scotland, following representations by the AMBS, the Secretary of State indicated that 'the time was not yet ripe to consider any large-scale extension and acceleration of the scheduling programme in Scotland' (AMBS 1986: 14–17). However, HS has made additional resources available internally and the annual target for newly Scheduled Monuments, which is being met, is now 300 cases a year. This is supplemented by the preparation of non-statutory registers of sites that may be worthy of scheduling. Two of Scotland's twelve regions have been completed and it is hoped to finish the project by 2000. In the meantime, the NMR of Scotland is the primary source of information for the scheduling programme. There are currently about 13,000 Scheduled Ancient Monuments in England, 5,300 in Scotland and 2,700 in Wales. In England, 60,000 sites may qualify for protection as being of national importance (Wainwright 1989: 167), in Scotland 18,000.

In all three countries there are monuments that are both scheduled and listed (Chapter 8). In such circumstances, scheduling takes precedence and Scheduled Monument Consent rather than Listed Building Consent is required for works (in England and Wales the relevant legislation is Section 61 of the Planning (Listed Buildings and Conservation Areas) Act 1990 and for Scotland Section 54 (1) of the Town and Country Planning (Scotland) Act 1972). One disadvantage of this situation is that, while both the ancient monument and the listed buildings legislation (AMAA Act 1979: Section 5 and the Town and Country Planning Act 1971: Section 99 (England and Wales), and the Town and Country Planning (Scotland) Act 1972: Sections 95, 97 as substituted by paragraph 20 of Schedule 9 of the Housing and Planning Act 1986) allows for the appropriate local or central government agency to undertake emergency repairs, only the listed buildings legislation allows such costs to be reclaimed from the owner. The overlap between scheduling and listing is being reduced as respective protection programmes proceed, though with certain monument types, for example castles, there may always be a degree of overlap, as the different legislations protect different parts of the monument.

Scheduling remains a strong protective measure. However, only archaeological (or architectural) features may be protected: the AMAA Act 1979 does not allow the protection of the setting of monuments. The AMAA Act 1979 abrogated that part of the Ancient Monuments Act 1931 concerned with 'preserving the amenities of any ancient monument' on the grounds that these matters are now best dealt with through the planning legislation. In fact, the only amenity area designated under the 1931 Act was for the protection of the amenity of part of Hadrian's Wall (roughly 17 miles of the 73-mile length of the Wall). 'The desirability of preserving an ancient monument and its setting . . . whether the monument is scheduled or unscheduled' receives explicit mention in PPG 16 (England), PPG 16 (Wales) and the draft NPPG, *Archaeology and Planning* (Scotland) (SOEnD 1992a, 1992b).

Under the Town and Country Planning General Development Order 1988 (England) and the Town and Country Planning (General Development Procedure) (Scotland) Order 1992, protection for Scheduled Monuments was improved by the requirement for planning authorities to consult the Secretary of State before granting planning permission for development that might affect the site of a Scheduled Monument.

Under the AMAA Act 1979 a plea of ignorance of scheduling is possible under certain circumstances. It was partly to try to ensure that owners and occupiers were cognizant of the existence of Scheduled Monuments on their land that monument wardens were appointed by all three bodies to visit sites regularly. Such visits are opportunities not just to inform owners or occupiers about monuments on their land but also to offer or arrange for advice about the best management for the monuments. The AMAA Act 1979 provides for access to land for the purpose of inspecting any Scheduled Monument (Section 6).

Scheduled Monument Consent (SMC)

The AMAA Act 1979 is not just a measure to protect monuments through scheduling, but also to control works affecting Scheduled Monuments. Thus the consent of the Secretary of State has to be sought for any of the following:

a. any works resulting in the demolition or destruction of or any damage to a Scheduled Monument;

b. any works for the purpose of removing or repairing a scheduled monument or any part of it or of making any alterations or additions thereto; and

c. any flooding or tipping operations on land in, on or under which there is a Scheduled Monument. (Section 2 (2))

These proscriptions lead to requirement for Scheduled Monument consent also to be sought for excavations.

It is illegal to undertake any of the above works at a Scheduled Ancient Monument (SAM) without consent, which must be sought through the provision of detailed proposals. The Secretary of State may grant consent for the execution of such works either unconditionally or subject to conditions, or can refuse outright. The consent, if granted, expires after five years. Compensation may be paid for refusal of consent or for conditional consent in certain circumstances, in particular if planning permission had previously been granted and was still effective (Sections 7–9). Failure to obtain SMC for any works of the kind described in Section 2(2) is an offence, the penalty for which may be a fine which, according to the circumstances of the conviction, may be unlimited. Provision is made for the inspection of work in progress in relation to SMC (Section 6 (3), (4)). Successful prosecutions of parties who undertook works without consent or broke SMC conditions have occurred.

Under the Ancient Monuments (Class Consents) Order 1981 as amended by the Ancient Monuments (Class Consents) Order 1984 (England and Wales) and the Ancient Monuments (Class Consents) (Scotland) Order 1981, certain activities do not require SMC. These are agriculture, horticulture and forestry works, provided that the activities formed the regular use of the land in the previous five years (but do not extend to major ground disturbance operations, such as drainage, subsoiling and tree planting); work carried out more than 10m below ground by the National Coal Board or its licensees; essential and certain repair works by the British Waterways Board; minor repairs to machinery; works essential for health or safety purposes; and, in England only, work carried out by EH. The Class Consents Orders are under review at present.

Considerable efforts are made to discuss proposals that affect Scheduled Monuments before works are carried out so as to best mitigate the effect of such works on the monuments. In some cases agreement is not possible and provision is made within the AMAA Act 1979 for a hearing. Such a public inquiry represents democracy at work in two ways: it allows the views of officials concerning a particular application to be scrutinized and tested; it also allows the general nature of the protection policy to be tested in a wider forum. In Scotland, for example, in 1991 a public inquiry on Arran accepted that it was possible to schedule areas between visible (and in this case upstanding) monuments because excavations elsewhere had demonstrated that archaeological remains do survive between such monuments.

Guardianship and acquisition

The AMAA Act 1979 allows for monuments (and land adjoining them) to be taken into State (or local authority) Care with the agreement of the owner through the signing of Deeds of Guardianship (Sections 12, 13, 15). This procedure was introduced by the 1882 Act (it is an indication of the importance of the monuments listed in the 1882 Schedule that most have now been taken into Guardianship). The officers charged with implementing the 1882 Act were placed within the existing Board of Works, the body that had long looked after royal castles and palaces in Britain (and some cathedrals and abbeys in Scotland). This body was the direct descendant of the Office of the King's Works which had been in continuous existence in England since the Middle Ages (MacIvor and Fawcett 1983: 9). Thus state organizations came to look after monuments held in a variety of ways, including ownership, guardianship and tenancy. Monuments are usually taken into State Care because of their signal archaeological, architectural or historical importance. There are 440 monuments in State Care in England, 330 in

Scotland and 125 in Wales, ranging in date from the Neolithic period to the present century. The presentation and interpretation of these monuments feature highly in the activities of the three state bodies.

The AMAA Act 1979 lays a burden to maintain the monument on the guardian who is given full powers of control and management (subject to any conditions in the deed), including the power to examine or excavate the monument or remove all or part of it for the purpose of excavation (Section 13). Provision is made for public access, its control and for charging for entry (Section 19).

The AMAA Act 1979 contains provisions allowing monuments to pass out of care: these have been used sparingly (Section 14). It also allows for the compulsory acquisition of 'any ancient monument for the purposes of securing its preservation' (Section 10). This was a development of the concept of Preservation Orders, originally introduced in the Ancient Monuments Consolidation and Amendment Act 1913 and further developed in the Ancient Monuments Act 1931 and the Historic Buildings and Ancient Monuments Act 1953.

Management agreements and grants to owners

Scheduling is an inherently passive form of legislation. Often further action is required to ensure the best protection of a monument. This was recognized by the Walsh Committee in its *Report . . . into the Arrangement for the Protection of Field Monuments 1966–68*. The resulting legislation, the Field Monuments Act 1972, introduced the concept of an acknowledgement payment to the 'occupier of land which is the site of a field monument'. This scheme was abrogated by the AMAA Act 1979, which introduced management agreements for ancient monuments, whether scheduled or unscheduled (Section 17). The AMAA Act 1979 also allows the Secretary of State to give grants for the acquisition or removal of a monument for the purposes of preserving it, or to ensure its preservation, maintenance and management (Section 24). In general, management agreements relate to ongoing maintenance and management, including fencing, clearance of scrub and pest control, while grants to owners encompass capital grants for works such as the consolidation of masonry structures and, in certain circumstances, grants for interpretative schemes (on management generally, see Darvill 1987).

The Secretary of State is also empowered to enter the site of a Scheduled Monument if it appears that works are urgently necessary for its preservation and to execute those works, after giving the owner or occupier seven days' notice in writing (Section 5).

Archaeological areas

The AMAA Act 1979 grants the Secretaries of State power to designate Areas of Archaeological Importance (Part II). The purpose of this section is to ensure that time is allowed for the investigation of archaeological deposits in towns before redevelopment takes place. Potential developers are required to give six weeks' notice to the relevant planning authority of any proposals to disturb the ground, tip on it, or flood it. Thereafter, the investigating authority has up to four-and-a-half months for archaeological investigation. In England, areas within five historic towns (Canterbury, Chester, Exeter, Hereford and York) were designated. In Scotland and Wales, the Secretaries of State took the view that existing arrangements between archaeologists and planners were so sound that implementation of Part II of the AMAA Act 1979 was unnecessary.

In some ways this part of the AMAA Act 1979 has been superseded by PPG 16 in England and Wales and in matters of working practice by voluntary codes of practice.

These include the *British Archaeologists and Developers Liaison Group Code of Practice* (BADLG 1991) and the *Archaeological Investigations Code of Practice for Mineral Operators* (CBI 1991; Chapter 16). These were agreed by developers and by both statutory and voluntary archaeological bodies, and set out to encourage good working practices. They operate primarily in relation to planning law, and extend to the whole range of archaeological activities on a site proposed for development or mining from first intimation of proposals to publication.

Metal detecting

Under the AMAA Act 1979 it is an offence for anyone to use a metal detector in a protected place (i.e. on a Scheduled Monument, or one in the ownership or Guardianship of the Secretary of State, or a local authority, or in an area of archaeological importance), or to remove any object of archaeological or historical interest found by the use of a metal detector from a protected site without the written consent of the Secretary of State (Section 42). Successful prosecutions of people in breach of Section 42 have occurred in both England and Scotland.

Excavation

During the Second World War the then Ministry of Works financed excavations in advance of the construction of defence installations and this role was expanded after 1945 to encompass the rescue excavation of archaeological sites, be they scheduled or not, in advance of developments. This work was encompassed by legislation in 1979. The AMAA Act 1979 allows the Secretary of State to 'undertake, or assist in, or defray or contribute towards the cost of, an archaeological investigation of any land which he considers may contain an ancient monument or anything else of archaeological or historical interest' (Section 45 (1)). The wording does not preclude expenditure on non-rescue investigations, though generally the call on excavation funds has been so great as effectively to restrict activities to the examination of threatened sites. The AMAA Act 1979 also indicates that publication is part of the excavation process (Section 45 (3)).

A review of archaeology in England during the last decade and a statement of EH's excavation strategies are set out in *Exploring Our Past* (English Heritage 1991a).

Ancient Monuments Boards

The Ancient Monuments Act 1913 established an Ancient Monuments Board, with separate provision for Scotland and Wales (Section 15). The Ancient Monuments Boards were continued under the AMAA Act 1979 (Section 22), though the National Heritage Act 1983 (Section 39) replaced the Board for England by the Commissioners of the Historic Buildings and Monuments Commission for England. The function of the Ancient Monuments Boards is to advise the appropriate Secretary of State with respect to the exercise of his functions under the AMAA Act 1979, and publish an annual report (Section 23).

Local authorities

The AMAA Act 1979 gives local authorities many of the same powers as it grants to central government (this authority was first introduced in the Ancient Monuments Act 1900).

These include Guardianship, the designation of Archaeological Areas, excavation, management agreements and grants, but not scheduling or compulsory purchase.

OTHER RELEVANT LEGISLATION AND REGULATIONS

The National Heritage Act 1983

The National Heritage Act 1983 established the Historic Buildings and Monuments Commission for England, popularly known as English Heritage (Sections 32–43). The duties of EH, as defined by the National Heritage Act 1983, are more wide-ranging than those formerly undertaken by the Department of the Environment. The primary duties, as set out in the Act, are:

> a. to secure the preservation of ancient monuments and historic buildings situated in England,
> b. to promote the preservation and enhancement of the character and appearance of Conservation Areas situated in England, and
> c. to promote the public's enjoyment of, and advance their knowledge of, ancient monuments and historic buildings situated in England and their preservation.

The National Heritage Act 1983 also encompasses the provision of educational facilities, information to the public, advice, the undertaking of research, and the creation and maintenance of records (Section 33 (2)).

Environment assessment regulations

The principles of environmental assessment were introduced by EC Directive 85/337 which holds that 'the best environmental policy consists in preventing the creation of pollution and nuisances at source, rather than subsequently trying to counteract their effects'. The Directive was implemented in Britain by several sets of regulations covering planning (including trunk roads, bridges and land drainage schemes requiring the consent of a Secretary of State rather than planning permission), electricity and pipelines, afforestation, and salmon farming in marine waters. Although provision is also made in the Directive for the environmental assessment of agricultural developments involving the breaking in of previously uncultivated land and the restructuring of rural landholding, these provisions have not been implemented in Britain (Macinnes 1990: 135–6; Lambrick 1992).

The regulations allow for the relevant authority to call for environment assessment (EA) of development proposals likely to have significant effects on the environment by virtue, *inter alia*, of their nature, size or location. Where EA is required, the developer must provide an Environmental Statement to supplement his normal application, setting out the information specified in Article 3 of the Directive about the site and the likely significant effects of the proposed development on the environment. This should include information relating to any significant effects on material assets and the cultural heritage, such as archaeological features and other human artefacts, and the measures envisaged to avoid, reduce or remedy adverse effects. The archaeological authorities in both central and local government are normally required to provide relevant information and advice for environmental assessments under preparation and also have the opportunity to comment on the adequacy of submitted statements.

The Agriculture Act 1986

Two sections of the Agriculture Act 1986 refer to the protection of the archaeological resource (Owen-John 1992: 92; Chapter 22). Section 17 makes provision for the 'conservation and enhancement of the natural beauty and amenity of the countryside (including its flora and fauna and geological and physiographical features) and of any features of archaeological interest there' and for 'the promotion of the enjoyment of the countryside by the public'. Section 18 provides for the establishment of Environmentally Sensitive Areas (ESAs) to protect, *inter alia*, 'buildings or other objects of archaeological, architectural or historical interest in an area' and to encourage 'maintenance or adoption of particular agricultural methods . . . likely to facilitate such conservation, enhancement or protection'. Ten areas have been designated in England, two in Wales and five in Scotland (Smith 1992: 131). A further twelve areas are proposed in England, two in Wales and five in Scotland.

Funds have been made available within the ESA scheme to allow the implementation of that part of the Agriculture Act 1986 dealing with the encouragement of the maintenance or adoption of particular agricultural methods that would lead to the conservation, enhancement or protection of the built heritage. In Scotland, most consultation is undertaken at local level, archaeological interests being represented by the regional archaeologists. Advice on policy, including implementation of Sections 17 and 18 is, however, undertaken at national level in Scotland, for example through training seminars in which HS officials participate together with colleagues from nature conservation. The situation is comparable in England and Wales.

Natural heritage legislation

In response to an amendment by Lord Walpole at the Committee stage of the Environment Protection Act 1990, the government gave an undertaking that the Nature Conservancy Council (NCC) would enter into a statement of intent with EH to ensure that archaeological features of interest were taken into account in the management of land notified as a Site of Special Scientific Interest so that damage to these features could be avoided. The Statement of Intent, approved early in 1991, was agreed by NCC, Cadw, the Council for British Archaeology, the Council for Scottish Archaeology, EH and HS.

The Natural Heritage (Scotland) Act 1991 states that 'it shall be the duty of Scottish Natural Heritage in exercising its functions to take such account as may be appropriate in the circumstances of . . . the need to conserve sites and landscapes of archaeological or historical interest' (Section 3). The arrangements for implementing this requirement have not yet been determined (Owen-John 1992: 90–1), though currently consideration is being given to a revised Statement of Intent for archaeology and nature conservation in Scotland.

The Electricity Act 1989

The Electricity Act 1989 charges licence holders (in effect the electricity companies), or equivalents, 'in formulating any relevant proposals . . . [to] have regard to the desirability . . . of protecting sites, buildings and objects of architectural, historic or archaeological interest' (Schedule 9, paragraphs 1 (1) (a) and 3 (1) (a)), while the licence holder before preparing or modifying a statement of intent shall consult with various bodies, including EH, the Historic Buildings Council for Wales and the Ancient Monuments Board for Scotland (Schedule 9, paragraphs 2 (2) and 4 (2)). AMBS has delegated this responsibility to HS, while in Wales the function is undertaken by Cadw.

The Water Resources Act 1991

The Water Resources Act 1991 requires the National Rivers Authority (NRA) in undertaking its duties 'to have regard to the desirability of protecting and conserving buildings, sites and objects of archaeological, architectural or historic interest' (Section 16 (1) (b)) and, with reference to the approval of codes of practice, requires consultation with EH and Cadw (Section 18 (4) (c)). The Act does not relate to Scotland. The NRA does not employ an archaeologist, but one of the water companies (Thames Water) does.

Inheritance tax

Owners of national heritage property are able to make a claim for capital tax relief (Capital Transfer Tax Act 1984: Section 31 = Inheritance Tax Act 1984 (the Act was renamed in 1986); Finance Act 1985: Section 94 and Schedule 26, 2. cf. Inland Revenue 1986). Exemption from capital taxes (capital transfer tax, inheritance tax, estate duty and capital gains tax) is conditional upon undertakings about the maintenance, preservation of, and public access to, the property. Conditional exemption can be claimed for, *inter alia*, SAMs or any other significant archaeological remains, amenity land (in order, for example, to protect views from or of a building), and land of outstanding historic interest. Advice on such matters is provided to the Inland Revenue by EH, HS and Cadw.

Forestry planting regulations

The Forestry Commission states in its *Grants and Procedures* booklet (Forestry Commission 1991) that 'it is the Forestry Commission's policy that tree planting should not damage any sites which are of archaeological importance' and that 'the Forestry Commission will not approve an application which does not provide for the protection of important archaeological sites': these statements encompass unscheduled as well as scheduled sites. Advice on archaeological sites will be sought from the county/regional archaeologists or, where these do not exist, the state agencies: EH, HS and Cadw (Barclay 1992b). Historic Scotland provides funds for any surveys required in advance of afforestation.

In 1990, two cases of unauthorized ploughing of archaeological sites (one scheduled, one unscheduled) by a private forestry company in receipt of Forestry Commission grants occurred in Scotland. In both cases the Forestry Commission withheld a proportion of the grant: the company was also fined under the AMAA Act 1979 for damage to the Scheduled Monument.

Planning policy guidance

In November 1990 the Department of the Environment issued, for England, PPG 16, entitled *Planning Policy Guidance: Archaeology and Planning* (DoE 1990a). This was followed in 1991 by a broadly similar document covering Wales (PPG 16 (Wales)). In Scotland a consultation paper in the form of a draft *National Planning and Policy Guidance* and *Planning Advice Note* (SOEnD 1992a, 1992b) on this subject was issued in August 1992 with a closing date for responses at the end of October. It is hoped to issue final documents early in 1993.

The English document sets out its purpose: guidance is for planning authorities, property owners, developers, archaeologists, amenity societies and the general public.

It sets out the Secretary of State's policy on archaeological remains on land, and how they should be preserved or recorded both in an urban setting and in the countryside. It gives advice on the handling of archaeological remains and discoveries under the development plan and control systems. The guidance pulls together and expands existing advice, within the existing legislative framework. It places no new duties on local authorities.

In particular PPG 16 emphasizes the fragility of the archaeological resource and the resulting necessity for sound management. The first priority, accordingly, is preservation and where this is not possible excavation must be undertaken ('preservation by record'). Much of the responsibility for the survival of archaeological sites and landscapes lies with local authorities through their development plans and development controls. Development plans should give appropriate cognizance to the protection and enhancement of archaeo-logical sites, and appropriate controls should be imposed, including provision for the excavating and recording of archaeological remains. While developers should not be required to finance archaeological works in return for the granting of planning permission, the onus is placed upon the developer to ensure that the conditions of the planning consent are met: this effectively requires the developer to fund any excavations or arrange for funding from elsewhere. These guidelines thus mark an important step in the move of the primary funding of rescue archaeology in Britain from the state to developers, be they public or private. One important aspect is that acceptance of the principle of developer funding will allow state resources for archaeology to be used on projects where there is no developer, such as coastal erosion.

THE FUTURE

Legislation enacted in the 1980s and 1990s points to the way forward in some aspects. The National Heritage Act 1983, the Agriculture Act 1986, the Environmental Protection Act 1990 and the Natural Heritage (Scotland) Act 1991 all include reference to one or more of the requirement to: disseminate knowledge, provide an education service, offer advice and undertake research. It seems possible that such activities might be extended to the core legislation concerned with the protection of ancient monuments.

The division between 'ancient monuments' and 'historic buildings' is largely a histor-ical accident: the protection of historic buildings was too sensitive to be included in the 1882 Act (Kennet 1972). However, the continuing existence of different legislation is seen as anachronistic in the present day. Thus, the creation of unified legislation is likely to be favoured, though such unified legislation needs to ensure that the existing protection is not diluted. The legislation allowing the protection of historic buildings already physically extends that protection more widely than the building itself through the concept of cur-tilage and through conservation areas. This wider concept could be usefully applied to the protection of archaeological sites, and especially landscapes, moving away from the nar-row focus upon unitary monuments that has governed the protection of archaeological sites since 1882 (Macinnes 1991: 200).

In 1882 there was only one item of conservation legislation. Now the protection of the built heritage appears in various Acts and agreements. This process started gradually, and more vaguely. The Telecommunications Act 1984 referred to the protection of the phys-ical environment (Part II, Section 9 (4) (a)) and since then balancing clauses have appeared in other legislation, including the Agriculture Act 1986, the Environmental Protection Act 1990 and the Natural Heritage (Scotland) Act 1991. Such requirements now refer much more specifically to the need to protect archaeological and historical sites and landscapes. Through such 'balancing' clauses, the protection of the built heritage is increasingly brought into wider countryside management and thus another development might be a move towards integrated designations (Miles 1992; cf. also Lambrick 1992).

Voluntary and formal agreements have developed additional methods of protecting archaeological sites. There may be further scope for expansion here.

Looking back, the variety of legislative measures, voluntary agreements, formal agreements and general co-operation, now so common within the wider framework of countryside protection, is remarkable to anyone who entered the archaeological profession more than ten years ago. This diversity is now balanced by the envelopment of concern for the protection of the built heritage within concern for the environment as a whole, as indicated by its inclusion within the White Paper on the UK's environmental strategy, *This Common Inheritance* (DoE 1990b).

ACKNOWLEDGEMENTS

I am grateful to colleagues both north and south of the Border for their comments on drafts of this paper: Mr J. R. Avent, Mr G.J. Barclay, Mr R.A.J. Dalziel, Mr R. Emerson, Dr N. Fojut, Mrs L. Linge, Mr R.A.C. MacDonald, Dr L. Macinnes and Dr G. Wainwright.

CHAPTER 6

PORTABLE ANTIQUITIES

Ian Longworth

Laws affording protection to portable antiquities vary widely in the UK. While in Scotland blanket protection is provided by the legal principle of *Bona Vacantia* and recent legislation has been put in place in the Isle of Man and Northern Ireland, in England and Wales only limited protection is provided for some objects of precious metal by the law of Treasure Trove and by regulations covering the export of national antiquities. In this, England and Wales are out of step with the rest of Europe, where all national antiquities either belong to the state as of right as in Scandinavia and Eastern Europe, or where the state reserves to itself powers of compulsory purchase to prevent export, as in France.

OWNERSHIP AND PROTECTION OF PORTABLE ANTIQUITIES

England and Wales

As a general rule objects of archaeological or antiquarian interest found buried in the soil are likely to belong to the owner of the land, with the exception of those made of gold or silver. These, whether coin, bullion or plate are deemed to be treasure and may belong to the Crown.

The concept of Treasure Trove is of considerable antiquity (Hill 1936). By the 12th century the medieval kings of England had established this right. This did not embrace all finds of gold and silver and never included jewels. To be deemed Treasure Trove two conditions had to be met. Firstly, that no one with better legal title to the objects could be found and, secondly, that there had to have been a clear intention on the part of those who had first deposited the treasure to repossess it at some future date. In effect the Crown was laying claim to treasure deliberately buried for safe keeping whose owner, for whatever reason, had failed to retrieve it. The law was seen to apply as much to objects concealed in above-ground structures as to deposits made in the ground.

Though no doubt a useful source of additional revenue, in practice the right of Treasure Trove may well have proved more rewarding in the expectation than in the receipt. Perhaps for this reason, the right to seek and retain treasure was sometimes assigned by the Crown to others. These franchise-holders became numerous over time (Hill 1936: 244) and included the Duchies of Cornwall and Lancaster, the Sees of Canterbury, York, Durham, Salisbury and Worcester; the cities of London and Bristol, some educational and ecclesiastical institutions and a number of private individuals. In some cases the rights of these franchise-holders have survived, but those of the Sovereign have been surrendered to the state in return for the Civil List. Treasure Trove seized on behalf of HM the Queen now passes to the Treasury on behalf of the nation.

By the 19th century it began to be appreciated that what had begun as a royal prerogative to raise revenue for the Crown could best be used to secure important treasures for the nation. In so doing no attempt was made to change the character of the law. Rather, the objects themselves were now simply seen as of greater value preserved than turned into cash. The arguments put forward were at first largely concerned with coinage and the desirability of studying the entirety of coin hoards to establish sequences within the earlier issues. By the middle of the 19th century, however, the need for a more organized procedure for regulating the law began to emerge.

Today the procedure is simple and straightforward. If gold or silver is found, it should be reported as soon as possible either to the British Museum (if in England) or the National Museum of Wales (if in Wales), to the police or to the coroner of the district in which the find occurs. The British Museum's Department of Scientific Research will weigh and assess the amount of gold and silver present. Reports are prepared for the relevant coroner both on the objects and on their circumstance of deposition where this can be established. If the coroner thinks on the evidence placed before him that there is a *prima facie* case that the objects may be Treasure Trove then he will call an inquest. It is then for the jury to decide at the inquest whether the objects are indeed Treasure Trove and to declare who was the finder. To do so the jury must satisfy themselves on three basic questions. Firstly, are the objects of gold or silver? Secondly, has no one come forward with better legal title to the finds and, thirdly, were the objects buried with an intention of future recovery? If the objects are declared Treasure Trove and there is no claim by a franchise-holder, then the coroner will seize them on behalf of the Crown and return them to the British Museum, or in Wales, to the National Museum. If either museum wishes to retain them, or, waiving their right, arranges for another museum to accept them, the objects are then valued and that valuation is scrutinized by an independent body set up by the Treasury: the Treasure Trove Reviewing Committee.

To encourage prompt disclosure of finds that patently have a monetary value, an *ex gratia* reward is paid to the finder. Since 1931 this has been set at the full market value of the finds. Only if the find has been concealed and not reported promptly will the reward be reduced, on the authority of the Secretary of State. A finder acting within the law cannot therefore lose financially but would almost certainly do so if an attempt was made to sell what would be in effect stolen property on the market. The money to pay the reward must be found by the Institution receiving the objects. No additional funds are provided by the Treasury. Should any objects or coins not be required by a museum then these can be sold on behalf of the finder or returned to the finder who is then free to dispose of them as he or she wishes. The basis of the law of Treasure Trove is then that objects of gold or silver that have been abandoned, though once buried with an intention of future recovery, belong neither to the finder nor the landowner, but to the Crown or franchise-holder; though finders will be fully rewarded for their honesty in reporting their discovery promptly.

While the Treasure Trove system has without doubt led to preservation for the nation of many of the finest objects discovered and has often permitted the prompt appraisal of the circumstances of their burial, weaknesses and problems with the administration of the law are all too obvious. The weight of case law, built up over the years, cannot conceal the fact that Treasure Trove springs from a medieval quest for extra revenue and is ill suited to the present need for legal protection for all portable antiquities. Many able commentators (e.g. Palmer 1981; Sparrow 1982; Cookson 1991) have pointed to the near impossibility of reconciling modern archaeological interpretation with the simplistic medieval concept of abandoned treasure. Two areas in particular have led to conflict. The definition of gold and silver, and the requirement to establish *animus revertendi*, that is, that the objects were deposited with an intention of later recovery.

In practice we are none too precise ourselves in the way we define objects as being made of gold. We willingly accept nine-carat items under this blanket heading, yet their actual gold content is only 37.5 %. Clearly in modern usage an object need not be made predominantly of a precious metal to fall within its definition. This, however, was not the view taken by the High Court in 1980 in the case of a hoard of debased coinage of the 3rd century AD found at Coleby in Lincolnshire (before Justice Dillon in *Attorney-General for the Duchy of Lancaster* v. *G. E. Overton (Farms) Ltd* – (1980) 3 All ER 503). Though the find was originally declared Treasure Trove and evidence was given to show that the coins in question would have been regarded as silver at the time they were being used, this verdict was set aside by the High Court on the grounds that to be deemed Treasure Trove the coins had to contain a substantial amount of gold or silver. This decision was later upheld by the Court of Appeal ((1982) 1 All ER 524 CA). No precise definition was offered by these courts. So it remains for the jury at each Treasure Trove inquest to decide for itself what it considers to be gold or silver. It is manifestly unsatisfactory that such a basic precondition for a declaration of Treasure Trove should remain unclarified.

Problems can also arise over the nature of the context itself. Archaeology is essentially an interpretative study and most observations are capable of more than one interpretation. We may note that objects have been carefully placed in the ground and there may be evidence to support the conclusion that effort has gone into seeking a place of deposition that is as discreet as possible. If the items are important and precious, more than simple concealment may be involved. In the prehistoric periods much ritual may have attended their burial. We have seen that for gold and silver to be declared Treasure Trove it is necessary to show that on the balance of probability the items are likely to have been originally hidden with an intention of subsequent recovery – that is, that this conclusion is more likely than one of casual loss or deposition of the objects as a non-recoverable votive deposit. If it has been possible to investigate the place of deposition or if the object is sizeable – a complete gold torc, for example – the likelihood of a casual loss can often be eliminated. It is in the case of deposits that have been placed in the ground with evident care that the question of intention arises most acutely.

The hiding of wealth in times of danger is well documented. One of the best recorded incidents in England can be found in Samuel Pepys's Diary (Latham and Matthews 1974). When in 1667 the Dutch fleet sailed into the Medway, Pepys took fright and arranged for his wife and father to carry his wealth (in coin) into the country and bury it for safekeeping. The account goes on to describe the difficulties that ensued when the time came to recover the deposit. Before the advent of the modern strongroom the ground, more rarely a standing structure, had to act as the equivalent of the safe deposit. Safer still might be ground dedicated to a deity, for here an element of divine protection could be added to the concealment. But on occasion items of value could also be offered to the gods themselves in the form of tribute and in the majority of these deposits there may have been no intention on the part of the donor to recover the items so offered. The two former contexts would clearly be Treasure Trove; the last would fall outside that law, though it must be stressed that unless a deposit can be shown to lie in direct association with a sanctuary or image of a god it seems extremely unlikely that only votive use could be inferred with any certainty. In this connection the recent trend to treat ritual and religious use as synonymous has only added confusion to uncertainty.

From the point of view of preserving information for posterity a third difficulty arises in the case of associated objects of non-precious metal. Though in many cases more than precious metal is involved, the law of Treasure Trove is confined solely to gold and silver. Thus the pottery vessel used to contain a hoard of silver coins cannot be declared Treasure Trove nor can any loose jewels not forming part of gold or silver jewellery. Associated finds are therefore at risk, for while the precious metal is claimed on behalf of the Crown (or a franchise-holder) the rest belongs to the landowner, who is free to do as he or she wishes. In the recent case of a hoard of bullion found at Snettisham (Hoard F), roughly two-thirds of the pieces were adjudged to be of precious metal while the remaining third were considered to be of base metal even though many of the pieces had considerable gold or silver in their content (Longworth 1992). Fortunately here as elsewhere the good will of the landowner allowed the purchase of the remaining finds so that the hoard could remain intact for future research, but such good will cannot in any sense be guaranteed.

The law of Treasure Trove in England and Wales can therefore be difficult to operate and offers no protection to associated groups whose content includes objects other than of gold and silver. Objects made from any material other than gold or silver have no statutory protection and can be held or disposed of at the whim of the landowner.

The Isle of Man

The law of Treasure Trove applies to the Isle of Man but here cases are decided by the High Bailiff in his capacity as Coroner of Inquests. A reward equivalent to the full market value is paid if the objects are retained by the Manx Museum or another museum and if the find has been fully disclosed and reported promptly either to the Government Secretary or to the police. The procedure is set out in Government Circular no. 66/72.

This circular also deals with the procedure for non-Treasure Trove items. Under Section 20 of the Manx Museum and National Trust Act of 1959 all archaeological objects must be reported to the Manx Museum or to the police. The legislation defines an archaeological object as 'any chattel, whether in a manufactured or partly manufactured or unmanufactured state which by reason of the archaeological interest attaching thereto, or of its association with any Manx historical event or person, has a value substantially greater than its intrinsic (including artistic) value, and the said expression includes ancient human and animal remains, but does not include treasure trove'. It further stipulates that objects must be reported within fourteen days, giving the nature of the object and how it was found. The finder must also permit examination of the object and photography if requested. These provisions, coupled with Section 22, which protects all archaeological objects from injury, defacement or destruction except under licence, and Section 23, which prohibits all unlicensed excavation, provide comprehensive cover for portable antiquities, further reinforced by Section 21, which prohibits all export of archaeological objects from the island without licence.

In an island with a relatively small population little is likely to escape the attention of the authorities, particularly as the resident Manx population takes an active interest in its own heritage and is keen to report any breach of regulations by non residents.

Northern Ireland

In Northern Ireland the definition of Treasure Trove also follows English law, the procedure being similar. Inquests are held by the local coroner (here sitting without a jury) and *ex gratia* rewards are paid at full market value, assessed by the Ulster Museum, for all discoveries promptly and fully declared. Uniquely, the reward is paid by the Department of the Environment (Historic Monuments Branch) but the Treasury retains title, the objects being placed on permanent loan in the Ulster Museum.

For other portable antiquities, the provisions of the Historic Monuments Act (Northern Ireland) passed in 1971 apply. The definition of an 'archaeological object' in Part V of the Act is similar to that employed in the Isle of Man but is drawn less comprehensively. Here the definition reads: 'any object, being a chattel (whether in a manufactured or unmanufactured state) which is, or appears to be, of archaeological or historic interest and which has, by reason of such interest, a value substantially greater than its intrinsic value or the value of the materials of which it is composed.'

Under Part IV of this legislation the finder of any archaeological object must report the find within fourteen days to the Ulster Museum or to the police, describing the circumstances of the find and the nature of the object. In Northern Ireland, the object itself must be forwarded unless there is difficulty over its removal. The Act lays down that the object may remain in the hands of the museum and/or the police for a period of up to three months. During this period ownership of the object cannot be transferred. As in the Isle of Man a licence is needed to excavate, issued by the Department of the Environment.

Scotland

In Scotland the Crown's claim extends through the concept of civil law '*quod nullius est fit domini regis*' (that which no longer has an owner becomes the Crown's) to all *Bona Vacantia* as well as objects of precious metals under Treasure Trove. In effect, all antiquities belong to the Crown and that right is in no way affected by the circumstances of their deposition. All finds must be reported to a museum or the police, whose duty it is to report the discovery to the local Procurator Fiscal. He or she in turn informs the Queen's and Lord Treasurer's Remembrancer (Q&LTR) as the Crown's official representative. A formally constituted committee, the Treasure Trove Panel (TTP), consisting of the Director of the National Museums of Scotland, together with two members appointed by the Chancellor of the Exchequer in consultation with the Secretary of State for Scotland, having the archaeological department of the National Museums of Scotland acting as its secretariat, advises the Q&LTR as to whether an item should or should not be claimed as Treasure Trove.

If such a claim is made the panel will go on to advise – should the find be required by a museum – as to which institution should receive the objects, and the value of the reward to be paid. This is normally set at full market value but may be reduced if the find has not been declared promptly or has been concealed in any way. The TTP in effect deals with all casual discoveries of sufficient interest to be claimed by the Crown.

Since 1981 finds from excavations financed in whole or in part by Historic Buildings and Monuments, Scottish Development Department, now Historic Scotland (HS) and casual finds made on monuments in its care, come before a Finds Disposal Panel (FDP). This is an informal advisory group consisting of a chairman and secretary drawn from HS, the Director of the Scottish Museums Council, the Director (or nominee) of the National Museums of Scotland and an independent assessor appointed by HS. Since all finds are the property of the Crown its role is simply one of assigning the finds to an appropriate museum collection. Where scheduled monuments are concerned, consent for excavation has to be obtained from HS.

Other legislation, achieved and proposed

Having read so far, an objective observer might be forgiven for thinking that the national heritage is ill served by such diversity in legislation devoted to portable antiquities. Put simply, there is no logical reason why objects of archaeological importance should be treated by different standards in the component parts of the UK. Such procedures can only give rise to doubts and uncertainty in the minds of the public. If the definition of an 'archaeological object' of the form favoured by the Manx and Northern Ireland legislation is acceptable and workable, then there are three basic strands to the question. Firstly, legal problems attendant upon the need to modify the prerogative of the Crown and constrain the rights of the individual (in England and Wales) under common law; secondly, the need to educate the general public as to what the law is and how they should react to it; and, thirdly, the ability to monitor and enforce any law which might be introduced.

At present portable antiquities are best protected in the Isle of Man and least so in England and Wales beyond those finds of precious metals covered by the provisions of Treasure Trove. Given the circumstances of the Isle of Man – a small island with a small but alert and co-operative population – Manx legislation has worked and worked well. But what of Scotland, where no new legislation is needed and where the problems have been well rehearsed now for almost a century and a half (Rhind 1858)? It must be admitted that here the situation is not entirely satisfactory (Sheridan 1991). Only following a major initiative in recent years by the staff of the National Museums of Scotland to promote public and professional awareness of the law has some improvement been seen in the reporting and processing of discoveries. Regular publication of Treasure Trove cases in the *Scottish Museum News* is slowly extending knowledge within the profession, but it has been shown that more direct methods are needed to reach the public at large. Yet the wider this knowledge extends the more work will be placed upon the administration of the system and further resources will be needed to cope with the increased work. One area in particular has already emerged: the disposal of finds from non-HS funded excavations which could swamp the work of the TTP. With widespread ignorance of the law, policing of the system in Scotland is yet to be tested.

Over the past thirty years archaeologists in England and Wales have been divided over how best to cope with the problems of securing better protection for portable antiquities. Some have felt that the best way forward was to retain Treasure Trove but to try to modify and extend its provisions; others have favoured a more root-and-branch solution, seeking totally new portable antiquities legislation. The latter camp is further divided between those seeking protection for the objects themselves and those for whom the recording of objects and their provenance is sufficient.

The only legislation actually passed in recent years directly affecting portable antiquities in England and Wales (and in this case extending also to Scotland) was the Ancient Monuments and Archaeological Areas Act of 1979 (AMAA Act 1979). Under Part III of this Act, Section 42 (amended for England by the National Heritage Act of 1983, Schedule 4, paragraph 60) it became an offence for any object 'of archaeological or historical interest' to be removed from a Scheduled Monument or Guardianship site while using a metal detector without written consent of the Historical Buildings and Monuments Commission for England (now English Heritage) or the Secretary of State. In the same year Lord Abinger introduced a Private Member's Bill in the House of Lords sponsored by the Council for British Archaeology. This sought to abolish Treasure Trove and replace it with legislation deeming that the Crown owned:

> any object lying in the earth or other private place without the owner being known which is:
> (1) made of gold or silver or an alloy containing either metal; or
> (2) lying with or adjacent to any object so made; or
> (3) contained in any class of object specified by order
> made under this subsection for the protection of portable antiquities by the Secretary of State for the Environment.

The Bill received its first reading in the House of Lords but lapsed when the government fell. Although it sought to abolish Treasure Trove, the protection of gold and silver objects and their alloys was restated but without the need to show *animus revertendi* and extending the provision to include associated objects of whatever kind. Many of the difficulties met at present in the administration of Treasure Trove would therefore have been removed, while clause (3) would have put in place a mechanism for extension of these provisions to embrace all or further categories of portable antiquities at some future date.

Although the concept of Treasure Trove was reinstated when the Bill was re-introduced in 1981, the legislation failed again. Having passed all its stages in the Lords, it was lost because of procedural problems in the Commons. It appears that the government did not favour the bill and in the Lords debate (9 February 1982) Lord Avon stated a view that promoters of future antiquities legislation must surely heed:

> If the bill is to secure its objective of getting more finds recorded and available for skilled investigation and display, then it needs to command the support of the people affected. We should not disguise the fact that the bill proposes a curtailing of centuries-old rights of ownership. I am sure it is wise to acknowledge this fully and openly.

But the need for revised legislation is pressing, as was underlined by events in 1986. A hoard of Iron Age silver staters had been discovered in 1985 and declared as having been found on the site of Castle Rings, Donhead St Mary, Wiltshire, a Scheduled Ancient Monument (SAM). At an inquest held in 1986 the hoard was declared Treasure Trove and the finder in due course received a reduced reward of £2,000. In the meantime, however, he had also been charged under the AMAA Act 1979 for using a metal detector and removing objects from a SAM without consent. He was convicted and fined £100 with costs. The perceived needs of the Treasure Trove system and of the protection of field monuments and their contents had finally come into conflict. The ensuing debate led in 1987 to widespread consultation following a statement by Lord Skelmersdale, the Under Secretary of State, in the House of Lords (26 January 1987). Having evaluated the submissions received, the preferred option adopted by the government, as stated by Lord Hesketh in the House of Lords (30 December 1989), was to be a code of practice rather than the introduction of new legislation. The terms of such a code have yet to be published. On the face of it, it might appear that such a position is difficult to justify given that the UK is a signatory to the European Convention on the Protection of the Archaeological Heritage, Valetta (CoE 1992). Article 2 of this convention commits each member state 'by means appropriate to the State in question' to the 'mandatory reporting to the competent authorities by a finder of the chance discovery of elements of the archaeological heritage and making them available for examination'. It must however be observed that the advisory notes accompanying the convention suggest that 'a State, however, may only require mandatory reporting of finds of precious materials or on already listed sites', thus reducing the provisions very much to the position already pertaining in England and Wales.

In the meantime proposals for new antiquities legislation have been drawn up by the Surrey Archaeological Society for introduction as a Private Member's Bill by Lord Perth. Like the Abinger Bills, these seek to meet the three most urgent requirements needed to improve the present system. Firstly, the proposed legislation offers precise definitions of gold and silver: a content of 0.5 % or more for coins and tokens, and 5.0 % or more for other objects. Secondly, it embraces all finds of gold and silver more than 100 years old, other than single coins or tokens, removing the need to show *animus revertendi*. Thirdly, it would include all associated finds. Treasure Trove would be retained with extended provisions, but the measure would also seek to introduce the offence of searching for treasure as a trespasser, aimed specifically at safeguarding the rights of landowners against metal-detector users operating on land without permission. As with its predecessors provision is made for discretionary extension of its provisions to embrace other categories of portable antiquities by the Minister of State.

THE EXPORT OF ANTIQUITIES

Under present regulations, all antiquities of whatever value (but excluding coins worth less than £35,000), found on UK soil or in UK territorial waters, need an individual licence before they may be legally exported. The legal basis for this system is an Export of Goods (Control) Order, issued annually under the terms of the Import, Export and Customs Powers (Defence) Act of 1939. Any request for an export licence has to be made to the Export Licensing Unit of the Department of National Heritage. Such requests are referred to the relevant expert advisor. For objects from the UK these are the British Museum's Keeper of Prehistoric and Romano-British Antiquities or the Keeper of Medieval and Later Antiquities, depending on the date of the object in question. The expert advisor then has to consider whether the items are of sufficient importance under one of the Waverley Criteria that an export licence should not be automatically granted. The criteria were devised in 1950 by a committee chaired by Lord Waverley, 'to consider and advise on the policy to be adopted by His Majesty's Government in controlling the export of works of art, books, manuscripts, armour and antiques and to recommend what arrangements should be made for the practical operation of policy'.

The committee decided on three questions to be asked: is the object so closely connected with British history and national life that its departure would be a misfortune; is it of outstanding aesthetic importance; and is it of outstanding significance for the study of some branch of art and learning or history?

If in the opinion of the expert advisor the answer to one or more of these questions is yes, then the case is brought to the Reviewing Committee on the Export of Works of Art, before whom the expert advisor and the would-be exporter argue their case. The Committee, having heard the evidence, makes its recommendations to the Minister of National Heritage. If the advisor's view prevails, then a period of time is allowed for an institution in the UK to make an offer to purchase the object. This period can vary, but is normally not more than six months. The applicant, however, is not bound to accept the offer, although a refusal normally leads to the licence being withheld. This procedure is geared towards the exceptional find, not the generality of archaeological discovery and in practice has two major drawbacks. Firstly, the licensing procedure is only of value if the regulations are observed. Unfortunately this is clearly not the case. Over the past three years, 1990–92, the number of licences actually requested has amounted to 34, 25 and 28, respectively. Secondly, once an antiquity has left the country, as the case of the Icklingham Bronzes has demonstrated, there are no powers to compel its return, though these powers may become available in the future embodied in a recent Council of the European Communities Directive if the object has been exported to a country within the European Community.

Under the Treaty of Rome, exports between member states were to become unrestricted. Article 36, however, empowered member states to prohibit or restrict the movement of goods on grounds of 'protection of national treasures possessing artistic, historic or archaeological value', provided that this did not 'constitute means of arbitrary discrimination or a disguised restriction on trade between member states'. While there appears at present to be no intention on the part of the European Community to harmonize individual member states' regulations controlling the export of their national antiquities, given this qualification to Article 36 it seems likely that individual national regulations could well be challenged in the future before the European Court of Justice (Goyder 1992). In the meantime, the removal of customs checks at national frontiers is likely to lead to still further antiquities leaving Britain illicitly and unlicensed.

The recovery of illicitly exported objects and stolen goods is a significant problem for the international community. This was addressed by the 1970 UNESCO Convention on the Means of Prohibiting and Preventing the Illicit Import, Export and Transfer of Ownership of Cultural Property, a convention yet to be ratified by the British government. In order to improve its implementation, UNESCO has recently provided resources for the International Institute for the Unification of Private Law (UNIDROIT) to draw up a further draft convention (Siehr 1992). This would place considerable responsibility on the purchaser to ensure that an object is not the product of illicit trade. It would require the return of stolen property, but compensation would only be paid if it could be demonstrated that necessary diligence had been exercised by the buyer to ensure that he or she was not acquiring property that had been stolen. Thirdly, it would seek arrangements for the return of illegally exported cultural objects when both states involved deemed the material to be of sufficient importance. Such an agreement will certainly be necessary if the trade in illegal antiquities is to be controlled outside the jurisdiction of the European Community.

ACKNOWLEDGEMENTS

I am most grateful for information kindly provided by Mr M. Brannon, Ms W. Horn, Dr A. Sheridan and Mr R. Warner.

CHAPTER 7

THE MANAGEMENT OF ARCHAEOLOGY UNDERWATER

Antony Firth

INTRODUCTION

The management regime affecting submerged sites is frequently different from that on land; we can start to talk of a distinctive management environment. Both the perception of remains rendered invisible by water and the regulatory mechanisms that apply below the water's edge contribute to this distinctiveness. The influence of problems of perception pervades all management, but the following discussion is restricted to the mechanics of managing archaeology underwater.

Management of archaeology underwater can be considered in terms of zones. The zones identified below correspond to differences in legal regime, rather than in the preservative environment or in the types of archaeological remains.

Inland waters

Rivers, lakes, reservoirs and other natural or artificial water bodies generally have the same status in law as land, so that all the procedures for dealing with archaeology on land can be applied to them.

Estuaries and ports

Estuaries and areas of sea near ports, including docks, harbours and marinas can be considered as inland waters for some purposes. Control of activities and developments may, however, lie with specific port and harbour authorities. For other purposes, their tidal nature means that they can be considered as territorial waters.

Inter-tidal areas

Legal regimes overlap in the inter-tidal area: low water is often used to define the seaward extent of land, and high water to delimit the landward extent of the sea. Care is required because the definitions used are not uniform and are based on average tides, not extremes. Tidal waters, a term used in some legislation, include tidal stretches of rivers, and the territorial sea. Archaeologists may find that they have recourse to two sets of management mechanisms, particularly on shallow shelving beaches or in areas of large tidal range.

Territorial sea

The territorial sea, from low water to the 12 nautical mile limit, and the seabed beneath it, form a significant proportion of UK territory (46 % according to Hildred and Oxley

1992). They are not subject to comprehensive planning and development controls. In the UK, the historical development of management of archaeology underwater has been dominated by wreck sites found by recreational divers in this zone. This emphasis is reflected in this chapter.

Zones beyond territorial waters

International law recognizes additional zones affecting both sea and seabed beyond 12 nm (Churchill and Lowe 1988), including the Contiguous Zone (12 to 24 nm), the Continental Shelf, and the Exclusive Economic Zone (to 200 nm). The UK, in contrast to some states, has not used its rights and responsibilities in these zones to try to exert control over archaeology underwater. Similarly, the UK has not attempted to manage archaeological material of UK origin or ownership lying beneath international waters.

RESPONSIBILITY

General responsibilities

A 1990 White Paper, *This Common Inheritance*, stated that the government is responsible for identifying and protecting archaeological remains on the seabed (DoE 1990b: 133). The Department of National Heritage (DNH) now has responsibility for nautical archaeology generally (DoE 1992a: 2). Although the government seems to accept that archaeology underwater is just as important as that on land, this concern has yet to result in comprehensive management of submerged remains.

Local planning authority (LPA) responsibilities and interests in archaeology are limited in their application below the low-water mark as their jurisdiction usually ends at this line. In consequence, developments and operations at sea are not subject to the archaeological controls that are integral to management on land. While planning jurisdiction appears unlikely to extend below the low-water mark in the near future, the issue is still under review, as are existing controls on developments and operations at sea (DoE 1990c). The government is, however, encouraging local authorities to take greater account of coastal development and the marine environment, so that LPAs may play an expanded role in archaeology underwater in future. This matter receives further consideration below.

Responsibilities for site protection

Ministerial responsibility for site protection has undergone several changes. It was transferred from the Secretary of State for Trade to the Secretary of State for Transport in 1983. The allocation of responsibility was a consequence of the particular development of archaeology underwater, and isolated it from the management of archaeology on land. In April 1991, responsibility was reallocated to the Secretary of State for the Environment, and was simultaneously devolved to the Secretaries of State for Wales, Scotland, and the Environment (Northern Ireland), respectively (Dromgoole 1992). One year later the responsibilities for wreck protection within DoE were transferred to DNH (DoE 1992a).

In England, wreck protection is dealt with directly by DNH, rather than English Heritage. In Wales and Scotland, this task is undertaken by Cadw and Historic Scotland respectively. In Northern Ireland, the Historic Monuments and Buildings Branch (HMBB) of DoE (NI) has a specific agency agreement with DNH on these matters.

The Advisory Committee on Historic Wreck Sites (ACHWS) is a non-statutory body that gives advice on matters relating to the Protection of Wrecks Act 1973; it makes recommendations regarding designation and licensing to the Secretaries of State. The Archaeological Diving Unit (ADU) is contracted to DNH to supply information derived from fieldwork relating to this legislation, and to provide such other advice as DNH may request.

Scheduling of monuments in inland, estuarine, inter-tidal or territorial waters under the Ancient Monuments and Archaeological Areas Act 1979 (AMAA Act 1979) is adminis-tered by the same bodies that are responsible on land.

Responsibilities for recording

The revised Royal Warrants of the Royal Commissions on the Historical Monuments of England (RCHME), Scotland (RCAHMS) and Wales (RCAHMW), issued in 1992, affirm the extension of their responsibilities to include ancient and historical monuments and constructions in, on or under the seabed within the UK territorial sea adjacent to England, Scotland and Wales, as announced in *This Common Inheritance* (DoE 1990b: 133; Chapter 3). In addition to the compilation of National Monuments Records (NMRs) on submerged sites, their duties now embrace identification, survey and interpretation of sites and monuments in, on or under the seabed. HMBB has taken on an equivalent task for Northern Ireland's territorial waters.

Responsibilities for determining ownership

The Department of Transport administers the provisions of the Merchant Shipping Act 1894, which affects ownership, salvage and the reporting of material removed from the seabed in UK tidal waters. The Ministry of Defence and the Foreign and Commonwealth Office maintain some rights to wrecks of vessels engaged in government service and British East Indiamen, respectively. A government statement in 1990 implied that the DoE (now DNH) would exercise any rights of ownership in each case, in consultation with rel-evant archaeological bodies (DoE 1990c: 4). In general terms the government is willing to exercise its powers of ownership, where these can be established, in favour of conserving wreck sites and artefacts recovered from them (Written answer, 20 December 1990, Official Reports, Parliamentary Debates (Lords) vol. 524 WA 59-60).

RECORDING

National Monuments Records

In England, submerged sites are recorded in the Maritime Section of the NMR. Both craft (known remains) and casualties (recorded losses) are included, as are other submerged sites. Efforts are concentrated on particular information sources, including the Hydrographer of the Navy's wreck records, records of losses, charted fishing-net snags, and the archives of independent maritime researchers. The Royal Commissions in Scotland and Wales may be expected to act similarly when resources become available. The record of sites in territorial waters adjacent to Northern Ireland will be compiled by HMBB.

Local records

Sites and Monuments Records (SMRs) play a central role in recording and managing archaeology on land, but a further consequence of the shoreline limit of local planning authorities is that SMRs rarely include submerged remains. This omission often extends upstream; records of sites and discoveries in inland, estuarine and inter-tidal waters are frequently poor. Important initiatives at SMR level include the Isle of Wight Maritime SMR; this formed the basis of RCHME's pilot project on national recording (DoE 1992d: 96). The compilation of records at local level has been shown to be effective in abstracting data from local archives, and in obtaining reports from recreational divers, fishermen and beachcombers.

SMRs can be expected to include records of marine and underwater material for a number of reasons. Firstly, the expanded role of local authorities in coastal zone management, and greater attention to the environment by other water-based operators, will create demands for information. Secondly, the work on sources and standards by the Royal Commissions, and possibilities of data exchange, should make it easier for SMRs to set up appropriate records. Thirdly, rising interest in the influence of water transport and other maritime activities in the past has implications for both management and research, and will require data.

Many museums hold artefacts recovered from underwater contexts in their collections. Their records of such material are often difficult to assess and interrogate.

REPORTING AND TREATMENT OF PORTABLE MATERIAL

Reporting

There is no scheme for the reporting of information or finds discovered underwater for archaeological purposes. However, the Merchant Shipping Act 1894 should act as a mechanism for registering finds from the sea as they come ashore. Salvaged material must be reported to a Receiver of Wreck, formerly a local officer of Her Majesty's Customs and Excise service. Current re-examination of the role of customs officers has led government to propose a central Receiver of Wreck to deal with all reports. This scheme seems likely to come into operation during 1993. Although the provisions of the 1894 Act are obligatory, the system has never been particularly effective. Most finds are probably not reported.

The requirement to report in the 1894 Act arises from salvage, and is a consequence of the obligation to deliver wreck to the Receiver. Material located but not recovered may not incur this obligation, so the Act does not furnish a mechanism for the reporting of archaeological remains generally, nor does it provide for preservation in situ. The provisions of the 1894 Act only apply to wreck, which includes items from a vessel or casualty, but not material that has been inundated or has come from the shore. The determination of what is or is not wreck may require careful interpretation, increasing uncertainty in specific cases and discouraging comprehensive reporting. Moreover, the 1894 Act does not cover inland waters, where land-based rules for the registration of finds apply.

The need to improve the reporting of archaeological information from underwater is widely recognized, but there are difficulties in devising a more effective scheme. The development of a comprehensive, effective system can be expected to continue to tax the patience of managers.

The treatment of portable material from sites designated under the Protection of Wrecks Act 1973 is clearer. Brief details of artefacts recovered from restricted areas should be contained in the licensee's report to ACHWS. Wreck that is raised must also be reported to the Receiver of Wreck in accordance with salvage law.

Salvors of wreck are entitled to a salvage award according to the 1894 Act. The government has been generous in its award of salvage to salvors of unclaimed wreck of historic or archaeological interest to encourage reporting, though there is little evidence that this policy has been successful.

Disposal

On its delivery, the Receiver must advertise any find and keep it for a period of one year to allow the original owner to make a claim. Resolution of ownership is dealt with below. The eventual owner must meet the Receiver's expenses in handling the material. Coins more than 100 years old and not purchased by a museum are subject to a levy of 25 % of their value. In cases of material requiring conservation, finders often keep possession but sign an undertaking to the effect that the wreck remains under the Receiver's control.

Prospective excavators of wrecks in areas restricted by the 1973 Act must indicate the ultimate destination of items recovered in their application for a licence. In the past, licences have been granted by the Secretary of State on the advice of ACHWS even where the licensee intended to dispose of material by public auction. There is no statutory protection against such disposal, but it is not anticipated that this practice will occur in future.

Resources for ensuring adequate conservation, publication and long-term storage are generally unavailable. While there are encouraging exceptions, these matters are often casualties of the lack of overall management and support for archaeology underwater.

SITE PROTECTION

The Protection of Wrecks Act 1973

Wrecks of archaeological interest can be subject to the Protection of Wrecks Act 1973. Protection comprises the designation of an area in which certain activities are restricted. Consequently, the position of the wreck must be known, but the name, origin and owner-ship of the wreck need not.

An offence is committed in a restricted area by any person who does, causes or permits any of the following things, otherwise than under the authority of a licence: tampering with, damaging or removing any part of the vessel, or any object formerly contained in such a vessel; diving or salvage operations, or the use of diving or salvage equipment; deposition of anything that would may obliterate, obstruct or damage any part of the wreck (Section 1(3)).

Activities such as bathing, angling and navigation are permitted provided there is no likelihood of damage to the wreck (Marine Directorate 1986: 1). Differences from the provisions of the AMAA Act 1979 include no right of public access (Section 19) and the absence of provision for any expenditure on acquisition and upkeep (Section 24).

Designation generally arises from an application by a member of the public, but emergency designation is possible. Advice on designation is given by ACHWS and ADU. There are no set criteria, except that the restricted area must be suspected to be the site of a vessel of archaeological, historical or artistic importance. The 1973 Act makes no reference to 'national importance', nor to age limits. The most modern pro-tected wreck dates from 1864. Most of the wrecks are post-medieval and the majority are located off the south and southwest coasts of England. There is neither a formal ranking of sites nor, at present, a programme to increase the representativeness of sites protected under the Act.

The 1973 Act can be applied throughout UK waters, which means the territorial sea, any arm or estuary of the sea, and any part of a river within the ebb and flow of ordin-ary spring tides. References in this Act to the seabed include any area submerged at high water of ordinary spring tides (Section 3(1)). The tidal reaches of rivers often extend far inland, so that the potential to make use of the Act is considerable.

Ancient Monuments and Archaeological Areas Act 1979

Archaeological remains underwater, including vessels, may also be protected using the AMAA Act 1979. Sites in inland waters, inter-tidal areas and other stretches of water within Great Britain are covered directly, but special provision is made for monuments in territorial waters in Section 53.

To date, no sites under territorial waters have been scheduled, but a number of inland or inter-tidal sites that are underwater or have underwater elements have been protected. The non-statutory criteria for scheduling ancient monuments might be expected to apply to the protection of sites underwater under the 1979 Act. Although the Act is applicable to vessels (Section 61 (7) (c)) and could be used to protect submerged wrecks it was stated (Under Secretary of State for the Environment 4 April 1979 Official Report, Parliamentary Debates (Commons) Fifth Ser vol. 96, col. 1363) that designation under the Protection of Wrecks Act 1973 would take precedence. As Departmental responsibility is no longer divided, there is no longer any reason to expect this statement to restrict use of the AMAA Act 1979.

Policing and enforcement

Offences against the 1973 Act are punishable by a fine not exceeding £5,000 in the case of summary conviction in a magistrate's court, and by an unlimited fine in the case of indictment. Policing of restricted areas is difficult, even if the area is within easy sight of land. Various offences, including unauthorized diving and fishing that causes damage, are known to occur. The first prosecutions under the 1973 Act took place in February 1991. DNH informs policing agencies of the designation of sites, and may request assistance in specific circumstances.

FIELDWORK

Control of fieldwork

On sites designated under the 1973 Act, archaeological investigation is prohibited except under the authority of a licence issued by DNH, Cadw, Historic Scotland or HMBB on behalf of the appropriate Secretary of State. The Secretaries of State may act on the recommendations of ACHWS or ADU. Licences are granted to named individuals and only authorize persons identified in an attached schedule to conduct the permitted activities. The licence may incorporate specific conditions. Virtually all licences are annual and must be renewed if work is to continue.

Information about research design, resources and equipment, conservation, archiving and publication is required in making an application for a licence. In almost all cases, the licensee must arrange for an archaeological advisor or director who will provide advice. However, such advisors and directors are not required to dive, nor to be in direct control of work on site. The government does not provide direct support or funding to satisfy licence conditions.

One licence condition is the submission of an annual report for consideration by ACHWS, which can request further information. This committee can recommend the refusal of applications to renew licences. ADU monitors and reports on work standards in restricted areas as part of its DNH contract. These procedures assist in the maintenance of archaeological standards on designated sites.

Activities on wreck sites of archaeological interest not designated under the 1973 Act may be constrained by common law. The relevant concept, 'salvor in possession', is widely misunderstood: far more than a simple claim or declaration by the would-be salvors is required. However, an approach based on salvage is incompatible with safeguarding the archaeological value of wrecks.

Health and safety

Archaeological fieldwork involving paid divers is subject to the *Diving Operations at Work Regulations 1981* (as amended), administered by the Health and Safety Executive (HSE). Regulations and guidance applicable in such circumstances, which also cover work by volunteers working with paid divers, are set out in *Diving Operations at Work: Guidance on Regulations* (HSE 1991). A General Certificate of Exemption (no. 1/81) relaxes many conditions required of most professional diving operations in the case of archaeological work, but is currently under review.

OWNERSHIP

In UK law, ownership of material lost at sea resides in original owners or their successors, unless it can be shown that abandonment has occurred. There is no provision to assume abandonment after any set period. The Crown has not claimed ownership of archaeological remains by virtue of their antiquity or the public interest. The Crown does, however, claim ownership of wreck from UK territorial waters that is salvaged and reported (see above), but remains unclaimed after one year, through the Merchant Shipping Act 1894. This mechanism is used to ensure good title on the disposal of wreck, rather than to benefit the Crown. Ownership is generally passed to the finder of historic wreck in lieu of a salvage award.

The 1894 Act has no bearing on the ownership of sites on the seabed. Claims to ownership by virtue of discovering a site are generally unfounded, as are claims to exclusive salvage rights based on finding a wreck and lifting a few objects.

Numerous wrecks still have current owners, because either ownership resides in the Crown (e.g. wrecks of Royal Navy ships), or rights of ownership have been acquired by successive individuals or organizations such as insurance companies. Such rights are not restricted to UK citizens; foreign governments have claimed ownership of wrecks of archaeological interest. The Netherlands is a prominent example, maintaining claims of ownership to wrecks of Dutch East India Company vessels.

The 1894 Act applies to wreck found in or on the shores of any tidal water within the limits of the UK. Wreck found outside the limits of the UK and brought within such limits is subject to the provisions on delivery (Dromgoole 1989: 29).

Inland waters are generally owned as land, with median lines where the dry land on each bank is in separate ownership (Howarth 1992). Ownership of material from inland waters is resolved as if it had been recovered on land.

Ownership and protection

Ownership of a wreck is not prejudiced by designation under the 1973 Act, but the owner is subject to that Act's prohibitions and licensing provisions. Material from restricted areas remains subject to the general rules of ownership. Remains removed to the surface become wreck for the purposes of the 1894 Act. In practice, licensed investigators retain possession of such finds in order to assure conservation. Usually a single report is made to the Receiver of Wreck to cover all material removed during the year. The relationship between the 1894 and the 1973 Acts has caused some difficulty in the past. Current interpretation is that the setting of conditions on the ultimate destination of finds in a licence to excavate inhibits commercial disposal, as had occurred previously.

The Government is not convinced that serious damage is done to archaeological material, nor that important material is lost to public collections, simply as a result of the requirements of salvage law (DoE 1990c: 2). There is some commercial salvage of material of archaeological or historical interest in UK waters. Its effects are unquantified, but several significant underwater sites in the UK have been and continue to be destroyed by salvage operations.

DEVELOPMENT CONTROL AND PLANNING

Until recently, management of archaeology underwater was almost entirely limited to dealing with sites affected by the provisions of the 1894 and 1973 legislation. But the emphasis is changing and it is likely that progress in archaeology underwater in terms of management, fieldwork and discoveries will be generated by procedures associated with development control and planning. These are very early days, however, so the following is only a sketch of some of the most important directions.

Locations and types of development

This section focuses on types of development and on the threats posed by particular processes. Inferences as to the potential archaeological impact of planned developments can be drawn from nearby sites on land, the presence of more recent material and casualties, and the likely character of remains that may be encountered. It may be difficult, however, to propose a reasonable archaeological response without being able to submit positions of known archaeological sites. In such situations, knowledge of the manner in which the development will affect the sea, river or lake bed may be critical in requesting additional information and in anticipating discoveries.

Table 7.1 illustrates the range of development types in relation to process and zone. Estuarine, port and inter-tidal zones are here merged as 'coastal', and developments in territorial and more distant waters are labelled 'marine'. The association between particular types of development and specific zones is illustrative and not absolute.

	Inland	Coastal	Marine
Extraction	Alterations to water courses	Maintenance dredging	Aggregate extraction
Construction	Bridges	Marinas Fish farms Port facilities	Offshore installations
Linear developments	Cable-laying	Outfalls	Pipelines Trenching
Shoreline	Embankments	Coastal defences	
Diffuse activities	Boat wash	Anchoring Recreational Diving	Trawling Dumping Commercial salvage

Table 7.1. Range of development types in relation to process and zone.

Effects of disturbance may occur over great distances as water is very efficient in transmitting energy and moving sediment. Hydrographic changes caused by dredging, or by coastal and riverbank defences, may affect both currents and sediment load, with consequences for erosion and deposition elsewhere. It is also necessary to consider the potential archaeological impacts in areas beyond the immediate environs of a project. In confined waters, effects on the local water table and on buried waterlogged deposits require consideration.

Equipment used in developments close to or under water can be massive and may require ancillary support over large areas. For example, a narrow linear development such as an outfall may be installed by a barge with large anchors extending hundreds of metres from the centre line marked on an application. Imprecision in position-fixing can also increase the area affected, as may the use of buffer zones.

Some offshore activities may not be subject directly to planning procedures, but their dependence on onshore facilities may bring them within the scope of development control. Access can be critical: plans to build or improve slipway, docking or berthing facilities imply increased levels of activity, which may have archaeological consequences and thus require comment. Shoreline erosion of archaeological deposits from the wash of boats and attrition attributable to recreational diving may be controlled in this way.

GUIDELINES AND CODES OF PRACTICE

The planning regime applicable to archaeology underwater is far from comprehensive and consists of many varied components. Best use should be made of whatever openings are available.

All manner of public, private, charitable and commercial organizations can draw up guidelines or codes of practice in relation to archaeology underwater or, more likely, to environmental and archaeological matters generally. Such statements lack the teeth of statutory controls, but indicate a degree of will or intent that may be absent under more formal systems. Guidelines and codes might be expected to cover the organization's own activities, the use of land, property or other rights that it owns or controls, and its dealings with other bodies and individuals.

The National Rivers Authority (NRA) presents an example of the role and potential importance of environmental policies applicable to water-based developments. In addition to having a general duty with respect to protecting and conserving sites and objects of archaeological interest, the NRA's Code of Practice on Conservation, Access and Recreation includes archaeological provisions (NRA 1991). The application of the Code to NRA activities can be enforced through directives issued by the Secretary of State for the Environment (Water Resources Act 1991: Section 18).

Voluntary procedures for developers and seabed operators also fall under this general heading. In 1990, the government intimated its readiness to develop a code of practice for seabed operators in discussion with relevant archaeological and industry-related organizations (DoE 1990b: 10). The code is being developed in line with similar codes for industry–archaeology co-operation on land, and its gradual introduction can be anticipated.

Planning policy

The government has recently set out guidance on coastal planning for local authorities in England and Wales in *Planning Policy Guidance Note 20* (DoE and Welsh Office 1992c). This extends the interests of LPAs beyond the low-water mark, although their jurisdiction remains firmly terrestrial. The planning system is presented as the primary means of reconciling development requirements with policies for the conservation and improvement of the coastal environment.

Archaeological aspects are reasonably well integrated in PPG 20. It makes systematic reference to historic landscapes particular to coastal areas and notes that the coastal zone has a rich cultural heritage both above and below the low-water mark. The relevance of PPG 16 to these matters is reiterated. The following comments should be considered in the context of government recognition in this guidance note of the significance of development control to remains below the low-water mark.

Development plans and management plans

Development plans have a dominant role in development control, supported by statute (see Chapter 8). Development plans are largely aimed at terrestrial concerns, but following PPG 20 they can be expected to take offshore matters into account, in line with overall coastal planning policy. PPG 20 sets out the role of development plans with respect to the coastal zone; it requires co-operation between LPAs, in the course of development plan preparation, to define policies for historic landscapes and archaeological sites and monuments, and refers to assessments of historic landscapes and sites of archaeological interest as necessary components.

Coastal management plans are discussed in detail in *Coastal Zone Protection and Planning* (DoE 1992b). The avoidance of environmental (including archaeological) damage is stated to be one of the chief aims of such plans. The government expects them to be prepared wherever there are demonstrable conflicts and pressures, with particular reference to estuaries (DoE 1992b: 8–9). They are not development plans as such, but LPAs are to take the lead in preparing them (DoE 1992b: 8) and their conclusions should be taken into account in preparing and reviewing development plans (DoE 1992c: 4.17).

At least 34 % of the coast of England and Wales is subject to specific management plans as a result of designation as Heritage Coasts. The Countryside Commission issued a new policy statement on Heritage Coasts in 1991 that recognized the value of archaeological features in objectives relating to conservation, protection and enhancement of natural beauty (Countryside Commission 1991a). The new objectives of the Heritage Coasts are to be included in management plans, including timetables for implementation, before 2000. The policy statement insists on rigorous control by the appropriate local and national authorities of developments affecting the inter-tidal strand of Heritage Coasts and their immediate inshore waters (Countryside Commission 1991a: 5).

Planning decisions

PPG 20 reiterated that decisions on proposed developments below the mean low-water mark generally fall outside the scope of the planning system. However, planning decisions are relevant to archaeology underwater, despite the lack of extensive jurisdiction, for several reasons. LPA decisions can affect areas of foreshore that contain remains submerged for much of the time. Moreover, LPAs may have direct jurisdiction over enclosed stretches of water and estuaries. Finally, PPG 20 states that LPAs should take offshore impacts of onshore developments into account when making planning decisions (DoE 1992c: 1.8).

In some cases, LPAs have the option to exercise control over specific activities offshore. For example, the Coast Protection Act 1949 gave local authorities some control over dredging activities within three nautical miles of their coasts. South Wight Borough Council made use of this to request remote sensing surveys and desktop archaeological evaluations before renewal of inshore dredging licences.

Developments within enclosed waters such as ports and estuaries are often controlled by specific authorities that do not fall within LPA jurisdiction. Coastal management plans are intended to be multi-agency and strategic, so that LPAs are encouraged to work closely with other interests, including port, harbour and other navigation authorities (DoE 1992b: 8). Decisions within the jurisdiction of authorities of these kinds may be expected to reflect policies expressed in coastal management plans and, by extension, other LPA policies.

Finally, some projects are not subject to general planning laws, but alternative arrangements (see below) exist that often require consultation with LPAs. This, too, may be expected to facilitate consistent consideration of the effects of specific developments on archaeology underwater.

Environmental assessment

Environmental assessment (EA) is particularly relevant to the management of archaeology underwater for two reasons. Firstly, many of the types of project for which EA is mandatory (Directive 85/337/EC Annex I projects) are often located at the coast or on rivers. In addition, several types of projects that may be subject to EA depending on their significance (Directive 85/337/EC Annex II projects) are directly concerned with water. Secondly, as marine developments are generally beyond normal planning jurisdiction, EA is one of the few means available of ensuring that possible environmental impacts are taken into account.

Procedures equivalent to EA are common among the wide range of authorities that take development-related decisions with implications for submerged remains. Government departments such as the Ministry of Agriculture, Fisheries and Food and the Board of Trade process such applications, as do agencies like the Crown Estates Commissioners. Some types of water-related development, such as salmon farms in marine waters and certain pipelines are covered by specific regulations requiring formal EA. Others, such as aggregate dredging, are subject to internal procedures intended to be the equivalent to EA (DoE 1989a: 16–22).

Some oil and gas companies have carried out comprehensive EA-related studies, notably where the proposal affects an area close to the coast and there is a local population to appease. Archaeology underwater has been included in these, involving desktop evaluations and some fieldwork.

The implementation of EA in coastal areas is variable, as the government has recognized (DoE 1992b: 12). Problems arise during scoping, and in considering inshore and offshore effects in the case of onshore developments. Archaeological remains underwater are particularly prone to these difficulties because the presence of sites in SMRs and NMRs acts as an important trigger in EA, and few underwater sites are currently included in these records. Without this, it is unlikely that archaeology underwater will be considered systematically in EA.

Marine protected areas

Coastal and marine areas are subject to many types of designation, some of which have already been cited. Marine protected area (MPA) is a generic term for schemes that designate areas of inter-tidal strand, and sea and seabed, generally for conservation purposes. The Marine Conservation Society has acted as a focus for discussions on MPAs in the UK, particularly with a view to promoting comprehensive, statutory systems to rationalize and improve on existing arrangements (Marine Conservation Society 1991; Firth and

Ferrari 1992). MPA schemes are often designed essentially for flora and fauna, but may provide a focus for information and control of developments that can be tapped for archaeological purposes.

Two forms of MPA of potential interest to the archaeologist are Marine Nature Reserves (MNRs) and Marine Consultation Areas (MCAs). MNRs are statutory reserves introduced under the Wildlife and Countryside Act 1981. Only two areas, around the islands of Lundy and Skomer, have been designated. The former includes two areas restricted under the Protection of Wrecks Act 1973. MCAs are a more recent DoE initiative, aimed at addressing some of the difficulties encountered with MNRs. They use a non-statutory consultative procedure to ensure that conservation interests are taken into account at an early stage in any form of development affecting the area. The MCAs proposed in 1992 cover extensive areas of sea and shore, including areas of significant archaeological potential (Wildlife Division 1992a, 1992b).

CHANGE IN THE MANAGEMENT OF ARCHAEOLOGY UNDERWATER

Archaeology underwater has benefited from a number of initiatives in recent years. Several of these changes were prompted by proposals formulated by the Joint Nautical Archaeology Policy Committee, published as *Heritage at Sea: Proposals for the Better Protection of Archaeological Sites Underwater* (JNAPC 1989). The transfer of responsibilities for site protection, the inclusion of marine sites in the NMR, and support for a training scheme for recreational divers were major results: other elements, such as the *Code of Practice for Sea-bed Developers*, are still in draft. However, changes to the principal legislation affecting archaeology underwater (the Protection of Wrecks Act 1973 and the Merchant Shipping Act 1894), the initial recommendation of *Heritage at Sea*, do not seem likely in the near future. It seems more probable that improvement to the legislative structure will arise from current initiatives on portable antiquities legislation (see Chapter 6) and the use of the relevant provisions in the AMAA Act 1979, rather than by means of new legislation aimed specifically at underwater concerns.

Most of the foreseeable changes in the management of archaeology underwater are related to the extension, in one form or another, of planning and conservation procedures to coastal and marine areas. There is a great variety of mechanisms already available or under development that make management of archaeology underwater a viable proposition. While early signs are very promising, it is yet to be demonstrated that archaeologists will overcome the problems of perception and take up the available tools to make best use of the opportunities for understanding that archaeology underwater presents.

CHAPTER 8

LISTED BUILDINGS
Roger W. Suddards

INTRODUCTION

The concept of protecting buildings in use for reasons of their special architectural or historic interest is of relatively recent origin when compared with the original legislation designed to protect ancient monuments, which was enacted in 1882. The 1932 Planning Act was the first piece of legislation designed to afford protection to buildings in general. Some fifty-eight years later the law relating to listed buildings in England and Wales has been consolidated in the Planning (Listed Buildings and Conservation Areas) Act 1990, hereafter referred to as the LBA (for Northern Ireland see Appendix, p. 134). There are at present 439,048 listed buildings in England and Wales.

The statutory provisions for the protection of 'buildings of special architectural or historic interest' are derived from our ancient monuments legislation and it is perhaps not surprising that it is possible for a building or structure to be both a Scheduled Monument and a listed building. However, Section 61 of the LBA provides that the legislative controls relating to listed buildings do not apply to buildings that are 'for the time being included in the schedule of monuments compiled and maintained under section 1 of the Ancient Monuments and Archaeological Areas Act 1979'. Buildings in ecclesiastical use and occupied dwelling houses cannot be scheduled but some buildings such as medieval barns are both scheduled and listed (see also Chapters 5 and 9). This chapter outlines the way listed buildings are selected and gives an overview of how they are protected. This will involve consideration of the following questions:

What is a listed building?
What is listed building consent and how does it afford protection?
What are the mechanics of control and enforcement?

WHAT IS A LISTED BUILDING?

The listing process

The listing of buildings of special architectural or historic interest is the responsibility of the Secretary of State. Central to the listing process is the list referred to in Section 1(1) of the LBA. It is the Secretary of State of the Department for National Heritage (DNH) who is responsible for compiling the list. Central government, not local government, has responsibility for listing.

Buildings appear on the list through one of three main methods: methodical resurvey, spot listing (an expedited procedure) and service of a building preservation notice by a local planning authority regarding a building that is subsequently added to the list by the

---

Author's note: this is a complex area of heritage concern, of which this is a general outline only. More detailed coverage can be found in Suddards 1988.

Secretary of State. There is no statutory right of appeal against listing. There is, however, power to amend the list and reference should also be made to paragraph 40 of DoE *Circular 8/87* (DoE 1987b).

The list is a control mechanism and is not a definitive assessment of quality. Lady Birk's description of the listing process as 'not a pickling policy' (1977: 5) reflects, in the writer's view, the correct position. Nowhere in the LBA is there a presumption in favour of preservation of listed buildings, but the DoE (and now the DNH) has always maintained this. There are now no buildings excluded from the possibility of being listed, but different consequences flow in respect of listing of churches in ecclesiastical use, ancient monuments and Crown property.

Buildings cease to be listed when listed building consent for demolition has been granted and fully implemented. Total demolition does not of itself cause the building to be removed from the statutory list but in practice a total demolition will be accepted as a 'delisting'. Where parts of the building remain in a reconstructible state the building continues to be listed.

What may be listed?

The simplistic answer to this question is 'a building which is of special architectural or historic interest'. The term 'building' is not defined positively in the LBA nor in the Town and Country Planning Act 1990. It is defined negatively by showing what is included in the definition and not what is in fact a building. A 'building' includes 'any structure or erection and any part of a building, structure or erection but does not include any plant or machinery comprised in a building'. One should also refer to Section 1(5) of the LBA which treats as part of a building:

a. any object or structure fixed to the building; and

b. any object or structure within the curtilage of the building which, although not fixed to the building forms part of the land and has done so since before 1 July 1948.

The listing may also embrace other buildings or structures that may be physically attached to a building but are themselves not separately listed. The interpretation of Section 1(5) of the LBA, particularly with regard to the question of curtilage, is not settled (Suddards 1988: Chapter 2).

Selection and grading

Listing is a two-stage process that considers whether the building should be listed in the first place and if so in what grade it should be placed. Selection of buildings for listing is the responsibility of the DNH. It is also important to note the provisions of Section 1(3) of the LBA. These provide that the Secretary of State may take into account not only the building itself but also:

a. any respect in which its exterior contributes to the architectural or historic interest of any group of buildings of which it forms part; and

b. the desirability of preserving, on the ground of its architectural or historic interest, any feature of the building consisting of a man-made object or structure fixed to the building or forming part of the land and comprised within the curtilage of the building.

It must be remembered that buildings, to be listed, must be of 'special architectural or historic interest'. In considering what constitutes 'architectural' interest, a view must be taken as to whether the term embraces the art and technique of building in its widest sense, or the design and appearance of a building in a more limited context. The assessment of these factors will be largely subjective and will inevitably stem from a particular inspector's specialist knowledge and aesthetic judgement.

The development of modern building techniques has created a number of potentially interesting situations. Could a building that is of great interest structurally be neither of historic nor of architectural interest? Would a novel technological development that was part of an ugly and modern building merit the listing of the building that reflected that technology? Some might aver that certain point blocks built in the 1960–70 period in the UK were of significance in the history of the development of concrete as a building material. Would the scarcity value of a particular type of concrete or the fact that the point blocks are no longer being built today justify the preservation of a last surviving example? Could such a building properly be listed? It is neither beautiful nor old, and could not be regarded as 'historic', but we believe it could be properly listed, since the word 'architectural' has the widest meaning and will embrace types of materials, methods of building expression and form, space, mass, light, scale, colour and the like.

The DoE *Guidance Notes* (1985) advise that in selecting a building for its association with technological innovation or virtuosity, it is essential that the information is absolutely accurate and dependable, as most of the buildings in this category are selected on the basis of historical fact, for example, the first example of its type or the first use of a material rather than on aesthetic qualities.

If it cannot claim any architectural interest, then it may qualify if it is of historic interest. The determination of what constitutes historic interest is eminently debatable and raises many issues. The DoE *Guidance Notes* suggest that an assessment of historic interest should deal with the importance of the person or event, and the importance of the building in relation to that person's life and work or that event. (The transient association of lodgers or tenants, however eminent, should be looked at critically.)

While these guidelines are helpful to a degree, they still leave considerable scope for individual interpretation.

How are buildings chosen?

The principles for selection or adding to the statutory list of a building are set out in Appendix 1 of DOE *Circular 8/87*. The principles are as follows:

a. All buildings built before 1700 that survive in anything like their original condition are listed.
b. Most buildings of 1700 to 1840 are listed, though selection is necessary.
c. Buildings dating from between 1840 and 1914 are only listed if of definite quality and character, and the selection is designed to include the principal works of the principal architects.
d. Selected buildings dating from between 1914 and 1939 of high quality are listed.

A few outstanding buildings dating from after 1939 are listed. The principal listing criterion remains the age of the building. The more recent a building is, the more selectively it is treated. Other relevant criteria are the state of preservation of the building when surveyed and its rarity within a building type. There is further guidance in Appendix 1 of *Circular 8/87* with respect to factors of social and economic history, technological innovation, well-known individuals and group value, although it should be noted that these principles of selection have no statutory basis.

English Heritage advises the Secretary of State on national criteria to be adopted in selection. The DNH keeps the listing standards under review and they are revised from time to time. The selection process has evolved over a considerable period. The process of revision has been demonstrated by the amendment to the selection criteria for inter-war buildings. Furthermore, all buildings of special architectural or historic merit over thirty years of age are now automatically eligible for listing. In very exceptional circumstances buildings of outstanding quality that are under threat will be listed provided that they are at least ten years old (DoE 1991).

Grading

When buildings are selected for listing they are placed in grades. There is no reference in the LBA to grading and the procedure is therefore non-statutory. Grading has administrative importance in relation to the awarding of grants and also in relation to listed building consent for demolition, alteration or extensions of listed buildings. Guidance is given in Paragraph 35 of *Circular 8/87* as regards how the DNH approaches the problem of grading.

Appendix 1 of *Circular 8/87* shows the present departmental approach to grading. Buildings are classified in grades to show their relative importance as follows:

Grade I. These are buildings of exceptional interest (only about 2 % of listed buildings so far are in this grade).
Grade II*. These are particularly important buildings of more than special interest (some 4 % of listed buildings).
Grade II. These are buildings of special interest, which warrant every effort being made to preserve them.

It should be noted that the criteria mentioned above are non-statutory and all that is required under the LBA is that a building must be of 'special architectural or historic interest'.

Deemed listing

Deemed listing is a process by which a building that is not listed either as part of the over-all survey of listed buildings carried out by the DNH, nor spot listed (see below), is deemed to be included in the list and has applied to it all listed building provisions. Two categories of buildings are deemed to be listed: firstly, those properties covered by building preservation orders made by local authorities under the pre-1968 legislation; secondly, those that are the subject of building preservation notices that may be served by a local planning authority in respect of a non-listed building that they opine is of special architectural or historic interest and is 'in danger'.

A building preservation notice is effective as soon as it has been served on both the owner and occupier of the building to which it relates and remains in force for six months from the date of service. The notice ceases to have effect if before the expiration of the six-month period the Secretary of State either lists the building or notifies the local planning authority in writing that he does not intend to list the property. If it appears to the local planning authority that it is urgent that a building preservation notice should come into force, it may, instead of serving the notice on the owner and occupier of the building, affix the building preservation notice conspicuously to some object on the building and this will count as valid service of the notice. Section 29 of the LBA contains provisions relating to compensation for loss or damage arising out of the service of the building preservation notice.

The mechanics of listing

Most listed buildings are added to the statutory list as a result of resurvey fieldwork undertaken by the DNH. An inspector will inspect the exterior of a building with a view to establishing its approximate date, form and function. Internal inspection, where this can be arranged, is important in situations where internal features survive but external features have been obscured by later alterations.

Each draft recommendation for listing accompanied by a photograph is submitted to a supervising inspector. Each entry is given a serial number, grid reference, address, proposed grading and a note of any group value. The list description details the most important features of the building but the listing covers the entire building. The list description may indicate what is not considered to be of special interest, such as a 20th-century extension.

The completed draft list goes forward to the Secretary of State for the DNH for signature. In most cases the decision to list is taken by the Head of the Department's Listing Branch, although controversial cases will be referred to the minister responsible for heritage matters. In a few cases the Secretary of State will make the decision whether to list, but this usually relates to spot-listing cases. In most cases the Secretary of State accepts English Heritage's advice whether to add a property to the statutory list but he is not bound to accept such advice.

Applications for 'spot-listing' can be made to the Secretary of State by any person. Paragraph 39 of *Circular 8/87* requests that applications are made well in advance of development proposals. Requests are sent to the DNH or its equivalents in Scotland and Wales and should include an address, location plan, recent photograph and information relevant to the age and history of the building. The Department assesses the urgency of the request, usually in conjunction with the local authority, then sends the request to English Heritage for action within a prescribed deadline.

Immunity from listing

Section 6 of the LBA provides a procedure designed to alleviate the risk of listing by enabling a person to apply to the DNH for a certificate stating that it does not intend to list the building within the ensuing five years provided an application has been made for planning permission or permission has in fact been given. If an immunity certificate is obtained then the Secretary of State for the DNH cannot exercise his powers of listing under Section 1 of the LBA and neither can the local authority serve a building preservation notice under Section 6(2)(b) of the LBA for five years from the date of issue of the certificate. Approximately 50 % of applications are successful (see Suddards 1988: Chapter 2).

WHAT IS LISTED BUILDING CONSENT AND HOW DOES IT AFFORD PROTECTION?

The principal mechanism used in the LBA to control demolition, alteration or extension of listed buildings is the requirement of listed building consent (LBC). Work carried out without an LBC authorization will be an offence. Consideration of listed building consent involves an understanding of both the criteria and procedure relevant to the LBC process. *Circular 8/87* sets out a clear and detailed policy statement regarding the DoE's current position with LBC.

Listing gives a building an important statutory protection but is not intended to be a process that involves an absolute ban on any future change. *Circular 8/87* contains details of the departmental thinking on the question of the criteria that it is suggested should be taken into account by local planning authorities or the Secretary of State for the DNH when considering LBC applications. The criteria for decisions are not necessarily closed, and over time greater sophistication of criteria may emerge. The statutory requirement for consideration of whether to grant LBC is for a local planning authority or the Secretary of State to have 'special regard to the desirability of preserving the building or its setting or any features of special architectural or historic interest which it possesses'.

The current departmental non-statutory criteria for LBC are contained in Paragraph 90 of *Circular 8/87* which emphasizes the importance of the building:

both intrinsically and relatively bearing in mind the number of other buildings of special architectural or historic interest in the neighbourhood. In some cases a building may be important because there are only a few of its type in the neighbourhood or because it has a fine interior, while in other cases its importance may be enhanced because it forms part of a group or series. Attention should also be paid to the contribution to the local scene made by a building, particularly if it is in a conservation area; but the absence of such a contribution is not a reason for demolition or alteration.

The problem of determining the importance of any building involves the question of differing subjective judgments. It is always open to the applicant to claim that the building should not have been listed. This is simply an assertion that the building should not have been regarded as of special architectural or historic interest. The question of the scarcity value of the building is often important, as is the contribution it makes to the local scene, particularly the street scene.

The circular goes on to discuss the architectural merit and historic interest of the building:

in assessing the importance of the building, attention should be paid to both its architectural merit and to its historical interest. This includes not only historical associations, but also the way the design, plan, materials or location of the building illustrates the character of a past age; or the development of a particular skill, style or technology.

Cases involving historic interest alone are rare. As far as the writer is aware there have been no Secretary of State's decisions on what is special or ordinary historic interest.

The condition of the building should also be considered, as well as:

the cost of repairing and maintaining it in relation to its importance, and whether it has already received or been promised grants from public funds. In estimating cost, however, due regard should be paid to the economic value of the building when repaired and to any saving through not having to provide alternative accommodation in a new building. Old buildings generally suffer from some defects but the effects of these can easily be exaggerated.

The condition of a listed building perhaps raises the most difficult issues, both for the applicant for LBC and for the local planning authority or Secretary of State. It is obvious that a route to demolition lies by way of neglect. The owner of a listed building may well allow the building to deteriorate to such an extent that it might fall down of its own accord, or hope that if it gets into a condition whereby an economic restoration is impossible, he will be able to persuade the local planning authority or the Secretary of State that he should be granted consent to demolish it.

Finally, the possibility of alternative uses for the site should be looked at:

> the importance of any alternative use for the site and, in particular whether the use of the site for some public purpose would make it possible to enhance the environment and especially other listed buildings in the area; or whether, in a rundown area, a limited redevelopment might bring new life and make the other listed buildings more economically viable.

Although the importance of an alternative use is a criterion relevant to an LBC application it is neither the only criterion, nor an overwhelming consideration. Finding an alternative use does not automatically mean that preservation must follow. For example, in 1985 Essex County Council advised that it would no longer be permissible to convert historic barns into housing in that county (EHM 1986: 8).

Replacement, replica and pastiche

The growth of interest in buildings of architectural or historic interest has lead to intense debates on questions of replacements and replicas and whether they should be encouraged or discouraged following the grant of LBC. The basic issue in many cases involves a consideration of whether a listed building should be retained and rehabilitated or replaced.

The retention of a façade of a listed building, often its most important and visible element, is at first sight an attractive solution to the question of choosing between rehabilitation or replacement. The retention of a façade often results in minimal disruption to the street scene and townscape. However, façadism raises a number of difficult questions. Should the façade remain listed or does the loss of the original building devalue it to such an extent that it should no longer be worthy of listing? Does the new building attached to the façade automatically become listed? Does a single wall façade constitute a sufficiently significant element of the original building or should a greater proportion of the building be retained, such as the façade and one room depth? It seems likely that if the façade of the building remains, 'the building' will remain listed, which will include any extension.

If it is not possible or desirable to retain the original façade or building, it may be possible to construct a replica, which for the purposes of the continuity of the street scene or the retention of an important landmark may merit consideration. However, for many reasons the introduction of a replica does not always find support. Why should a replacement building be a replica of an original? The proposed new building has often been designed for a different function from the building it is to replace and is very likely to benefit from modern design and construction techniques that bear no relation to those used in the original building. Thus in some cases a replica may be regarded as merely a pastiche and undesirable.

Replicas are likely to maintain architectural interest, but it is doubtful whether the 'historic' interest would have been maintained in a replica for the simple reason that such interest largely disappears if the original building is removed.

Alterations and extensions

LBC is required for any works for the alteration or extension of a listed building 'in any manner which would affect its character as a building of special architectural or historic interest.'

Potentially, any alteration to a listed building may require consent, internal alterations included. This applies regardless of the grade of the building. As a broad principle, it is stated in *Circular 8/87* that alterations affecting the character of a building as one of special architectural or historic interest should be kept to a minimum, and that repair is preferable to replacement where possible.

WHAT ARE THE MECHANICS OF CONTROL AND ENFORCEMENT?

We deal here with the mechanics of an application for LBC to demolish, alter or extend a listed building. The LBC procedure provides an additional planning control in addition to the requirement for planning permission in respect of development.

Demolition of listed buildings causes contention and can only be authorized if:

a. the local planning authority or the Secretary of State has granted written consent (LBC) for the execution of the works and the works are executed in accordance with the terms of the consent, and

b. notice of the proposal has been given to the Royal Commission on Historical Monuments, and either

i. for at least one month following the grant of consent and before commencement of the works reasonable access has been made available to the Commission for the purpose of recording the building, or

ii. the Commission have by their Secretary or other authorized officer stated in writing that they have completed their recording of the building or that they do not wish to record it.

Where the demolition or the alteration or extension requires a specific grant of LBC to authorize it, the procedure for obtaining this is dealt with in Paragraph 76 of *Circular 8/87*. It is necessary for the local planning authority to examine applications for planning permission and LBC separately and to give separate decisions. It should be noted that the setting of a listed building is a criterion that must be taken into account in the consideration of both applications for LBC and applications for planning permission. Sections 16(2) and 66(1) respectively of the LBA 1990 are the operative provisions.

LBC normally is granted for the benefit of the building. Personal planning permissions are granted very rarely, if at all, and it is believed that personal LBCs are granted even more infrequently.

The procedure

The procedure for obtaining LBC is to be found in Sections 10 and 11 of the LBA 1990 and in the Town and Country Planning (Listed Buildings and Buildings in Conservation Areas) Regulations 1990, which also provide the form of an application for LBC, how it should be made, the advertisement of it by the LPA, and the time for dealing with it. Retrospective consent is also possible.

Section 15(5) of the LBA gives the Secretary of State power to direct that local planning authorities should notify bodies of persons specified by him of any applications they receive for LBC and of their decision. Such a direction is given in Paragraph 81 of *Circular 8/87* which requires that notice of all applications for consent to demolish a listed building, and the decisions taken thereon, should be given to the following bodies: The Ancient Monuments Society, The Council for British Archaeology, The Georgian Group, The Society for the Protection of Ancient Buildings, The Victorian Society, and the appropriate Royal Commission on Historical Monuments.

Except in the case of The Royal Commission on Historical Monuments (which is notified because of the possible need to record the building, should consent to demolish be granted), the notifications of the applications are accompanied by the relevant extract from the list describing the building. Any representations received in response to these notifications must be taken into account when the application is being considered.

Paragraph 82 of *Circular 8/87* contains the further direction that local planning authorities shall notify English Heritage of all applications for listed building consent to alter, extend or demolish, first, any Grade I or II* building outside Greater London and, secondly, any grade of listed building in Greater London. There are supplementary directions relating to London Docklands.

English Heritage performs an advisory role in relation to cases notified to it by local planning authorities. English Heritage's views are therefore available to be taken into consideration by the local planning authority when it reaches a decision upon an application for LBC for full or partial demolition. English Heritage's intervention at this stage is as advisor to the local planning authority, but negotiation with the owner of a listed building is common.

If a local planning authority refers a case for possible call-in by the Secretary of State, the Secretary of State will invite English Heritage to advise whether he should determine the case himself. English Heritage acts in an advisory capacity and the ultimate decision on an application will be that of the Secretary of State if the case is called-in and that of the local planning authority if it is not. At this stage English Heritage is acting in its capacity as advisor to the Secretary of State so that negotiation with the local planning authority and the owner of the listed building is not possible ('the silent period'). Once the DoE has considered English Heritage's advice and has reached a decision on whether to call-in the application, English Heritage is again free to negotiate.

The decision of the Secretary of State on a called-in application is final, save of course on an appeal to the High Court by a person aggrieved under the provisions of Sections 63 and 65 of the LBA.

Conditions in a listed building consent

LBC may be granted unconditionally, or subject to conditions. Under Section 17(1) of the LBA conditions may in particular include:

(a) the preservation of particular features of the building, either as part of it or after severance therefrom;

(b) the making good, after the works are completed, of any damage caused to the building by the works;

(c) the reconstruction of the building or any part of it following the execution of any works, with the use of original materials so far as practicable and with such alterations of the interior of the building as may be specified in the conditions.

Section 17(2) of the LBA provides that a condition may also be imposed requiring specified details of the works (whether or not set out in the application) to be approved subsequently by the local planning authority or, in the case of consent granted by the Secretary of State, specifying whether such details are to be approved by the local planning authority or by him.

Mention should also be made of the time limits for listed building consents under Section 18 of the LBA. The normal time limit is set at five years, but the period can be longer or shorter. If consent is allowed to lapse an application for further consent may be made; although the danger for the applicant will be that the local planning authority's policy may have changed since the original consent was issued.

Rights of appeal

The applicant has a right of appeal to the Secretary of State for the DoE where the local planning authority refuse LBC or grant it subject to conditions, or if no decision is given within the prescribed eight weeks or any such extended period as the applicant may have agreed to. The applicant may appeal within six months of the receipt of the decision or of the date of failure by the local planning authority to give notice of a decision.

The notice of appeal may include a claim that the building is not of special architectural or historic interest and ought to be removed from any list.

Unless the appeal relates to an application to demolish any listed building, to alter or extend a Grade I or Grade II* listed building, or to an enforcement notice in connection with either case, the Secretary of State may appoint someone to determine the appeal instead of doing so himself. In practice, most listed building appeals have so far been determined by the Secretary of State. Before determining the appeal, the Secretary of State must, if either party so desires, afford both the appellant and the local planning authority the opportunity of appearing before and being heard by a person appointed by him.

Notification to the Royal Commission on Historical Monuments of the decision

Where LBC to demolish is granted, local planning authorities are asked in *Circular 8/87*, Paragraph 117 to include a statement in their decision notice to indicate that the applicant must permit the Royal Commission on Historical Monuments to record the building before demolition. The recommended wording is:

> Attention is drawn to [section 8(2) LBA, formerly 55(2) of the TCPA 1971], the effect of which is that demolition may not be undertaken (despite the terms of the consent granted by the local planning authority) until notice of the proposal has been given to the Royal Commission on Historical Monuments, and the Commission subsequently have either been given reasonable access to the building for at least one month following the grant of consent, or have stated that they have completed their record of the building or that they do not wish to record it.

However, the above three requirements do not apply to demolition of unlisted buildings in conservation areas.

Alterations and extensions: the general principles

The principles relevant to the alteration and extension of listed buildings can be set out as follows:

a. Demolition now constitutes a 'building operation' requiring planning permission. However, *Circular 16/92* contains a direction that excludes all demolitions except those of dwelling houses from the effect of changes to the definition of development introduced by the Planning and Compensation Act 1991 (PCA).

b. Demolition of a listed building requires listed building consent.

c. Demolition is not a term defined in the LBA, nor is there a definition or guidance in the regulations nor in *Circular 8/87*. *Circular 16/92*, however, now addresses the issue of planning controls over demolition.

d. The problem arises in determining the line between demolition and partial demolition (neither phrase being used in the LBA) and the line between demolition and the removal of materials that is required for the purpose of an alteration or addition to a listed building.

e. If demolition only is concerned, that is, there is no extension or alteration involved, then listed building consent will be required, however small the extent of the demolition. 'Building' includes in its definition 'part of a building'. Partial demolition cannot be justified as avoiding the need for LBC on the grounds that only a few stones are removed: they might be the vital ones. But this will not apply to free-standing structures built after 1948 within the curtilage nor to the other exemptions in *Circular 8/87*.

f. Applying a *qualitative* test to what might be considered to be an alteration or extension of a listed building we would expect the DoE to view as alterations and not as demolition: the replacement of one type of roofing material with another (e.g. asbestos tiles for slate), the removal of part of the fabric of a building purely to facilitate the carrying out of alterations or extensions (particularly the removal of part of the roof or wall to enable an extension to be constructed), new windows in enlarged openings or new doors, if the alterations or extensions would affect the character as a building of special architectural or historic interest.

g. To apply a *quantitative* test to what might be considered to be an alteration or extension of a listed building rather than demolition, it might be helpful to consider 10 % of the cubic content basis – 10 % or less would not be demolition. The genesis of this (perhaps not unreasonable) basis is that 10 % is that element of the cubic content of a Grade II (unstarred) listed building that does not require LBC. A further example of the use of 10 % as a *de minimis* criterion is the direction that exempts the necessity for a conservation area consent in relation to the demolition of 10 % of a building used for an industrial process.

Ancient monuments

The provisions of Sections 7–9 of the LBA do not apply to 'a building for the time being included in the schedule of monuments compiled and maintained under section 1 of the Ancient Monuments and Archaeological Areas Act 1979.'

The provisions for the authorization of works affecting ancient monuments (it is an offence to effect certain specified works without such authorization) are contained in Section 2 of the Ancient Monuments and Archaeological Areas Act 1979 (Chapter 5).

Ecclesiastical buildings

Ecclesiastical buildings have always presented particular problems in planning terms (see Chapter 9). There are three main aspects to this issue. The first is that no one is sure what the term 'ecclesiastical' covers; while one might expect that all Christian denominations of all kinds might fall within this definition, what about buildings of non-Christian religions? The second is that churches in the Anglican community have, since 1913, been treated in a special way. The third aspect is that churches are such an essential part of our rich architectural heritage. There are probably 20,000 or so churches belonging to Anglicans, non-conformists and Roman Catholics alone. Of these, more than 12,000 are listed and 2,500 or so are listed Grade I (or A – an earlier category of listing, most such former Grade A buildings having now been replaced by the Grade I category in England – see Suddards 1988: Chapter 8).

Listed building enforcement notice

Carrying out works without LBC (in breach of Section 7 of the LBA) or in contravention of a condition attached to a consent (in breach of Section 9(2) of the LBA) can lead either to prosecution or the issuing of an enforcement notice or both. However, in relation to an enforcement notice, the Secretary of State considers it beyond the powers provided in the LBA to require reinstatement of property damaged or destroyed by accident.

Section 38 of the LBA provides for the issue of a listed building enforcement notice. This is the main weapon in the enforcement regime available to local planning authorities. Section 38 has been amended, particularly in relation to the penalties for breach of the provisions of the LBA, the withdrawal of listed building enforcement notices, appeals under Section 39 of the LBA, and variation and enforcement provisions relating to such notices.

Criminal matters

There are five principal sanctions in the LBA by way of criminal prosecutions in relation to listed buildings:

  a. unauthorized work to a listed building;
  b. acts causing or likely to result in damage to listed buildings;
  c. non-compliance with a listed building enforcement notice;
  d. non-compliance with a building preservation notice;
  e. non-compliance with a dangerous structures notice.

Criminal sanctions generally

Following the implementation of the Planning and Compensation Act 1991 (PCA) criminal sanctions for breach of listed building controls are now more likely to be an effective deterrent. Schedule 3 of the PCA increases the maximum fine in Section 9 of the LBA on summary conviction for unauthorized works to a listed building from £2,000 to £20,000. A similar increase applies in respect of summary conviction for an offence under Section 43 of the LBA (failure to comply with a listed building enforcement notice). On conviction on indictment the penalty is an unlimited fine.

Schedule 3 of the PCA extends to the Magistrates Courts the existing Crown Court power in Section 9(5) of the LBA. This provides that, in determining the amount of any fine to be imposed on a person convicted on indictment of an offence under Section 9 of the LBA, the court shall have regard to any financial benefit that has accrued or is likely to accrue to the defendant in consequence of the offence.

There are other criminal sanctions in relation to listed buildings but these (e.g. failure to permit entry) are only an application of the criminal offences relating to planning law generally.

CHAPTER 9

ECCLESIASTICAL BUILDINGS IN USE

Carl Bianco

INTRODUCTION

Great Britain enjoys a rich inheritance of historic ecclesiastical buildings. The Church of England alone supports some 16,400 churches, of which about 12,200 are listed as being of special architectural or historic interest, over 2,600 at Grade I. The Church of Scotland and the Church in Wales also own many listed buildings, as do the non-conformist churches and the Roman Catholic Church. Together, these represent a unique and highly significant part of Britain's heritage.

However, while these sites are indeed immeasurably important from an architectural, archaeological, historical and artistic viewpoint, they are not museums. They are the centre of living, growing communities, their form shaped by the needs of those who have worshipped in them over the centuries. As with most historic sites, a great deal of their value (both academic and aesthetic) lies in the evidence they display of change. Whether the result of major rebuilding, repair or internal re-ordering, any alteration to the fabric and setting of a church can reveal much about its community's response to shifting climates of religious, social and political feeling. At the same time, however, the very change that has made these buildings what they are also has the potential, if uncontrolled, to destroy forever their historic character.

The standing fabric of a church, its contents and its surroundings (both above and below ground) constitute an archaeological entity. Any work in and around a church therefore has the potential to destroy valuable evidence for the evolution of that site. The provision of new heating or drainage systems, the digging of foundation trenches for an extension, the relaying of floors or the disturbance of monuments or ground levels within a churchyard can all have major archaeological implications. Equally harmful are works to the standing fabric of a church. The piercing of historic masonry to form a new entrance, the stripping of unwanted plaster, the repointing of stonework or the alteration or removal of internal fittings; all these can be highly damaging from an archaeological viewpoint if undertaken without appropriate advice (for a detailed discussion of the archaeological study of churches, and the threats to which they are vulnerable, see Morris 1989; Parsons 1989; Rodwell 1989; and for cathedrals in particular, Tatton-Brown 1989).

The archaeological management of these buildings and their surroundings must therefore balance the interests of conservation with the needs of an evolving, dynamic faith. It cannot seek to prohibit change, but must ensure that all work is controlled and that, where archaeological evidence is to be unavoidably destroyed, appropriate provision is made for its recording. Of course, this problem of potentially conflicting interests is not in itself unique to church archaeology. What is unique, however, is the special legal status afforded to ecclesiastical buildings in use which places them outside the secular system of listed building control. This 'ecclesiastical exemption' will now be discussed in general terms before exploring its practical application, primarily through reference to the Church of England's internal systems of control.

ECCLESIASTICAL EXEMPTION

When the Ancient Monuments Consolidation Act 1913 was introduced, the Archbishop of Canterbury, Randall Davidson, requested that the Church of England be exempt from its provisions in order to safeguard its freedom of worship. In return, he gave an undertaking that the Church would review and enhance its own existing system of building control, the faculty jurisdiction (of medieval origin). Ecclesiastical exemption was thus granted on the understanding that the Church of England would provide a system of protection for its historic buildings comparable to that exercised by the state, and since that time the Church has developed and expanded its internal administration to meet this requirement. Curiously, however, the non-Anglican churches – while they made no such promise of good conduct – have managed to shelter under the umbrella of the exemption for more than seventy years, despite the fact that they operate no equivalent internal controls (although current discussions seek to rectify this anomaly).

Section 60 of the Planning (Listed Buildings and Conservation Areas) Act 1990 states that any 'ecclesiastical building which is for the time being used for ecclesiastical purposes' is exempt from listed building control except where the Secretary of State provides by Order (the extent of such an Order being an issue currently under discussion). The term 'ecclesiastical purposes' is not defined, although it excludes any building used by a minister of religion primarily as a residence. Cases from the courts have, however, demonstrated that the term 'ecclesiastical' does not solely mean Anglican, nor even necessarily Christian.

There is no such exemption from the Town and Country Planning Act 1990, and planning permission is still required for any 'development', defined as 'the carrying out of building, engineering, mining or other operations in, on, over or under land, or the making of any material change in the use of any buildings or other land' (Section 55 (1) 3). Thus, for example, the extension of a church building would require applications under both secular planning law and the relevant system of ecclesiastical control. Maintenance, internal works, and works that will not materially affect the external appearance of a building are excluded from this definition. There is similarly no exemption from Scheduled Monument Consent, although the Ancient Monuments and Archaeological Areas Act 1979 prohibits the scheduling of 'an ecclesiastical building in use for ecclesiastical purposes' (Section 61 (8)). However, work to any Scheduled Monument within the consecrated area of a church (for example an Anglo-Saxon cross or a lych gate) would still require Scheduled Monument Consent.

The exemption has, not surprisingly, had its share of opponents from the outset. These consider that the interests of conservation would be better served by removing churches from internal control and making them subject to the same secular legislation as other historic buildings. In January 1984 this concern prompted the Department of the Environment (DoE) to issue a consultation paper on the subject. Subsequent discussions with representatives of the Church of England and of the Churches Main Committee (a body representing all main denominations) resulted in a decision by the government that the exemption should be generally retained, subject to certain amendments. This decision was announced by Lord Skelmersdale in the debate on the Housing and Planning Bill in the House of Lords (see *Hansard* for 13 October 1986, and also DoE 1987b). The two major points arising from the Skelmersdale statement were that the exemption would not cover the total demolition of a church (except, in the case of the Church of England, as part of a redundancy scheme under the Pastoral Measure 1983, see below); and that further discussions should take place on how far the exemption should extend to objects or structures within the curtilage of a church (such as a church hall), a point to which we shall return.

The Church of England had, by the time of the Skelmersdale statement, conducted its own review through a commission established under the Bishop of Chichester in response to the introduction of government funding for church repairs. The final report of the Faculty Jurisdiction Commission (FJC 1984) made a number of recommendations for improving the Church of England's system of control, and was influential in persuading the government of the validity of the exemption. These recommendations finally achieved statutory authority in the Care of Cathedrals Measure 1990 and the Care of Churches and Ecclesiastical Jurisdiction Measure 1991, which will now be discussed (for those unfamiliar with the organizational structure of the Church of England, see Welsby 1985 for a good introduction).

THE FACULTY JURISDICTION

The principles of faculty jurisdiction are set out in the Faculty Jurisdiction Measure 1964, now partly amended and supplemented by the Care of Churches and Ecclesiastical Jurisdiction Measure 1991 (hereinafter referred to as the Care of Churches Measure 1991). Measures and their associated Rules are passed by the General Synod (the governing body) of the Church of England, but are also ratified by Parliament, and thus have the full force of English law. Under this law, any parish within the Church of England must apply for a faculty (licence) if it intends to make any change, internal or external, within its consecrated area. Faculties are granted by the chancellor of the diocese, a barrister-at-law acting on behalf of the bishop, although the authority to grant faculties may be delegated to archdeacons in uncontentious cases. Proposals must be formally advertised, and all interested parties are at liberty to make representations regarding those proposals.

Before determining any faculty case the chancellor must seek the advice of the Diocesan Advisory Committee (DAC), a body comprising representatives of all fields relevant to the care and conservation of churches, including nominees from English Heritage, the national amenity societies and the local planning authority. Legally established under the Faculty Jurisdiction Measure 1938 (and with their role newly defined by the Care of Churches Measure 1991) the DACs had developed informally in the wake of Archbishop Davidson's undertaking to the nation. Their advisory responsibility extends to all interested parties; in particular they can provide valuable assistance to individual parishes in the formulation and execution of proposals. Indeed, the Faculty Jurisdiction Rules 1992 establish a system whereby a parish can submit its proposals direct to the DAC before lodging a faculty application, thereby allowing the DAC to express its support or otherwise at the outset.

Particularly complex or sensitive cases can be referred to the Council for the Care of Churches (CCC) for further advice. This body was formed in 1921, and has a number of statutory functions under the Faculty Jurisdiction Measure 1964, the Care of Churches Measure 1991 and the Pastoral Measure 1983 (see below). In addition to providing a wide range of expert advice, it co-ordinates the work of the DACs, liaises with national and regional organizations and administers grants for the conservation of church furnishings.

In the majority of cases the chancellor will accept the advice of the DAC (taking into account all comments received from other agencies and individuals) but is not obliged to do so. Where there is opposition to a proposal, the chancellor may convene a Consistory Court hearing (usually at the church in question) at which he or she may call upon witnesses to give evidence; and where the granting of a faculty is contested there are provisions for appeal to higher ecclesiastical courts (for a comprehensive description of the faculty system, see Newsom 1988).

REDUNDANCY

When a parish church within the Church of England is deemed to be surplus to requirements (either because of pastoral concerns or because the cost of repair is considered to be
too great) it can be declared redundant under the Pastoral Measure 1983. This provides the
legal framework for the disposal of such buildings and ensures that conservation issues
are given a hearing.

Before putting forward a proposal for the redundancy of a church, the Diocesan
Pastoral Committee must ascertain the views of the local planning authority, and obtain
from the Council for the Care of Churches a report on the historic and architectural qualities of the church, its contents and its churchyard, and of other churches in the area. After
possible amendment the proposal is then sent to the Church Commissioners, who will
consult the Advisory Board for Redundant Churches (ABRC) before sending the draft
pastoral scheme to all 'interested parties'. Any comments received will then be considered
by the Commissioners when finalizing the scheme for formal approval by Her Majesty in
Council.

The pastoral scheme itself is primarily concerned with the future of the parish as a
whole, while the fate of the building is normally handled through a redundancy scheme
made under Section 48 of the Pastoral Measure, which requires that notices be served on
the diocesan Board of Finance, the ABRC and the local planning authority. The proposals
are also advertised in the local press, and any interested party is eligible to comment.

One of three courses may be advocated at this stage: that the building be demolished;
that an alternative use be found; or that the building be vested in a guardianship body,
most commonly the Redundant Churches Fund (RCF). This last course (and the most
desirable from an archaeological viewpoint) is taken if the ABRC advises that the church
'is of such historic and archaeological interest or architectural quality that it ought to be
preserved in the interests of the nation and the Church of England' (Section 47). The RCF,
funded jointly by the DoE and the Church Commissioners, currently cares for some 250
former parish churches, and aims to maintain a church broadly as it was at the time of its
redundancy (see Redundant Churches Fund 1990).

If the ABRC considers that a church is of insufficient interest to warrant guardianship,
or if the Church Commissioners are themselves satisfied as to the proposed course of
action, the Commissioners may recommend that an alternative use for the building be
found or, more rarely, that it be demolished. There then follows a 'waiting period' that,
because of the often protracted process of seeking a new use, can afford plenty of opportunity for the abandoned church to fall into ruin through neglect or vandalism, ultimately
increasing the likelihood of its eventual demolition, as at Holy Trinity, Birkenhead.
However, even if a new use is found, as is generally considered desirable, the result can
often be highly damaging archaeologically. Conversions (for example to office, residen-
tial, or community use) often display a striking insensitivity to the internal space of the
building and to its historic fittings, and many fine churches – even if not fine enough to be
placed in guardianship – have been ruined in this way (for examples of conversions, good
and bad, see Powell and de la Hey 1987; for the problems of redundancy in general see
also Binney and Burman 1977a, 1977b; Rodwell and Rodwell 1977). Of course, once a
church has formally been declared redundant the exemption from listed building control
ceases to apply – it being no longer a building in ecclesiastical use – and planning permission will always be required for any change of use or material alteration.

However, if total or partial demolition is ultimately recommended under a redundancy
scheme the exemption still applies. In return, the Church Commissioners have agreed to
notify the Secretary of State in all cases where the proposed demolition of a listed church

(or an unlisted church in a conservation area) is opposed by English Heritage, the ABRC, the local planning authority or the national amenity societies. The Secretary of State is then empowered to convene a non-statutory public enquiry, and may recommend either that the building be vested in the Redundant Churches Fund or that further efforts be made to find an alternative use. The first such enquiry was held over the future of Holy Trinity, Rugby, in 1980 and, despite the recommendation of the Secretary of State that it should be preserved, the Commissioners finally secured its demolition in 1983. However, the Commissioners have since undertaken to accept a recommendation for transfer to the RCF (see DoE 1987b).

ARCHAEOLOGY IN THE DIOCESES

The Dibdin Commission of 1913–14, conducting the first review of the faculty jurisdiction as promised by Archbishop Davidson, stated clearly that both the Chancellor and the DAC had a duty to have regard to matters architectural, archaeological, historic and artistic. In 1986 the CCC and the then Cathedrals Advisory Commission established a working party to review the Church's response to archaeology in the light of these clear obligations. Its report, *Archaeology and the Church of England* (CCC 1988), made a number of recommendations regarding archaeological management at parish, diocesan and national levels, but many of these have yet to be implemented.

However, with the approval of the Care of Churches Measure 1991, archaeology has at last received the formal recognition promised by the 1913 Commission. Under its provisions DACs are required to have within their membership at least one person 'with a knowledge of archaeology', and are to advise on all matters relating to 'the architecture, archaeology, art and history of places of worship'. They must also:

> review and assess the degree of risk to materials, or of loss to archaeological or historic remains or records, arising from any proposals relating to the conservation, repair or alteration of places of worship, churchyards and burial grounds and the contents of such places. (Schedules 1 and 2)

When the Council for British Archaeology (CBA) established its Churches Committee in 1972, one of its earliest initiatives was to compile a list of those archaeologists who would be suitable to serve as consultants to DACs. In conjunction with the then Council for Places of Worship (now the CCC) the CBA urged each diocese to appoint one of these nominees as a full member of its DAC, or at least to recognize him or her as an independent consultant. Consequently, by the advent of the 1991 Measure, most DACs were provided with some form of archaeological support (for further background see Jesson 1973; Addyman and Morris 1976; Rodwell 1987). However, while the Measure itself requires a member with a knowledge of archaeology, there is no statutory requirement for this to be a CBA-nominated consultant. The effectiveness of the system is thus dependent to a large extent on the attitude of the individual DAC and the ability of the archaeologist involved. In cases where the CBA nominee is used only as an external consultant, the extent of his or her involvement in faculty cases will be dependent upon either the DAC's discretion in inviting such involvement or upon the sheer determination of the consultant to take a proactive role.

Of course, archaeology in the dioceses can be most effectively managed through proper consultation from an early stage, a principle stressed in current national policy. The DoE Planning Policy Guidance Note 16: *Archaeology and Planning* (PPG 16) is a highly influential document, giving archaeology long-overdue recognition as an integral part of the planning process (DoE 1990a), and its basic principles apply as much to the ecclesiastical sphere as to the secular. In the same way that a local planning authority is required under PPG 16 to ensure that archaeological considerations are taken fully into account (and that appropriate mitigation strategies are incorporated into all developments) so the Chancellor, on the advice of the DAC, can attach archaeological conditions to the granting of a faculty. This principle has received formal recognition in a recent case concerning St Mary, Thame, in which the Chancellor of the Diocese of Oxford ruled not only that the Consistory Court had the power to attach to a faculty an archaeological condition, but that the requirements of the Court should be at least as stringent as those of the County Archaeologist. The same principle applies to redundant churches, and the ABRC is also paying increased attention to archaeological issues, recommending that appropriate recording forms an integral part of any proposed demolition or conversion, as at St Mary, Thetford, and St Martin, Colchester (ABRC 1992).

However, the financial implications of current national policy are rather less easy to translate to the ecclesiastical sphere. Under PPG 16 there is a clear obligation upon the developer to bear the cost of archaeological work arising from a project, but it is widely argued that churches (and indeed other charities), while they may assume the role of developer in a technical sense, should receive special consideration as they are non-profit-making. On the other hand, it can be argued that it is equally unreasonable to release churches from all financial obligations and thereby to encourage a situation in which it becomes expected that some external agency will foot the entire bill for consequential archaeological work.

When considering this sensitive issue, it is necessary to bear in mind an important distinction between 'development' and 'maintenance/repair'. With the former it can be argued that, if a parish can afford to make some addition unrelated to the general care of the fabric (such as an extension for pastoral and social use), it is only reasonable to expect that the church should bear the costs of any resultant archaeological work. Indeed, if an archaeological evaluation is conducted at the outset, as recommended by PPG 16, the foundations of a new building can often be modified to minimize archaeological disturbance, and thus reduce costs (see also English Heritage 1992b). If, however, the work is in response to the poor condition of the existing fabric (for instance a decaying roof or unstable tower) then a parish will often find it difficult to raise the money for even essential repairs. To then expect the church to fund the associated archaeological recording is plainly unreasonable. Even relatively small repair and maintenance works can have a significant archaeological impact, and there is therefore the potential for a parish's archaeological bill to exceed that of the main work.

Since 1978 English Heritage has administered a system of State Aid for Churches in Use, with an allocation of £10.5 million for the financial year 1992/93. These funds are specifically for repair and not for archaeology, although English Heritage will grant-aid agreed items of recording at the same percentage as the associated repairs (on average about 40 %). However, grants are only awarded if strict criteria are met, which means that there is no provision for grant-aiding archaeological recording where the repair itself is not eligible. In particular, English Heritage will generally only consider 'outstanding churches', that is those listed at Grade I or II*. This effectively excludes a huge number of churches on the basis of a criterion that does not specifically reflect the archaeological value of the building at all.

The CBA Churches Committee has long campaigned for specific consideration to be given to rescue archaeology in churches, but although English Heritage may exceptionally offer additional funds to any 'developer' in financial difficulty (English Heritage 1991c) it has declined to make a special case for ecclesiastical sites in use. However, with the widespread application of PPG 16 within the diocese, the requirement for archaeological work will continue to grow, and the development of a national policy for the realistic funding of church archaeology is a priority, and a challenge, for the coming years.

It has been suggested that, at least in relation to churches of known archaeological importance, there should be a regular archaeological involvement in the process of general fabric maintenance (CCC 1988). Under the Inspection of Churches Measure 1955, every parish church must be inspected by an approved architect every five years, and a report submitted describing the state of the fabric and prioritizing any remedial works that are necessary. Clearly it would be valuable for there to be an archaeological input into this quinquennial inspection process. The resultant report could then identify particularly sensitive or vulnerable areas of archaeological importance and could help to reduce both damage and costs, or at least enable a parish to be aware of the possible implications of certain works. However, although this has been recommended as good practice it has yet to gain widespread recognition.

Ultimately, the importance of a parish's own input into the archaeological management of its church cannot be overemphasized. Indeed, the 1988 report stated that 'the primary responsibility for the archaeological care of a parish church rests with the PCC [Parochial Church Council], under the guidance of the faculty jurisdiction' (CCC 1988: Section 5.1). The fact that this responsibility is rarely appreciated only highlights the generally low recognition that archaeology receives within the Church. This lack of popular awareness presents a challenge to the archaeological community, and recent years have seen a number of initiatives by individual diocesan consultants to promote such awareness (see e.g. Hunter 1992). The effective management of the archaeological resource is ultimately dependent upon the goodwill and support of the people in the pews.

CATHEDRALS

Church of England cathedral churches lie wholly outside the scope of the faculty system, and until very recently had no equivalent accountability whatsoever. The Cathedrals Advisory Commission, established under the Cathedrals Measure 1963, existed to offer expert advice to cathedral chapters, but it had no statutory authority; in practice each cathedral could do as it pleased. The obvious potential for abuse prompted the Faculty Jurisdiction Commission to recommend in its 1984 report that works to cathedral churches be brought under statutory control. The result was the Care of Cathedrals Measure 1990, which came into force on 1 March 1991. The corresponding enforcement legislation (Care of Cathedrals (Supplementary Provisions) Measure) is currently awaiting parliamentary ratification.

Under this Measure the administrative body of a cathedral must obtain external approval for any works that would:

materially affect the architectural, archaeological, artistic or historic character of the cathedral church or any building within the precinct of the cathedral church which is for the time being used for ecclesiastical purposes, the immediate setting of the cathedral church, or any archaeological remains within the precinct of the cathedral church. (Section 2)

Approval must also be sought for the sale or permanent disposal of any object of architectural, archaeological, artistic or historic interest, and for the permanent addition of any object. Applications for approval must be made to either the Cathedrals Fabric Commission for England (CFCE), or the cathedral's own Fabric Advisory Committee

(FAC) (depending on the exact nature of the proposed works), and there is a right of appeal against their decisions.

The CFCE is a national body established under the Care of Cathedrals Measure 1990, and replaces the previous Cathedrals Advisory Commission. Its function is to ensure the highest possible standards of care and conservation, while recognizing the primary role of the cathedral as the centre of Christian worship and mission. Its members are chosen after consultation with a wide range of specialist national bodies representing the interests of both conservation and religion; the CFCE maintains close links with these organizations in both its judicial and advisory roles.

The CFCE determines all applications for proposals that would involve the permanent alteration or demolition of the fabric, the disturbance or destruction of archaeological remains within the cathedral precinct, and the sale or loan of objects designated as being of outstanding interest. It also has the authority to call in for its own determination any proposal deemed to give rise to special considerations. When an application is made to the CFCE, notices must be placed on public display and also sent to the local planning authority, to the national amenity societies, and to English Heritage. All interested parties have a right to make representations, and any comments received must be taken into account by the CFCE when determining the case.

Each cathedral has its own FAC, half of its members being nominated by the administrative body and half by the CFCE. The FAC's primary role is to advise the administrative body upon all proposed works, and it has power to determine all those applications that do not require referral to the Commission. Notices of all such applications are placed on public display and sent to the CFCE and (in certain instances) the local planning authority for comment.

Listed building consent is still required for all buildings not in use for 'ecclesiastical purposes', and scheduled monument consent must also be obtained where necessary. The provisions of the Town and County Planning Act 1990 also apply to all developments, and in cases where planning permission is required, cathedral bodies are encouraged to seek approval from the CFCE first. This is desirable from a practical viewpoint, since applications under the Measure can be processed far quicker than secular planning applications, and it also enables the local planning authority to ascertain the views of the CFCE before reaching its own decision.

Since the Cathedrals Measure 1963 the administrative body of every cathedral has been required to appoint an architect. Now, under the new Care of Cathedrals Measure 1990, archaeology has received similar recognition, and the appointment of an archaeological consultant is a statutory requirement. The 1990 Measure also provides for the architect's quinquennial inspection of the fabric to be undertaken in consultation with the archaeological consultant, and both these specialists are obliged to attend all FAC meetings. An effective working relationship between the two can therefore ensure that the archaeological implications of all proposed works to the fabric or within the precinct are identified at an early stage. The statutory post of Cathedral Archaeological Consultant is one of the most significant developments in the legislative standing of archaeology in the Church of England, and certainly gives the cathedral consultant an authority denied to his or her diocesan counterpart.

Indeed, the Care of Cathedrals Measure 1990 as a whole provides a far more secure framework for the control of archaeological projects than exists in the dioceses. Since all proposals involving the disturbance or destruction of archaeological remains require approval at a national level by the CFCE, the Commission is able to implement the principles of PPG 16 to a consistent standard. It will insist upon a full evaluation of the site and the formulation of a proposed mitigation strategy before considering any scheme, and may then attach such conditions as it deems appropriate (as at Bristol, Canterbury, Hereford and Winchester). Early consultation is encouraged, and standards of project management are required to conform with current national guidelines (see English Heritage 1991b).

Many cathedrals have taken readily to the requirements of the Measure, although in some cases there exists a lingering resentment at the loss of previous autonomy. However, the introduction of government funding for cathedrals has eased the transition. Administered by English Heritage, the grant scheme covers both Anglican and Roman Catholic cathedrals and involves an initial grant of £11.5 million phased over three years, with a review promised thereafter. Allocation of funds is determined on a means-related basis, and archaeological recording is eligible for funding as a part of any grant-aided repair. English Heritage and the CFCE work closely together on all projects of mutual concern and, although both the cathedrals grant scheme and the Care of Cathedrals Measure are only a few years old, the partnership is proving a fruitful one, and the future care and conservation of cathedrals looks encouragingly secure.

NON-ANGLICAN CHURCHES AND THE FUTURE OF ECCLESIASTICAL EXEMPTION

It will by now be apparent that, at least in so far as it relates to the Church of England, the term 'ecclesiastical exemption' is something of a misnomer, for the Church is in no way exempt from legal control of its historic buildings. Rather, it has been given leave to administer its own system of control and this has in turn been ratified by Parliament. Indeed, it can be argued that the Church of England's controls are actually superior to those exercised under the secular system in a number of respects. Firstly, listed building control is concerned specifically with matters of architectural and historic interest, while the Church's system also makes provision for safeguarding the archaeological and artistic character of a building. In addition, while listed building consent is concerned only with demolition, alteration and extension, and internally only with 'fixtures', ecclesiastical control also covers repair and extends its protection to moveable contents.

The same basic principles apply to the Church in Wales, since the faculty system survived the Disestablishment of the Church in 1919. However, it has not been revised significantly since that time, and in 1991 the Governing Body of the Church in Wales established a Commission on Faculties to review both the faculty jurisdiction itself and the overall framework for the care of churches (Church in Wales 1992). The Commission will take into account the new Measures of the Church of England, and will consider not only parish churches but also cathedrals, for which it proposes the formation of a central advisory and regulatory body along the lines of the CFCE. CBA Wales now has its own Churches Committee, and this will doubtless pursue archaeological interests with the same vigour as its counterparts in England and Scotland.

However, as has already been mentioned, the exemption relates to all ecclesiastical buildings in 'ecclesiastical use', and not simply to those covered by the faculty system or the cathedrals legislation of the Church of England (or the Church in Wales). Consequently, all the other major religious organizations in Britain have until now reaped the benefits of the exemption without ever having established suitable alternative systems of control (never having made the promise of good conduct given by the Church of England). For the position in Northern Ireland see Appendix (p. 134). The limited controls that do exist elsewhere vary widely in standard, and are nowhere comparable to those exercised under faculty jurisdiction or the Care of Cathedrals Measure 1990.

In the Church of Scotland the alteration of fabric and fixtures in a church requires the consent of the Presbytery (a smaller unit than a diocese of the Church of England), which is also responsible for arranging for the quinquennial inspection of all church properties (see Church of Scotland 1983). The Advisory Committee on Artistic Matters exists at a national level to advise Presbyteries and Kirk Sessions (the lowest court of the Church of Scotland, comprising the minister and the elders), and although its involvement in conservation issues has been limited in the past, it currently has a member from Historic Scotland who also represents the interests of the Council for Scottish Archaeology (CSA) Churches Committee. In addition, each Presbytery has an Archaeological Advisor, whose role the CSA is working to enhance.

The CSA Churches Committee also nominates Honorary Archaeological Advisors to the Scottish Episcopal Church, and is currently in the final stages of compiling a computerized inventory of Scottish Church Heritage, which will offer the first uniform list of data on all ecclesiastical sites in Scotland. This data has been gathered with assistance from a network of volunteers, whom it is hoped will now go on to support the work of the various Archaeological Advisors, a system that could be valuably employed elsewhere.

However, the Scottish system is the only one of the other denominations that provides an even remotely comparable system of control. In the Roman Catholic Church there is no central administrative structure for monitoring works to its buildings, and individual dioceses are almost wholly autonomous, arrangements being made predominantly at the discretion of the bishop. In the principal non-conformist churches (the Methodist Church, the Baptist Union and the United Reformed Church) control is more hierarchical in nature, with works requiring internal approval at local and regional levels, but although conservation issues may be taken broadly into consideration they have no formal place in the system (for a helpful summary see Mynors 1989). Buildings belonging to other faiths, such as synagogues and mosques, are also included under the exemption, although they likewise provide no control.

In February 1992 the DoE issued a consultation document aimed primarily at resolving this unsatisfactory situation, proposing that the exemption should only continue for those religious organizations able to demonstrate that they have a formal system of control that meets certain standards. Its suggested Code of Practice requires that proposed works should be submitted for prior approval to a body that is independent of the local congregation or community in question. This independent body should take into account conservation issues; should consult with the local planning authority, English Heritage, and the national amenity societies; should advertise the proposals publicly; and should have appropriate procedures for enforcement and hearing appeals (DoE 1992e).

The document further proposes that, where an ecclesiastical body fails to provide an appropriate system of control, it should lose the exemption in respect of all external works, but that internal works will remain exempt. However, it is often internal fixtures and fittings that are at greatest risk; the notorious gutting of the interior of the Fournier Street Mosque, East London, in 1986 is a frequently cited example. Similarly, in 1989 an important tomb was removed from the Roman Catholic Church of St Charles Borromeo prior to its being made redundant (at which point it would have become subject to listed building control), and in 1991 the interior fittings of the 1790 Baptist Chapel, Great Gidding, Huntingdonshire, were removed without any wider consultation. The irony in this latter case, as in so many others, is that it was the fittings for which the building was listed in the first place. This aspect of the document is plainly unacceptable, and will need serious reconsideration.

Another concern relates to the issue of curtilage buildings, and thus impinges as much upon the Church of England's existing system as upon other churches. In order to rationalize what it sees as a confusing situation, the DoE propose to limit the exemption to the 'principal ecclesiastical building', thus presumably returning such structures as church halls, chapter houses, and so on to listed building control. However, approval for works to these buildings would still be needed under the relevant ecclesiastical procedures as well, thus necessitating a dual system of control. This would not only add unnecessarily to the administrative burden, but would inevitably lead to dispute over the definition of the term 'principal ecclesiastical building'.

CONCLUSIONS

At a time when British archaeology is coming of age professionally, it is encouraging to observe both the increased awareness of archaeological issues in the Church of England and the corresponding move to increase the accountability of the non-Anglican churches. However, legislation can only go so far, and it is now the responsibility of the archaeological community to develop the potential offered by the legal framework. The problem of funding is crucial, but there are also academic and theoretical issues still to be addressed. There is as yet no strategic research agenda for church archaeology, and thus no basis for formulating the academic priorities that should drive all archaeological work. Archaeology for its own sake is simply not a realistic option, and the particular resource constraints of church archaeology make the need for prioritization all the more urgent (and in fact this issue is being addressed by the CBA Churches Committee).

But if one were to select a single aspect of church archaeology that requires particular attention it would be that of raising public awareness. Care for the archaeological resource is ultimately the responsibility of those for whom these buildings are primarily places of regular worship. The archaeologist must therefore convey to these people the value of that resource, not only from an academic and educational viewpoint, but as a testimony to the history of the community and its faith. If the archaeologist is sensitive to the needs of the church, and the congregation is made to feel sympathetic to the interests of archaeology, the battle to save this precious resource will be more than half won.

CHAPTER 10

LOCAL AUTHORITY OPPORTUNITIES

David Baker
with Ian Shepherd (Scottish dimension)

This is an inopportune moment to write about local authorities. A three-fold review is in progress: of tiers, boundaries and structures. The first and second are expected largely to replace the 1974 two-tier system of counties and districts with all-purpose unitary authorities of as yet uncertain size and area; the third is converting councils to enablers of hitherto in-house services, either redeployed as internal trading groups or ejected into the private sector.

Amid such uncertainty it is convenient to consider 'local authority opportunities' not through the unstable departmental structure or the rather limited legislation but in terms of the processes of historical conservation itself. This chapter concentrates primarily upon the historic landscape and archaeological sites rather than historic buildings, which are covered elsewhere (see Chapter 8).

THE PURPOSES AND PROCESSES OF HISTORICAL CONSERVATION

A local authority perspective reinforces the ubiquity of the historic environment in time and space: each region, county, district and parish has a historic landscape with settlement patterns, settlements, sites, buildings and artefacts. Although the cultural resource is finite and non-renewable, it is not exempt from the impact of land-use competition, the give-and-take of conflict resolution and the need to justify allocations of accountable funds.

Historical conservation is a continuous, multi-staged process, involving a variety of organizations, and serving a range of social interests. It can be presented in model form as a continuous cycle of broad conservation containing within it a narrow cycle of management (Figure 10.1). At the outset, classes of features are identified as survivals of historic interest. The population of survivals is then located through survey, whose information product is stored in record systems with dual functions as archives and management tools.

The management cycle draws upon understanding of historical identity. Whether it is characterized as preservation or conservation depends upon the extent to which it simply attempts to slow down decay, or whether it also uses repair, adaptation and alternative uses. The management process generates new information to be fed back into the records system: some of it documents what has had to be destroyed for some reason or other, thus adding to knowledge of class, place or period; some of it adds information about the surviving resource, thereby increasing potential understanding for future management.

Authors' note: David Baker (Bedfordshire County Council) and Ian Shepherd (Grampian Regional Council) both write in a personal capacity. The views expressed in this chapter are not necessarily those of the planning departments in which they are employed.

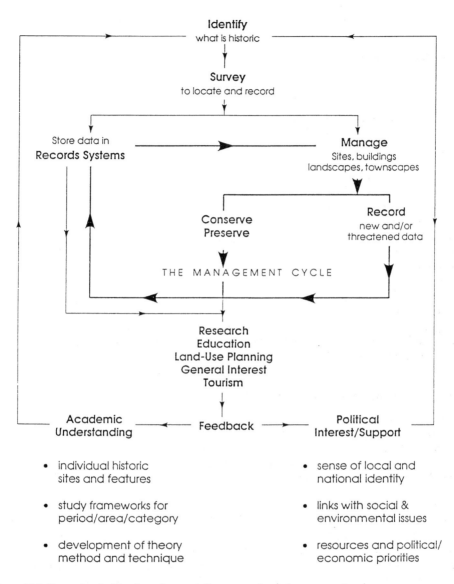

Figure 10.1. Conserving the historic environment: the conservation and management cycles.

All this is done for a diverse set of reasons. They include research as an activity to find out more about the human past, education to give the rising generations historical awareness and appreciation, satisfaction of the curiosity of local people and tourists, and management of the environment through the land-use planning process. Together, these outputs contribute to the human cultures whose remains they contain, and to general interest and support that can be expressed through the political process. In turn, they can feed back to the general awareness of heritage and its value, which is the basis of the conservation process. Much of this can be achieved through the broad spread of services provided by local authorities.

ORGANIZATIONAL REQUIREMENTS

Successful conservation depends upon a combination of information and expertise. Accessible information is the basic intelligence about landscape, habitation, fabric and deposit, without which decay cannot be slowed, or character and appearance enhanced. It is also the basis for continuing research into subject, period and place, whether professionally or privately, through academic project or casual enquiry. The expertise using that information for those tasks must cover a range of skills to match a range of distinctive local heritages.

Continuity of care and explanation requires a network of accessible information and expertise deployed at national and local levels. In the locality, this means a maintained information system that documents archaeological and architectural identity, together with a dossier of management history. It also entails teamwork by grouped experts dedicated to an area large enough for the effective deployment of their skills and accumulating knowledge, as well as being able to interact with local societies and individuals.

Such requirements exist only patchily at present, and it must be a key conservation aim to influence the local government review so that the scope for local arrangements improves, even if it takes time for all the resources to become available. English Heritage's recently announced strategy, *Managing England's Heritage – Setting Our Priorities for the 1990s* (English Heritage 1992a) also recommended that more work be done at local level, and this is a further reason to strengthen the provision.

IDENTIFICATION

At first glance local authorities have a largely passive role in the identification of features in the environment as types having historic value: the most familiar response is the incredulity of some senior councillors concerning the latest national-level decree that something they can remember being built is now of historic interest. There is a duality of attitude: on the one hand industrial archaeology can be hated for its association with the dereliction and redundancies of deindustrialization; on the other, an almost universal awareness of 'heritage' too easily leads to an unfocused confusion of history and fiction. The negative result is a resistance to change in the familiar scene just because it is familiar; a failure to perceive how it is actually the product of many changes over a long time. The positive side comes with the cherishing of local landmarks and scenes, as much as for their contribution to a distinctive locality as for any intrinsic academically defined merit.

Here local authorities can provide a guiding hand in various ways through schemes for identifying 'countryside treasures' or 'heritage treasures'. Well-written and detailed descriptive documents for conservation areas can also help. These can enable individuals, members of local amenity and archaeological or historical societies, or classes from local schools, to identify for themselves that some things are historic, thus gaining personal ownership of discovery.

On a more formal level, the mere act of developing record systems like the Sites and Monuments Records (SMRs) raises local questions about what is historic. There is an interestingly wide range of official cut-off dates for data collection by SMRs, especially those that include buildings, ranging from 1700 to the 1970s. Involvement in assisting English Heritage with the Monuments Protection Programme (see Chapter 17) and with revising the lists of listed buildings also gives local authorities the opportunity to define classes of site or building or examples of types that do not qualify for national designation but are significant elements in the local scene.

SURVEY

Local authorities tend to become involved in two kinds of identification survey: basic work to develop local record systems and work to extend statutory protection by means of listing buildings or scheduling ancient monuments. There is now a complete coverage of SMRs in England and Wales, but the survey work for their basic development has been very uneven. In pump-priming the network, the Department of the Environment (DoE) and English Heritage (EH) were driven initially by the need to have something in place for planning purposes, and more recently to assist the Monuments Protection Programme (MPP).

Survey work for basic SMR development usually has an objective of general awareness of everything that it is reasonable to know for planning purposes. Achieving it requires a process that can be undertaken in one or two stages. In the first stage, all the readily available, mostly published, data is rapidly accumulated to provide a working basis, creating a coverage whose unevenness reflects the sum of past individual interest in various subjects and places. In the second, some kind of systematic survey is undertaken to provide a minimum common level of awareness across the area, filling in or confirming the apparent gaps. In Bedfordshire, conveniently one of the smallest shire counties, it proved possible to carry out two county-wide systematic surveys between 1975 and 1985, one for archaeological sites and the historic landscape, and the other for the majority of listed or listable buildings.

The parish survey, for archaeology and the historic landscape, covered each parish with a standard three-stage procedure of pre-field, field and post-field checklisted activities, starting and ending with the SMR. The aim was to cover certain standard local printed and documentary sources so that they did not need to be recombed for every new planning case. Fieldwork was restricted to checking the condition of known sites and identifying suspected ones in places of potential archaeological sensitivity; detailed recording was deliberately avoided. The SMR holdings were revised, and historic map transcripts prepared on the modern Ordnance Survey (OS) base. A written essay on each parish was prepared but not published, apart from seven state-of-the-art productions at the end of the programme: these demonstrated the impracticability of trying to combine rapid record enhancement with systematic survey publication in any finite timetable.

The programme for historic buildings was derived from Bedfordshire Planning Department's assistance to DoE with list review. This work was also primarily concerned with identification rather than detailed analysis, but it provided a fine opportunity to look systematically at each building of any age, parish by parish. Photographs were taken, and this collection, which now stretches back over twenty years, is of growing value for both archival and planning purposes.

DATA STORAGE

Securing SMR coverage of England and Wales took over twenty years, from Oxfordshire in the mid-1960s to Kent in the late-1980s (ACAO 1984; RCHME 1993). Mentioned in despatches by the General Development Order of 1988, the White Paper *This Common Heritage* in 1990, and Planning Policy Guidance Note 16 (PPG 16, DoE 1990a) (but not yet a statutory function), SMRs have developed variously according to local circumstances, influenced by EH and its predecessor as paymaster until 1989.

The existing collection, mostly in planning departments or museums, ranges from simple planning tools with little more than the basic material already in the National Archaeological Record (which the Royal Commission on the Historical Monuments of

England (RCHME) took over from the former OS Archaeology Division, see Chapter 4), to well-developed multi-purpose systems. RCHME's recent survey has found significant variations between SMRs in the spheres of archaeological and architectural interest, sources of information and methods of recording, size and quality of the resulting databases, supporting records and archives, and progress with computerization. A further major issue is the working out of a mutually beneficial relationship with the RCHME's National Monuments Record (NMR). Local SMRs must aim to become the comprehensive detailed record for the historic environment of their areas, containing all relevant information or at least references to where it can be found. They are not complete after the initial period of development; professional maintenance is needed for their use which in turn causes further development through the contributions of casework consultations and designed research programmes.

SMRs must store all local data on the historic environment in a sufficiently analysed form to permit retrieval in response to a wide variety of enquiries. It was the potential for multi-factoral retrieval that distinguished the better earliest records from local single-field card-indexes, though a surprising number had no retrieval other than by map location until well into the 1970s. The Royal Commission survey (RCHME 1993) clearly shows the currently unsatisfactory state of index computerization: there are more than half a dozen different database systems in use, some the product of the entrepreneurial cost-cutting at which archaeologists have had to excel. There is now an obvious opportunity for convergence in retrieval systems under the lead of RCHME as SMRs progressively update hardware and software. In conjunction with this there is a need to develop common data standards and apply recently compiled thesauri of terms to bodies of records perhaps initially collected and first analysed up to twenty years ago.

Other, local, developmental forces are pulling at SMRs. Links must be established with museums to cross-reference provenanced material in their artefact-led records. Direct communication with units operating in the locality must be ensured so that fieldwork results are routinely accessed: analysis should however be confined to the usual fields of site type, period and artefact categories, acting as an index to the full detail of a separate excavation archive. SMRs ought perhaps to avoid entanglement in the databases for types of excavated finds and structures, which local organizations must construct as the basis for ensuring consistent standards of reporting from all projects undertaken in their areas.

There is also pressure for SMRs to become part of wider-based environmental databases, going beyond the inclusion of historic buildings. Systems for the natural environment are less easy (see Chapter 22). Some, like surveys of ancient and semi-natural woodlands, have community of interest with systems containing historic landscape features; others, for features like Sites of Special Scientific Interest (SSSIs) and Prime Sites of Nature Conservation Interest (PSNCIs) deal with matters sufficiently different to make any detailed integration difficult. Perhaps it is best to merge records covering dissimilar topics at a generalized level only, with the limited objective of defining potential conflicts or conjunctions of interest for further consideration.

The aggregation of county SMRs has been contemplated mostly in terms of relations with the NMR rather than on a regional basis, although regional SMR working parties have existed for some time. The concept of a national–local network of records for the historic environment, each with its distinct leading functions, emerged during the mid-1970s (Baker 1977). It has taken a long time to get rooted, but RCHME's new recommendations following its survey of SMRs (RCHME 1993) ought to provide a way forward. The NMR is seen as a core index record to the whole intercommunicating national–local network, with a sensible division of labour between the two levels, and a commitment from RCHME, subject to funding, to assist the less well-developed SMRs over initial development.

The local government review is a potential wild card. SMRs were set up on a county basis, but spend most of their time providing information to district planning officers. Few districts have viable SMRs, apart from some large historic urban centres (EH is to fund others following the York model). Yet the review has set up an obvious tension between counties and districts competing to be the future unitary authorities for their areas. EH and RCHME have stated that SMRs and their related functions cannot be run cost-effectively for an area much smaller than a shire county, but not even the most blinkered archaeologists could reasonably expect the outcome of the review to pivot on their minority interests.

Problems will arise where a motley collection of small new unitary authorities implies the fissioning of existing SMRs into sizes that cannot support basic staffing levels. Opportunities will arise in those areas where the new unitary authority is of county or large city size, with the possibility of developing SMRs towards proper historic environment records, including historic buildings. In between, fancy footwork will be demanded of those that survive intact under some kind of joint arrangement between adjacent authorities. The best guarantee for what seems likely to be an untidy situation would be the achievement of statutory recognition for a network established and led through RCHME so that there was 'system' support for the weaker links.

PLANNING

It is through the land-use planning system that the greatest opportunities arise for the beneficial management of the cultural resource, given its primary concern with the balance between the economic benefits of development and the conservation of the physical environment. The key documents are, for archaeology, the Ancient Monuments and Archaeological Areas Act 1979 (AMAA Act 1979) and the PPG 16 of November 1990 (DoE 1990a). The latter's comments on archaeology in development plans have recently been amplified by an Advice Note prepared by EH in conjunction with the Association of County Archaeological Officers (English Heritage 1992c).

Scheduled Monument Consent (SMC) is administered at national level, by the DoE on the advice of English Heritage, unlike Listed Building Consent, which is handled by district planning authorities (see also Chapter 8). A case is being made increasingly frequently that SMC ought also to be handled at local level, with the same kind of reserve powers for the Secretary of State as exist for buildings (Scrase 1991). There is not space here to deploy the arguments, beyond commenting that the workload likely to be generated by the fruits of the MPP (Chapter 17) will greatly strengthen the case for local administration, but that it would not be practicable without an increase in the quantity and quality of local resources.

Plans

The planning system has an impact on the historic environment as a series of decisions about proposals for development. However, the Planning and Compensation Act 1991 clarified the importance of development plans by stating a clear presumption in favour of granting permission for proposals that conform to their policies. Thus plans at all levels can between them set a framework capable of ensuring that most aspects of the historic environment are at least taken into account when considering site-specific issues.

The DoE's *Development Plans and Regional Planning Guidance*, published in February 1992, identifies conservation of the natural and built environment as one of nine key topics for Structure Plans whose task is to set the framework for the local plans within their area. It also advocates sustainability as a key concept, but this ecological concept has not yet been worked through properly in the context of historic survivals, whose decay can be slowed by conservation, but which cannot be regenerated or transplanted. The problems of cross-environmental communication are being considered jointly by the Countryside Commission, English Heritage and English Nature; a jointly commissioned study on strategic planning guidance is expected shortly (LUC 1992).

Strategic policies in Structure Plans and any regional planning guidance need to express the nature, significance and value of the historic environment, and its relationship with other environmental matters. Statements must be sufficiently clear to ensure that its various aspects are considered in more detail in local plans. The Structure Plans for Hereford and Worcester, and for Bedfordshire, provide examples:

> Features of historic and/or architectural importance listed below which contribute to the landscape quality of the county will be perpetuated by enhancement and management (where possible and appropriate by agreement) and any development, operations or activities which would permanently and adversely affect those features will not normally be allowed:
> a. listed buildings, conservation areas and their settings
> b. historic landscapes, including parks and gardens, commons and village greens
> [Explanation: In some respects the whole county is an historic landscape with each period of man's activities reflected . . .] (*Hereford and Worcester Structure Plan* Policy CT7)

> When considering proposals for development the local planning authorities will seek the preservation of Scheduled Ancient Monuments and other sites of major archaeological significance and their settings through:
> a. ensuring the availability of sufficient information to valuate the importance of the site and assess the impact of development proposals;
> b. seeking to resist or modify development proposals likely to have an unacceptably adverse effect upon sites and their settings;
> c. the use of management agreements to mitigate the effects of potentially conflicting land uses upon standing structures, including earthworks, and on buried deposits;
> d. seeking to ensure that provision is made for an appropriate level of investigation and recording in advance of the destruction of those sites which do not merit permanent preservation. (*Bedfordshire Structure Plan* Policy 14)

District local planning authorities are required to produce general district-wide local plans, and county minerals and waste disposal authorities to provide county-wide local plans, for those topics. There used to be considerable enthusiasm for subject plans, dealing with aspects of land use, and a feeling that they were the answer to an archaeologist's prayers. They have value for defining scope, determining priorities and resolving conflicts within a particular interest, but the arena of most significance is the district-wide local plan which provides the framework for resolving conflicts between interests whose general importance has already been defined at the strategic level. Alternative approaches are informal papers as part of wider initiatives: an example is Norfolk's Countryside Strategy, based on a series of about a dozen consultative topic papers which included *Historic Landscapes & Archaeology* (Norfolk County Council 1988). Sector-based studies for countryside conservation can also take an area and deal with it in a multi-disciplinary framework.

Local Plan policies affecting the various aspects of the historic environment may be divided into those that aim to protect and enhance its elements, and those that seek to control development that might affect it. Policies for archaeological protection might include:

Development which adversely affects the sites or settings of scheduled ancient monuments, other nationally important archaeological sites and monuments, and monuments of especial local importance will not normally be permitted.

The local planning authority will encourage owners of important archaeological sites to maintain them in good condition and to adopt sympathetic land management regimes.

Examples of policies for development control are:

The local planning authority will require sufficient information from applicants, including where necessary the results of evaluation by fieldwork, in order to assess the potential impact of their proposals upon important archaeological sites.

The local planning authority will seek to lessen the impact of acceptable development proposals upon important archaeological remains and their settings by, as appropriate:
a. negotiating their modification to increase preservation.
b. not permitting development to commence until satisfactory provision has made for an agreed programme of archaeological investigation and recording.

More detailed policies could be devised to suit the special circumstances of particularly sensitive areas. York City Council has produced one such set (Arup 1991) that tries to deal with reconciling the need for development with deep and rich deposits, and all within an explicit justifying research framework (see Chapter 12).

Development control

Development control provides opportunities for conservation in the positive as well as the negative sense. Regrettably too much turns out to be no-saying, in defence of site, building or area, but this is often because the developer has either not consulted at an early enough stage in the process, or is hoping to bulldoze the opposition. In many cases negotiation, including communication of the value of what might be at risk, can lead to either an acceptable compromise or otherwise unlooked-for gains all round.

Successful development control of cases involving conservation interests requires good communication between planning officers and specialist conservation and/or archaeological officers with their own information systems. The identity of significant items recorded on the information system must be registered on the overall planning constraints maps maintained within the planning department. It is important that depiction is restricted to an area of unspecified identity or importance so that a potential impact triggers off a specialist consultation that allows the extent of any problem to be fully explored.

Defining what ought to be registered as a constraint is a difficult exercise requiring judgement and a measure of realism, bearing in mind the intensity and variety of survivals in most areas of England. Listed buildings and Scheduled Ancient Monuments are obvious, but other categories are more problematical. Important unlisted buildings might be caught through an unofficial 'local' list or by their location in a conservation area. Important unscheduled sites might have already been identified through the scoring processes undertaken by county archaeological officers participating in the MPP: however, if a realistic threshold is not adopted, too much land may appear to be constrained, with a corresponding loss of credibility. To justify landscapes as constraints requires that they are distinctively identifiable or have been designed in some way.

In order to assess the impact of any planning application affecting any aspect of the historic environment it is essential to have sufficient information about what is proposed and what will be the impact of its implementation. It might affect a place where there may be a site, a building that might have as yet unidentified qualities, or a landscape whose spatial and temporal components have not yet been identified. The requirement for information now seems obvious, but getting it accepted in practice has been a long swim against many tides: these have included generalized presumptions in favour of development and against aesthetic control, and the political wish for rapid processing of objection-free applications to keep a council high in the league table of nimble bureaucrats.

The provision of sufficient information has for some time been established as a principle for listed buildings and conservation areas: applications have been refused for lack of it, and appeals against refusal dismissed. The case is more difficult for archaeological sites whose significance (or even existence) is often not knowable in advance. Despite the statement in DoE *Circular 8/87* that the existence of an important archaeological site was a material consideration in the determination of a planning application, it was not until the issue of PPG 16 (DoE 1990a) at the end of 1990 that there was clear government guidance about the need for sufficiency of information prior to determination. It has been impressive how rapidly previously frustrated local authority archaeology officers have been able to get the necessary procedures generally accepted.

At the time of writing, terminology, methodology and roles are being painfully defined for a flexible staged approach to the investigation of land threatened by development. Classically, it involves an appraisal to see if there is a potential problem, an assessment of all existing readily available information, and, if needed, a programme of fieldwork evaluation. The latter can involve a combination of documentary research, aerial photography, fieldwalking, earthwork survey, geophysical prospecting and test pits or trial trenches. The overall result is intended to underpin proposals for mitigation of impact that can range from amendments to increase preservation, through securing provision for recording in advance of destruction, to outright refusal of consent.

This new procedure has opened up tremendous opportunities but also conferred new and heavy responsibilities: it is the key indicator of archaeology's political arrival. However, acceptance of those responsibilities has to carry with it an awareness of the interests of others, together with a sense of values that helps to integrate rather than divide archaeology and society. It is not enough to say that all Britain is a palimpsest of archaeological survivals, thus justifying possibly expensive fieldwork evaluation of all major proposals, whether or not there is any predictive archaeological information. Similarly, the extent of programmes required to assess and evaluate impact must have regard for economy, not only of the resource under investigation, but also of the developers' resources, which may be limited in some cases where otherwise acceptable proposals are economically marginal. Only if credible balances of this kind can be struck and consistently maintained will it be possible to wean some local planning authorities from refusing to ask for evaluation prior to consent, and only imposing it as a condition to allow post-determination recording; this leaves no room for manoeuvre on mitigation by preservation except on a voluntary basis.

This leads to the other major provision of PPG 16, government acceptance that application of the 'polluter pays' principle to archaeology licenses the use of a 'negative' planning condition to ensure that important evidence is recorded in advance of its destruction by development. The model condition, now engraved upon the professional heart, requires the implementation by the applicant of a scheme of work approved by the local planning authority in advance of the commencement of development, for the purpose of recording important evidence affected by it. Many feel this is a better way of handling the archaeological dimension than through a freely concluded Section 106 Planning Obligation. Matters of current debate within the profession include the format and content of this scheme of works, which is being increasingly associated with the procedures outlined in English Heritage's model published as the *Management of Archaeological Projects* (English Heritage 1991a).

These new procedures have bestowed the role of 'curator' on the local authority archaeologist in a new network of relationships between curators, contractors and consultants (see also Chapters 14, 15 and 16), evolving in response to archaeology's new involvement with the world of commerce and development. Though archaeologists might naively argue that their primary ethical devotion to the finite non-renewable resource places them above conflicts of interest arising from the giving of planning advice that leads to fieldwork funded by a prospective developer, world-weary developers familiar with desperate stratagems to maintain continuity of work for under-sized and under-funded units tend to think otherwise. Their response is often to reach for assistance from a new form of an old profession, and one of archaeology's newest variants, the consultant: at the time of writing these vary in quality as much as the other players on an uneven playing field whose earthworks are often at risk of being levelled without proper evaluation.

The local authority archaeologist (or curator) has a new and heavy workload arising from the procedures introduced or consolidated by PPG 16. This was recognized in a study commissioned by English Heritage from Pagoda Associates a mere twelve months after the introduction of PPG 16. It found that as a result of the archaeological significance of most planning proposals being properly considered in advance of determination, there had been a noticeable increase in the requirement to produce briefs and specifications for archaeological work, as well as to monitor such activities on site: many local authority archaeologists were simply overwhelmed.

Not all the local authority archaeologist's casework comes through the planning system. Public utilities like British Gas and the regional water companies carry out work that can have an archaeological impact, yet usually do not need planning permission. However they are producing codes of conduct, such as the Water Act Code of Practice (1989) that require them to behave in an environmentally conscious manner, and this usually involves consultation at scheme design stage. The Forestry Authority has also built up a significant track record of consultation about grant-aided schemes for planting. Road schemes ultimately require planning permission, but only at the stage the route is finally fixed: there can be a heavy archaeological input to the previous stages.

PRESERVATION AND MANAGEMENT

PPG 16 correctly stresses the primacy of preservation *in situ*, but it tends to be perceived as putting into place arrangements for mitigating potential damage and underlining the 'polluter pays' principle for the funding of 'preservation by record'. Yet there is a whole suite of work beyond development control, beginning with preventative measures incorporated in development plans, such as the ability to identify in Minerals Plans areas of sensitivity to be evaluated before any application to extract can be considered. Local authorities are also empowered under the AMAA Act 1979 to give grants to assist with the cost of the preservation, maintenance or management of any ancient monuments in their areas, and with the costs of archaeological investigations (see Chapter 5).

There are other facilitating possibilities for the local authority archaeologist. Counties and districts with active countryside interests have a tradition of working with landowners and the farming community across a broad range of environmental matters. There is tremendous scope for promoting the interests of historical conservation in the range of agricultural initiatives that have been sweeping across the countryside, many sprouting from the European Commission (English Heritage/MAFF n.d.; see also Chapter 22). The new agricultural landscapes of the 1970s immediately raised the question as to what of the old enclosed or pre-enclosure landscapes had survived the onset of prairie farming. More recently, Set Aside has emerged as a device of obvious potential that somehow must be converted into a non-rotational mechanism so that historically sensitive land can be taken out of persistently threatening uses such as ploughing and tree-planting.

The basis for all such countryside work is information about sites and understood landscapes, which provide both a context and a predictive framework for as yet undiscovered sites and features of significance. These can be expressed in the Farm Plan, which includes a general environmental audit as the basis for management proposals. The ultimate objective must be the preparation of a management plan for every Scheduled Ancient Monument and locally important site: such plans could be backed up by management agreements for scheduled sites, grants for repair of erosion on earthworks and ruins, and grants for the provision of interpretative facilities. This kind of work is supported by initiatives like the Countryside Stewardship scheme, which provides grants and advice to help conserve landscapes of particular character together with the natural and historic features they contain. Though organized at national level, they provide local authorities with a mechanism to make significant progress in consciousness-raising and management in their areas.

Positive management of archaeological sites can be dovetailed neatly into other major local authority programmes. Hampshire has become a major partner in the care, investigation and interpretation of Danebury hillfort in one of its country parks. Cambridgeshire, one of several councils with an extensive Farms Estate, has undertaken a systematic survey to identify archaeological sites, assess their importance and condition, and to make recommendations about their management, protection and public presentation (Malim 1990).

The AMAA Act 1979 permits local authorities to take scheduled sites into their guardianship. This has happened only to a limited extent, and there are particular problems in retaining the expertise to look after ruins. Bedfordshire County Council sought from the late 1970s to take into its care those ruins that the old DoE was not prepared to accept: action was necessary if collapses were to be averted. Ultimately, the county's two ruined medieval churches, a 15th-century brick gatehouse and chapel, and part of a secularized monastic building, were acquired or taken into guardianship. The last took over ten years to achieve and all received significant basic repair grants from DoE and English Heritage. This example is not provided out of domestic smugness, but to point up the real problems in counties like Norfolk and Suffolk, where even the most well-funded local authority could not expect to cope with hundreds of ruined churches of architectural and landscape merit.

Some local authorities, particularly those adjacent to, or overlapping with, National Parks, may have the opportunity to become involved in more extensive management regimes for designated land such as Areas of Outstanding Natural Beauty and Environmentally Sensitive Areas (see Chapter 22). The uplands of Dartmoor, Exmoor and the Peak, coinciding with some of the rich areas of prehistoric and medieval settlement, remain relatively undamaged by the impact of repetitive lowland cultivation.

OUTPUT AND FEEDBACK

Local authorities can make a fundamental contribution in outputs on historical conservation matters to a variety of customers. This facilitates feedback to the other stages in the overall process of historical conservation.

As far as education is concerned, the effects of local management of budgets (LMS) and 'opting-out' to grant-maintained status cannot yet be properly assessed. It is uncertain whether teachers' advisory services, including those concerned with aspects of the historic environment, will survive in the face of new dependence upon purchase by shrinking devolved school budgets. Leisure services, including museums, are directly involved as promoters and custodians of local heritage resources. Planning departments, as advocates of environmental conservation, are in a key position to influence others as long as they survive privatization or externalization.

Local authorities have traditionally produced leaflets and booklets about their services and aspects of their areas; some are simply descriptive or interpretative and intended to increase environmental awareness; others deal with specific issues and legal obligations. Many are ephemeral, the range of quality in design and content can be considerable, and by no means all seem to be very clear about the audience they are addressing: getting the balance between words and pictures is often a problem, with slabbiness of text a common failing.

THE SCOTTISH DIMENSION

The picture in Scotland is rather different, partly because of a fundamental contrast between official aspirations and political indifference (cf. Breeze 1988: 4; AMBS 1988: 27), partly through the characteristics of local government, population and geography. In sum, gross inequalities of provision now exist between the local authority archaeological services in Scotland and England.

By way of introduction the slowness of uptake must be emphasized. In 1975, on local government reorganization, only one out of twelve regional and island authorities – Grampian – appointed an archaeologist, in spite of the promotion of a comprehensive system of archaeological provision by the Society of Antiquaries of Scotland (SAS 1974). By 1980, two other regions had created single posts (and the Orkney Heritage Society had also appointed an archaeologist who is yet to be adopted by his islands council), but it was not until the late 1980s that four others followed. Two major regions – Lothian and Tayside – have yet to appoint archaeologists (as have the Western Isles): Historic Scotland provides cover in these areas. In general, one can say that these nine posts have been established in often hostile circumstances.

This sparseness of cover is compounded by the sheer scale of most of these regions, as has recently been vividly illustrated in another context by comparing the provision for archaeology in Highland Region (2.5 cultural resource managers/three museum curators) with that in a similarly sized area, the whole of Wales (Cadw, four trusts, The Welsh Royal Commission and the University Colleges. See Barclay 1992c: 106–7, fig. 38).

The Local Government and Planning (Scotland) Act 1982 and the Town and Country Planning (Scotland) Act 1972 are the basis of the planning system in Scotland. The system splits responsibility, allocating strategic planning to the regional councils, and local planning and most development control to the districts, although certain regions (Highland/Borders/Dumfries and Galloway/the island authorities) perform both functions.

It is probably true to say that structure plans have survived better in Scotland than in the south (SO 1992: 48), although the use that has been made of them for archaeological purposes is limited, but now generally sufficient. In the first round of structure plan creation, in the late 1970s, several had no archaeological dimension whatsoever (e.g. Strathclyde and Tayside: both were amended after receipt of vigorous responses to public consultation exercises in the early 1980s). Now, most plans contain basic policies to protect archaeological sites of national and regional significance. Grampian, Strathclyde and Fife make use of this last concept, referring to lists devised during plan preparation: the Fife list defines Areas and Sites of Regional Importance (FRC 1992). The plans also set the framework for the preparation of local plans by district councils (in areas of 'two-tier' planning), as well as providing a policy context for development control by both levels of the planning system.

111

Only in Strathclyde, where policy formulation has been refined further than in most other regions, has a wide range of policies for the historic environment been promulgated, although the rural conservation areas defined in the Highland Region Structure Plan are an interesting attempt to integrate historic and natural landscape conservation and interpretation. These are not formal designations under the Civic Amenities Act, but rather expressions of interest that Highland Regional Council has not so far been able to progress further.

The current round of structure plan revision generally preceded the publication of the first draft of the *National Planning Policy Guidelines: Archaeology and Planning* (NPPG; SOEnD 1992a, 1992b) and hence their provisions, which entrench archaeology within the planning system, are not yet reflected in every plan. The revised Central Region Structure Plan is, however, a good model for the future, covering as it does preservation *in situ*, developer funding and local plan guidelines (CRC 1992: 7.42).

The structure plans may be linked to related documents of strategic intent such as indicative forestry strategies (promulgated in *Scottish Office Circular 13/1990*), minerals or interpretative strategies, although Strathclyde prefers to keep all its approved policies in the one document.

The AMAA Act 1979 gives wide powers to local authorities in the field of heritage management. Certain authorities are exercising their powers of acquisition: for example, in Grampian the Regional Council's Heritage Fund (itself established as a result of a Structure Plan proposal) has been used to purchase a recumbent stone circle, while the Highland Heritage Network in Highland Region links features in the natural and cultural landscapes. Part II of the Act was never implemented in Scotland, in spite of calls in several Structure Plans for this to happen.

The insertion of archaeological policies in the Structure Plans has been a vital first step in setting the context for safeguarding archaeology at the local planning level (Shepherd 1988: 31). The most typical Structure Plan policy is one stating that there will be a presumption against development that would destroy or adversely affect Scheduled Ancient Monuments (SAMs) or sites of regional significance. There is now a considerable body of experience throughout the country in translating such a general statement into effective protection within the district councils, both at local plan formulation and during development control. An excellent example of the new breed of local plans is the one for Clydebank District, which covers part of the Antonine Wall and includes policy to ensure that developers meet their obligations to archaeology (CDC 1992: E10). This experience extends to defending the local plan policies at public local enquiries.

Other recent statements of local authority policy, notably environmental charters (Raemaekers 1992), represent an extension of ways of promoting the protection and management of archaeological resources that confirm archaeology as the essential time dimension of environmental planning (cf. Shepherd 1988: 27).

The fundamental source of archaeological advice for planners is, as in England, an active SMR, maintained by the regional archaeologist. Although at varying stages of development, most are already invaluable, not merely within the planning system, but also for assessing notifications of forestry proposals. This system, hard-won after considerable vicissitudes (Shepherd 1989, 1992) means that the single most extensive and destructive land-use change in Scotland now takes account of the archaeological heritage.

Currently, Historic Scotland has begun to commission assessments of data held in SMRs in order to provide a non-statutory list of sites of national importance (AMBS 1991: 5). Avowedly not a Monuments Protection Programme, the pilot study, in Grampian, has recently identified over 600 such sites to add to the 330 currently scheduled (out of a total of 8,500 SMR entries).

The provisions of the Environmental Assessment directive (see Chapter 22) have recently been greatly strengthened by the publication of the draft NPPG (SOEnD 1992a, 1992b) which recognizes archaeology as a material consideration in planning issues. Several aspects are already in everyday use, such as the suspensive condition that ensures archaeological investigation prior to development and the briefs and specifications required for developer-funded projects. There is, in Scotland, a complete split at regional level between curators and contractors: this has been encouraged by Historic Scotland.

Some reservations about the NPPG remain, particularly in relation to the funding of small but socially desirable developments in rural Scotland, while Malcolm Rifkind's refusal in 1988 to countenance developer-funding within the forestry industry appears increasingly anomalous in the light of the NPPG (AMBS 1988: 28; Shepherd 1992: 166).

Overall, the considerable improvement on the situation of archaeological resource management in Scotland as described in 1980 (Brand and Cant 1980) has been gained all too slowly and represents but the beginning of a process that is somewhat unstable in a time of rapidly changing balance between the archaeological responsibilities of central and local government. There is certainly a need for a clearer definition of the responsibilities of each tier of government; it is no longer acceptable for the present confusion to continue. This is all the more pressing in the context of local government reorganization and the need to strengthen local resources consequent on the National Planning Guidelines.

THE FUTURE FOR LOCAL AUTHORITY ARCHAEOLOGY

What does the future hold for local authority archaeology? Much depends upon political stance. The further down the road to privatization, the greater might be the difficulty for the service-purchasing client side in the new slimmed-down authority to ensure the continuity of maintained information systems and local expertise that are fundamental to historical conservation. Providing such services through the crude mechanisms of competitive tendering, which nearly always pivots on price, is incompatible with that continuity. The short-termism of arrangements depending upon frequent combats of uncertain outcome in the marketplace must prevent the introduction of basic systems in areas still lacking adequate provision, and may even encourage the dismantling of existing linked expert teams and record systems.

Already there are worrying developments. In some English counties SMRs are being seen as external services capable of provision through competition, ignoring the question of archival continuity. Units bidding competitively against each other for growing quantities of PPG 16-related fieldwork are stacking up an impressive pile of completed contracts, but the process is inevitably geared more to developers' needs than to increasing local archaeological understanding (the reason for doing it in the first place).

Yet historical conservation must earn its exemption from the full blast of a force basically legitimized through the push to achieve value-for-money, by showing that it can achieve its targets economically, efficiently and effectively by other means. This will involve a willingness to look hard at the range of conservation activities that can be undertaken at local level, as discussed in this chapter, and at the tasks within them, in order to decide which can still contribute to the overall objective as it is now defined, and whether those are better done in-house, by external consultants, or by collaboration with neighbouring organizations.

It may well be that the local archaeological (or historical conservation) organization cannot achieve the minimum critical mass without combining so-called 'curating' and 'contracting' roles (a serious oversimplification that does not equate with the purchaser–provider divide sweeping through local government). A wide range of expertise is required of the local authority archaeologist, in subjects and periods of time, and in technical matters. An individual with relatively little personal experience of major fieldwork projects will have difficulty in approving a detailed specification of works and monitoring to certify compliance with it.

Combined organizations must be structured so that at financially sensitive points in the conservation cycle they are, and can be seen to be, separate and independent, yet on other matters are able to communicate as needed on academic and professional matters. The prize of success in such self-regulation will be the opportunity to develop a coherent understanding of the local historic environment and a consistent approach to its conservation. Such systems will usefully demand coordination between planning archaeologist, fieldwork unit and museum, and have the potential to benefit a wide range of customers now and in the future.

CHAPTER 11

BRITISH ARCHAEOLOGY IN A WIDER CONTEXT

Henry Cleere

Legislative and administrative structures for the protection of the archaeological heritage are now in place in virtually every country. Their diversity and efficacy reflect political and historical contexts. In Sweden, for example, where the world's first monuments protection law was promulgated by Royal Proclamation in 1666, the concept of archaeological remains as part of the cultural heritage of the nation is deeply entrenched in the national consciousness and is given material substance through strong legislation and a comprehensive antiquities service. Cambodia, by contrast, which is painfully emerging from decades of civil war and totalitarian rule, has no monuments protection legislation and a wholly inadequate antiquities service. The former communist countries of the now defunct Eastern Bloc are in the process of readjusting their systems to the realities of an economy in which priorities are set by market forces.

It would be impossible within the compass of this chapter to provide a comprehensive overview of all the systems operating in the last decade of the 20th century. Instead, it is proposed to describe broad categories, with examples from individual states, in the fields of legislation and organization, concluding with a section on international and interregional legislative instruments and institutions.

LEGISLATION

A comparative study of world antiquities legislation reveals gradations of scope, from state ownership of all types of antiquity, whether portable or monumental, to the application of protective measures for selected categories. A number of surveys of antiquities legislation have been published, both regional (e.g. Hingst and Lipowschek 1975; CoE 1979) and international (e.g. Burnham 1974; UNESCO 1985) but unfortunately these are soon out of date, since there is a continuous process of revision of laws springing from political changes and new approaches to heritage protection. Of more value, perhaps, are the comparative analytical studies, such as that by Tesch (1984) and above all the monumental work of O'Keefe and Prott, which is still in progress (1984; also Prott and O'Keefe 1989).

The most comprehensive form of legislative protection for the archaeological heritage is unquestionably that in countries with a communist form of government. Put quite simply, these laws assert a state title to all archaeological materials, both portable and monumental, along with severe penalties for destroying, damaging, or stealing them and regulation of any works that may have an impact on them. This was the case in the countries of the Eastern Bloc (e.g. Herrmann 1981; Jaworski 1981; Princ 1984) but in most of them plans are being made to replace this strong legislation with more selective protection comparable with that in western Europe. Only in the People's Republic of China is strong legislation of this kind likely to survive to the end of the 20th century (Zhuang 1989).

Comprehensive legislative protection of this kind is, however, not confined to Communist states. The Scandinavian tradition, stemming from the Swedish Royal

Proclamation of 1666, is equally emphatic in maintaining a public interest in all aspects of antiquity. The Norwegian Cultural Heritage Act 1979 extends protection to any example from an exhaustive list of monument categories from the earliest times to AD 1537 (Section 4) and to all portable antiquities over the same period for which no owner can be identified (Section 12). The situation in Sweden and Denmark (Kristiansen 1984) is comparable with that in Norway; in Germany a similar form of protection applies in Schleswig-Holstein, because of its historical links with Denmark (Reichstein 1984: 40). In the Scandinavian countries this protection extends to undiscovered antiquities: they are automatically protected from the moment of their discovery and there is a presumption in law that they are protected before the moment of discovery. A number of other countries have similar legislative protection, but there are few where it is effectively implemented. Greece is one such example; of those in the Third World, Mexico is another (Lorenzo 1984).

A more restricted form of legislative protection is that which applies not to all objects and monuments in specified categories but only to those that are identified by means of registers of protected monuments and objects. This is the system in operation in, for example, Italy (d'Agostino 1984) and Japan (Tanaka 1984). In Italy landowners are obliged to notify the competent authorities of discoveries of archaeological material, but it is necessary for the authorities in turn to inform the owner of the state interest in the discovery for full legislative protection to be extended to it; this principle is known as the *vincolo*, and applies equally to works of art and antiquities. The Japanese system, based on the 1975 revision of the Law for the Protection of Cultural Properties 1950, is broadly similar to that in Italy. A similar protection system applies in Europe in Austria, the Republic of Ireland, Spain (García Fernández 1989), and Switzerland, although in the case of the last two, responsibility is delegated to *Comunidades Autónomas* and *Cantons*, respectively.

In many countries, there is little, if any, protection extended to portable antiquities, and only those monuments on statutory lists are protected. This is, of course, the situation in Great Britain (but not Northern Ireland, see Appendix, p. 134) if the archaic nonsense of Treasure Trove is disregarded (Palmer 1981; Sparrow 1982; Chapter 6). Among European countries such a system applies in most of the German *Länder* (Hingst 1964; Brönner 1982; Reichstein 1984), France, The Netherlands, and Portugal. Belgium is an interesting case: until recently, the legislative protection of the heritage was minimal, but constitutional changes have resulted in the creation of three separate legislative codes, for the Flemish- and French-speaking regions and for multilingual Brussels, respectively. The new legislation in French-speaking Wallonia is on the Italian model, but at the time of writing no details are available for those of the other two regions, where drafting is still in progress.

Finally, there is the situation where there is legislative protection for both monumental and portable antiquities, but where this applies only to a portion of the land surface of the country. This is the case in the USA (King *et al.* 1977; McGimsey and Davis 1984; Carnett 1991), where federal legislation, such as the Antiquities Act 1906, the Archaeological and Historic Preservation Act 1974, and the Archaeological Resources Protection Act 1979, applies only to federally owned or Indian lands and to projects funded by federal agencies. The National Historic Preservation Act 1966 (as amended) creates procedures for approved state programmes, and this initiative has resulted in effective legislation being enacted by a number of states. Federal and Indian lands represent only some 40 % of the land surface of the USA, and the protection afforded to antiquities on them is becoming stronger every year with the increasingly successful enforcement of the Archaeological Resources Protection Act 1979 (Smith and Ehrenhard 1991). Sadly, however, the rate of erosion of antiquities on the remaining 60 % shows no signs of slackening.

One factor common to the great majority of national legislations is the requirement of authorization to excavate. In some legislations (e.g. Great Britain and the USA) this applies only to excavations on protected monuments, but in others, such as France, any archaeological excavation, whether on a protected monument or not, requires official authorization, a point that is picked up in the 1992 European Convention (see below).

Any study of comparative antiquities legislation highlights one basic fact: there is an inverse relationship between the effectiveness of the legislation and the length and complexity of the laws themselves. One extreme is that represented by Scandinavian legal texts. The Norwegian Cultural Heritage Act 1979 encompasses protection of ancient monuments, historic buildings, and portable antiquities in a mere twenty-nine clauses, supported by regulations set out in six clauses. The Danish Conservation of Nature Act, which covers the entire field of cultural and natural conservation, devotes no more than six clauses out of a total of seventy-one to archaeological monument protection. At the other end of the scale is the UK Ancient Monuments and Archaeological Areas Act 1979, with its sixty-five clauses and five schedules (to which must be added the lengthy provisions of town and country planning legislation in respect of historic buildings). In Spain the admirable Spanish Historic Heritage Law 1985 runs to sixty-six clauses plus three lengthy annexes, but to this have to be added seventeen provincial statutes. The total assemblage of national and provincial laws and regulations covering the protection of Spain's historic heritage fills a volume of more than 1,000 pages (García Fernández 1987) yet archaeologists visiting Spain will be acutely conscious of the inadequacy of the protection currently available to much of that heritage. The corpus of US federal legal instruments is equally gargantuan.

ORGANIZATION

The kaleidoscope of antiquities protection laws around the world is mirrored by the organizational structures in place to implement them, though only perhaps in France is there one that is as complex as that in the UK, with its government heritage agencies (English Heritage, Cadw, DoE (NI) and Historic Scotland), Royal Commissions, National Trusts, museums, county archaeologists and units. All of these organizations undertake the basic heritage management functions of survey and inventory, statutory protection and conservation, rescue archaeology, monument management, and control of portable antiquities. Broadly speaking, they fall into three main categories: centralized national organizations, decentralized national organizations, and federal or quasi-federal organizations.

Typical of the centralized structure is that in Sweden. The *Riksantikavieäbetet* (Central Board and Museum of Swedish Antiquities) is based in Stockholm. It is responsible for all aspects of implementing the comprehensive Swedish legislation. Much day-to-day work is handled through a network of regional offices, and contracts for rescue excavation and other activities are also placed with local museums and universities. Recently, with the advent of competitive tendering, aspects of market economics have been introduced into the traditional Swedish system.

Norway has a similar system, with the headquarters of the Central Office of Historic Monuments (*Riksantikvaren*) based in Oslo. Here, too, there is some measure of decentralization, with certain functions delegated to the five major regional museums in Oslo, Stavanger, Bergen, Trondheim, and Tromsö. In addition, *Riksantikvaren* has a number of permanent excavation teams in historic town centres such as Oslo, Tonsberg, and Trondheim. In Denmark responsibilities are divided between the National Forest and Nature Agency (*Skov- og Naturstyrelsen*) of the Ministry of the Environment and the National Museum. The museum is responsible for excavations (often working through local museums) and the agency covers other aspects of heritage management such as survey, inventory, and involvement with planning authorities (Kristiansen 1984). Other centralized systems of this kind exist in Czechoslovakia (or now, rather, the component states of the Czech Lands and Slovakia), Hungary, Ireland, Sri Lanka, and a number of countries in Africa and Latin America. Recent reforms in Poland have brought together the appropriate elements of the former Institute for the History of Material Culture of the Academy of Sciences and the State Conservation Workshops (PKZ) to create a new Polish Archaeological Service (Schild 1993).

There is a greater level of decentralization in other centralized states. In India the Archaeological Survey of India (ASI) has its headquarters in New Delhi and specialized branch offices in various parts of the country, but its work on the ground is the responsibility of its *Circles*, of which there are eleven covering the whole country (Thapar 1984). A number of state governments have archaeological services, but these are largely underfunded and under-resourced: the decision-making body is unquestionably the ASI. In France responsibility for heritage management is divided between a number of centralized organizations based in Paris – *Monuments Historiques, Musées de France*, etc – most of which report to different ministries. The nearest approach to a state antiquities service is the *Sous-Direction de l'Archéologie* of the *Direction du Patrimoine*, which comes under the Minister of Culture and Communications. This body is responsible for all rescue excavation in France, working through a number of *Circonscriptions*. Until comparatively recently the *Circonscriptions* were headed for the most part by part-time directors who doubled as university professors and museum directors. Over the past decade, however, the funding of this work has been greatly increased, and this has permitted the appointment of younger *Conservateurs Régionaux de l'Archéologie* to the twenty-five *Circonscriptions* (which include Guadeloupe, French Guiana, and Martinique) and the four national *Centres* devoted to specialized research. They also now have substantial permanent professional staff. Another new feature of French archaeology is the increasing number of permanent archaeological posts at *Département* and municipal level.

An increasing amount of French rescue archaeology is now developer-funded and as a result there is a floating population of contract excavators, similar to that in Britain. The fragmentation of French archaeology between bodies such as the *Sous-Direction* and research bodies such as the universities and the *Centre National de la Recherche Scientifique* (CNRS), to say nothing of the museums and the substantial French archaeological effort overseas funded by the Ministry for Foreign Affairs, has been a source of concern to archaeologists there for a number of years. These two factors have resulted in no fewer than five reports being produced over the past seventeen years, beginning with that by Jacques Soustelle in 1975, all aimed at improving the structure of French archaeology. However, little has been done to implement their recommendations and as a result the confusion and resentment remain. The situation was compounded early in 1992, when the *Conseil Supérieur de la Recherche Archéologique*, which was charged with co-ordinating archaeological effort, resigned *en bloc*. These periodic crises in French archaeology are regularly reported in the columns of the lively *Nouvelles de l'Archéologie*. The grossly under-resourced Archaeology Department of the Portuguese Cultural Heritage Institute (*Instituto Portugues do Património Cultural*) has a similar structure, as do those in Greece and The Netherlands, where the *Ephorate* and the *Rijksdienst voor het Oudheidkundig Bodemonderzoek* respectively operate through regional offices.

The Italian system takes this type of devolved structure a stage further. Heritage matters are primarily the responsibility of the *Ministerio per i Beni Culturali ed Ambientali*

(Ministry of Cultural and Environmental Property), but all field activities are channelled through the regional *Soprintendenze* (d'Agostino 1984), of which there are currently twenty-three. The *Soprintendenti* are responsible for all aspects of antiquities protection in their regions, with total administrative and financial autonomy. The field of operations is broad: monitoring of construction and highway projects, rescue and research excavations, field survey, inventory, restoration of monuments, and application of the *vincolo* (see above). Until recently, virtually all archaeological work was carried out either by *Soprintendenze* staff or by universities and museums, but now a considerable amount of work in fields such as rescue excavation and restoration is being handled by private organizations on contract.

Austria is constitutionally a federal state, so many functions are delegated to the nine *Länder*. Under the 1929 Constitution, however, the protection of monuments (*Denkmalschutz*) is a matter for federal concern alone and so heritage matters are covered by the 1923 federal law on the protection of monuments (*Bundesdenkmalschutzgesetz*), as amended in 1978. Basic decision-making rests with the Federal Monuments Office (*Bundesdenkmalamt*) based in Vienna. However, a number of the *Länder* have created provincial legislations and established strong provincial archaeological services to which matters of inventory and rescue excavation are delegated by the *Bundesdenkmalamt*, notably Steiermark and Salzburg.

Since the end of the Franco era Spain has increasingly moved in fact, if not in law, towards a federal state, with the delegation of substantial powers to the *Comunidades Autónomas*. The 1985 Law (García Fernández 1989) assigns primary responsibility for implementation to the central government. Archaeology and antiquities are the concern of the Institute for Conservation and Restoration of Cultural Property (*Instituto de Conservación y Restauración de Bienes Culturales*) of the Ministry of Culture. That body is, however, concerned more with overall supervision and policy-making; work on the ground is now largely the concern of the *Comunidades Autónomas*. Here, unfortunately, there is a wide variation in commitment and provision. Most of the individual provincial legislation is directed principally to the monitoring of excavations, to the exclusion of all else, and few have more than a handful of archaeologists in post. However, the situation is slowly improving, not least because of the influence of the heritage in emphasizing provincial cultural identity.

Other examples of centralized systems with a substantial measure of decentralization to provincial administrations are those in Japan (Tanaka 1984) and the People's Republic of China (Zhuang 1989).

The final group of countries covers those that have wholly federal constitutions. The principal example in Europe is Germany, where the Federal Constitution specifically reserves all cultural activities to the *Länder*: there is no federal antiquities legislation nor any federal antiquities service in the *Bundesrepublik*. The spectrum of provision at state level is almost as broad as that across the world, ranging from the excellent structure in Schleswig-Holstein inherited from earlier Danish administration to the minimalist approach in Hesse or the overcomplexity of the system in Lower Saxony (Reichstein 1984). While field survey, inventory, excavation, and monument protection all figure in the tasks assigned to *Land* archaeological services, the attention given to them differs greatly.

These comments relate essentially to the eight *Länder* and three independent towns that made up the former Federal German Republic. The German Democratic Republic, as might be expected, had a very different system before reunification. It was a centralized structure with positive and effective decentralization to five heritage management centres, which combined and integrated archaeological and historical monument conservation and protection, inventory, excavation, museums, and research very efficiently. This wholly admirable structure has now been dismantled and adapted to conform with the requirements of the federal constitution.

The USA, too, has a federal constitution which delegates certain activities to states. There is no central federal antiquities service as such, although the National Park Service of the Department of the Interior has a long and distinguished record in this field, and acts as lead agency for all archaeological projects in which federal agencies are involved. One of the most impressive developments in US archaeology over the past two decades has been the way in which federal agencies have acknowledged their responsibilities towards the archaeological heritage and have built up substantial professional archaeological divisions: especially noteworthy are the Department of Defense, the Bureau of Land Management, and the US Department of Agriculture's Forest Service, which employ several hundred full-time professionals among them.

Following the passage of the Archaeological and Historical Protection Act in 1974, which provided for up to 1% of the costs of federal projects to be made available for archaeological mitigation work (survey and excavation), the long-established contracting bodies, largely associated with universities and museums, were unable to cope with the sudden exponential increase in demands for their services. As a result many private archaeological contracting firms were set up. Few US archaeologists would deny that the outcome was a great deal of bad archaeology, inadequately reviewed and largely carried out mechanically to meet the statutory duties imposed upon federal agencies. Reports were produced to conform with statutory requirements in a handful of copies and then buried in agency archives, without being made available to the archaeological community at large. That deplorable situation has considerably improved over the past decade: there is better supervision and monitoring of projects by agency archaeologists and the surviving contract groups work according to infinitely higher standards than their predecessors in the 1970s. Here again, unfortunately, the market economy of the Reagan years has influenced federal procurement regulations so that there is an obligation on agencies to accept lowest tenders irrespective of the quality of research design or resources.

Outside federally owned lands, the level of heritage management varies enormously. The National Historic Preservation Act 1966 established a federal policy of co-operation with state and local governments to protect historic sites and values. Procedures were created for approved state and local government programmes, under the supervision of state historic preservation officers. During the Reagan and Bush administrations federal funding for this work dwindled, but most state administrations have maintained the programmes from their own resources to lesser or greater degrees.

In Australia, as in Germany, there is no federal antiquities legislation that is a state responsibility. The Australian Heritage Commission's primary responsibility is that of inventory, the compilation of the Register of the National Estate. The states all have their own monuments services, each responsible for implementing state legislation. Canadian federal legislation covers certain aspects of the protection of historic sites and Indian artefacts, but here again the main thrust is via the provinces, with their own legislations and antiquities services. The Alberta Heritage Act 1973 must be among the most comprehensive anywhere in the world and it is very effectively implemented by the provincial antiquities service.

It has been possible in this chapter only to highlight certain national structures in order to illustrate the range of possibilities in use across the world. Unfortunately the literature on this subject is relatively slight, with very few detailed accounts of individual systems. Those wishing to learn more about the systems in use in individual countries should consult the invaluable *Directory of Archaeological Heritage Management*, produced by the

International Committee on Archaeological Heritage Management (ICAHM) of the International Council on Monuments and Sites (ICOMOS), which lists the addresses of antiquities services in most of the countries of the world (ICOMOS 1990).

INTERNATIONAL CONVENTIONS AND ORGANIZATIONS

At the European level, heritage protection and management is considered to be a component of culture and so falls within the province of the Council of Europe. This organization is long on ideas and ideals but short on funds. Its main contribution in the field of heritage management has been the promulgation of conventions, of which the revised European Convention on the Protection of the Archaeological Heritage, signed in Malta in January 1992, is the most important.

Following Council of Europe custom, an international group of experts in heritage management and law was responsible for the drafting of this instrument, which was then submitted to Council members for comment. The final version lacks some of the sting of earlier drafts, though it is an infinite improvement over the 1954 Convention which it supersedes.

Like all international conventions it begins with a preamble in which the importance of archaeology for the study of the prehistory and history of mankind is underlined. It also emphasizes the many threats to the heritage that become apparent as development schemes and natural hazards increase. Perhaps the most important statement in the preamble is that the protection of the archaeological heritage 'should rest not only with the State directly concerned but with all European countries, the aim being to reduce the risk of deterioration and promote conservation by encouraging exchanges of experts and the comparison of experiences.'

The Convention defines the archaeological heritage as 'all remains and objects and any other traces of mankind from past epochs' that can illustrate the history of mankind and its relation to the natural environment. Of great importance is the new concept that such remains may be situated both on land and under water, which means that even shipwrecks are now acknowledged as forming part of the heritage.

Among the measures proposed for enhancing protection is the creation of legal instruments, listing protected areas and reserves. Another provision is that anyone who comes across an archaeological object is obliged to report the find. The States Parties must also ensure that only competent persons are permitted to carry out archaeological excavations and non-destructive techniques must be used as far as possible, rather than excavation.

One article deals with ways of integrating archaeology into physical planning procedures. Another addresses the question of who should pay for archaeological excavations resulting from changes in land use. The principle that 'the polluter pays' (i.e. whoever causes the destruction of an archaeological site should pay the excavation costs) was put forward in an earlier draft of the Convention, but it had to be modified for the final text, since it was too extreme and provocative for certain countries (among them the UK). The Convention in the event merely mentions the need for 'suitable measures to ensure that provision is made in major public or private development schemes for covering, from public sector or private sector resources, as appropriate, the total costs of any necessary related archaeological operations.'

All costs for practical field operations and publication are considered to form part of the excavation costs, but not subsequent scientific studies. The Convention refers cautiously to 'a publishable scientific summary record before the necessary comprehensive publication of specialised studies.' The obligation to disseminate information to colleagues and to the public at large is also laid upon archaeologists.

Trade in archaeological objects is not illegal or immoral as such, but illicit excavation is a growing activity. The Convention lays particular stress on museums and similar institutions under state control not acquiring elements of the archaeological heritage with illicit or questionable backgrounds; other institutions, whose acquisition policies are not under state control, should also be influenced to act in a similar way.

The Convention also aims to stimulate mutual technical and scientific co-operation between States Parties in the form of exchange of experiences and experts.

One of the main problems with the earlier Convention was that it made no provision for monitoring and continuous updating. It is hoped that this will be remedied by the creation of a standing committee with instructions to monitor the application of the Convention by States Parties, to report to the Committee of Ministers on the state of archaeological protection policies in those countries, and to make proposals for better implementation of its provisions.

The 1992 Malta Convention marks a significant step forward in archaeological heritage protection and management in Europe. Signature of a convention is only the first step, however: it does not have the force of law in individual countries until it is ratified by them. In the case of the 1954 Convention, for example, it was not until 1975 that it was ratified by the UK government. However, with the likely expansion of membership of the Council of Europe with the inclusion of the former Communist states of central Europe and some at least of the components of the former USSR, hopes for a more effective and better-integrated approach to the European archaeological heritage must be high.

The Council of Europe has no more than moral force. Financial clout resides with the twelve countries of the European Community (EC). Although the Treaty of Rome is broadly drafted enough to bring cultural matters, and especially heritage protection and management, within the purview of the EC, it has been reluctant to involve itself to any great extent with such matters in the past. There is a small cultural budget that has largely been applied to prestige projects such as the restoration of the Athens Acropolis. These funds are now being applied on a more systematic basis, a specific theme being chosen for each year (that for 1992 was the industrial heritage). However, the EC's potential role in heritage matters is much greater in other areas, albeit in a more oblique form. Directives such as those on Environmental Assessment and Environmentally Sensitive Areas (ESAs) provide opportunities for archaeological elements to be introduced, either in Brussels during the drafting procedure or when these are introduced, as they must be, into national legislation: the inclusion of archaeological factors in the definition of ESAs in the UK resulted from concerted action on the part of the natural and historical environmental lobbies. Other areas of EC activity that offer opportunities for better archaeological heritage protection are the regional policies, especially those relating to Least Favoured Areas, which in many cases coincide with areas of high archaeological potential, and those relating to tourism and urban planning.

At the international level UNESCO (United Nations Educational, Scientific, and Cultural Organization) is the UN lead agency for heritage matters. It has been responsible for a series of important recommendations and conventions since its foundation in 1947 (UNESCO 1985). These include:

Convention for the Protection of Cultural Property in the Event of Armed Conflict, 14 May 1954 (the Hague Convention)
Conventions on the Means of Prohibiting and Preventing the Illicit Import, Export and Transfer of Ownership of Cultural Property, 14 November 1970
Convention concerning the Protection of the World Cultural and Natural Heritage, 16 November 1972

Recommendation on International Principles Applicable to Archaeological Excavations, 5 December 1956

Recommendation concerning the Preservation of Cultural Property Endangered by Public or Private Works, 19 November 1968

Recommendation Concerning the International Exchange of Cultural Property, 26 November 1976

Recommendation for the Protection of Movable Cultural Property, 28 November 1978.

The 1954 Hague Convention has been demonstrated by the Gulf War and the civil war in Yugoslavia to be something of a dead letter. Steps are being taken at the present time to prepare a revised and much tougher version for eventual submission to the General Assembly of UNESCO. The 1956 Recommendations on archaeological excavations are also somewhat outdated, referring to a postwar period when a considerable measure of anarchy reigned in archaeology, especially in the countries of the Third World. It is planned to begin work on a drastic revision of these Recommendations in the foreseeable future.

It is the 1970 and 1972 Conventions, with their concomitant Recommendations, that are most relevant to the present-day situation. The problem of illicit trade in antiquities is one that still needs to be tackled in practical terms. It is no coincidence that the countries in which the main centres of the international trade in art and antiquities are located, such as Germany, The Netherlands, Switzerland, and the UK, have still failed to ratify the 1970 Convention. It is to be hoped that the Malta Convention will persuade them that the time has come to do so. The passage of the Single European Act by the members of the EC, with the consequent abolition of tariff and customs barriers between the twelve member states, has also resulted in intensive study being given to its implications so far as the illicit trade in cultural property is concerned.

The 1972 World Heritage Convention remains somewhat controversial among archaeologists: it is still seen by some as a 'beauty contest' between nations. Nonetheless, since it came into force in 1975, nearly 300 heritage monuments from over 100 States Parties have been included on the World Heritage List, to represent, as the preamble to the Convention describes it, 'this unique and irreplaceable property, to whatever people it may belong'.

There is a rigorous system of evaluation of nominations made by States Parties for inclusion on the List, involving three stages of assessment, first by ICOMOS as an independent non-governmental organization and then by the World Heritage Committee, elected by the States Parties. The primary criterion for inclusion is 'outstanding universal value' in one or more of six precisely defined categories. However, this must be supported by evidence of adequate conservation measures and management plans being in place. States Parties make regular contributions to the World Heritage Fund, which is used to provide technical assistance for work on World Heritage Monuments, principally in the Third World.

The secretariat for this work is provided by the recently created Centre for World Heritage of UNESCO, but the Convention is autonomous and not subject to decisions of the UNESCO General Assembly. There is, however, another area of UNESCO's work in heritage matters which is its direct responsibility. It has run a number of major international campaigns, largely financed by contributions from member states, over the past forty years: these include the massive campaign in Nubia in advance of the completion of the Aswan Dam, the restoration of temples at Borobodur (Indonesia) and in the Katmandhu Valley (Nepal), and the excavations at Carthage (Tunisia).

There is one final international document that should be known to all archaeologists, whether involved in heritage management or not. In 1985 ICOMOS created an International Committee on Archaeological Heritage Management (ICAHM), which identified three major initiatory tasks. It compiled a directory of heritage institutions (ICOMOS 1990), it held the first international conference on the subject in Sweden in 1988 (ICAHM 1989), and it drafted a Charter for the Protection and Management of the Archaeological Heritage, which was approved by the ICOMOS General Assembly in Lausanne in 1990 (ICAHM 1990). The Charter is the seminal doctrinal document for this sphere of professional activity.

Its nine articles cover the whole range of activities and issues with which heritage managers should be concerned. They lay down ethical and professional standards and goals in clearly defined fields: integrated protection policies; legislation and economy; survey; investigation; maintenance and conservation; presentation, information, and reconstruction; professional qualifications; and international co-operation. It is intended that the Lausanne Charter should, like the Venice Charter of 1964, which established standards for the conservation of historic buildings, become the gospel, code of practice, and Hippocratic Oath of all professional archaeologists and heritage managers.

CHAPTER 12

CURATION OVERVIEW

Jane Grenville

This chapter introduces a degree of critical comment into some of the issues raised in this part of the book and considers some longer-term implications. This might be most clearly approached by asking a series of questions:

Who identifies and controls the destiny of sites?
Who excavates them?
How should they be investigated/how are assessments made?
How is the money controlled?
What is the relationship of curation to research?

WHO IDENTIFIES AND CONTROLS THE DESTINY OF SITES?

Clearly (see Chapters 5 and 8 on the respective legislation for ancient monuments and listed buildings), the answer to this question depends to some extent upon whether the site is above or below ground, and upon the level of protection afforded to it. It is arguable that in all cases the powerful actor is the landowner, in whose hands lie the initiative for change or neglect. It is perhaps interesting to note, in this context, the varying effects of action or neglect upon upstanding and subsurface sites: lack of direct human intervention upon a subsurface site may be benign, but the effects of natural agents such as rabbits, bracken and water erosion cannot be minimized (see also Chapter 22). In a building, the failure to undertake routine interventionist maintenance is usually a major cause of decay, yet neglect may also prevent the worst excesses of 'modernization' and loss of original features. Active conservation measures to prevent natural and artificial acceleration of decay are therefore essential for both subsurface sites and buildings. Having said that, once the decision to seek change has been taken, the destiny of the site lies within the control of external agencies (although the wishes of the owner undoubtedly remain a material consideration to be balanced against other matters in the determination of the case).

Two-track legislation presents some difficulties in disentangling this situation: intervention on a Scheduled Ancient Monument requires Scheduled Monument Consent (SMC) and this is determined by appropriate agencies under the provisions of the Ancient Monuments and Archaeological Areas Act 1979 (AMAA Act, see Chapter 5). By contrast, intervention in a listed building, whether for purposes of repair or alteration, requires Listed Building Consent (LBC), which is granted by local planning authorities under the Planning (Listed Buildings and Conservation Areas) Act 1990. It is in advice, rather than legislation, that the two systems seem to be converging. A comprehensive guide to the provisions for listed buildings and conservation areas was issued by the Department of the Environment (DoE) in *Circular 8/87*. Notwithstanding the fact that this relates primarily to historic buildings, it contains, tucked away at Paragraph 52, the advice that 'Ancient monuments, and their settings, whether scheduled or not are *of course* a material consideration in the determination of planning applications' (my italics). The appearance of this advice was of the utmost importance. While it appeared simply to formalize best practice in the most efficient local authorities, it was by no means a matter of course, as implied, to regard archaeology as a material factor in the planning process, although by the mid-1980s most counties held Sites and Monuments Records (SMRs) and the checking of planning applications against this information to look for archaeological significance was becoming more common (see Chapter 10). With the formal blessing of the DoE for this practice, the possibilities for the protection of the archaeological resource seemed to be greatly enhanced.

The introduction of Planning Policy Guidance Note 16 (PPG 16, DoE 1990a; also Welsh Office 1991; SOEnd 1992a, 1992b) has shifted the balance yet further towards the inclusion of archaeology as a material factor in the planning process. PPG 16 advises that 'archaeological remains should be seen as a finite and non-renewable resource . . . Appropriate management is therefore essential to make sure that they survive in good condition.' (Paragraph 6). The baseline for this management is clearly set out in Paragraph 8: 'Where nationally important archaeological remains, *whether scheduled or not, and their settings*, are affected by proposed development there should be a presumption in favour of their physical preservation.' We will return to the matter of physical preservation for it has wider implications. The point to note here is that the archaeological resource is being flagged up, in a major document dedicated to that purpose, as a material factor within the planning system: 'developers and local authorities should take into archaeological considerations and deal with them from the beginning of the development control process' (Paragraph 18). The relevant personnel are clearly identified: 'All planning authorities should make full use of the expertise of County Archaeological Officers or their equivalents'. There is no obligation to consult English Heritage in the case of non-scheduled monuments although 'local planning authorities may find it helpful' to do so (Paragraph 23). By contrast, as discussed above, they are required to do so in the case of a proposal likely to affect the site of a Scheduled Ancient Monument (Paragraph 23).

Over the last few years then, without any legislative changes, there has been a significant shift in the perception and treatment of the archaeological resource. While the involvement of central government remains mandatory in the case of SMC, the broadening of the net to include non-scheduled sites has brought with it a devolution of powers to the local authorities, hence bringing archaeological planning practice in line with listed buildings.

There are, however, significant differences. Firstly, all 'archaeological' remains may be regarded as material factors, but nowhere does the definition of archaeology suggest that the resource might include listed buildings. PPG 16 might be stretched to include buildings, and indeed comments by English Heritage in its 1991 annual report suggest that it should. Nevertheless, it seems likely that a more traditional definition of archaeology as subsurface sites and ruins will prevail, at least in the near future. This leaves an anomaly between the buried/ruined resource and the historic building stock. Among the former, the historical and archaeological significance of all sites, whether scheduled or not, is a material factor. Among the latter, only those that are listed are singled out for such attention. Secondly, Paragraph 81 of *Circular 8/87* requires local authorities to consult five national bodies (The Council for British Archaeology, the Ancient Monuments Society, The Society for the Protection of Ancient Buildings, the Georgian Group, and the Victorian Society) in the case of application for LBC to demolish or partly demolish listed buildings. There is no parallel mandatory consultation system built in to PPG 16. Paragraph 23 suggests that county archaeologists 'may wish to consult locally based museums and archaeological units and societies', but there is no absolute requirement that they do so. In terms of the original question, 'Who controls the destiny of sites?', this seems to be a very significant difference in the treatment of the two parts of the resource.

It is not difficult to see the historical circumstances that give rise to such an anomaly: at the time that LBC became compulsory (Town and Country Planning Act 1968), there was little expertise within local authorities to assess the historical merits of individual buildings, whose selection for listing had been made not by the authority, but by the Inspectorate of Ancient Monuments and Historic Buildings (then a part of the DoE and now reconstituted as English Heritage). Consultation was introduced at the specific request of the planners. By contrast, at the time of the introduction of PPG 16 in November 1990, every county had an archaeological officer, and the SMRs were, to a large extent, locally generated. The soliciting of friendly advice from interested parties might therefore safely be left to the discretion of individual county archaeologists; whether or not the sometimes less benign policing function of statutory consultation might usefully be extended into the realms of PPG 16 is a matter for debate.

It is arguable that the academic archaeologist plays little part in this process (but see Chapter 2). Rather, it is his or her role as the developer of new research strategies that ought to be important, to the extent that current research interests might logically be expected to affect the perception of what is archaeologically important. Nor is this wishful thinking; the recently published *York Archaeology and Development Study* (hereafter referred to as the *York Study*) bases its definition of archaeological importance very firmly upon the results of a research exercise undertaken by the Department of Archaeology at the University of York, using data collected over twenty years by the York Archaeological Trust (Arup 1991).

Having said that, it appears that collaboration of this kind is the exception rather than the rule. As one who moved from academic research into the world of curation of listed buildings with very little understanding of how that world was structured, then back to mainstream archaeology, albeit in a consultative role at the Council for British Archaeology (CBA), and then finally back into a university, my overall impression is of a profession in which curation and research are largely decoupled, to the very great disadvantage of both. This is an issue that seems to require urgent action, and is one to which I shall return.

WHO EXCAVATES?

Excavation in the 1970s and 1980s was largely a matter of territoriality (see Chapter 14). Local units were set up to meet the challenge of rescue archaeology. Some were funded by local authorities, others supported by museums or university departments. Yet others formed as independent charitable trusts. Each confined its activities to its home town (e.g. York or Winchester), county (e.g. West Yorkshire), or region (e.g. Wessex). Some university units effectively became regional or county units (Birmingham covering the West Midlands, for instance, or the Institute of Archaeology Field Unit, which concentrated operations in Sussex). The only true 'roving' unit was the Historic Buildings and Monuments Commission's Central Excavation Unit, which acted in the capacity of a national flying squad. The 'territorial' norm, however, was sanctioned in the framing of the AMAA Act 1979, for when areas of archaeological importance were to be designated, a local unit was to be named as the investigating body, setting the brief and carrying it out.

The advent of large-scale developer funding at the end of the 1980s led to the adoption in some cases of competitive tendering systems. This is, perhaps, hardly surprising, given that it would not occur to a property developer to use a particular firm of architects or engineers simply because they happened to operate locally. Nevertheless, for a profession like archaeology, which has always regarded itself as fundamentally research-led, the change has proved to be somewhat traumatic. The debate continues over the relative importance of the need for firmly based local knowledge upon which to build an effective research programme versus technical/financial efficiency (Swain 1991). Suffice it to point out at this juncture that as more and more units take on contracts well away from their 'home' areas, there are implications for research that we would be unwise to ignore, and to which I will return.

It would, however, be misleading to suggest that all excavation is carried out under contract and funded by developers. Units, universities, and amateur societies are still able to undertake research excavations and surveys where funding is available. Such finance may emanate from English Heritage, university research funds, the learned societies and local or county-based amateur societies. Such ventures tend on the whole to be fairly small-scale: it seems doubtful that a private research project on the scale, for example, of Sutton Hoo, would be commissioned in the present recession.

Although concerned with survey rather than excavation, the work of the Royal Commissions should be mentioned at this point, as bodies undertaking major research programmes themselves, and funding and supervising those of others. In recent years, while not abandoning their principal role as bodies of record, the Commissions have altered their strategy by moving away from county-by-county inventories, and concentrating their efforts instead on thematic studies of threatened categories of monuments or landscapes (Chapter 3).

HOW SHOULD SITES BE INVESTIGATED?

With the squeeze on research funding and the strictures of PPG 16, increasingly intervention is restricted to small-scale evaluations. PPG 16 sets out a clear decision-making route along which planners, advised by archaeologists, should travel. A desk-based assessment of the site (trawl of the SMR, other relevant documentation and geophysical survey) precedes an evaluation, 'normally a rapid and inexpensive operation, involving ground survey and small-scale trial trenching' (DoE 1990a: Paragraph 21). Having established the importance of the archaeological deposits, and hence the weight that should be accorded to them in the planning process, various outcomes are possible:

The archaeology is considered to be of insufficient importance to affect the progress of the planning application.

Mitigation strategies are identified. These include moving the site of the proposed construction or re-designing foundations so as to minimize damage.

If this is not possible and the deposits are of sufficient importance, a large scale excavation precedes construction. This, of course, results in the removal of the deposits, and does not accord with the stated first aim of PPG 16, which is to preserve important archaeological deposits *in situ*. Nevertheless, information about those deposits is recovered. For this reason, the process of comprehensive excavation has been termed 'preservation by record', an expression that has lately come to be regarded with suspicion on the grounds that the phrase stretches the meaning of the word 'preservation' to unacceptable limits.

If the deposits are of such high quality that their retention *in situ* is merited, and there are no engineering solutions to the safe construction of the proposed development, then planning permission may be refused on archaeological grounds.

In the case of the first and last options, no further archaeological work will be undertaken on the site. The same outcome, then, results from diametrically opposed archaeological situations: sites of very high or very low research potential receive no further archaeological investigation. Some might perceive a paradox here, while others regard the preservation of the best sites as entirely logical, the conservation of the database being an essential responsibility. This is where the *York Study* and PPG 16 part company, since the former recommends the excavation of sites of high research potential and the preservation of all others whose potential, as currently perceived, is either low or unknown. The practical results of the research bias of the *York Study* are outlined below.

The second option, for the redesign of foundations, follows an archaeological evaluation that has shown the site to be of archaeological significance. A common engineering solution to such a condition is to build on a piling system, which offers minimal disturbance to the ground surface.

This system has been formalized in York as a result of the *York Study*. Within the AMAA Act 1979, archaeological significance is established by means of desk-based survey and field evaluations where necessary, and matched to perceived research priorities. The new York City Council policy states that 'developments which disturb or destroy more than 5 % of the archaeological deposits contained within the boundaries of an application site will normally be refused' (YCC 1992: Policy Statement A2). Where it is impossible to design a project to destroy less than 5 % of the archaeological deposits, two options exist:

a. planning permission is refused;
b. the redevelopment may be approved with a requirement for the developer to fund a rescue project and its publication and the deposition of the archive in an approved museum.

Significantly, however, where 'the evaluation indicates that the site has the potential to meet the criteria contained in the Research Framework' (a research agenda generated by the *York Study* and updated by a YCC-convened archaeological forum for the city), 'York City Council will advise the developers that they have the option of offering the site to the archaeological community so that it can attempt to raise the necessary funds to undertake a research excavation' (YCC 1992: Paragraph 8.13). No such opportunity has yet arisen. It will be interesting to see whether developers react favourably when it does.

Setting aside the example of York to return to the more widely implemented provisions of PPG 16, the third option, that of total excavation, is one that is likely to be avoided in future in urban situations, where alternative foundation systems provide a cheaper option for developers. However, in situations where the geology of the site is unsuitable for piling, or in rural cases, where the development may be for gravel or mineral extraction, total excavation remains the only option. Nevertheless, it should be remembered that, by definition, the sites with the greatest archaeological potential will remain uninvestigated, as planning permission for archaeologically destructive development is likely to be refused.

Where, then, might we expect to see the major research excavations of the late 1990s? Will there be any? With the operations of the units and private consultants so dictated by particular planning circumstances, it seems likely that the impetus must come from central government, from the universities or from the learned societies. Funding for such exercises will surely be difficult to secure during recession, yet the potential for research-led excavation, unhampered by the exigencies of development, is attractive.

Alongside this diminution of excavation must be set an increase in archaeological recording of standing buildings. There are both intellectual and practical reasons for this: the perception of historic buildings as archaeological artefacts has sharpened over the past decade, and the rate of attrition of the stock of historic buildings has accelerated. Archaeologists have, in response to this, increasingly turned their attention and technical

129

know-how to the study of standing fabric. The cynic might also point out that there are certain other advantages to pursuing this study: it is largely non-destructive, thus avoiding some of the ethical problems that have arisen in the excavation of the subsurface resource; and on the whole it is less labour-intensive and therefore less expensive to carry out than excavation.

HOW IS THE MONEY CONTROLLED?

Other chapters in this volume cover the problems of funding and they should be referred to for a broader discussion (e.g. Chapters 4 and 13). Nevertheless, it is important to allude to them here, for there are implications for the relationship of curation to research.

Developer funding seems, at the moment, to be the accepted form of financing the bulk of archaeological rescue work. As a result, the archaeological field profession has become locked into broader economic cycles more tightly than hitherto. As in the building trade, cyclical boom and bust have severe implications for the retention of a skilled workforce and the dispersal of such a workforce must surely carry implications for the quality of research.

Central funding comes in the form of grants from English Heritage. As the system of developer funding has gained ground, so central government expenditure on rescue archaeology has been systematically reduced over recent years. Against this reduction in the rescue budget, we might compare the increase in grant aid to buildings of outstanding importance (Section 3A grants), and the introduction of a budget ring-fenced for the recording of buildings in advance of such grant work.

Some financial support, particularly for survey work, comes from the Royal Commissions. Their own role as compilers of the database has already been discussed, but it is worth mentioning here that they also grant-aid other archaeological bodies in compiling surveys. Examples include the Chester Rows Research Project (jointly funded by English Heritage) and the East Cheshire Mills Survey. Such surveys enhance research; they also provide a valuable database upon which curatorial decisions may be based.

Funding by the research councils might be regarded as another source of central support for the profession. On the whole, however, grant aid from the Science-Based Archaeology Committee of SERC and from the British Academy tends to support individual projects at doctoral or post-doctoral level. It is the responsibility of the profession to ensure that such work has relevance for the wider research agenda. Mechanisms for the necessary flow of information implied by this exist within the specialist committees of the CBA, among whose stated aims is the active promotion of research. The problem was approached from another direction by the establishment in 1987 of the Forum for the Co-ordination in the Funding of Archaeology (Pollard 1990, 1: 4). Its aim was to be a co-ordinating body for archaeological research by improving the flow of communication between the various funding agencies. A further refinement to this structure might sensibly be to establish formal communication between the Forum and the research community (and the CBA and the Institute of Field Archaeologists (IFA) might be seen as the mouthpiece of the research and field communities, representing as they do archaeologists from all sections of the community: academic, curatorial, contracting and amateur).

THE RELATIONSHIP OF CURATION TO RESEARCH

The implications of the foregoing summary for the relationship of research to curation are formidable. Various trends have been identified:

    a. The introduction of preservation *in situ* as the preferred option for important archaeological resources;

b. The formalizing of archaeology as a material consideration within the planning system;

c. The move away from central funding towards developer funding;

d. The increase in archaeological attention paid to standing buildings.

Taking these in order, then, let us consider the significance of each for curation and research.

Preservation in situ

PPG 16 is unequivocal in its advice that 'where nationally important archaeological remains, whether scheduled or not, and their settings, are affected by proposed development there should be a presumption in favour of their *physical preservation*' (my italics). Called upon to define 'archaeological importance' to the wider world, the profession generally invokes two main criteria: degree of preservation of deposits and their suitability for answering present research questions. With this definition to hand (and it is broadly that used in the *York Study*) a potential clash between the aims of research and curation may be easily identified, for it is precisely those most interesting deposits that are withheld from research by PPG 16.

How has this state of affairs come about? There seem to me to be two chief reasons. Firstly, as research questions were refined and changed through the 1970s and 1980s, archaeologists came increasingly to regret the damage caused to the archaeological resource by, for instance, the single-minded pursuit of urban Roman levels at the expense of the medieval material above. The conclusion was drawn that, if previous generations had destroyed levels we would have wished to investigate, then the onus is upon the present generation not to destroy evidence our successors might wish to study. Rather than second-guessing future research interests, the important parts of the resource should simply be left intact.

Secondly, and again contingent upon the finite nature of the resource, is the argument that future generations will have such vastly improved techniques of data capture, that the more important sections of the record should be left for their investigation.

There are other issues, perhaps more politically sensitive, involved here as well. The failure of some researchers to publish their findings has meant that key sites have been destroyed without record as effectively as if the bulldozers had moved in. There is a justifiable feeling that the rate of excavation should slow down, until the backlog of publication is substantially reduced.

Further, where sites have been published, the quality of the publication has, in some cases, been regarded as inadequate (see also Chapter 19). Where this is contingent upon a poor archive, the situation is yet more dire, as the possibilities offered by returning to the material are severely curtailed (Chapter 21). A response to this problem has been the ever-increasing refinement of data-capture techniques and recording systems, and with them an ever-rising cost of projects. Excavation is now an extremely expensive operation and it is cheaper simply to leave the deposits in the ground undisturbed for future archaeologists.

The logic of all this is fairly clear and yet I would argue that the profession runs the risk of stagnation. If we do not follow up our present research interests, then how can the future research agenda develop? If we do not continue to address the problems of large-scale data capture and analysis, then how will improved techniques be developed? One might draw a parallel here with the issues facing the zoologists over vivisection: how far is it acceptable to maim your research base, the better to understand it? If we take the worn-out cliché of archaeology as the unrepeatable experiment, do we follow that to the conclusion that we should not do it at all?

These are broad questions that the archaeological community should and does address continually. My point in raising them here is simply to emphasize how our present curatorial stance subtly influences the way we answer them (and, of course, vice versa).

Archaeology in the planning process

The arrival of archaeological evaluation as a standard procedure within the planning cycle is undoubtedly welcome. It is to be hoped that fiascos such as the Rose Theatre incident will become things of the past, as the archaeological significance of a site is assessed before construction work begins.

That said, the system of 'rapid and inexpensive' evaluation recommended in PPG 16 could, if not carefully monitored, descend into a purely mechanistic exercise, in which the information gathered may be quickly compared with the existing archive in order to assess its significance, but which is of such an ephemeral nature that it is unlikely to enter the corpus of received knowledge itself. In other words, archaeological endeavour could be reduced to a form of stamp-collecting, in which ever greater mountains of information are excavated, but in which synthesis is scarcely attempted. Field archaeologists would become technicians and the study, as opposed to the practice, of archaeology would stagnate. Only if we take seriously the need for evaluation to state the research context and potential can we hope to avoid this state of affairs.

There seem to be two ways of addressing this problem. The first might be through the process of tendering for contracts. If, rather than tendering for carefully delimited briefs drawn up by the curatorial archaeologist (normally the county archaeologist), bids were always invited for full project design including research objectives, this concern would largely evaporate. English Heritage already demands detailed information on research design before offering funding for archaeological projects, whether rescue or survey; asking contractors to offer such designs rather than accepting the assumptions implicit in a simple specification would ensure that the field profession continued to maintain contact with the realms of pure research. The flip-side is that developers would find themselves facing larger bills, which they might not be prepared to foot.

Secondly, the volume of small-scale evaluations is unlikely to be reduced in the near future. In order to ensure that they do not become 'dead knowledge', funds must be set aside to pay for their exploitation for regional assessment and large-scale research design. This might be a fruitful area of co-operation between the universities and the field units.

Developer funding

Developer funding has been adopted in a political climate that favours the removal of responsibilities from state institutions into the hands of individuals and private companies. This philosophy suggests that, while the heritage itself may be regarded as a common asset, responsibility for damage to it must rest with the agency inflicting that damage. It is mirrored in the principle of 'polluter pays', widely accepted in environmental circles.

This approach is heavily dependent for its logic upon a universal acknowledgement of the value of the archaeological resource. While research may in the past have been hampered by lack of public funding, it is the lack of private and commercial sponsorship that now needs to be addressed and undoubtedly that involves a battle for hearts and minds. Dissemination of results to a broad public is no longer simply a reasonable duty for an archaeologist in receipt of public funds. It has become an absolute economic necessity for a subject increasingly dependent upon a credible image for its survival. While the 'heritage industry' is regarded with healthy suspicion in many quarters of the profession, archaeologists must accept that the accurate and entertaining dissemination of knowledge at a popular level is essential for the health of the subject.

From a rather different angle, the combination of developer funding and the materiality of archaeology in the planning cycle has very direct effects upon research, one of which I have alluded to above. It is an important point, however, which bears repetition: the sample of sites investigated is skewed towards those upon which major development is being undertaken. The preponderance of excavation is therefore urban or on rural gravel terraces and takes place in areas of relative 20th-century prosperity. Furthermore, non-profit-making organizations or individuals may carry out operations that are highly damaging to the archaeological resource, and may reasonably argue that they are unable to foot the archaeological bill. Without a solution to this problem, a good deal of church archaeology, for example, may be lost as a result of the withdrawal of public funding. Finally, but crucially, on the matter of the skewing of the research agenda by modern circumstances, it should not be forgotten that agricultural and forestry operations are not subject to planning controls: the deep-ploughing of unscheduled sites without archaeological mitigation is currently legitimate.

The archaeology of buildings

It might be argued that it is the pressures associated with the study and curation of the sub-surface resource that have led to the renewal of interest in the archaeology of standing buildings. Churches have always been regarded as legitimate research fodder for archaeologists as much as architectural historians, as the work of H.M. and Joan Taylor (amateurs by definition, if not in approach) on Anglo-Saxon architecture demonstrates. Nevertheless, it cannot be denied that academic interest in buildings archaeology, secular as well as religious, is increasing, and that in the field recording projects are multiplying.

There are considerable implications for both research and curation here. Taking research first, it seems that a research agenda that is explicitly archaeological needs to be formulated. This has been an area of concern for the CBA since its foundation in 1944, and one upon which it has turned particular attention since the creation of a post dedicated to historic buildings work in 1988. The recent formation by the IFA of a Special Interest Group for Standing Buildings is an encouraging sign, as is the introduction of specialist courses into some undergraduate and post-graduate degree courses.

In curatorial terms there are difficulties inherent in the two-track legislation. Listed buildings have long been the responsibility of conservation officers or non-specialist planning officers within local authorities. They may not be within the same department as the county archaeologist and they operate within different legal frameworks. There are significant differences in the advice given in PPG 16 and *Circular 8/87* on the place of archaeological recording; the *Circular* advises that LBC may be made conditional on archaeological recording, but the model condition attached as Appendix VII stresses that the expense of the record must not be passed on to the applicant, a direct reversal of the advice of PPG 16. The current rewriting of the *Circular* as a new *Planning Policy Guidance Note* should be seen by the archaeological community at large as a crucial opportunity to set the recording of buildings on a level with that of the buried resource.

These are some of the issues raised for research by the present regime of curation in this country. Principal among them is the fact that, as archaeology takes its place within the planning system, academia and the field profession cannot afford to operate in mutual isolation: such a course would without doubt lead to the terminal stagnation of the discipline.

LEGISLATION IN NORTHERN IRELAND

Ann Hamlin

Apart from the Ancient Monuments Protection Act 1882, Ireland has had a quite different history of legislation from Britain. Official care of monuments in Ireland goes back to the disestablishment of the Church of Ireland and the Irish Church Act in 1869. This made provision for the future upkeep of certain important ecclesiastical sites: 137 ruined churches and crosses were vested in the Commissioners of Public Works to be maintained as 'national monuments', 17 of these being in what is now Northern Ireland.

This Irish precedent was quoted in the debates on what eventually became Sir John Lubbock's Ancient Monuments Protection Act in 1882. This legislation applied to Britain and Ireland, and there were eighteen Irish sites in its schedule (three in the north). The Ancient Monuments Protection (Ireland) Act 1892 increased the scope for protection beyond the sites in the 1882 schedule, and under the Irish Lands Acts of 1903 and 1923 the Land Commission was given the power to vest important monuments in the Commissioners of Public Works.

After the partition of Ireland, the twenty-two sites in the six northern counties passed from the Commissioners to the Ministry of Finance for Northern Ireland, and in 1926 the Ancient Monuments Act (Northern Ireland) was passed, giving the state a greatly increased responsibility for the care of monuments. This act provided for State Care through acquisition and guardianship, protection through scheduling and preservation orders, the setting up of an Ancient Monuments Advisory Committee, and the reporting of all archaeological finds to that committee. A supplementary Ancient Monuments Act (Northern Ireland) 1937 introduced a provision from the 1930 Ancient Monuments Act of the Republic of Ireland: the restriction of excavation for archaeological purposes except under licence issued by the 'Ministry' (now the Department of the Environment for Northern Ireland). The Republic's 1930 Act had introduced the reporting of finds, and in these two areas – finds reporting and licensing excavations – Irish legislation, north and south, still differs from the law in Britain.

The next landmark was the Historic Monuments Act (Northern Ireland) 1971, legislation still in force. This is a fairly short piece of legislation, in the tradition of the 1926 and 1937 acts, but it increased the effectiveness of protection through scheduling, provided for the registering of scheduling in the Statutory Charges Register, introduced powers of compulsory acquisition of monuments, and provided for the appointment of an advisory Historic Monuments Council.

The 1971 legislation has served Northern Ireland well for more than twenty years, but it lacks some of the powers of the 1979 GB Ancient Monuments and Archaeological Areas Act, and new Northern Ireland legislation is now in preparation, for planned completion in 1994. Under the prevailing system of governing Northern Ireland this will be an Order in Council rather than an Act. The draft order proposes Scheduled Monument Consent and restrictions on the possession and use of metal detectors, and strengthening of the Department's powers to provide facilities at State Care sites, as well as a number of other changes.

Although the 1971 Act deals with the reporting of finds, and the proposed new order will also include a section on archaeological finds, these have no bearing on the ancient 'law' of Treasure Trove. DoE (NI) is responsible for administering Treasure Trove in Northern Ireland on behalf of HM Treasury.

The work of protecting archaeological sites and monuments benefits from several other pieces of Northern Ireland legislation. The Nature Conservation and Amenity Lands (Northern Ireland) Order 1985 empowers DoE (NI) to designate Areas of Outstanding Natural Beauty (AONBs) and to make proposals for positive conservation. Four areas have so far been designated under the 1985 Act, and the man-made elements of the landscape – monuments and buildings – are embraced within the AONB management concerns. Also within DoE (NI), under the Planning (Northern Ireland) Order 1991, the Town and Country Planning Service prepares area plans which, when formally adopted, become the statutory planning framework. Measures for the protection of historic sites and monuments within this framework have been developed over many years. The Armagh Area Plan, which is in its consultation stage (December 1992), has identified an Area of Significant Archaeological Interest to embrace the Navan complex, large enough to protect the monuments and their landscape setting. The Plan proposes particular policies to protect the sites and the landscape and also to promote positive management and enhancement. Article 19 of EC Council Regulations 797/85 and 1760/87 provides for financial support for farmers who agree to certain conservation measures. These regulations were implemented in Northern Ireland by Article 3 of the Environmentally Sensitive Areas (Northern Ireland) Order 1987. This empowers the Department of Agriculture to designate ESAs. Good management of historic monuments by participating farmers is a compulsory element in the new phase of ESAs launched in autumn 1992, covering 11 % of the farmland of Northern Ireland.

The protection of historic buildings came late to Northern Ireland, and was preceded by much vocal lobbying by conservation bodies, especially the Ulster Architectural Heritage Society, founded in 1967. The Planning (Northern Ireland) Order 1972 provided for the listing of buildings of special architectural or historic interest, for grant-aid for conserving listed buildings, and for the designation of conservation area. The Historic Buildings Council was appointed in 1973 and the first conservation areas was designated in 1975. Grant-aid to listed churches was made possible by the Historic Churches (Northern Ireland) Order 1985. Powers of protection for listed buildings were increased in 1990 with the Planning and Building Regulations (Amendment) (Northern Ireland) Order. This provided for urgent repairs to endangered buildings and the serving of repair notices on owners of neglected properties. The historic buildings work is now carried out under the Planning (Northern Ireland) Order 1991, a largely consolidatory measure that embraces the work on churches. The Planning Order also provides for an opportunity to record listed buildings when listed building consent (to alter or demolish) has been granted.

Part Three: PRACTICE

CHAPTER 13

ENGLISH HERITAGE FUNDING POLICIES AND THEIR IMPACT ON RESEARCH STRATEGY

Roger Thomas

INTRODUCTION AND BACKGROUND

Introduction

Throughout the UK, the postwar decades, and the years since about 1980 in particular, have seen both a remarkable level of fieldwork and the transformation of a wide range of organizational structures, policy frameworks and areas of technical and intellectual expertise concerned with the management of the nation's archaeological heritage. Many of these topics are described in more detail elsewhere (including Chapters 1, 4, 14). These developments, taken together, have provided a firm basis for the continuing development of archaeological resource management in the UK: they have to a large extent been made possible by sustained funding and support from the various central government agencies concerned with archaeology. This chapter considers the archaeological policies of English Heritage (EH), the agency responsible for England, and its predecessor bodies in central government. It will discuss the development of these policies and the ways in which they have been implemented, examine the range of activities towards which funding and support has been directed, briefly review achievements to date and consider the prospects for policy development in the 1990s.

English Heritage (statutorily known as the Historic Buildings and Monuments Commission for England: HBMC) came into being on 1 April 1984 (Chapter 5). The statutory duties of HBMC as laid down in the National Heritage Act 1983 (NH Act) include the duty ('so far as practicable') to 'secure the preservation of ancient monuments . . . situated in England' and to 'promote the public's enjoyment of, and advance their knowledge of ancient monuments . . . situated in England and their preservation'. 'Ancient monument' in this context has a similar, although not identical, definition to that contained in the Ancient Monuments and Archaeological Areas Act 1979 (AMAA Act; Chapter 5) and is sufficiently broadly defined to encompass most kinds of remains of archaeological interest.

The NH Act confers a range of specific functions on the Commission; it also amended the AMAA Act so as to transfer certain powers contained in that legislation to the Commission, including the power to undertake archaeological investigations and to publish the results. Ancient monuments and archaeological work therefore forms an important component of EH's activities. However, EH has a wide range of other responsibilities so that archaeological concerns are only part of the overall spectrum of its work (detailed in EH's *Annual Reports* from 1985 onwards).

English Heritage is a large organization, with a staff of some 1,600 and a budget of slightly over £100 million in 1991/92. The bulk of its income is an annual grant from central government, with which the organization, while independent, has close links. In

1992 responsibility for EH, which had lain with the Heritage Division of the Department of the Environment (DoE), was transferred to the newly created Department of National Heritage (DNH). As the department of state responsible for heritage matters, DNH has an interest in broad questions of archaeological policy and funding; it is also responsible for the administration of some aspects of ancient monuments legislation, which it does with professional advice from EH (Chapter 5).

Until the mid-1980s, central government responsibility for archaeology in England lay with the Directorate of Ancient Monuments and Historic Buildings (DAMHB) within DoE. In effect, EH was created by transferring the staff and organization of this body and giving them independent status. Responsibility for ancient monuments and archaeology had earlier lain with the Ministry of Public Buildings and Works, and its predecessors the Ministry of Works and the Office of Works, before the creation of DoE in 1969. The strand of continuity through these departmental changes has been the Inspectorate of Ancient Monuments. The Inspectorate originated in 1882; it is this body that has been the engine of the development of the funding and other archaeological policies of EH and its predecessors.

Background: funding policies before 1980

Government financial support for archaeology really began during the Second World War, with resources being provided for the rescue excavation of sites threatened by wartime activities (e.g. Grimes 1960). Support continued through the 1950s and 1960s. During this period, rescue excavations were generally carried out either directly by the ministry itself or under the auspices of local excavation committees. Ministry excavations were undertaken either by inspectors or by fee-paid supervisors – sometimes academics or museum staff, sometimes itinerant excavators (Rahtz 1974a: 59) – aided by volunteers or paid labourers. Fee-paid supervisors were normally engaged solely for the duration of an excavation; support for subsequent post-excavation work and publication was not always adequate. In a number of places, notably in historic cities, local initiatives led to the formation of excavation committees in response to development threats: examples include the Roman and Medieval London Excavation Committee (Grimes 1968), the Winchester Research Unit (Biddle 1974) and the Canterbury Excavation Committee. Funding for the activities of such bodies came from the ministry, from local authorities and from a range of other sources. Again, infrastructure and resources were rarely adequate for the tasks in hand. Elsewhere, archaeological responses to development threats at this period were made, on a more or less ad hoc basis, by museum archaeologists or by local amateurs.

In the late 1960s and early 1970s, there was a considerable upsurge of public and professional concern about the loss of archaeological sites through development of all kinds. The level of government funding began to increase (largely as a result of pressure from the newly formed organization RESCUE, see Barker 1974). Many more local excavation support organizations and trusts were established, some in particular towns or cities, some in rural areas and some in response to specific threats (notably motorway construction). These bodies derived the bulk of their funding from DoE grants, enabling them to employ professional archaeological officers and to mount excavations. However, not all areas enjoyed such cover. During this period, too, the scale of DoE's direct archaeological programme increased as well, including the major campaigns of excavations by Wainwright on prehistoric monuments in the south and by Stead on Iron Age and Roman sites in Yorkshire.

The organizational and funding arrangements for archaeology in England before 1973 were embryonic, small-scale (especially early in the period in question) and, by today's standards, ad hoc. However, much important work was done; many sites were excavated which would otherwise have been lost without record. The greatest problems arose in the area of post-excavation and publication work, and it was not until the 1980s and 1990s that many of the excavations carried out at this time were published.

From 1973, DoE planned to establish a network of regional archaeological units that were intended to provide comprehensive archaeological coverage across the country (Chapters 4 and 14). Their organization was variable: some were independent trusts; others were based on local authorities; and others on museums or, in some cases, universities. Eventually some eighty such organizations were receiving annual DoE grants towards their running costs. The hope that local authorities would assume more responsibility for these costs in due course and the underlying intention of creating a comprehensive archaeological service were not fully realized.

POLICY DEVELOPMENTS 1980–90

The move to project funding

In 1980, DoE announced its intention to end annual grants to organizations and to move to a system in which funds were made available for specific projects of agreed scope, duration and cost. This move from core funding (for establishment costs) to project funding marked a major change in government policies in support of archaeological activity: the move was also, for obvious reasons, widely unpopular. There were two reasons behind it.

The first was that all public expenditure generally requires specific statutory authority. Before 1979, however, there was no explicit statutory basis for central government spending on field archaeology; support was, administratively, more or less ad hoc. The passage of the AMAA 1979 Act changed this; its Section 45 (as amended by the NH Act 1983) provided that EH:

(1) . . . may undertake, or assist in, or defray or contribute towards the cost of, an archaeological investigation of any land in England which they consider may contain an ancient monument or anything else of archaeological or historical interest . . .

(3) . . . may publish the results of any archaeological investigation undertaken, assisted, or wholly or partly financed by them under this section . . .

This section, which gives the same powers to local authorities, furnished, for the first time, a clear statutory basis previously lacking for government support for archaeology. The manifest intent of this section is to provide for the funding of specific projects but not for general subsidies to organizations.

The second reason to adopt project funding was professional and operational. By 1980, approximately 85 % of the archaeology budget was taken up with recurrent establishment costs to the aforementioned eighty organizations; a form of stagnation had arisen that was reflected in the ever-increasing backlog of unpublished excavations and the concomitant lack of uncommitted funds assignable to new projects. Project funding would ensure a regular release of funds that would give new ideas, projects and organizations a chance (English Heritage n.d.).

Behind the legal and policy reasons for this change is a sound academic rationale. It has long been recognized that rescue archaeology must be 'a research activity with an academic basis, the aim of which is to add to the sum of human knowledge' (Wainwright 1978: 11). The move to project funding made it possible for DoE to stipulate that, before a proposed project would be considered for funding, the project director had to provide a written statement (or research design) setting out its aims and justifying its importance in its regional and national academic contexts. This stipulation was designed to improve the quality and direction of the research problems that were to be addressed through archaeological work by ensuring that each project was planned within the framework of a well-designed problem-oriented research strategy. A formal research design has been required for each grant-aided project since 1980.

The context of policy development 1980–90

The project funding system provided a framework within which particular policy objectives could be pursued, to ensure the best use of archaeological resources based on correctly identified strategic priorities. The policies that have been followed, the criteria employed in the allocation of DoE and EH archaeological funding, and the patterns of funding and activity during the 1980s, will be examined. As background, this section considers the range of influences that have affected the development of archaeological policies since 1980.

The archaeological policies of EH and its predecessors did not develop in isolation, but reflect, *inter alia*, wider trends in public policy, the views of advisory bodies and the outcome of consultation and discussion with external archaeological interests. These various influences may be briefly examined.

(i) The 1980s saw a continuing emphasis on the need for careful control over, and accountability for, public expenditure and on the need to ensure 'value for money'. Trends in environmental policy, notably the 'polluter pays' principle, have also been of importance. Wider policy trends relating to public expenditure have manifestly had an impact on the development of archaeological funding policies.

(ii) Before 1984, DAMHB was an arm of central government; its policies had to evolve within the overall framework of government policy as determined by ministers. Contrastingly, policy and strategic direction at EH is its commissioners' responsibility; archaeological policies are developed within the context of EH's overall remit for the historic environment.

(iii) Two statutory advisory bodies composed of eminent individuals from the archaeological world successively played an important role in determining and reviewing archaeological policy, including funding policy. Before 1984, the Ancient Monuments Board (AMB) was responsible for advising on the archaeological work of central government. In the 1970s a National Committee on Rescue Archaeology was established as an AMB sub-committee, to advise on the issues arising out of the rescue archaeology programme: for instance, a working party of the Committee produced the Frere Report (DoE 1975a) on publication problems (Chapter 19). Area Archaeological Advisory Committees, established in the 1970s, were disbanded in 1979. On the creation of EH, the AMB was replaced by the Ancient Monuments Advisory Committee, a statutory advisory body that provides independent expert advice to the commissioners of EH on ancient monuments and archaeological matters.

(iv) EH, and DoE previously, has regularly consulted the national archaeological societies and special interest groups about policy matters and individual cases. These groups have also produced statements of academic priorities (e.g. Prehistoric Society 1988) that have helped to inform decisions about resource allocations. Since the inception of project funding, an annual report including expenditure information has been published, enabling the profession to keep in touch with policies and to comment on them.

(v) Consultation, both formal and informal, between different sections of the profession is an important mechanism by which policy is developed. EH liaises regularly with Cadw and Historic Scotland, with the Royal Commissions and with a range of bodies such as the Council for British Archaeology, the Association of County Archaeological Officers (ACAO), the Standing Conference of Archaeological Unit Managers and the Institute of Field Archaeologists.

(vi) Discussions between EH's professional staff and those of archaeological organizations (especially grant recipients and local authority archaeological officers) working 'on the ground' are important for exchanging views on policy and for reviewing the implications and results of particular approaches.

The archaeological funding policies of EH and its predecessors have therefore evolved within a wider policy context and have been developed in consultation with others. The resulting policies therefore reflect a variety of imperatives, views and opinions.

Archaeological policy statements 1980–89

At a time of rapid change in archaeology in the UK, policy has been kept under fairly close review, and has also been implemented reasonably flexibly in response to changing circumstances. A number of clear statements of policy were published during the 1980s and these have provided the framework within which the patterns of funding for particular activities and projects have developed. These set out the purposes towards which available resources would be directed and the criteria by which decisions about allocations would be made.

In considering this framework, it is important to stress at the outset that, ever since the passing of the first Ancient Monuments Act in 1882 the primary objective of government in this domain has been to secure the preservation of important monuments and archaeological remains. Government involvement in archaeological rescue excavation arose because, where it was not possible to preserve monuments and remains physically, the appropriate response was to excavate and record that which could not be preserved – the policy of 'preservation by record' is a well-used (and sometimes criticized) phrase. Archaeological excavation has been a last-resort substitute for preservation *in situ*, rather than being a primary objective of policy. This fundamental point is one that it was possible to lose sight of in the rapid expansion of rescue archaeology in the 1970s and 1980s.

A second key point is that government concern has always focused on monuments and remains of 'national importance'. This is the criterion that monuments must meet if they are to be scheduled under the ancient monuments legislation; archaeological projects must also fulfil it if they are to receive funding from EH.

The first such policy statement was the announcement of the change to project funding. DoE stated concurrently that its archaeological funding during the 1980s would be based on a strategy encompassing a set of priorities established by the national period and topic societies in conjunction with the AMB. These priorities were:

a) Sites and Monuments Records (SMRs): the compilation of records of identifiable sites was recognized to form an essential database for preservation, management and excavation policies. Increased resources were to be directed towards SMRs in order to facilitate the identification of a representative sample of the features that make up the historic environment.

b) Monument selection procedures: it was proposed that the selection of monuments for scheduling should be within the framework of a sampling policy to ensure the preservation of a representative sample of each class of monument.

c) Environmental evidence: more resources should be directed towards projects with potential for recovering environmental information, particularly in wetlands and water-logged sites.

d) Landscape archaeology: the investigation of areas of historic landscape should receive increased emphasis.

Stress was again laid on the importance of formulating proper research designs for rescue archaeology projects (English Heritage 1991a: 4–5).

In 1983, the Secretary of State published non-statutory criteria (Chapter 5) governing the selection of monuments of national importance for scheduling. The same criteria, with the accompanying explanatory texts slightly modified, are used to determine whether proposed archaeological projects are of national importance and therefore eligible for funding (for further discussion see Chapter 17). They are as follows:

a) Survival/condition. The survival of archaeological potential is a crucial consideration.

b) Period. It is important to consider the record for the types of monuments that characterize a category or period.

c) Rarity. There are monument categories that are so rare that any destruction must be preceded by a record.

d) Fragility/vulnerability. Important archaeological evidence may be destroyed in some cases by a single ploughing episode or similar unsympathetic treatment and must be preceded by a record.

e) Documentation. The significance of a project may be given greater weight by the existence of contemporary records.

f) Group value. The value of the investigation of a single monument may be greatly enhanced by association with a group of related contemporary monuments or with monuments of other periods. Dependent on the nature of the threat, in some cases it may be preferable to investigate the whole rather than isolated monuments within the group.

g) Potential. On occasion the importance of the remains cannot be precisely specified, but it is possible to document reasons for anticipating a monument's probable existence and so justify the investigation.

In 1986, EH published *Rescue Archaeology Funding: A Policy Statement* (English Heritage 1986). This set out the background to EH's policies, the principles on which funding decisions would be based (including the criteria just described), consultation arrangements and the categories and mechanisms of funding. The document also included the following statement (English Heritage 1986: 7):

4.4 It is important to emphasise that English Heritage allocates the funds at its disposal for recording those archaeological sites which cannot be preserved and whose destruction is taking place beyond the control of agencies with the powers and resources to deal with the problem. The Commission welcomes participation by developers and other bodies in the funding of rescue programmes for its resources are inadequate to carry that burden alone. In particular local planning authorities have a clear role to play in ensuring that the archaeological implications of planning decisions are properly assessed; and, that where destruction of important archaeological sites is unavoidable, due provision for essential archaeological recording is agreed and made before permission for a particular development scheme is given.

This important statement presaged the basic principles of DoE's Planning Policy Guidance Note 16 on *Archaeology and Planning* (DoE 1990a) (see below).

EH produced *The Management of Archaeology Projects* in 1989 (English Heritage 1989). This document emphasized the need for sound management of archaeological projects and was felt to be necessary because of the growing complexity, scale and duration of projects (especially urban post-excavation ones) supported by EH. The document, which reflected the broader requirements of control, accountability and value for money in public expenditure, was the forerunner of a much fuller second edition entitled *Management of Archaeological Projects* (English Heritage 1991b). Further important policy statements, published in 1990 and 1991, are considered below.

POLICIES IN PRACTICE 1980–90

The archaeological activities of EH

The foregoing discussion of EH's archaeological policies in the 1980s provides the background for a consideration of the pattern of activities and funding in practice. Archaeological considerations are central to EH's work in preserving and presenting ancient monuments and historic buildings. The investigation of sites and buildings (whether by survey, excavation, or the archaeological analysis of standing structures), the recording and interpretation of such work, and the publication of the results, account for a significant part of EH's budget. Table 13.1 provides a summary of the allocation of financial resources by EH to archaeological activities during 1990/91.

Rescue grants	£5,550,837
Ancient Monuments Laboratory contracts	678,278
Properties in Care: archaeological recording	973,848
Monuments Protection Programme	440,713
Publications	241,341
Storage grants	51,566
Backlog report grants	100,209
Consultants and fees	341,432
Oxford Training Course	27,540
Central Excavation Unit	132,036
Ancient Monuments and Historic Buildings recording	165,296
Total	£8,703,116

Table 13.1. Summary of the allocation of financial resources to archaeological activities by English Heritage in 1990/91. (Source: Wainwright 1991: 4.)

The categories used in Table 13.1 may be explained in slightly more detail:

Rescue grants are grants to archaeological projects carried out by external organizations. This budget includes an annual transfer of funds (£500,000 in 1990/91) from the Department of Transport for archaeological work on road schemes: in practice expenditure on such work has consistently exceeded the sum transferred.

Ancient Monuments Laboratory contracts are contracts, mostly with universities, under which archaeological scientists (mainly environmentalists and conservators) are employed to provide expertise in archaeological science to archaeological projects grant-aided by EH, and to provide specialist advice to archaeological organizations in their areas. These contracts are a substantial additional input of resources to projects.

Properties in Care: archaeological recording. This is work to record the fabric of standing monuments in the care of EH, as part of programmes of consolidation and repair of those monuments.

Monuments Protection Programme. This programme of scheduling enhancement is described in more detail in Chapter 17.

Publications. Grants are made for the publication of reports on archaeological projects that have been supported.

Storage grants are made to approved museums for the permanent storage and curation of the archives of grant-aided projects.

Backlog report grants. The 1980s saw a major programme of work to publish the results of a backlog of excavations undertaken before 1973. This programme has now been largely completed.

Consultants and fees. Consultancy fees are incurred through the use of consultants for specific projects and pieces of work.

Oxford Training Course. Support is provided for an in-service training scheme for archaeologists at the University of Oxford's Department of External Studies.

Central Excavation Unit. This is EH's 'in-house' archaeological field unit. The unit carries out selected fieldwork projects and other activities. Now renamed the Central Archaeological Service to reflect a changed role within EH, it is a central source of advice and expertise on the execution of archaeological projects.

Ancient Monuments and Historic Building recording. Resources are made available for recording work necessitated by programmes of repair to monuments and buildings where those programmes are grant-aided by EH.

Funding for archaeological projects 1980–90

Grants to external organizations for archaeological work have formed the largest part of EH's support for archaeology since 1980. The level and pattern of this expenditure has had a significant impact on the development of archaeology and the archaeological profession in the country as a whole.

The total archaeological grants made by DoE and EH have increased fairly steadily over the years. Between 1972 and 1980 the rate of growth was remarkable – from less than £500,000 in 1972–73 to about £3.5 million in 1980–81. By 1989–90 the figure was just over £7 million. (See Chapter 14, Figure 14.1.) The rise in available resources has underlain many of the most important developments of the past two decades.

The rescue archaeology programme of the 1980s was largely demand-led and, the increase in funding notwithstanding, demand for funds invariably outstripped availability. Selectivity therefore had to be exercised (in accordance with the criteria discussed above). Many projects had to be funded from a variety of sources, with contributions being obtained from developers, local authorities and elsewhere to complement funding from EH.

In terms of purposes and objectives, it is possible to divide EH's archaeological grants into four categories:

a) SMRs: support for the establishment or enhancement of comprehensive and retrievable databases.

b) Surveys: grants for extensive strategic surveys (including aerial photographic ones) to identify and record the archaeological resource in particular areas as an aid to management strategies. Such surveys have generally been carried out in close conjunction with SMRs.

c) Excavations: grants for the excavation and recording of archaeological remains threatened with destruction and not open to preservation *in situ*.

d) Post-excavation: grants for preparing the results of excavations for publication. Unless the results of an excavation are published, there is no general public gain in knowledge or understanding to justify the expenditure of resources on the excavation.

Categories (c) and (d) can really be considered together: Ancient Monuments Laboratory contracts for archaeological science and grants for publication and for museum storage also relate principally to excavation/post-excavation projects.

The apportionment of funding between the various categories in the period 1982–90 is depicted in Figure 13.1. The pattern is a striking one. Excavation (X), and post-excavation (PX) work in particular, has absorbed by far the largest share of resources and in percentage terms the expenditure on SMRs, surveys (S) and aerial photography (AP) has been small (responsibility for the last-mentioned was transferred to RCHME in 1986: Chapter 18). The costs of post-excavation work have been particularly heavy and, within this category, urban post-excavation projects have accounted for between 35 % and 60 % of total annual project funding (Fig. 13.2). The importance of careful control of post-excavation projects is obvious. Urban projects of course arise almost entirely from developments under planning control, and the significance of the archaeological planning policies now enshrined in PPG 16 (DoE 1990a) for future funding is clear.

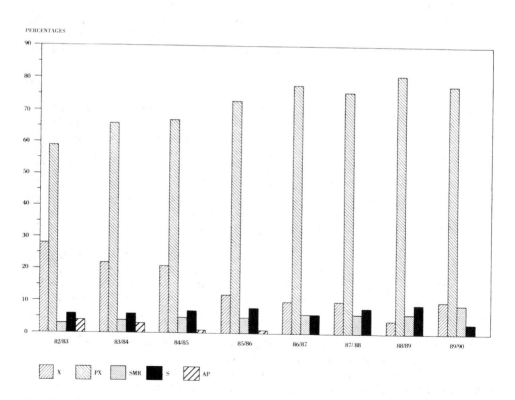

Figure 13.1. Categories of projects funded 1982–90 as a percentage of costs (English Heritage 1991a, fig. 2).

PERCENTAGES

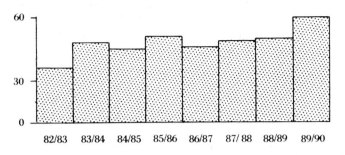

Figure 13.2. Urban post-excavation funding expressed as a percentage of annual project grants (after English Heritage 1991a, fig. 6).

The products of funding

The results of EH's archaeological funding in the 1980s have been substantial. The archaeological infrastructure – in terms of staff and the information base – has been strengthened, especially through support for SMR and survey projects. A very wide range of important monuments and remains of all periods and types has been excavated and recorded in advance of destruction, and analysis and publication of the results has greatly increased our knowledge and understanding of the past and of the character of the archaeological record. These achievements may be briefly reviewed. A fuller account may be found in *Exploring our Past – Strategies for the Archaeology of England* (English Heritage 1991a).

The pursuit of preservation policies through the funding of SMRs, in association with ACAO, has resulted in important developments. These essential databases, on which policies are founded, have been strengthened. SMRs are also important for the prosecution of archaeological planning policies, and have underpinned EH's Monuments Protection Programme. Funding for SMRs has often been linked to agreements on 'pump-priming' funding to assist local authorities in establishing permanent posts, mostly in planning departments, for county archaeological officers and SMR officers. With support from EH, the number of archaeological posts in local authorities rose substantially in the 1980s. All county councils now employ archaeological officers, as do some district and borough councils, such as York and the London Borough of Southwark.

Preservation policies have also been pursued through project funding of survey and aerial reconnaissance. Some surveys have been commissioned in response to the need to develop scheduling and management policies for areas of high potential. Into this category fall surveys on claylands (Raunds, Stansted, the Weald), upland areas (e.g. the Lake District, the Mendip and Quantock Hills, Salisbury Plain, Dartmoor, West Penwith), coastal zones (the Avon Levels, the Essex and Lindsey coasts) and river valleys (the gravels of the Upper Thames, Cambridgeshire and Herefordshire). Other surveys, such as the Stonehenge Environs Project, have had more direct relevance to the rescue programme and have been combined with excavation. Projects in wetland landscapes, such as those in the Fenlands and Somerset Levels, fall into this category.

The execution of surveys, combined where appropriate with excavation, has offered an opportunity to integrate archaeological considerations with changing countryside policies, reducing the threat to vulnerable areas (Chapter 22). Such initiatives have been taken for

instance in the Somerset Levels and West Penwith, where the recognition of the archaeological importance of the landscapes has been subsequently confirmed by designation as
Environmentally Sensitive Areas.

Excavations in advance of development and other threats, and the associated post-
excavation work, consistently absorbed the bulk of EH's archaeology budgets in the
1980s. This investment has enhanced our knowledge of the monuments and remains of
every period, from the Palaeolithic to the post-medieval, in every region. Projects have
ranged from fairly modest investigations of individual sites to major, long-term and multi-
disciplinary landscape projects such as those at Raunds in Northamptonshire and West
Heslerton in North Yorkshire. Space does not permit more detailed consideration of the
results of the rescue archaeology programme of the 1980s, but published analyses of funding and reviews of results can be found in *Exploring our Past* (English Heritage 1991a), in
Wainwright (1984) and in the *Archaeology Review*, which has been published annually by
EH since 1989 (e.g. English Heritage 1991e).

INTO THE 1990s   *to end of chapter*

Archaeological policies in the 1990s

The years since 1990 have seen further important developments in archaeological policies,
springing mainly from the publication by DoE of PPG 16 (DoE 1990a). From about 1985,
a number of county councils (working in conjunction with EH) began to develop archaeological planning policies that put the onus on applicants for planning permission to assess
and accommodate the archaeological implications of their proposals. Uncertainty about
the precise extent of the powers of planning authorities in this area led to pressure for DoE
to publish a circular on archaeology and planning. The Rose Theatre controversy in the
summer of 1989 added impetus to this call and, following discussions between EH and
DoE and wide consultation by DOE on a draft, PPG 16 was published in 1990.

PPG 16 emphasizes a number of basic principles: the importance government attaches
to archaeological remains and their preservation; the need for local planning authorities to
take account of archaeology in strategic planning and development control work; the need
for the archaeological implications of planning applications to be assessed before applications are determined; the need wherever possible to preserve important remains threatened
by development and the expectation, where preservation *in situ* is not possible, that developers should make adequate provision for archaeological excavation and recording. This
last policy is usually termed 'developer funding'.

In many ways, PPG 16 can be seen as a culmination of policy directions pursued through
the 1980s. The implications of PPG 16 (and comparable instruments such as the
Environmental Assessment Regulations – see Ralston and Thomas 1993) for the funding,
organization and practice of archaeology are profound, and are still unfolding. A full consideration of this subject is beyond the scope of this chapter. However, PPG 16, with its
emphasis on the developer's responsibilities for archaeological work made necessary by
development, has significant implications for the future role of EH funding. Following the
publication of PPG 16, EH has published a further series of policy statements on archaeology.

The first is *Rescue Archaeology Funding: a Policy Statement* (English Heritage 1991c).
This replaces the 1986 statement, and modifies funding policy in the light of PPG 16.
English Heritage funding may be appropriate where developer-funding is not a possibility
(perhaps because of the nature of the threat) and in cases where, despite proper prior
assessment, important archaeological remains have unexpectedly come to light after planning permission has been granted and which it would not otherwise be possible to record.

In addition, EH will commission projects that will enable it to carry out its statutory duties, and will direct funding to particular problems with this in view.

A major statement of future policy is made in *Exploring our Past – Strategies for the Archaeology of England* (English Heritage 1991a). This paper analyses the achievements of the 1980s and sets out an agenda for the 1990s in the light of achievements and policy changes such as those contained in PPG 16. A framework of academic objectives, focusing particularly on processes of change, is developed and a range of operational aims concerned with identifying, protecting, managing and analysing the archaeological resource is set out. Among the roles envisaged for EH in the 1990s are those of helping to define and monitor standards for good professional practice in an era of developer funding and competitive tendering, of carrying out reviews of current knowledge in various areas as an aid to determining future priorities (e.g. Fulford and Huddleston 1991), of promoting syntheses of work undertaken in the past (including work supported by developers) and of informing the public about archaeology through publication, education and presentation projects.

A second important publication that year was *Management of Archaeological Projects* (English Heritage 1991b). This is a greatly expanded version of *The Management of Archaeology Projects* (English Heritage 1989) and is widely known as MAP 2. MAP 2 attempts to analyse the processes, both intellectual and managerial, involved in carrying out archaeological projects, and to provide advice and guidance on this subject. MAP 2 is intended as a manual of good practice for archaeological projects regardless of how these may be funded, and has provoked widespread discussion in the profession. The existence of such documents is of particular importance when many of the clients for archaeological works are non-archaeological bodies such as developers.

Finally, EH has recently announced its intention to support the production of archaeological assessments and strategies for around thirty major historic towns and cities over the next five years (English Heritage 1992a) as part of the response to PPG 16. This programme will be undertaken in conjunction with the local authorities concerned.

Future roles

EH's archaeological policies are thus developing in response to changing circumstances, and will continue to do so as the need arises. The developments of the 1980s have resulted in a great increase in the overall level of activity nationally. EH funding now only accounts for perhaps 30 % of the annual total (cf. English Heritage 1991a: 12). This, however, implies a changed role for EH funding, not a diminished one. Some threats (such as coastal erosion and some wetland desiccation) do not derive from development, and funding from EH may be appropriate in such cases. There is also still a significant (although diminishing) commitment to post-excavation work, some of it relating to sites excavated in the 1970s and 1980s. In future, however, perhaps the most important part of the role of EH and its funding will be to provide the strategic framework within which individual projects funded by other agencies can be designed and executed, and to provide a central source of advice, guidance and support nationally.

SUMMARY AND CONCLUSIONS

This chapter has attempted to outline the development of central government's policies for the support of archaeology, and the role of that support in the development of our present approaches to archaeological resource management in England.

In the 1970s, DoE was by far the largest funder of archaeology, and the pressing need at that time was to establish structures and to respond reactively to immediate threats to the archaeological heritage. The 1980s in particular saw the emergence and consolidation of a coherent organizational and policy structure, much of it local-authority based, for the management of the archaeological resource. Project funding from DoE and EH was important in making this possible.

The 1990s have seen the burden of the costs of archaeological work occasioned by development lifted from EH, enabling resources to be redirected to other activities. Archaeological resource management is now a diverse and often decentralized activity, and there is an important place for a central agency that can provide strategic overview, direction and support. The 1990s seem certain to see further developments in the role of EH as the practice of archaeological resource management continues to evolve in a rapidly changing world.

CHAPTER 14

ENGLISH ARCHAEOLOGICAL UNITS AS CONTRACTORS

Andrew J. Lawson

The title of this chapter encapsulates two significant developments in British archaeology in the past two decades. Firstly, it acknowledges professional teams of archaeologists (units) as an element within the structure of the discipline, particularly in England (see also Chapter 4). Secondly, it recognizes that in the 1990s archaeologists play different roles, among which is that of 'contractor'. This chapter explains the implications of that role. However, before exploring these implications, it is instructive to consider the current situation in a historical perspective.

The rise of rescue archaeology was conveniently chronicled in 1974 in a small volume edited by Philip Rahtz (1974b). At that time, Professor Charles Thomas noted that in order to respond to the 'rapid and tumultuous change' in society, 'progressively minded archaeologists should welcome new thinking and should realise that we have already set a foot on the path in the shape of "archaeological units"' (Thomas 1974: 12–14). Earlier, specific threats to archaeological sites had led to localized responses. For example, in York, one of many historic towns threatened by postwar redevelopment, the York Archaeological Trust for Excavation and Research was constituted in 1972, drawing heavily on the experience over the previous decade in Winchester. From October of that year it employed a unit of eleven people (Addyman 1974: 162). Similarly, the establishment of the network of British motorways led to the formation of committees intent on tackling the situation in advance of (or more often during) the destruction of rural sites (Fowler 1974: 114–29). Threats of all kinds were obvious throughout the nation and local initiatives spawned units. The reaction in Kent epitomized the concerns:

> By the end of 1971 it had become clear that, with the ever-increasing threat in Dover and on so many other sites in Kent, the situation had changed out of all recognition . . . For years several of the leading individuals had grossly neglected their business affairs and full-time jobs, but now even this was not enough. The never-ending work of rescue demanded a greater sacrifice, and so four of the team forsook their own professions to become full-time rescue archaeologists, hoping to survive on a small subsistence level wage. (Philp 1974: 77)

Professional archaeology has progressed enormously in the realization that it would neither attract nor retain the best qualified staff on a subsistence-level wage. Archaeology is now an accepted profession that commands reasonable fees. However, a debt is due to the sacrifices of the first unit archaeologists who were prepared to dedicate themselves to their subject without expecting a large financial return.

Elsewhere, as in Norfolk, a number of archaeologists individually investigating different sites within the same geographical area came together to pool resources and expertise so as to make professional cover more effective. The structure for an archaeological unit designed to cover the breadth of archaeology with different staff specializing in different periods was defined in Norfolk in 1972. Staff were recruited to fill gaps in expertise and the unit was formally launched in April 1973. Here it was realized by an enlightened county council that the newly formed unit provided a valuable service to the community and in consequence it was prepared to underwrite certain salary costs initially, and eventually to absorb the unit totally as part of its Museums Service. Suffolk and Essex did likewise. For various reasons, however, not all counties could offer such support for a team dedicated to their area.

Where gaps in district or county provision necessitated the establishment of a unit, regional bodies were established, such as CRAAGS (the Committee for Rescue Archaeology in Avon, Gloucestershire and Somerset) and Wessex Archaeological Committee. In each, a centralized organization was regarded as a better structure than dealing with a number of dispersed individual archaeologists.

By 1975 the proliferation of units was coming to an end despite the fact that coverage was not comprehensive. It was also said that because these teams were largely committed to work in specific localities, the system had 'an inherent lack of flexibility' (Hinchliffe 1986: 2). The solution from the Inspectorate of Ancient Monuments (IAM) was to establish the Central Excavation Unit (CEU). It was to fill the gaps, to excavate on nationally important sites and to ensure that where the Department of the Environment was obliged to excavate (as a result of notice served under the contemporary Ancient Monuments Acts) provision had been made. The unit was based at Fort Cumberland near Portsmouth (hardly a 'central' location), from which projects throughout the country were mounted.

The concept behind the local archaeological units was that they should become centres of local excellence as experience grew. Accrued knowledge would lead to a more efficient selection of priorities, especially in post-excavation studies. Many management committees and units produced policy documents to focus attention and energy on the most important areas for research (e.g., in East Anglia, the Scole Committee 1973; and for Wessex, Ellison 1981). Although these laudable aims in many instances remain valid, the orientation of funding strictly towards threatened sites meant that the research directions advocated sometimes became longer-term objectives than the more academically minded might have liked (Lawson 1987). Nonetheless, one fundamental principle was established and continues to underpin excavation strategy: the selection of any archaeological site for investigation, and the diverting of hard-won resources to it, must be academically justified.

FUNDING

The establishment of a network of units and a steady expansion in the work they undertook was only possible because of an increase in central government funds. A lecture delivered in 1982 by Geoffrey Wainwright was the first exposition and analysis of the allocations made from the Department of the Environment since the rescue budget was created in the 1950s (for further details see Chapter 13). Subsequently, expenditure has been published annually (Fig. 14.1). In this series of annual statements it is important to note the changing role of government funding. In the 1970s, block grants were made to units, which essentially underpinned the costs of the unit. Work was focused on certain agreed projects, whether survey, excavation or post-excavation, selected on the advice of regional advisory committees. However, a modification of legislation (in the form of the Ancient Monuments and Archaeological Areas Act 1979) meant that government funds could only be used for specific pieces of work and not to pay directly for the maintenance of institutions. 'Project funding' became the norm from 1981: it required much closer attention to the management of units and passed the problem of seeking sufficient paying work to sustain unit staff from the funder to the employer. Exceptionally, as in the case of

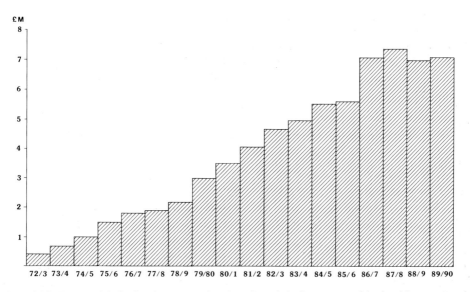

Figure 14.1. The growth in funding for rescue archaeology through the Inspectorate of Ancient Monuments and English Heritage (from English Heritage n.d. and English Heritage 1991a).

CRAAGS, units that could no longer propose projects attractive to the IAM for funding went into liquidation (see also Chapter 15).

In the early 1980s government funds were acknowledged as the major source of revenue for rescue archaeology either through the IAM, employment initiatives such as the Manpower Services Commission, or local authorities. However, government policy, in line with the increasing influence of the European Community, tended towards holding developers responsible for the effects of their respective schemes. In short, if private companies were to profit from the development of land, the tax-paying public should not have to bear the expense of any necessary archaeological work. Instead, this should be paid for by the developer. In 1983 the duties of the IAM were transferred to a new body, the Historic Buildings and Monuments Commission for England (HBMC, popularly known as English Heritage). Immediately it was clear that government funds were no longer to be the only source of revenue. 'The role of the HBMC is that of joint funder of individual projects . . . participating in discussions with other sponsors where this can be helpful' (English Heritage n.d.: 1). In 1986 a strong indication of the change of funding policy was given: 'The Commission welcomes participation by developers . . . in the funding of rescue programmes'(English Heritage 1986: 7). Because most developments are controlled by local authorities, the 'participation by developers' was seen to be best negotiated during the planning process and, hence, the part that could be played by local authorities was highlighted. In 1990, the government issued guidance on archaeology (DoE 1990a) and English Heritage confirmed its view that: 'It would be entirely reasonable for the planning authority to satisfy itself before granting permission that the developer has made appropriate and satisfactory provision for the excavation and recording of the remains' (English Heritage 1991c). Although it is not explicitly stated, 'satisfactory provision' must be taken to mean arranging for the financing of the required work.

Because of the variety of funding sources it is difficult to be precise about the total sums spent by archaeological units. Nevertheless, in 1988/89 government spending

151

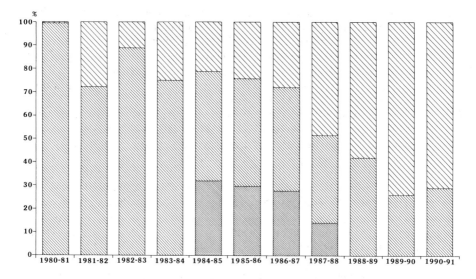

Figure 14.2. The changing proportions of funding to the Trust for Wessex Archaeology Ltd from three principal sources: Manpower Services Commission (darkest); Inspectorate of Ancient Monuments/English Heritage (medium); developers including local authorities (lightest).

through English Heritage was £7.1 million, while 'developers contributed an estimated £14M' (HBMC 1989: 20). The change in the proportions of income from different sources is reflected in the accounts of many archaeological units (for example, the Trust for Wessex Archaeology Ltd; Fig. 14.2). The change in funding policy has necessitated the establishment of a means of implementation through local authority planning departments (see Chapter 10). It has also meant that archaeological units have had to develop skills in negotiation and contracting common to their new sponsors, which are predominantly commercial companies.

The results of this policy have meant that financial provision for rescue archaeology can be commensurate with the size of the threats, and that the ability of archaeologists to respond is not unacceptably restricted by limited government funds. Although holding developers responsible for the archaeological work necessitated by their proposals may be morally correct, units have had to learn to respond to the fluctuations of income resulting from variable rates of development, which are themselves heavily influenced by the state of the national economy. In the early 1990s those units that had previously expanded to respond to vigorous redevelopment have been faced with the need for reduction because of a development slump precipitated by an economic recession. In London, for example, the size of the Museum of London's excavation staff was halved in 1990.

THE DEFINITION OF 'UNIT' IN THE 1990s

For more than twenty years the term 'archaeological unit' has normally been used to describe a team of professional archaeologists working together to identify the need for archaeological intervention, to undertake rescue recording and subsequently to report on the results. Traditionally they have worked within defined geographical areas, and have sought the necessary funding possibly from a variety of sources. Local solutions differed, so that the committees or employed units were affiliated to local authorities (e.g. Norfolk County Council, Winchester District, Poole Borough), universities (e.g. University of Birmingham, Institute of Archaeology), or were independent bodies (e.g. Trust for Wessex Archaeology Ltd). Some units, such as the Oxford Archaeological Unit, were able to attract resources from several sources in return for various services: in that example, the county council, city council and district authorities.

Many committees wished to be independently and properly constituted to take full advantage of tax concessions and to protect their members. Their ambitions were broadly to undertake archaeological research and to educate the public, in all its guises, in archaeology and, hence, it was appropriate that some became charitable trusts. However, once employers, they became liable for many things, including the taxation of their employees. Consequently, many committees have also become limited companies. This refers to the limited liability that the members of a company have in the event of an inability to pay its debts. Their work may have included some or all of a range of tasks including the maintenance of Sites and Monuments Records (SMRs), the monitoring of planning applications, advising on appropriate archaeological action, fund-raising, excavation, publication, public education, conservation, storage, etc.

Placing the responsibility for funding archaeology with developers has, however, led to significant changes in archaeological unit practice necessitating a careful definition of the roles played during the negotiation for planning consent. The Local Government Act 1988 wishes to see the separation of the 'enabler' and 'provider' because the government has been concerned about restrictive practices that might prevent a funder getting the best value. It has also been argued that a developer should be at liberty to choose whom he likes to do the required work to an appropriate standard. Developers who had little know-ledge of units or of the prices they charged have frequently established competition among units to attract the best value for their money (Chapter 16). The result has been that some units have been asked to work outside the geographical 'territory' in which they had traditionally worked.

Such changes have caused considerable concern among many archaeologists, who have warned of the possible erosion of work quality and of the continuing viability of existing organizations. Some have objected to the principle of free-ranging professional teams on the basis that local knowledge and experience is essential in the interpretation of discoveries. Conversely, many have seen the employment opportunity presented by these more commercial practices for individuals or new 'units'. The early 1990s have witnessed the establishment of small private companies, partnerships or self-employed individuals trading as archaeological contractors in a commercial way in competition with the existing units. Hence, in the 1990s although the term 'unit' can still be applied to teams of professional archaeologists, the basis under which they trade and the services they offer vary greatly. Indeed, the term occurs less and less commonly in the official title of an organization, being sometimes replaced by 'Services' (e.g. Thames Valley Archaeological Services) or 'Associates' (e.g. Oxford Archaeological Associates), or being dropped altogether.

ROLES

The establishment of a network of archaeological units throughout Britain did not follow a preconceived cohesive strategy. In consequence, the nature, scale and conditions under which they were established were disparate. Those charged with the running of the units found it essential to learn of the experiences of others and to unite to standardize working practice and conditions, especially because at that time all units were dependent upon funds from central government. In 1975 the Standing Conference of Unit Managers (SCUM), now the Standing Conference of Archaeological Unit Managers (SCAUM), was constituted to enable constructive debate between colleagues, the IAM, government and others. This organization published advice on many topics such as wages, agreements with mineral operators, and health and safety in an attempt to mould corporate good practice.

More recently, the Institute of Field Archaeologists (IFA), established in 1982, has played an extremely important part in the development of archaeological professionalism. Its *Code of Conduct* (IFA 1988a) which all subscribing members must abide by, spells out a number of principles governing the ethical behaviour of archaeologists. Whereas SCAUM remains a forum for the discussion of topics of mutual interest, the IFA comprises individual members who are validated and controlled by its Code. Although English Heritage and its predecessors have always played a pivotal role in the growth of the profession because they were the principal sources of revenue, it was most important that the profession became sufficiently mature to control itself. The part played by the IFA has become more important as the network of units, each traditionally working within restricted and defined areas, has become less rigid. To help its members cope with the situation, the *Code of Conduct* has been amplified with bylaws to cover, *inter alia*, disciplinary regulations and a *Code of Approved Practice for the Regulation of Contractual Arrangements in Field Archaeology*. The practical implications of these are amplified in Chapter 16.

During the discussions over the formulation of the bylaws the responsibilities of archaeologists working in field archaeology were identified and titles given to different role players. There were:

curators – responsible for the conservation and management of archaeological evidence, e.g. county archaeological officers

contractors – those undertaking work, e.g. field units

clients – those paying for the work, e.g. developers, English Heritage

consultants – those offering independent advice

Because planning control and the establishment of projects are systematic, the definition of these roles helps to explain the way in which different parties fit into the system. However, because of the unique nature of every archaeological site, considerable professional judgement is required in decision-making at all stages; hence the system cannot become totally mechanistic. Many of the units established within local authorities have undertaken the full breadth of archaeological roles, offering a single integrated service. Some, such as in Norfolk, have now allocated specific staff to specific tasks in order that there should be no confusion in the mind of an outsider of the role played by each. Similarly, the integrated service of the Museum of London, which previously covered all archaeological functions in the capital, has been fragmented. Now English Heritage acts as a planning adviser, MOLAS (Museum of London Archaeological Service) acts as a contractor and the Museum itself safeguards and displays its collections.

UNITS AS CONTRACTORS

Under the structured system outlined above, the scope for archaeological work is defined by the curator. Because the curator must safeguard the resource he or she must set out precisely what must be done to satisfy this concern. The work required may be set down in outline as a brief; for example, 'the site should be excavated using an appropriate sampling strategy'. The brief must then be expanded through a 'specification' to be precise about the requirements. The 'specification' has to be a very carefully thought-out strategy, its requirements being both reasonable and sustainable. The importance of the specification must be stressed because it dictates what will happen to a site and may prescribe the final opportunity for recording irreplaceable evidence. It may be very time-consuming even for an experienced fieldworker to produce a well-thought-out specification and frequently help from others may have to be sought. It is always wise to identify the need to vary the work in the light of unforeseeable discoveries because by its nature archaeology is not totally predictable.

Contractors are invited to consider doing the work defined in the specification. The IFA bylaws dictate that only those with the requisite qualifications, expertise and experience should take up the offer. Consequently, the contractor has to demonstrate that he or she has the qualities to meet the criteria and can undertake the work cost-effectively at the appropriate time.

The decision of which contractor to use will be the client's. It may be guided by advice on a variety of aspects, such as the suitability of the contractor, previous employment or price. The price for the work is usually submitted as a tender and where prices are sought from several units the process is referred to as 'competitive tendering'. Once a tender is accepted the agreement reached between client and contractor is usually confirmed in a binding contract, the form of which can vary from a simple exchange of letters to long, complicated documents that cover every circumstance (Darvill and Atkins 1991; see also Chapters 15 and 16 for further discussion). Once a contract has been won the unit will use its best endeavours to discharge its obligations in a way that reflects well on itself and its client. The work to be done will have been defined in the specification and any variation from it, possibly necessitated by discoveries on site, will have to be negotiated with the client and the curator. Variations in work may lead to a variation in cost and time, and consequently agreements may also have to be modified. The contractor will have to comply with all appropriate legislation governing employment, taxation, working conditions, etc. For example, it is a statutory requirement for contractors employing more than five people to implement a health and safety policy. The demands of safety and the avoidance of risks are high but are essential for the protection of employees and the public.

MANAGEMENT

Guidelines on the way in which projects should be managed have been set out by English Heritage (English Heritage 1991b). The way in which a unit organizes itself to manage projects successfully is its own concern. Nonetheless, it will wish to ensure that it is so structured, and has working practices understood by all its staff, such that individual tasks can be undertaken and controlled effectively. For example, 'Wessex Archaeology' is the abbreviated name used by the contracting unit maintained by the Trust for Wessex Archaeology Ltd. It employs about seventy people and undertakes a hundred projects each year.

In Wessex Archaeology the responsibility for running projects is delegated to a series of project managers, each of whom controls several projects simultaneously. Other specialist managers have responsibilities for aspects of work common to many projects. Whereas these specialist managers control the standard of work in their sphere and advise project managers on the best approach to individual projects, it is the latter who have overall responsibility for the projects. Exceptionally, because the manager in charge of administration also contributes to corporate strategy, his status is enhanced. The work of the project managers is controlled by two assistant directors who are answerable to the unit director. The latter is answerable for all activities of the unit (Fig. 14.3). Different management systems are used in other units.

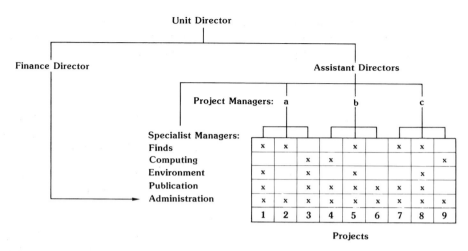

			Projects						
Specialist Managers:	1	2	3	4	5	6	7	8	9
Finds	x	x			x		x	x	
Computing			x	x					x
Environment	x		x		x			x	
Publication	x		x	x	x	x	x	x	
Administration	x	x	x	x	x	x	x	x	x

Figure 14.3. Simplified management structure within the Trust for Wessex Archaeology. The diagram shows the way in which nine hypothetical projects, represented as a series of tasks in vertical columns, are managed by three project managers (a, b and c). Specialist tasks common to several projects are overseen by specialist managers (for example, finds in projects 1, 2, 5, 7 and 8) who assist the project managers: the latter have overall responsibility for the projects. The project managers are monitored by the assistant directors who, with the finance director overseeing administration, are answerable to the unit director.

ACCOUNTABILITY

While undertaking a contract, a unit has responsibilities in a number of different directions. It may be obliged to carry out the work specified in full to an appropriately high standard in the agreed time and for the agreed sum. This obligation is to the client who is paying for the work. A good working relationship and successful outcome will stand the unit in good stead, especially if further contracts might be let by the client.

The unit will also be held to account by the academic community, which seeks new information to help solve problems in interpretation and whose advice has been sought in formulating strategies that direct the selection of sites meriting investigation. It is in order to satisfy this broader interest that the dissemination of results is so important. The length of any published report should be commensurate with the importance and complexity of the project. The most important sites will merit publication as a monograph. Yet it is the quality of all reports and the interpretation contained in them that will determine the unit's academic reputation.

The principle that archaeological records must be interpreted and disseminated and the fact that it is the contracting unit that is obliged to compile the report that brings this about means that units can not be merely technicians in the art of excavation (*pace* Frere 1988: 34). The contracting unit also has an ethical responsibility to the public. Archaeological remains are seen as a limited and unrenewable national resource. Excavation is inherently destructive and therefore no archaeologist should squander the resource. Similarly, grants made to contracting units through English Heritage are public funds derived from taxes. Those spending grants have a moral obligation to ensure that they are used diligently for the purposes they have been granted. Although detailed technical publications are usually produced for the academic community (above), it is frequently desirable to disseminate the results of important discoveries in a non-technical fashion that will be attractive to a wider, public readership.

Many contracting units take out insurance policies to safeguard themselves lest they inadvertently default on their obligations. Usually insurance will cover accidents; liability to employees, third parties or the public; or professional indemnity.

CONTROL

Concerns about the performance and quality of work are normally addressed through monitoring. All interested parties will wish to ensure that their interests are satisfied. When acting as a contractor the unit will wish to satisfy itself that it is conducting work to its own predetermined standard. New national quality assurance schemes, such as British Standard 5750, are popular in large manufacturing companies because accredited organizations comply with standardized internal vetting. However, such systems are not yet established in British archaeology. Externally, the client will wish to be satisfied that the contractor is keeping to time, doing the required work and will complete on schedule. The curator will wish to ensure that the specification remains correct and is being professionally discharged. Those who do not perform in a correct fashion may face disciplinary action. For example, a client may sue for breach of contract or a case may be brought through the IFA's Disciplinary Procedures because the individual responsible for particular work has acted unethically. Units that recurrently perform badly or unprofessionally are not likely to be recommended or engaged again, and, hence, will find survival difficult.

The more flexible working arrangements brought about by units being less territorial has in part removed the *raison d'être* of the CEU, and, in consequence, its staff have been redeployed in monitoring units contracted by English Heritage. With its redefined brief, the CEU has become the Central Archaeological Service.

VIABILITY

For any unit to be viable it must command the resources necessary to undertake the work required of it. The resources are likely to include staff, equipment, premises, services and so on. The unit will need to have employment agreements with sufficient funds to honour them. It will need to buy or rent equipment, premises and other services necessary to complete a variety of projects. In some units certain costs may be underwritten or paid, for example, by local authorities or universities, but for the independent organization without financial support all revenue must be gained from the projects and sufficient projects won to cover the full costs of maintaining the unit. The managers responsible for the viability of the organization therefore need to plan carefully and to introduce a pricing strategy that is attractive to clients and will secure enough contracts to cover the financial needs of the unit. The pricing must balance competitiveness with a fair reward to staff.

Traditionally, archaeologists have not sought to make profits from their work. However, profit is what enables commercial companies to weather temporary lulls in their markets, to research and develop new ideas, to improve working practice and standards and to allow for capital investment. If archaeologists are to survive in a commercial milieu they must embrace this concept of profit. Under these circumstances all units acting as contractors will have to agree an acceptable formula that generates reserves enabling them to maintain future efficiency and viability. But as long as some archaeologists pretend that they are working purely for the love of it, and seek only a subsistence wage, there will be limited scope for the advancement of the profession and an equal status with disciplines such as architecture or engineering, which have become allied through working in a development-led world.

CHAPTER 15

THE ARCHAEOLOGIST AS CONSULTANT

Simon Collcutt

INTRODUCTION

Any expert may give advice when asked, a reactive role. Consultants offer advisory services as a part or the whole of their function, a proactive role highly dependent upon situation and vested interest. There are no significant overview texts on British archaeological consultancy; indeed, there are surprisingly few books on consultancy in any sphere. There are some interesting reports from the USA but the context is so very different that the American experience cannot be discussed here (cf. *BAN* Editorial 1988; Burrow and Hunter 1990). Lack of references in mainland European literature gives the false impression that archaeological consultancy is not practised at all outside these islands. Consultants do not, as a rule, talk openly about their activities; they publish only on procedural aspects and, until very recently, they have had no specific professional forum or association. There is thus no way of estimating how many archaeological consultants are currently practising, in one capacity or another, in Britain. Above all, there is the question (as yet unanswerable) of how much the present visibility of consultants is a fad, a transient reflection of factors outside archaeology, and how much a real phenomenon, representing significant shifts in professional philosophy and structure.

This book is an 'Introduction' but, from the consultants' viewpoint, they are living that introduction. This chapter cannot be set out in formal textbook style, each section constructed around received wisdom. The current concerns of and about consultants are described, drawing upon the experience of the author, a practising consultant. The result is a collection of observations and assertions, many more questions than answers.

DEFINITIONS

An archaeological consultant provides expert archaeological advice. Terminology is currently very broad and imprecise. The definitions given below are as self-explanatory as possible, and will be used consistently in the present chapter; used elsewhere, these terms will not automatically communicate the desired meaning. Each category has been included on a de facto basis, as, in every case, practitioners have used the terms consultant or consultancy to refer to some aspect of their work in the published literature.

A freelance consultant offers consultancy services as an unattached individual. A part-time consultant offers services that are (presumably) merely incidental to other employment. An institutional consultant offers services from within an archaeological organization with wider objectives than consultancy; for instance, many archaeological units and trusts now supply consultancy services. A mixed-practice consultant is an archaeologist operating from within a broader-based consultancy firm: examples include practices specializing in tourism, town and country planning, environmental monitoring or engineering. An archaeological practice consultant operates from within a specifically archaeological (or heritage) consultancy firm. The commercial status of archaeological consultancy practices is varied but there has been a tendency for private limited companies to appear over the last few years.

Consultants are expected to have a broad grasp of all archaeological issues but a consultant specialist concentrates on particular areas of expertise, often involving artefact studies. The phrase consultant technical specialist may be useful, referring to firms with archaeological personnel that provide scientific support. Non-archaeologists who supply advisory services directly to archaeology may be called ancillary consultants: there are a growing number of aerial photographers, geophysicists and remote-sensing specialists in this category (Chapter 18), as well as solicitors and barristers who specialize in listed-building and other archaeology-related legislation.

Individuals in all these categories provide advice to external organizations. However, some consultants hold posts in-house. A public tied consultant operates within and provides advice more or less exclusively to a public organization. A commercial tied consultant operates from within and provides advice exclusively to a single developer firm; so far such positions are very rare. Some consultants may be partially tied through an exclusivity contract with a particular developer; this entails both a pre-emptive right (to exclude other archaeological advisers) and an obligation (to provide advice to that developer) and would usually also involve an agreement to avoid contracts with other parties when there might be competition or conflict with the interests of that developer. An advisor is usually a relatively senior, experienced archaeologist who provides occasional advice to a public organization (the term will be written thus here, leaving the more common spelling 'adviser' to denote an unspecified role); remuneration for such a role may range from zero to full fees.

A consultee is a person or organization with the non-commercial right (statutory, delegated or otherwise) to be consulted in a given situation; consultees will often have vested interests different from those of consultors. Planning authorities and other governmental agencies are usually the formal consultor but other individuals (developers and their agents) would do well to contact consultees directly. The most obvious examples of consultees include central government organizations (including 'quangos' and departmental sections) or archaeological organizations appointed by local authorities that have no internal archaeology sections. The advice of consultees is usually free (i.e. costs are borne by the consultee organization) but there are situations in which costs may be recovered. For instance, a consultant may be given temporary powers (subject only to the High Court or equivalent) to act (under statute) for the purposes of arbitration and is entitled to include his or her fees as part of the taxation, or he or she may be appointed with a set honorarium as a professional witness (e.g. by a coroner) or as assessor (to assist the planning inspectorate). Included in the category of consultees are those persons normally called curators (e.g. county or regional archaeologists, governmental agencies with specific curatorial responsibilities, or managing archaeologists appointed by a landowner) whose advice, when based upon policy, statute and property law, has the power of a directive subject only to public inquiry, ministerial veto or the courts.

Certain university posts have recently been created with roles that are either not yet clear to outsiders or are still actively evolving. For instance, the Executive Directorship of Archaeological Research and Consultancy at Sheffield University may in part reflect an institutional consultancy, while the British Property Federation Chair of Property Development and Archaeology at Bournemouth University would seem to have been constituted in part to facilitate synthetic research into the performance of archaeologists, including consultants, within the planning system.

The reader is encouraged to search such publications as *British Archaeological News* or

The Field Archaeologist for examples of practitioners in the categories defined above; this is a valuable exercise that will demonstrate the levels of expertise involved, the increasing rate of personnel transfer from other roles to consultancy, and the growing willingness to use the label consultancy to cover existing activities. However, it should not be assumed that individuals can be permanently labelled using the above classification: many persons have multiple roles, with the proper classification being dependent on the situation in a particular application. There has also been a shift in stress from the individual (a person with a known history) to the organization or firm, a more anonymous unit.

THE HISTORICAL CONTEXT

Archaeological consultancy is the result of a number of trends, more or less directly related to factors inherent in the development of the discipline itself. The story is too convoluted to attempt a linear history here; many of these matters are dealt with from different perspectives elsewhere in this volume (Chapters 1, 4, 14 and 16).

There has been a steady decline in the vigour of many learned societies since the Second World War, due both to intrinsic factors (e.g. competition from home-based interests such as television) and to growing friction between amateurs and professionals. With the boom in university posts in archaeology in the 1960s and earlier 1970s, the demand for advice could be satisfied but, over the last decade, academic priorities have changed. This source of expertise is no longer generally available at the consultancy level and few academics have an understanding of how public archaeology is practised – so much so that the present author feels justified, at least in the shorthand of this chapter, to exclude mainstream university activity from the term public archaeology.

A parallel boom-and-retrenchment development occurred in public archaeology. The good years saw an increase in the influence of the Royal Commissions and the establishment of a system of Sites and Monuments Records (SMRs), county and regional archaeologists and fieldwork units. The raised profile of archaeology eventually brought new legislation and planning policy. Advice was readily available from consultees but, probably by default rather than design, with an increasingly authoritarian tenor, unqualified from any other quarter. Then the public money began to dry up. Units lost much local and central government funding, many struggled to become financially independent and some went to the wall. Curators are having to cope with decreased resources and increased workload. The lead role of central government bodies has been redefined and loss of confidence has occurred, especially in England, as first the profession and then the public have perceived the new agenda, epitomized in such cryptic statements as: 'We will privatise our direct labour force over the next three years' (English Heritage 1992: 5; Chapter 1).

Another consequence of the raised profile of public archaeology in the 1970s was the crystallization of the concept of professionalism, the most obvious result being the establishment and increasing influence of the Institute of Field Archaeologists (IFA). Such a movement has three aspects: the search for standards, the formulation of career structures and the exclusion of non-professionals (not of amateurs or academics *per se* but of persons unable or unwilling to meet emerging standards) – which, no matter how regrettable under certain circumstances, are inseparable.

It is the author's experience that, on the whole, private developers have reacted as reasonably as could be expected to changing planning requirements. It is unfortunate that many public development agencies have so often dragged their feet. However, even less enlightened firms could not fail to have noticed the fact that the price of public acceptability is increased developer funding, and this since the later 1980s during a seemingly endless and deepening slump. Developers, needing assurances over cost-effectiveness and avoidance of delays, regularly express distrust of the motives of archaeologists (*all* archaeologists) and concerns over their managerial abilities; the commercial consultant is made aware, on an almost daily basis, of the full extent of this distrust. Despite early enquiries by developers concerning the viability of commercial tied consultants (the normal response to a need for expertise in larger development firms), very few such posts yet exist, probably another reflection of distrust which, in general, seems mutual.

The fortunes of public archaeology are not simply a function of the economy. As archaeological standards have risen and it has been admitted that field archaeologists and their families might be allowed to live in something more substantial than tents, public archaeology has certainly become vastly more expensive, making this the major preoccupation of all concerned. However, the economic link may sometimes be less direct and predictable. The Green issue, from which archaeology has benefited so much (even a little improperly at times), is a case in point. Born during the good times and quickly sending an offshoot to integrate with the postwar town and country planning initiative, the environmental movement seems to have gained strength during the slump, although this vigour cannot last for ever if starved of funding. Each of the trends noted in this section has a particular but different momentum, producing a constantly shifting situation as positive and negative feedback drifts into and out of play.

By the mid-1980s, there was conflict between, on the one hand, raised professional standards, career expectations and university output of graduates and, on the other, shrinking employment prospects in many areas of archaeology. The more or less arbitrary nature of salary freezes, resource shrinkage and actual cuts in posts meant that there was little correspondence between the quality of personnel and the fact of dissatisfaction or redundancy. These problems caused a toughening in the call for further standards and increasing resentment of amateurs and academics who might threaten job prospects in other sectors; competition between surviving organizations became acute (cf. Baker 1987). Indeed, it may be suggested that the proper evolution of the IFA towards a chartered institute representing the profession as a whole has been seriously damaged as the gulf between members and non-members has widened.

The frustration of the undervalued and the unemployed can have only one of two possible results, in archaeology as in any other sphere. The disillusioned left the profession. Those who refused to abandon their self-esteem and the belief in the worth of their expert knowledge gained through long vocational training, started to offer their services directly in the marketplace where demand was growing for advice in the face of rising costs.

The massive growth in all types of consultancy in British industry and commerce since 1980 is no accident but a consequence of our current society. Space to discuss this broad topic is lacking here, although the key factors may be listed: the shifting economics of in-house versus external expertise, economics based upon increasingly short-term criteria; employers' increasing inability or unwillingness to shoulder the rising cost and complexity of training; the dangers to employees of participating in the training of potential younger or cheaper replacements; the expertise famine in the early boom years; the later expertise glut following rationalization, merger or bankruptcy; the replacement of employer loyalty by the ethos of sustainable profit, causing decreasing job security; the replacement of employee loyalty by the ethos of personal development, causing decreased employee reliability; the decreasing willingness to allow downward delegation of decision-making; the appalling social strain caused by the geographical mobility (job-hopping) now required to attain advancement; the philosophy that job satisfaction can be more closely equated with financial success; the value placed by our society upon assertiveness; and the total uncoupling between salaries and the hours white-collar staff are expected to work – in brief, the perceived personal risk now involved in putting all one's eggs in one basket with a single primary- or secondary-sector employer. After a little thought, reasonable archaeologists will admit that many of these factors are not so different from those operative in their own profession.

The archaeologist contemplating unattached consultancy is usually faced with the following realities: little or no capital; expertise, possibly in public archaeology, but no experience in accountancy and cashflow management, employment and contract law, marketing, or the workings of the businesses of prospective clients and co-consultants; immediate infrastructure needs (office space, computing, communications, transport, insurance); no commercial reputation; and absolutely no safety net. Anyone who thinks that taking this course is an easy way to fortune is a fool. Given very hard work over several years and good luck, a degree of security may be achieved. There are no yuppies in archaeological consultancy and certain trappings (car, mobile phone and business suit) are necessary tools of the trade and not indicators of individual affluence.

Career prospects in archaeological consultancy are already changing because those who have survived from the earliest ad hoc stages have perforce taught themselves and clients to anticipate high professional standards, in both archaeology and commerce. Any fledgling consultant who cannot contrive to spring more or less fully armed into action now has a poor life expectancy. The establishment of new consultancies will inevitably slow; personnel will be drawn into existing practices at trainee or probationer level. When a qualified consultant is ready to move on, he or she will find that there are increasing opportunities in mixed and tied situations as an alternative to unattached practice. The move to consultancy must not be seen as an irrevocable step. There are already a few examples of individuals transferring back from consultancy practices to units, universities or museums; although reasons for transfers so far have perhaps most commonly been negative, the broadening of experience accumulated as the profession increasingly finds it natural for individuals to move between roles can only benefit the subject.

THE ROLE OF CONSULTANT

Consultancy represents a spectrum that may be subdivided according to two criteria: vested interest and intrinsic powers. On the one hand, there are consultants whose responsibilities (apart from allegiance to professional ethics, general to all archaeologists and currently best articulated in various IFA Codes) are to a specific organization with a set of defined objectives; from these objectives flow more or less explicit powers that require that the opinions expressed be given weight, not necessarily in proportion to the purely archaeological merit of the argument. On the other hand, there are consultants whose responsibilities are commercial: to the financial wellbeing of their own organizations and to the fulfilment of particular contracts; such consultants have no intrinsic powers beyond those conferred by reputation, competence and force of argument. In reality, most consultants (or, more properly, individual consultancy situations) fall somewhere between these two extremes, although there is indeed a degree of polarization.

It will be useful to discuss the concepts of 'independence', 'impartiality' and 'objectivity' here. An independent organization is one that is self-contained (*pace* Selkirk 1988), while an impartial one has no vested interest in the outcome of a particular issue. English Heritage, a state-dependent organization, is not impartial when advising on the importance of an unexpected find if there may be compensation or project-funding implications for the public purse, just as independent consultants are not impartial when advising on a project costing that their own firm proposes to implement. Again, the degree of impartiality has nothing to do with actual performance; a consultant in any position may decide to let vested interest govern decisions entirely or may try to keep such interest at a distance and reach a decision more nearly based upon the facts, an approximation to an objective decision. Financial interests are not the only issue; for instance, if one seeks advice from an expert in a particular field, there is a trade-off between increased depth of understanding and increased myopia on judgment of comparative importance.

The crux of the matter is that all archaeologists have vested interests of various kinds that cannot be ignored. The relevance of interests is conditional on the situation in each case; the wise sponsor should recognize these interests while the wise consultant (considering long-term benefit) should make sure that relevant interests are fully declared, a point of particular importance for independent consultants where there is less immediate peer oversight. There should be no *a priori* problem with Chinese walls (the internal separation of functions, such as that between development control and contracting arms in local authority archaeology sections) as long as they are explicit; such arrangements can often have compensatory advantages with respect to continuity and efficiency.

As long as archaeology has a reasonably high profile there will be conflicts of interests, irrespective of the particular economic or political climate. Shifting combinations of advisers are useful, even indispensable, for all parties in order to help balance the interests sufficiently for those parties to feel able to reach a consensus in each case (cf. Redman 1990; Griffiths 1991); that many advisers will style themselves consultants is merely an honest statement that someone must pay to keep the service operative. Rational archaeological decisions cannot stem from monopoly nor the free market but only from a guaranteed mixed economy – a suggestion that goes beyond fashionable metaphor to pragmatism (cf. Addyman in CAWP 1988).

Since the nature of consultancy is so situation-dependent, it would be futile to try to describe representative cases, although archaeological consultants are not involved only with the planning system (for instance, there are practitioners who deal with taxation, insurance and even forensic science). However, there are broad categories where the responsibilities are materially different, not necessarily as a function of the type of consultancy organization involved. The most obvious category is that of adviser, involving first-data retrieval and interpretation, followed by project design and logistics; the role may develop into that of supervisor, with implementation of management or monitoring strategies. When the agreement of others besides the sponsor or client must be sought, the consultant becomes a negotiator. The consultant always has the task of mediator, and should ensure that he or she has both the data and the understanding to improve communication between the different parties involved. If agreement cannot be achieved, the consultant must become an advocate, not of the sponsor or client but of his or her professional opinion as a consultant. The adversarial situation thus precipitated is a basic and necessary mechanism of the British planning and legal systems, designed to break deadlock; however uncomfortable the role may become at times, it would be professional cowardice to refuse to participate (cf. Dalwood 1987; Chippindale 1991). In rarer cases, the consultant may be an arbitrator, with powers to judge between opposing advocates, an even more uncomfortable position owing to the responsibilities involved.

Leaving aside tasks related to individual projects, the consultant has an ambassadorial role, striving to earn the developer's respect for archaeology and archaeologists. This is a difficult job when so many archaeologists seem to have a constitutional disrespect for the objectives of developers. The consultant may also be a fund-raiser, showing clients how to instigate projects of public benefit (and what rewards might be expected in publicity terms); however, the consultant who abuses the position by failing to define the exact boundary between statutory responsibilities and benefaction is no better than the consultant who neglects to bring material facts to the attention of curators. There is also the role of popularizer: in education, the media, display and tourism. This is perhaps the least formalized but most responsibility-laden task of all, since it will be the main (in some cases, only) point of contact with the public in general – the ultimate if often unwitting, even unwilling, sponsors of archaeology.

What sort of person will make the best consultant? Many people (including a few practitioners) have an image of consultants as pushy, arrogant and confrontational individuals. It is true that the effective consultant needs a robust line in argument, an ability to project the voice and a very thick skin in order to survive the daily onslaught, often simultaneously from different quarters. However, it is surely the qualities of perseverance and self-assurance, continually justified by thorough preparation, that are most valuable. Few women have so far chosen to become consultants, especially in the commercial sector, probably because the aggressive image is unattractive – all the more reason why their greater involvement would be welcome.

THE STATE OF PLAY

Opposition to archaeological consultancy is articulated most strongly by other archaeologists. Calls for restrictive practices are endemic in the literature, with talk of 'approved organizations' or 'regulation and procurement' (cf. CASG 1988; IFA 1988b; Gater 1990; BADLG 1991). Some such practices have been officially adopted, for instance, in local authority select lists of 'approved' contractors with a rigid closing date for admittance (e.g. West Sussex County Council 1988; Staffordshire County Council 1991). Tender competitions that categorically require that the proposed project be directed by an IFA member are increasingly common. The English case of statutory Areas of Archaeological Importance is a salutary example of the limitations of the closed shop; on balance, the legally designated monopolies have produced satisfactory services on a day-to-day basis (cf. *BAN* Editorial 1989 for a note on some problems) but consultants have often had to be used to help cut through conflicts of interest with respect to general policy (cf. Arup 1991). Even when appointed to given tasks, archaeologists do not have an exclusive position; they must resign themselves to monitoring, either by quantity surveyors (cf. Lawrence 1989) who have no archaeological priorities whatsoever, or by archaeological consultants trained to understand the priorities of both the archaeologist and the client or sponsor.

Developers rarely perceive archaeological consultants as independent; the consultant is usually treated either as employee or Trojan Horse. Developers themselves tend not to express their opinion of archaeologists in print (but cf. Edwards 1989); it has been left to the pastiche that is the 'Developer Column' in *The Field Archaeologist* (see especially 'Fitzpatrick' 1991, 1992) to warn of the very real preconceptions, biases and legitimate worries of developers.

Consultants themselves are becoming justifiably annoyed at the tawdry image imposed upon them, as can be seen for example in the recent call to use the phrase 'consulting archaeologist' (Strickland 1992b). The move by so many county archaeologists and senior unit and museum staff to consultancy both underlines the quality of personnel now to be found in this specialization and begs the question of what intolerable resource and intellectual constraints have prompted what is still a very risky career shift. The formation of the Association of Professional Archaeological Consultants (APAC) in December 1992, as a specific forum in which consultants can discuss their mutual concerns, will hopefully promote coherence and facilitate both internal and external communication.

There has been encouragement for consultants from several quarters in the last few years but, superficial antagonisms aside, attitudes have not always been unequivocal. In the section 'Who is it for?' of a pamphlet (IFA n.d.) designed to encourage archaeologists to join the IFA, thirteen different types of archaeologist were listed, with no mention of consultants: it has taken a new edition (October 1992) to rectify this omission. The first IFA *Directory of Members* (IFA 1989) contained a list of those members available for consultancy, a well-meaning but useless step, since there was no clear indication of vested interests. The structure of the profession is sufficiently awkward that the IFA has been unable to carry out earlier plans (cf. IFA Council 1987; Darvill 1991b) to produce a comprehensive directory of contractors, including consultants. Again, PPG 16 and PPG 16 (Wales), but not the Scottish consultation draft PAN or NPPG on *Archaeology and Planning* (DoE 1990a; Welsh Office 1991; SOEnD 1992a, 1992b) suggest that developers might wish to make use of consultants for advice during the planning process. However, government commissions to consultants send a different signal. Why was a report on 'best practice' for mineral operators with respect to archaeology included in a commission to a non-archaeological environmental consultancy (Roy Waller Associates Ltd 1991) and why was a report on the performance of PPG 16 commissioned from a non-archaeological planning consultancy (Pagoda Projects 1992), both with predictably bland, uninformative and occasionally inaccurate results? Individual antipathy is one thing but organizational reluctance or paralysis is another and cannot be shrugged off simply as a perceptual problem.

Moving to more specific problems, it can be suggested that consultancy practices cream off the more profitable aspects of contracts, leaving fieldwork and the even more financially risky post-fieldwork projects to units (as implied in *BAN* 1990). On the face of it, this is quite true, but the real situation is not that simple. First, it is common practice for consultants in non-archaeological disciplines to gather information, from the field if necessary, upon which to base their advice; it is permissible for archaeological consultants to do the same, to carry out certain forms of field evaluation if adequately qualified. Second, most units now provide consultancy services. Third, from a commercial viewpoint, field evaluation is seen by many units as a troublesome, scrappy process, necessary in order to win commissions for more substantial excavations. Evaluation is arguably the most important yet most underrated aspect of modern public archaeology (cf. Darvill and Gerrard 1992), and requires a special set of skills (in both desktop and fieldwork modes) from totally committed teams, however constituted. It would be damaging, and quite unnecessary, to let an artificial demarcation dispute develop here: all types of organization must recognize that a reliable operating surplus can only stem from solutions that are both academically sound and cost-effective for sponsors or clients.

It is obvious that archaeologists in tied and mixed practices must come to terms with a strong set of vested interests in their parent organizations, although it would be unfair to assume that they necessarily lack objectivity. However, the problem, if problem it is allowed to become, is in fact much wider. Most larger projects involve a consultancy team, usually with either a planning consultant or barrister as lead; the pressures upon an archaeologist to conform are likely to be even greater in this situation than in a mixed practice. Archaeologists must clearly be prepared to work conscientiously in the team environment. However, it is imperative that the concept of planning and management balance be maintained (cf. Davies 1991) and that there be no invisible trawl of issues, no setting aside of minor constraints until they have been openly weighed against all other material considerations. It should not be forgotten that the team context also provides the invaluable opportunity for archaeologists to inform their team colleagues (and vice versa) in a confidential setting where all parties can safely expose and examine their motives.

Allied to the above problem is the issue of data suppression (Heaton 1988; Hinton 1992). When the consultant has presented a report to the client, the contract is fulfilled. The client is not entitled to edit the report and pass it on as the consultant's work, but the client may legally decide not to pass on the report at all or to edit it to remove all reference to the consultant. The latter practices are much more common than the reader might think, and it is important to realize that few non-archaeological consultants see any ethical dilemma in such actions. The IFA *Code of Conduct* (IFA 1988a) is generally applicable to this problem but is currently not specific enough. It is a legal fact that a consultant's advice is given in confidence and must remain confidential if the client so wishes. However, during a project the archaeological consultant may gather field data. It is advisable that a clear statement be included in all contractual arrangements that any 'primary archaeological data', together with 'proximal interpretation' (the basic commentary that renders bare facts useful), must be released to the relevant SMR before a planning or management decision is taken regarding the land in question (cf. Collcutt 1991). The concept may be widened to 'primary archaeological documents' (those not yet recorded in the SMR but clearly containing data relevant to a decision); a list of such documents, with no comment, may be sent to the SMR if the consultant's report has not been made available.

Contracts present another problem for consultants. There are a number of complex model contracts and contract guidelines in circulation (cf. Darvill and Atkins 1991). However, clients for consultancy will not use these forms and any attempt to force the issue may lose the consultant the contract. The consultant will normally discuss the project with the client (possibly after receiving documentation) and will then send a free-style letter of proposal, including any specific conditions relevant to the particular case (consultants should include general statements upon contract conditions, such as adherence to professional codes or standards, in their publicity brochures, which are a legal part of all contractual agreements); the client will then reply with a free-style letter of commission. When a client has earned a degree of trust, the consultant may even be expected or willing to act upon verbal instructions. Formal contracts may of course be necessary when imposed by clients, as is often the case on private infrastructure and government projects. Nevertheless, the nature of most consultancy tasks, commonly involving intermittent or emergency input over long periods in response to changing situations, is not amenable to prior formal contractual definition. Since it is the consultant who takes the commercial risk (and all consultants should learn their contract law thoroughly), the profession must allow consultants to use their judgement on the conditions of contract in any particular case and not try to impose pro forma documents. The only situation in which more rigorous definition (usually in the form of a detailed specification) is systematically needed (to safeguard the archaeological resource rather than the consultant) is when the consultant proposes to carry out significant fieldwork.

The matter of contract is different from that of brief. A brief is a statement of objectives, stripped of administrative and financial provisions (Chapter 16). Whatever method is used to establish the brief, the consultant should make sure that both he or she and the client understand and agree on its meaning. This is not usually a problem, except in the case of competitive tendering (CT). There has been much discussion of the latter topic in archaeology (e.g. Hobley in CAWP 1988; Richard Hughes reported in Marvell 1990; Watson 1990; Heaton 1991; Swain 1991). The IFA *Code of Approved Practice for the Regulation of Contractual Arrangements in Field Archaeology* (IFA 1990) is a laudable attempt to mitigate the worst possible effects of CT (cf. also Lawson 1989; English Heritage 1990, 1991) – an attempt which is not yet working. Both public and private sectors are resisting proper tender practices every inch of the way, and archaeological tenderers are letting it happen. The main problem is that many developers seem to think that they can both write the brief and judge the tenders themselves. If the IFA really wants to make design rather than cost the competition criterion, more forceful action must be taken to ensure that members maintain solidarity and refuse to tender to briefs that have no input from a qualified archaeologist, either curator or consultant. Similarly, it is good practice for a brief to state the name(s) of the competition judge(s), the period during which requests for further details may be made (and answers circulated equally to all tenderers), the tender deadline and the judgment date; these provisions are not mandatory but many people (archaeologists and developers) do not seem to realize that any demonstrable instance of unfair tender practice is potentially cause for civil action. This is not an attempt to drum up business for consultants; consultants running a tender competition are automatically disqualified from competing themselves, other than under the most exceptional and explicit circumstances (including prior warning to other prospective tenderers). The use of tendering is definitely on the increase, now including even minor projects. Many conscientious firms of consultants and fieldwork teams put very considerable effort into tenders; if the ground rules are not equitable, this effort (and the money it entails) is wasted. CT briefs must contain a statement of the full objectives of a project (including contingencies), together with a thorough set of rubrics indicating the different types of information the tenderer should submit. If no fee has been paid, the specification submitted by a tendering firm is that firm's copyright; all archaeologists should be very wary of any specification that has obviously been prepared by someone with archaeological expertise but which has no acknowledgement of the author.

The question of legal liabilities arises in any consultancy context. Consultants are extremely exposed when advising on archaeological matters affecting the viability of multi-million-pound projects. All contractors will carry substantial public liability insurance, sometimes with special clauses to cover fieldwork. Such insurance is affordable since it has a relatively low premium-to-cover ratio. Advice is quite another matter, requiring full professional indemnity (similar to that held by solicitors) at a premium of tens and even hundreds of thousands of pounds per annum for relatively low cover. There are partial solutions, with various legal insurance packages at premiums of a couple of thousand pounds. This is a topic for the IFA to consider, with a view to publishing recommendations on a range of options that would be affordable for different practitioners. Persons wishing to work on major projects will soon have no choice in this matter; demonstration of full professional indemnity cover of a minimum of £5 million is becoming a routine prerequisite.

Consultants cannot ignore the questions of standards and quality assurance (Chapter 16). Especially when at draft stage, certain IFA documents may fail to appreciate the gamut of constraints upon commercial practitioners (cf. SIBA 1992); the IFA should bring a wider range of expertise to bear upon the matter of standards. A formal standard must be viable in contexts rarely under the total control of archaeologists, and must, by very definition, contain mechanisms for at least qualitative measurement of performance. As for quality assurance (QA), British Standard 5750 is a daunting prospect, especially when one realizes that eligibility for the kitemark will cost a minimum of £2,500 per year. There are, however, several consultancy practices that already have a QA scheme in place (cf. Strickland 1992a). The important point is that BS 5750 and the relevant supporting documentation (especially Parts 1, 1/2 and 8, and Doc No E000146) contain a clear statement of what is involved in quality assurance, under the two main rubrics of 'Procedures' (explicit instructions to staff on how to go about a task and how to document progress) and 'Audit' (checking and improving performance at various project stages or before subsequent projects). Any archaeologist can set up a rudimentary QA scheme that can be refined and expanded (incorporating detailed professional standards as they appear) over a period of years, indeed, logically for ever. It is not difficult to devise formal written procedures to cover many aspects of consultancy work, together with simple internal audit mechanisms. Compact questionnaires may be issued with reports, so that both clients and curators can contribute external audit statistics.

Consultants operate in the marketplace and must be allowed to set their fees as they see fit. Commercially acceptable fee rates have risen steadily in real terms over the last few years, so that archaeological consultants can now attract remuneration (from which all overheads must be financed) comparable with the lowest rate for, say, generalist solicitors (but still significantly below those for most other types of professional consultant). Larger developers or projects can pay such rates but small developers and most members of the general public cannot. Similarly, some local planning authorities do not yet consider archaeologists to be in the same category as other planning consultants and will usually balk at the cost of archaeological support at public inquiries (Saville 1990). Consultants must decide under what circumstances they are available to advise upon the public heritage. The interim solution already adopted by some firms is a *pro bono* allocation from operating surplus, with all non-profit-making applicants eligible but choice of projects to receive partial or full subsidy being made by the consultancy management on criteria of pure archaeological merit. Given assurances of proper administrative structure and sound ethical base, consultants might be willing to subscribe to a centralized archaeological aid fund, similar to (but a little less pernickety than) the mechanism operating in the legal profession.

Finally, there are the problems inherent in consultancy training. The IFA *Directory of Educational Opportunities* (IFA 1992) contains many items of interest, while individual events are advertised in a variety of archaeological journals and newsletters; the *APAC Newsletter* will seek to collate relevant material. Consultants should give more lectures and seminars aimed primarily at training rather than publicity. Personnel exchange and on-the-job training schemes may be difficult to organize because of commercial issues and confidentiality; nevertheless, at least larger firms should be able to find some occasions when such training might be possible. In-post continuous or upgrade training will be easier within firms, through shadow and post-mortem systems, but should also include as much exposure as possible to relevant colloquia. Every individual should be encouraged to maintain a project-by-project appendix to their curriculum vitae, noting precisely the nature of their input. This will be useful to a current employer, in order to check for and rectify any imbalance in experience, and also invaluable (supported by references or certification) if the individual changes employment or needs to demonstrate competence for a particular contract.

CHAPTER 16

WORKING PRACTICES

Timothy Darvill

INTRODUCTION

Among the most pervasive changes to have occurred in archaeological resource management over the last decade are those relating to working practices, here taken to mean the professionally accepted, normal arrangements and frameworks for the performance of archaeological tasks. The causes of these changes are numerous and complicated, but some are relevant to an understanding of the present situation. Principal among these is the proliferation of legislative measures that bear on archaeological work and the tighter definition of roles and areas of responsibility. Other matters of importance are noted in later sections.

Inevitably this short account is a highly selective outline of a wide topic. It is divided into three main sections. The first deals with operational matters connected with the main areas of current archaeological endeavour; the second with relationships of various sorts within the profession and between archaeologists and other parties; and the third with the general regulation of archaeological work. Specifically excluded is any consideration of employment arrangements; the important matter of health and safety is only given cursory treatment.

Matters discussed here are subject to almost constant modification in the light of shared experiences and collective debate. This reflects the relative youthfulness and buoyancy of the profession. Change is not always welcomed by all, and can sometimes be hard to accommodate quickly within local working environments while maintaining professional dignity, the authority of advice already given, and indeed the *raison d'être* for a particular existing organizational structure or arrangement. For this reason, both the stimulus for, and the implementation of, changes in working practices in archaeology are generally incremental rather than radical in nature, and localized rather than widespread in their effects.

OPERATIONAL CONSIDERATIONS

With changes to the funding structure, increased diversity in the tasks required, and the tendency for archaeologists to work within multi-disciplinary teams, the day-to-day running of archaeological organizations has become a complicated matter. Regardless of whether the organization is concerned with contracting, curating the resource, consultancy, presentation and display, academic research, or a combination of these, tried and tested working practices are essential. The following sections focus on selected key topics within which working practices have, largely through consensus, become established.

Project management

Projects come in many shapes and sizes, but all are journeys into the unknown, fraught with risk, whose exact course can never accurately be predicted and whose final outcome is never completely guaranteed. Project management aims to minimize risks, order and direct resources, and relate objectives to attainable goals so that work is finished on time, within budget, and to an acceptable standard.

All projects need managing, but the more complex the project the greater the need for a trained project manager. Complexity in such cases can be roughly measured in terms of the number of task-sets, the number of individuals and organizations who will perform those tasks, and the degree of co-ordination required between task-sets.

Four main sorts of project are generally recognized, each with its distinctive type of management system (Lock 1988). The execution of archaeological fieldwork projects is most closely allied to the kind of management system associated with construction projects, and this is the path that has been followed by English Heritage in its recommended approach to the management of archaeological projects, colloquially MAP 2 (English Heritage 1991b).

The project management system proposed in MAP 2 comprises five successive phases:

1 Project planning
2 Fieldwork/data collection
3 Assessment of potential for analysis
4 Analysis; report preparation
5 Dissemination

Activities appropriate to each phase are divided into a series of four successive steps: proposal, decision, data-collection, and review. The whole process can be seen as cyclical: each phase begins with a proposal and ends with a review that in turn defines the proposal for the next phase. Each phase should have clearly defined objectives and be appropriately resourced in terms of staff, equipment, time and costs.

All projects need to be executed by a qualified, competent and motivated team, but the key figure is the project manager (see also Chapter 14). He or she leads the team and takes overall responsibility for the success of the project. The project manager is concerned with optimizing and co-ordinating resources of all kinds to achieve the defined goals. The project manager's authority can vary from executive responsibility in a line management sense through to co-ordinator by persuasion.

Project management increasingly involves the use of sophisticated techniques for analysing a proposed project, computing possible routes that increase the likelihood of success, and modelling resource requirements as the project unfolds. Such management tools include critical-path analysis, network analysis, and cascade diagrams of various sorts (especially Gantt charts).

Briefs, specifications and project designs

The terms brief, specification, and design, often prefaced by 'project', are sometimes used interchangeably, although each has an accepted meaning acquired by usage within archaeological project management. Each kind of document should only be employed for its intended purpose; thus it is important to know and recognize the differences.

A brief is an outline for an archaeological project (IFA 1990: 6), usually little more than the definition of objectives, the rationale or justification for their pursuit, an indication of the methods that might be used, and the operational parameters on the execution of the work. A specimen brief has been published (Chadwick 1991).

A specification is usually taken to mean a detailed statement of the necessary works associated with the undertaking of a particular project (IFA 1990: 6). It might form the basis for soliciting competitive tenders. Both the brief and the specification are normally prepared by or agreed with the relevant curator before implementation.

A project design is the outcome of a phase of project planning within the accepted framework of archaeological project management and as such is a phase-related piece of project documentation (English Heritage 1991b: 9–10). It specifies the objectives of the whole project and outlines the resources likely to be needed to achieve them. English Heritage has published a checklist of the main items to be included in a project design (1991b: 27–9).

Estimating

Costing archaeological projects in terms of the resources required to achieve set objectives is far from easy. It needs a considerable input of time, consultation with all members of a project team, and the use of results from the tracking of similar projects previously undertaken. There is no common method for costing archaeological work, nor are there generally available price guides for regularly executed operations.

There are also different ways of specifying the price of a task or service detailed in a project specification. The most straightforward way of specifying costs is as a fixed price. Here the contactor undertakes to execute an agreed project for a specified sum, this being set down in a contract (see below). Where the full extent of the work is uncertain at the time a contract is made, the contract may provide that the price be ascertained by measuring the work actually done against items in a bill of quantities or a schedule of rates.

Adjustments to a fixed-price contract may be permitted if there is: (1) a fluctuation clause in the contract entitling the contractor to be reimbursed for any increase in labour or materials costs, or giving the client the benefit of any decrease therein; (2) a clause requiring adjustment to the fixed price where there is any variation; and (3) a general clause whereby contractors may claim an increase in the actual work such as may be caused by late instructions from the client.

Where no price is fixed, the contractor is entitled to claim a reasonable amount from a client. Determining what is reasonable must depend on circumstances but may include payment for the skill, supervision, experience, and services of the contractor as well as materials and labour supplied. It should be noted, however, that market prices used to calculate a price set down in a contract are taken to be those at the time the contract is signed, unless the contract itself says otherwise.

Another method of calculating price is the costs-plus principle. Here the contract contains detailed provision for the calculation of costs with an agreed additional percentage of costs to cover overheads (including a profit margin if that is appropriate). The contract may provide for the contractor to be paid an additional sum in the event of the completion of work before a stipulated date.

Competitive tendering

Competitive tendering (CT) for archaeological projects is relatively new, at least in the commercial sense; its introduction has caused considerable debate (Swain 1991). The system, which provides for a number of contractors to submit quotations for undertaking a piece of work defined by a specification, is basically straightforward and perfectly legal so long as tendering is undertaken in an even-handed way. English Heritage has issued a policy statement on CT (1991a: 27–8), and Historic Scotland has circulated a draft policy for comment.

The Institute of Field Archaeologists' *Code of Approved Practice for the Regulation of Contractual Arrangements in Field Archaeology* (IFA 1990) includes the following clauses relating to CT:

12. An archaeologist involved in commissioning or undertaking works will satisfy himself or herself that the scope of any agreed brief or specification is adequate for the declared purpose, conforms with accepted academic standards and does not needlessly place the resource at risk.
13. An archaeologist involved in seeking tenders must endeavour to ensure that all potential contractors consider the same brief, are provided with the same information regarding the criteria for selection, form of tender and deadline, and are clearly notified of the selections procedures and who will select tenders. An archaeologist must treat each such tender as a confidential document unless otherwise specified and the contents of the tender must not be divulged to other tenderers prior to the selection of a contractor.
14. An archaeologist shall not select a contractor or recommend a contractor for selection on the basis of price alone. Having satisfied himself or herself that competitors are adequately qualified and are available to undertake the work, an archaeologist will select or recommend for selection from competing tenders those which: meet the brief; are least damaging to the resource; are the most comprehensive; and are the most cost effective.

Of these, clause 13 is probably the most onerous. It requires careful documentation of the tendering process lest procedures are later called into question. Clause 14 has proved slightly more problematic in practice than its drafters expected because one interpretation of its wording essentially allows competition by design: devising an acceptable specification becomes part of the competition itself. This is less than ideal since it encourages specifications that involve the minimum work possible rather than an appropriate and realistic response to the problem in hand. Moreover, contractors find it hard to justify the commitment of resources to the preparation of detailed specifications in a competitive situation when, probabilistically, the chances of success are stacked against them. Currently, the trend seems to be towards greater attention to the preparation of a single project specification (usually by a curator or consultant), this document being used as the basis for all tenders. To judge from practice in other professions, however, even this is unlikely to prevent submissions of non-conforming tenders.

Obligations to other parties and the declaration of interests

Archaeological organizations typically either work for a number of clients or carry out a range of roles. Whichever, overlaps of interest are likely to occur; it is important that these are declared before conflicts arise. The IFA's *Code of Approved Practice for the Regulation of Contractual Arrangements in Field Archaeology* includes the following clauses to deal with these matters:

22. An archaeologist whose professional responsibilities combine recommendations about preservation and recording with its execution must clearly indicate the combination of these interests to all relevant parties in order that any potential conflicts of interest can be clearly identified.
23. An archaeologist will declare to other parties within a contractual arrangement any other relevant business interests, and will execute the contract faithfully, conscientiously, fairly and without inducements to show favour.
24. An archaeologist should exercise caution in undertaking, for different organizations, a series of contracts relating to a single site or monument where conflicts of interest may arise.

Clause 22 applies, for example, in the case of integrated archaeological organizations that both provide planning advice to local authorities (curatorial role) and offer an archaeological contracting service. Many developers are distrustful of such arrangements even when there is an apparent organizational distinction between the two sections. The trend is towards the complete separation of curatorial from contractual responsibilities; this already applies in many parts of the country.

Territoriality

Closely linked to the issue of CT has been that of territoriality (see also Chapters 4 and 14), particularly the notion that where an archaeological unit has been practising for a considerable time, accumulating a database and providing a community service, then it is the most appropriate body to undertake archaeological contracts in its own neighbourhood. The idea that any archaeological organization should enjoy exclusive rights over a defined area was never really sustainable in the economic and political climate of the UK in the late 1980s. Discussions of territoriality were rather sterile: a useful summary of the arguments has, however, been presented by the Council for British Archaeology (Lambrick 1991: 23–4).

Proponents of territoriality generally oversimplified the complex, but essentially divisible, roles undertaken by most archaeological organizations. In practice, it is now widely accepted that curatorial responsibilities are best executed on a territorial basis or at least on that of a series of geographically interlocking areas of responsibility. The debate has now shifted to the question of where within local government is the most appropriate locus for archaeological advisers: the County/Region/Islands Area, or the District/National Park, or some other area (e.g. a unitary authority), or a mosaic of different levels in different places.

Equally, it is accepted that most contractors have the qualifications, skills, and capability to work in a range of regions and situations. Many contractors have freed themselves from ties to particular geographical areas, although most retain a core operating area while accepting that they do not have exclusive rights within it. To assist clients and consultants with the selection of appropriate contractors, many curators maintain lists of contractors who would be acceptable to them for projects within their area of responsibility. How such lists are established is not always clear, although some authorities have advertised for submissions from contractors who would like to be so listed.

Competency and qualification

Importance is attached to being qualified and competent for the kinds of archaeological work expected of individuals and organizations, as poorly executed work by unqualified and incompetent practitioners would bring the whole profession into disrepute. The IFA's *Code of Approved Practice for the Regulation of Contractual Arrangements in Field Archaeology* includes the following relevant, and fairly stringent, clauses:

> 10. An archaeologist may advertise his or her services but must ensure that the services offered are consistent with the Code of Conduct and that claims of competence match the task in hand.
> 11. An archaeologist shall not offer, recommend the offer of, or accept a contract of work unless he or she is satisfied that the work can be satisfactorily discharged. The archaeologist undertaking the work should have the requisite qualifications, expertise and experience and be able to meet the projected timescale.

Attaining appropriate levels of competence and experience is not simply about qualifying and then practising but rather about gaining proper experience and then maintaining skills through continuing professional development (CPD). The various classes of corpo-

173

rate membership of the IFA (in ascending order: practitioner, associate, member) recognize accumulating experience through time-service. An increasing number of curators insist that project managers and staff superintending archaeological works are members of the IFA at an appropriate level (identifiable by the distinctions: PIFA, AIFA and MIFA).

Some professional bodies require that qualifications are maintained through the annual accumulation of CPD credits for courses and training programmes attended. In archaeology at present, attending training programmes is voluntary, although it is likely that it will become compulsory within the foreseeable future.

Best practice and quality assurance

Closely related to the matter of qualifications and competency is the question of quality. IFA council has set up a working party that is currently drafting a series of standards documents for archaeological work. Seven such documents are envisaged:

1 Desk-based studies
2 Field evaluations
3 Structural surveys and standing building recording
4 Excavations
5 Watching briefs
6 Artefact and ecofact study and curation
7 Study of excavation records

These documents are intended to state the key principles for different types of project, and deal with outcomes rather than technical details on the achievement of those outcomes. The aim is to make good practice the norm, and to promote best practice wherever possible.

Internally operated quality assurance checks frequently form an element of project tracking procedures used by archaeological organizations. Indeed, Total Quality Management (TQM) is now an ambition for some archaeological organizations; it is expected that before long successful ones will be awarded a 'kitemark' for quality assurance under BS 5750 recently introduced by the British Standards Institution. The principal advantage of such quality assurance systems is that procedures can be audited through a formal review system.

Subcontracting

One way of increasing the scope of work that an archaeological organization can discharge is through subcontracting elements of projects. This generally works well, although there are important contractual implications that are sometimes overlooked (Darvill and Atkins 1991: 2).

Any archaeological organization may secure assistance with the performance of part of a project through subcontracting except where there is an express prohibition in the contract itself or it is a personal contract. It should be borne in mind that an archaeological organization will be liable for defects in a subcontractor's work as if it had performed it itself. There should be a clause in the subcontract indemnifying the archaeological organization for any loss arising as a result of the subcontracted work. If the subcontractor breaches the main contract the archaeological organization can recover from the subcontractor losses suffered as a result. It may be expedient to include a clause in the subcontract whereby the subcontractor agrees to be bound by the main contract, but this will not necessarily incorporate all the terms of the main contract. Terms must be expressly incorporated to apply to the subcontract.

Professional indemnity

Much archaeological work is based on professional judgement and inevitably there will be occasions, rare it is to be hoped, when such judgements are found to be deficient. For this reason all archaeological organizations (including individuals in private practice) should be covered by professional indemnity insurance. Premiums are usually linked to annual turnover, degree of risk, and the nature of the work.

RELATIONSHIPS

Tighter definition of roles among archaeologists, more closely defined responsibilities and the fuller integration of archaeological work with that of other professions mean that the question of relationships between parties, whether they are all archaeologists or not, has become more critical in recent times. The main players in such networks of relationships are the four 'Cs': curators, contractors, consultants and clients. Areas where working practices impinge on the question of relationships between parties are now considered.

Contracts

Contracts of various sorts form the most common means of regulating and defining relationships; their use in archaeology has recently been reviewed in some detail (Darvill and Atkins 1991). A written contract may range from an informal letter through to a tightly structured document compiled by a solicitor. In all cases a contract must contain:

1   The names of the parties, or a sufficient description of them
2   A description of the subject matter
3   All material terms
4   Details of any consideration

A 'standard form' contract is a pro forma document regularly used in particular situations to which it specifically relates, although it may be necessary to vary some clauses according to the requirements of a particular application. Such contracts are likely to be useful for routine, well-defined tasks such as watching briefs, evaluations and the recording of standing buildings. Many archaeological contracts undertaken today are of the 'design and execute' type. In these, the contractor devises a programme of work (described in a specification), agrees it with the employer and appropriate archaeological curators, and then carries it out.

The three basic elements of any contract are: the agreement, the contractual intention, and the consideration. The *agreement* involves the unqualified acceptance by one party of an offer made by another party, this acceptance being brought to the attention of the party making the offer. A tender may be invited from potential suppliers of goods and/or services. In such cases each tender submitted is an offer: the organization that invited the tenders can accept any tender to bring into existence a binding contract. For this reason it is important to include with any tender the terms and conditions under which it can be fulfilled. A *contractual intention* must exist to create a legally binding contract. If there is no intention then despite the existence of an apparent agreement supported by a consideration there will not be an enforceable contract. The *consideration* is a benefit that one party must confer on the other in return for the benefit received. Whether the consideration is a promise, goods, or services, it is usually of considerable value although the benefits conferred need not be of the same value (e.g. cost), or the same kind (e.g. financial as against intellectual), as the benefits received. Where an archaeological organization has been granted charitable status the nature of any consideration has to be examined very closely.

For example, a developer may agree to make a donation to an archaeological organization which then carries out the tasks for which it has been set up. The archaeological organization should approach the Inland Revenue and Customs and Excise in advance to check that exemption from VAT will be granted. In such circumstances, any contract should not contain provision to acknowledge the sponsor, for example in press coverage, as this may be deemed a supply of services and give rise to a liability for VAT.

It is also important, irrespective of whether the consideration is deemed a donation or a payment for services, that it is clearly stated that costs or sums payable are inclusive or exclusive of VAT (even if VAT is not being charged) in order to reduce the possibility of a VAT liability arising subsequently.

Contracts are not just records of agreements. Their construction should be regarded as a useful exercise in thinking through the circumstances of a project, how it will be executed, and the various effects that it might have on other people. Their negotiation provides an agenda for discussions between the main parties and the chance to express views on particular points. Their implementation may be used as a management tool to keep the project on course.

Most important, however, is that contracts should not simply be documents familiar to project managers and negotiators. In order that a contract for services can be fully executed it is vital that each level of management is aware of those elements of the contract that are relevant to their responsibilities. Many archaeological organizations use contracts to regulate work undertaken for developers and other non-archaeological organizations. Contracts are also used for subcontracted work between archaeological organizations and specialists of various sorts. Specimen model contracts for archaeological services have been published (BADLG 1989; Darvill and Atkins 1991). A review of the main components of the contract and an outline checklist of points to consider follows (and see CBA 1982; Atkins and Darvill 1991).

Definition of site or area for investigation

Any archaeological contract must specify precisely where the land to be investigated lies. A scaled plan of the site and its environs is often helpful. Where possible the plan should include: delineation of the area(s) to be excavated; information on access; land ownership; adjacent holdings and surrounding structures; proposed locations of spoil heaps and on-site accommodation for the archaeological organization; and known live services. It is often necessary, having regard to the design of the proposed development or subsequent land use, to specify a maximum depth of archaeological investigation, related to a datum point. A procedure for reviewing this restriction may also be agreed.

Purpose and scope of contracted work or services

Obligations imposed on developers by clauses in a development agreement, conditions of planning consent, or conditions attached to a Scheduled Monument Consent may be the reason for engaging an archaeological contractor. In such cases it is often helpful to make this clear in preliminary sections of a contract, not least so that it can be used to demonstrate intent by a developer to statutory bodies and/or local authorities. The works to be undertaken should be listed in a schedule. The importance of a well-considered specification that includes a provisional programme can not be underestimated; extracts from such a document may usefully be included in the schedule. In adapting the project specification to the requirements of a contract, however, there must always be adequate account taken of the need to retain some flexibility for the post-excavation and publication programme as well as the site-works proper.

Licence period and work programme

It is important to state when work will start, either as a date or as a time determined by the completion of some other task, and how long the work will take. A summary programme will frequently be included in the project specification that forms part of the schedule. In order to control work schedules, it is usually helpful to specify the notice period that a developer is required to give before works commence. Arrangements for changes in the duration of the work programme, premature termination or postponement must be made. Arrangements for checking standing buildings before or during demolition must be specified. This provision allows observations that may help with subsequent interpretation of excavated features; detailed recording of standing buildings or remains of historic interest would be contained in the specification. Arrangements for any continuing observation of the development by the contractor after the conclusion of the agreed archaeological programme must be specified, including statutory safety provisions and indemnity for consequent delays.

The following points might be considered when establishing the length of a contract:

1 Date of commencement on site
2 Dates of phased sectional entries/completions
3 Dates of final completion on site
4 Date of interim report to client
5 Date of final report
6 Extensions to contract period (reasons/agreements required/consequential costs)

Consents and access

Responsibilities for obtaining any licences or consents required need to be specified. Who undertakes such duties as organizing disconnection of live services should be specified. Arrangements for access need to be defined, including the following:

1 Kinds of access point(s) (vehicular, pedestrian) and kinds of access required (e.g. for lorries, caravans)
2 Wayleave restriction(s) on site
3 Wayleave restriction(s) over adjacent properties (who pays?)
4 Sites for infrastructure works (offices/soil heaps/finds processing/stores/parking)
5 Invited visitors/sponsor's representatives
6 Access by the general public
7 Access for contractors (shared use of space/access points?)
8 Licences

Ownership and disposal of finds and records

The ownership of finds and responsibilities for the costs of conservation of such finds, where appropriate, should be established before excavation commences. Special permission may be required for the archaeological contractor to take temporary custody of finds and structural remains for the purposes of study and reporting. Arrangements for the final disposal of finds, any structural remains recovered, and the records relating to the archaeological work should be agreed.

Financial arrangements

It is important to establish who is paying for the work, how much they are paying, how they are to pay it, and whether the amounts payable include VAT or not. All sources of finance for a given project forming the subject of a contract should be declared. The following points may be considered when looking at the financial structure:

1   Price: fixed price/contract price plus market fluctuations/costs-plus/contingency sums (percentage or flat rate)
2   Payments: in advance (part or whole)/interim payments (frequency?/dates due?)/basis of claim (costs or programmed payment)/minimum amount of interim claim/final account due
3   Retentions: interim claims/on completion of reports
4   Interest: on overdue payments/cost of project finance (cashflow)
5   Penalties: late completion/non-performance/delays to the archaeological programme
6   Extras: publication costs/storage grants/special conservation work/displays/receptions and publicity
7   Compensation: tenant's rights/grazing/loss of crops/damage to land drains, fences, access, etc.
8   Reinstatement: compaction/surfaces/imported aggregate, etc.

Developer's assistance

It is often cost-effective for developers to offer assistance in kind, especially things that an archaeological contractor would probably have to subcontract anyway. Lighting, fencing/hoarding, shoring, sheet piling, spoil removal and effluent disposal (ground water, chemical toilet waste, rubbish etc.), the provision of facilities (e.g. shelters, offices, toilets) and plant (e.g. mechanical excavators, pumps, dumper-trucks) might be considered. Agreed forms of assistance should be specified.

Site condition before and after licence period

Agreement should be reached on the site's condition when taken over by the archaeological contractor (e.g. cleared of buildings, levelled, topsoil removed) and on its return to the owner and/or developer at the conclusion of work (e.g. wholly/partially backfilled, degree of compaction, topsoil correctly replaced, resurfaced). It is good practice to photograph the site before and after archaeological work.

Arrangements for inspection and monitoring

The developer or his representative must have the right to inspect the site and the archaeological activities at any time. Where works are carried out in fulfilment of a planning consent or Scheduled Monument Consent some monitoring of the progress and standard of the archaeological work will often be required. This is almost always in the interest of both parties: in many cases such monitoring would be undertaken by the county archaeological officer or an English Heritage/Cadw/Historic Scotland inspector. In some cases, all parties concerned may agree to engage an independent archaeological consultant to monitor the work at the expense of one or more of the parties (this work would be the subject of a separate contract). Exact arrangements for such monitoring should be set out in the specification, but the contract must always state arrangements for access to the site by the person undertaking the monitoring.

Security

Agreement should be reached on responsibility for and the nature of site security, given that sites may be in joint occupation. The following aspects might be taken into account:

1　Boundary features, e.g. fences, hedges
2　Stock fences
3　Hoardings
4　Gates and entrances (locks, bolts, availability of keys, etc.)
5　Lighting
6　Temporary trench protection
7　Public viewing areas and platforms
8　Offices, stores and displays
9　Mobile equipment and vehicles
10　Shoring

Size of team, safety and work practices

In some cases the number of people (including visitors) permitted on site may be limited. General safety considerations will be an implied term in most archaeological contracts, although reference may be made to areas of responsibility. Special consideration may be given to matters such as:

1　Keeping paths and roads clean
2　Noise pollution (night operation of machinery)
3　Support for surrounding buildings
4　Reductions in ground-water levels
5　Silts and sludge entering drains
6　Special shoring

Insurance and liabilities

Most projects will require various types of insurance (e.g. public liability, employer's liability, plant hire, special conditions/equipment). Limits and areas of liability may usefully be specified in the contract.

Assignment, subletting and subcontracting

The extent to which these aspects need to be controlled varies greatly by project. These matters should be dealt with in the contract. Subcontracting will often feature in major projects and might include fencing, earthmoving, dewatering, geophysical and academic inputs among other things.

Change of site ownership

On occasion, archaeological projects have started, but during their execution the freehold, leasehold or other interest in the site has changed, thereby necessitating renewed negotiations at inopportune times, at considerable extra cost, and with potentially serious consequences. It is better if the terms of contract can be tied to the site.

Termination or suspension of construction work

If the archaeological organization has the power to stop construction work that is putting in peril archaeological remains it is important to specify exactly who can issue a stop command; and the consequent procedures. This section of a contract would normally conform with and be cross-referenced to, for example, a development agreement.

Termination or suspension of archaeological work

The possibility that one or other party to a contract may wish to terminate or suspend work must be considered along with the financial and timetabling implications. The most likely causes of such an eventuality include:

1 Little of archaeological importance being found
2 Major change in development plans and/or changing threat to the site
3 Land-use restrictions

Publication and publicity

The need for publications of various sorts, films, information packs, reports for the client, and data to update the Sites and Monuments Record should be reflected in the contract and specifically in the project design. Publicity is a special problem with much archaeological work and requires careful control so that neither party to the contract has cause for complaint. Special care is needed in the case of work funded from charitable donations.

Arbitration and settlement of disputes

Provision should be made for any dispute that arises to be settled by a third party.

Monitoring and tracking

Four principal kinds of monitoring can be identified in archaeology today:

1 Curator monitoring
2 Client monitoring (including monitoring by a consultant acting as agent)
3 Project tracking (i.e. internal monitoring)
4 Third-party monitoring

The last is rare; such monitoring mainly relates to cases of dispute or disagreement. Project tracking is something that organizations should undertake as part of their internal project management system. Both curator and client monitoring usually involve regular liaison with contractors and periodic inspections of ongoing work.

All monitoring has three facets: observation, recording, and reporting. The three elements most likely to be the subject of attention are: performance, time and cost. Assessment of performance includes its quality and is measured with reference to the expectations included in the project design. Time is a measure of progress and can be gauged with reference to 'milestones' identified at the project planning stage. Cost can be calculated in real terms but is more likely to be measured as the proportion of the budget actually used.

Reports from monitoring and tracking exercises give insights into project progress. Decisions can be made about any changes necessary to keep the project on target.

Confidentiality

As archaeological work is brought further forward in the development process so the question of confidentiality becomes more important. Archaeological assessments and field evaluations may be carried out before land is purchased or options exercised. In such circumstances archaeological information has financial implications as well as academic value. Information is power: even when the outline of a scheme is publicly known there may be tactical reasons for making technical information available in a predetermined order and under controlled circumstances, as for example in a consolidated report containing information on all technical studies undertaken. Sometimes the archaeologist may be caught between the client's need to work or negotiate with the archaeological information generated by initial investigations kept in-house, and the wider professional obligations to make results available. Given that archaeologists have been notoriously bad about making publicly available the results of their work the idea that everything should be disclosed immediately seems rather hypocritical. Equally though, improvements on past performance must be sought and item 27 of the IFA's *Code of Approved Practice for the Regulation of Contractual Arrangements in Field Archaeology* suggests six months as a reasonable period after which access to primary records should be allowed. Thought may be given to exactly which elements of a project are confidential: that a given kind of archaeological operation has taken place at a particular locality is unlikely to be privileged information, although exact details of the findings may be sensitive. Throughout, a pragmatic line agreeable to all parties concerned is needed.

REGULATING WORKING PRACTICES

Everything that professional archaeologists undertake occurs within frameworks of regulatory measures of greater or lesser stringency. Some frameworks relate to the definition and scope of operations, others to the acceptability and quality of performance. Four main regulatory mechanisms are explored hereafter.

Legislation

Field archaeology is not a regulated profession (cf. medicine, law), but archaeological resources and their treatment are determined by provisions scattered through a substantial raft of primary legislation, supporting instruments, and associated guidance notes. The general impact of these on working practices may be gauged from the descriptions of the legislation in Chapters 5 and 10. A few specific provisions can, however, be highlighted, especially those contained in the Ancient Monuments and Archaeological Areas Act 1979 (AMAA Act 1979).

Permissions are required under statute to carry out some kinds of archaeological work. The most notable of these is Scheduled Monument Consent: the definition of 'works' extends to archaeological investigations and many kinds of management operation (AMAA Act 1979: Section 3). The use of geophysical equipment within 'protected places' (Scheduled Monuments, Guardianship Monuments, Areas of Archaeological Importance (AAIs)) also requires prior written consent (AMAA Act 1979: Section 42).

Licences are also normally required under Section 25 of the Burial Act 1857 for the removal of the remains of any body from any place of burial; full details and variations in Scotland have recently been summarized by Garratt-Frost (1992)

Licences for other kinds of archaeological excavation are required in Northern Ireland (see Chapter 4 and Appendix, p. 134) and the Isle of Man, but not in England, Wales or Scotland. When, in due course, the UK government implements the revised European Convention of the Protection of the Archaeological Heritage, signed in Malta in January 1992, provisions will need to be made for the authorization and supervision of further archaeological activities (CoE 1992: Art 3).

Within AAIs, some aspects of working practice are defined by legislation (AMAA Act 1979: Part II), among them timetables for responding to operations notices and the scope of works that can be carried out by an investigating authority (see Chapter 5).

Although rarely used, powers of entry to private property may be authorized by the

181

Secretary of State for the purposes of inspecting Scheduled Monuments and recording matters of archaeological or historical interest (AMAA Act 1979: Sections 6, 26). Provision also exists for the temporary custody of finds and objects of interest recovered during visits under such powers for the purposes of investigation, analysis, restoration or preservation (AMAA Act 1979: Section 54).

Discretionary expenditure on the acquisition and preservation of ancient monuments (AMAA Act 1979: Section 24) and on archaeological investigations (AMAA Act 1979: Section 45) is provided through the legislation. In England, a policy relating to the disbursement of such 'rescue' funding has been issued and subsequently reinforced by a full strategy document (English Heritage 1986; 1991a). Three special areas for funding are established: projects where all possibilities of saving a site or for obtaining funds elsewhere have been exhausted; commissioned projects that enable English Heritage to carry out its statutory duties, including funding research work with such duties in view; and projects where it is not practicable for the developer to make full provision for the kind of archaeological works required (English Heritage 1991a: 33–4).

Other areas of legislation have a bearing on working practices in archaeology, most notably that dealing with health and safety at work. The Health and Safety at Work Act 1974 provided for a comprehensive and integrated legal framework for dealing with the health and safety of virtually all people at work, while also providing for the protection of members of the public where they may be affected by work activities; it also set up a Commission and Executive responsible to ministers for administering the legislation. A manual on these topics from an archaeological perspective has been published (Allen and Holt 1986) and a useful guide to safe working during field survey is also available from the Council for British Archaeology (Olivier 1989b).

Codes of practice

There are three main codes, drawn up to assist in the definition and regulation of work within particular industries, in routine use.

The code promulgated by the British Archaeologists and Developers Liaison Group (BADLG 1991), and supported by a wide range of archaeological organizations, sets out to define areas of responsibility and acceptable means and procedures for the integration of archaeological recording and investigation in the development process.

The second code, published by the Confederation of British Industry (CBI 1991), considers similar issues with respect to minerals operations. Finally, mention may be made of the *Code of Practice on Conservation, Access and Recreation* for the water industry, published by a number of government departments (DoE 1989b). The man-made environment receives special attention in this code.

Professional regulation

The need for a professional institute for archaeologists had long been recognized, although it was not until 1982 that the Institute of Field Archaeologists (IFA) finally came into being. Its objectives, as defined in its Memorandum of Association (IFA 1987: 1) are:

> to advance the practice of field archaeology and allied disciplines, to define and maintain proper professional standards and ethics in training and education in field archaeology, in the execution and supervision of work, and in the conservation of the archaeological heritage; to disseminate information about field archaeologists and their areas of interest.

Field archaeology is broadly defined by the IFA. Its membership, which now exceeds 1,000 individuals, includes practitioners working in units, local authorities, government departments, government-sponsored organizations, museums, universities, and those in private practice.

On joining the IFA members agree to abide by the Code of Conduct and all other bylaws. There is a disciplinary procedure open to members and non-members alike to investigate allegations of misconduct by members; if allegations are upheld then sanctions can be brought against the member concerned. At the core of the Code of Conduct (IFA 1988a) are four principles:

1   The archaeologist shall adhere to the highest standards of ethical and responsible behaviour in the conduct of archaeological affairs.
2   The archaeologist has a responsibility for the conservation of the archaeological heritage.
3   The archaeologist shall conduct his or her work in such a way that reliable information about the past may be acquired, and shall ensure that the results are properly recorded.
4   The archaeologist has a responsibility for making available the results of archaeological work with reasonable dispatch.

Each principle is developed as a set of rules. Collectively they serve as a foundation for the development of other bylaws relating to specific areas of working practice, for example on contractual arrangements (IFA 1990).

Peer review

Much archaeological work is subject to peer review, although not always visible as such. Applications for grants and for membership of learned societies and the IFA are based on peer validation of documentation and peer approval of proposals. The same applies to briefs and specifications relating to fieldwork programmes. Most manuscripts are refereed before acceptance for publication. As an academically based discipline, printed reviews of published works are commonplace.

Peer review serves to regulate archaeological work by promoting innovative and forward-looking projects, endorsing good work practices, and supporting what are collectively regarded as worthwhile endeavours. Looking into the future it will be interesting to see whether archaeologists in Britain are sufficiently confident to allow more penetrating peer review of their work, perhaps along the lines already practised in the USA (Burrow and Hunter 1990: 196).

CHAPTER 17

ASSESSMENT OF FIELD REMAINS

Bill Startin

INTRODUCTION

Archaeological resource management involves many judgements and decisions. Is a site of sufficient importance to qualify for legal protection? Should a proposed development be allowed to go ahead and destroy archaeological remains? Which sites should have a priority claim on scarce funds for excavation, conservation action, or presentation? Which sites can be excavated now and which should be preserved for the future? Do we know enough about the remains and their survival to make the required decision or is further field evaluation necessary? This chapter is about the assessments that are required to inform these judgements and decisions. They are a routine part of archaeological resource management and are normally made on the basis of current knowledge, although this is known to be very incomplete, and especially on the basis of the data that have been recorded in local and national Sites and Monuments Records (SMRs).

The word 'assessment' is used in this chapter in the sense of 'give a value to'; the question may often be asked in the form 'how important is this site?' Words like 'value' and 'importance' are comparative terms and it is necessary to examine our frameworks for comparison. How, for example, is the judgement made concerning the relative importance of a proposed supermarket and the archaeological remains that would be destroyed by its construction? To examine the issues involved we must consider why archaeological remains are important (i.e. why we seek to manage the resource), how judgements are made, the criteria used, and the role of consensus.

Many of the decisions in archaeological resource management concern specific archaeological sites and, for clarity, this chapter explains assessment largely in terms of single sites or monuments. However, field remains can be identified at different scales and in many different forms. Accordingly, the final section considers the interrelationship between assessment and our understanding of the archaeological resource, whether in the form of single sites, groups of remains, historic towns, or as part of the wider landscape.

The issues outlined above identify assessment as a complex task; this chapter has been written, unrepentantly, to reflect that complexity. In particular, the relationship between assessment and our understanding of the resource raises some awkward questions and the non-specialist should become convinced that the assessment of field remains is a professional task. On the other hand, the writer is concerned to demonstrate that the task is not too complex and that professional advice should be capable of clear explanation to the non-specialist; assessment is not simply a matter of recondite expert opinion. Some jargon terms are necessarily introduced, such as 'academic value' and 'monument discrimination', which it is hoped the reader will find helpful as labels for important concepts or procedures.

It should be noted that extensive reference is made in what follows to procedures that have been developed by English Heritage (EH) to undertake its Monuments Protection Programme (MPP), a review of the archaeological resource in England to identify which monuments qualify for legal protection or other action through being of national importance. While these references give the chapter an English flavour, they help to make the assessment process evident in a way that has UK-wide validity.

WHY ARE THE ARCHAEOLOGICAL REMAINS IMPORTANT?

To explain assessment we cannot, as is so often done, use the word 'important' without supporting argument. The principal reason why archaeological remains are important is for the information they contain about the past. Within archaeological resource management this can be termed academic value since the remains will require examination and interpretation before their value can be made apparent to a wider audience. However, the use of this term must not disguise the wider public interest and the place archaeology holds, alongside history, anthropology and sociology, in the study of past and present societies. Surviving archaeological remains are additionally important because they are fragile and irreplaceable; each site contains unique information that will be lost forever, unless recorded, if that site is damaged or destroyed. Already, only a fragmentary record of our past survives.

For sites that are totally buried, with no surface features, academic value is the only importance. For many remains, however, there are other values. The modern landscape has been heavily influenced by human activity and archaeological sites, individually or in groups, form an important visual component. As such, their academic importance must be judged alongside other factors, including their contribution to the aesthetic values of landscape and townscape. Visible sites also provide a direct educational resource and, more generally, contribute to the recreational activities of modern society. Finally, many archaeological sites either have or gain a symbolic importance, either through standing as symbols for the past or past events or because they were deliberately created as monuments, as with the Cenotaph or the war cemeteries in northern France.

These other values are less tangible than academic value but not less important. For example, the debate over the remains of the Elizabethan Rose Theatre in London illustrates emphatically how strongly values such as 'sense of place' can be held – to tread the ground that Shakespeare trod. We should also not forget the power of 'curiosity value' (Darvill 1992a), fascination with the unfamiliar nature of archaeological remains. Taken together, these various values make the assessment of importance a testing task; indeed, given the diversity of the archaeological resource, even academic value is difficult to estimate. But what do we really mean by 'value' and how do we make the necessary judgements?

What is value?

Full consideration of this topic lies outside this chapter – it would be a chapter in itself – but the word 'value' is used so frequently that some further explanation is required. In the modern, materialistic world, 'value' is often used in a restricted economic sense and, indeed, since it would make certain cost–benefit comparisons easier (e.g. preservation versus development), there is pressure to try to find economic equivalents for the values outlined above. In practice, this is not just the case for archaeology but applies to environmental assessment in general, including ecological, geological and landscape considerations (Coker 1992). Some economic equivalents have been noted: an excavation can be costed; visitors may be willing to pay an entrance fee and/or bear the cost of travel to a site; a site will have a purchase value. In addition, other concepts have been invented to aid such economic assessments (Darvill 1992a), including 'option value' (I may wish to visit the site) and 'existence value' (I don't wish to visit the site but I value its existence).

However, not only are most economic measures of only short-term validity (e.g. based on levels of compensation payments), while conservation is a long-term need, but important aspects cannot be given an economic value. For example, the research value of irreplaceable data is incalculable (Coker 1992: Fig. 6.3).

More detailed discussion of these issues can be found in the references given above (Darvill 1992a; Coker 1992) but it is important here to accept that archaeological sites cannot be given absolute values and that this has an effect on the form of assessment, which may be described as 'procedural' rather than 'economic'. To quote Coker (1992), discussing environmental assessment in general: 'the recommended procedure represents a valuation process, even though the values that are derived are implicit since at this point there is no appropriate methodology for measuring environmental values in money terms'. In short, 'value' is described in comparative terms, the best known of which for archaeological sites is whether or not a given example is of 'national importance' as denoted within Section 1(3) of the Ancient Monuments and Archaeological Areas Act 1979 (AMAA Act 1979).

HOW ARE PROFESSIONAL JUDGEMENTS MADE?

Some forms of assessment are relatively easy. For example, the value of a sack of potatoes can be calculated by considering its weight and the market price for potatoes. Assessing the severity of a patient's illness may be a much more difficult matter, where the evaluation of some of the indicators, such as pain, has to be based largely on subjective observation, and it is common to talk of a doctor's 'professional judgement'. The study of such judgements is of sufficient interest that there is now an Open University course on the subject (Open University 1988).

Figure 17.1, taken from the Open University course, illustrates a range of modes of enquiry, depending on the nature of the task and the mode of cognition involved. For example, projecting an object of known size and weight a certain distance is a well-structured task involving an analytical mode of cognition; scientific experiment may be the appropriate mode of enquiry.

Assessing archaeological remains is not a well-structured task and the mode of cognition will necessarily be more intuitive, although this should not be taken to imply an absence of analysis. 'Intuitive judgement' is, in effect, recognized in the AMAA Act 1979 (Section 1(3)): 'the Secretary of State may on first compiling the Schedule or at any time thereafter include therein any monument which appears to him to be of national importance'. In practice, the Secretary of State takes advice and the mode of enquiry can be identified as 'peer-aided judgement'. As these observations show, there should be no embarrassment in presenting professional judgements in archaeology as being subjective to a greater or lesser degree. However, just because the assessment of archaeological remains can be described as 'ill-structured' is not an excuse for ill-structured thinking: explicit criteria that inform our judgements can be identified, the judgement process can be explained, and, as demonstrated below, to some degree we can also undertake 'system-aided judgements'.

Except at the most general level, for example from the perspective of an uninterested supermarket developer, individual archaeological sites are not particularly alike. Assessing the relative importance of, say, an Iron Age settlement site and an area of 19th-century lead-mining remains presents difficulties; they are sufficiently unlike that we value them for different reasons. The lead-mining remains may provide a very visible link to the period that put the 'great' into Great Britain; the Iron Age settlement may be much less obvious but will hold information about a period for which there are no written

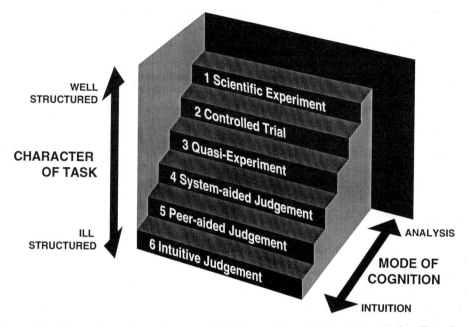

Figure 17.1. The cognitive continuum. Reproduced by kind permission of the Open University from Figure 3, Introductory Text 1, D321, *Professional Judgement* (1989).

sources. To help get over such difficulties, the assessment can begin by comparing like with like: for example, how important are the lead-mining remains in comparison with other lead-mining remains?

In practice, it is useful at this stage to recognize two different scales of comparison: individual monuments can be classified in order to group similar examples (e.g. long barrows) together into monument classes and comparisons can then be made at one scale between individual examples within specific monument classes and at a second scale between the classes themselves. Within the MPP, these two scales, discussed in more detail below, have been identified as 'monument discrimination' and (monument) 'class characterization'. In fact, at least four important aspects can be identified in the process of applying professional judgement to the archaeological resource: classification, monument discrimination, monument class characterization, and, finally, assessment.

Classification is required in order to break up the total archaeological resource into smaller data sets capable of being recorded and studied; the need to distinguish between the remains of long barrows, round barrows, hillforts, Roman forts, castles and so on is so obvious that it is rarely discussed, except in relation to the terminology used for computer-based records. However, classification is not an end in itself; it is required in order to make clear which sites are being assessed as broadly similar – as belonging to the same monument class – and the diversity of types and components within that class. This process is a necessary preliminary to 'monument discrimination'. Within the MPP, this issue has been covered by the production of a set of monument class descriptions. These represent a synthesis of our current knowledge and, since they expose limitations in our understanding, will obviously be subject to change through time as new data come to light and further research and synthesis are undertaken.

Finally, assessment will involve combining the results from monument discrimination and class characterization. These aspects of the judgement process need to be examined initially in relation to the criteria that inform them.

Assessment criteria

The criteria that inform the judgement of whether or not a monument qualifies for scheduling were first published in 1983 (DoE 1983) and have been widely promulgated since (e.g. DoE 1990a). The version of the criteria given here adapts them to assessment and omits those concerned with management action (Darvill *et al.* 1987 offer a fuller explanation).

The 'monument discrimination' stage of the judgement process has been identified with the following criteria, listed in no particular order (Darvill 1988):

Survival. Within any given class of monument, extant examples will survive in many different states of completeness. The area of a site may have been reduced by hostile land use and/or erosion, while remaining features may be regarded as being of less value if they have been heavily disturbed by robbing, ploughing, animal burrows, etc. Extensive archaeological excavations will also diminish the 'survival' of a monument.

Potential. Each class of monument provides a slightly different range of contexts for the preservation of archaeological and paleoenvironmental evidence. The nature of the evidence itself cannot always be specified precisely, but its probable existence and importance will have a bearing on the value of the monument as a whole.

Diversity (features). Most monument classes can be broken down for study into a number of smaller parts or components, not all of which will be demonstrated equally well at different examples of the monument class. The value of a monument will be enhanced if it demonstrates a good range of significant components.

Amenity value. Some monuments may be given high amenity value because they are particularly characteristic of a class or type and therefore provide good examples for use in education and display. Other sites may be accorded high value because of their strong historical associations, because of their accessibility, or because they are landmarks in their own right.

Documentation (archaeological). For any monument, archaeological study through excavation, field survey or environmental analysis can represent a gain in our understanding of the importance of the surviving remains.

Documentation (historical). This criterion is only applicable to some classes of (mainly medieval and post-medieval) monuments. Historical records can represent a gain in our understanding of the importance of the surviving remains.

Group value (association). The value of a monument may be enhanced by its association with other monuments of different classes (association with monuments of the same class is considered separately). Two kinds of association must be recognized: contemporary associations involving monuments of broadly the same date and non-contemporary associations involving monuments of earlier and/or later date.

Group value (clustering). The value of a monument may be enhanced by its association with other monuments of the same class. Clustering may have occurred for a variety of reasons, chronological or cultural, and will allow inter-site studies on sites preserved in comparable environments.

It is, of course, not immediately clear whether these criteria are equally important and it will be noted that seven of the eight are most directly concerned with academic value and only one with the other values identified at the start of this chapter. Certain criteria may also be interdependent: for example, the 'survival' of a site might be reduced as its 'documentation (archaeological)' is improved through excavation. The task of applying these criteria will be returned to below.

The 'class characterization' part of the judgement process involves four further criteria:

Period (currency). It is important to consider for preservation monuments of all dates; accordingly, the age and period over which any particular class of monument was constructed and used are important characteristics. In general, the longer the chronological span of construction and use of any given monument class the more examples will need to be included to make a representative sample.

Rarity. Some monument classes are represented by very few surviving examples, others by a great many. Clearly the loss of one example of a rare class is more significant than the loss of an example of a numerous class.

Diversity (form). Some classes of monument are represented by a variety of types that may be chronologically, regionally, or culturally defined. The more diverse a monument class, the more examples will need to be included to make a representative sample of the past.

Period (representativeness). Some classes of monument represent the principal source of information about their period while others are just one of a wide range.

Consideration of these criteria, again largely concerned with 'academic value', facilitates the assessment of the importance a monument may have through belonging to a more-or-less important monument class. As with the discrimination criteria, no one criterion necessarily takes precedence. For example, Roman amphitheatres are very rare in England (six examples) and there are about 100 times as many recorded Neolithic long barrows (although this is still a relatively rare monument class); however, long barrows are much more representative of their period, were constructed over a much longer timespan, and show a greater diversity of form. Arguably, we can learn much more about Neolithic society from the study of a long barrow than we can about Roman society from the study of an amphitheatre.

Having identified the relevant criteria, we can now examine the process through which they are applied.

The judgement process

It is useful to recognize at least two levels of assessment at this stage. At the more detailed level, there is the hard-edged assessment of an individual site or part of a site required, for example, when that particular site is threatened. More generally, there is the level of assessment that only seeks, for example, to identify all sites of national importance. Explicitly or implicitly, the broader assessment forms the context for the more detailed one (as, for example, identification by scheduling forms the context for scheduled monument consent procedures) and it makes sense to work from the general to the particular.

General assessment

The process by which monuments are assessed to identify those of national importance has received detailed consideration as part of the MPP. A general outline has been published (Darvill et al. 1987) with detailed explanation being provided by manuals, which have so far only been circulated as working papers (Darvill 1988, 1991, 1992b). The account given below is intended to demonstrate both how MPP procedures work for relatively well-defined monument classes ('system-aided judgement') and, importantly, that they do work. In short, it is contended that we can understand the nature of the judgements we make, that we can identify and agree the relevant criteria, that we can analyse retrospectively how previous judgements may have been made, and that we can see how explanation and feedback lead to a consensus as to what is important. It should be noted in passing that the form of system-aided judgement outlined below is not the only procedure used within the MPP; for industrial remains, for example, no adequate database is available and the mode of enquiry involves an ordered sequence of data-gathering, synthesis and peer-aided judgements.

Plunging straight into 'monument discrimination' using a scoring system, Table 17.1 gives the scores for the top 57 of 200 moated sites in a particular county. Identifying details (e.g. the site names recorded in the county SMR) have been omitted to prevent this particular record-based evaluation becoming fossilized. Each of the discrimination criteria has been scored, on the basis of guidelines provided within the MPP in the monument class descriptions, as good (3), average (2) or poor (1), with the exception of 'group value (clustering)', which has been scored on a presence (2) or absence (1) basis; in this example, the two 'documentation' criteria have been taken together. Each moated site has then been given a total score by adding the squared values of the individual criterion scores (values are squared to increase the dispersion of the total scores). Also shown in the table are the type of moat, where known (based on RCHME 1968 and Le Patourel 1973), whether or not it was scheduled (S) at the time of evaluation, which non-scheduled sites had been identified by county archaeological staff as being of national importance (A) in an independent assessment that preceded the MPP, the approximate threshold for national importance, and which sites (E) below the threshold were subsequently also thought on the basis of informed judgement to be more important than their scores suggested. The setting of the threshold for national importance and the nature of the subsequent informed judgement are discussed further below.

Table 17.1 is very useful in bringing together a wide range of information for further analysis and in illustrating certain significant conclusions. It appears to show a high level of consensus over the sites that are most important, with previously scheduled sites (S) and those identified from earlier evaluation (A) grouped at the top of the ranked list.

Although this consensus certainly exists, there is, admittedly, a degree of circularity in the argument because the criteria were identified on the basis of past assessments. This is in itself an important point since the system enables us to 'capture' how past assessments were made; this can be termed 'past policy capture' (Open University 1988, Introductory Text 2). Unsurprisingly, those sites that were best preserved (scoring 3 for 'survival') were ranked highest, especially if they exhibited a diversity of component features, good documentation, and/or good 'potential' (e.g. for the survival of organic remains through waterlogging). This seems to fit with current perceptions and the overall consensus illustrated by the scored evaluation would suggest that we have, indeed, identified the relevant criteria correctly.

The system illustrated by Table 17.1 appears to outperform earlier intuitive and peer-aided assessments by identifying other important sites that had previously been missed. Consultation with those who had undertaken these assessments confirms that these other sites are considered genuinely important. However, this does not mean that the results can simply be taken at their face value – far from it.

The system generally has the effect of identifying groups of sites with the same total scores, the totals themselves being separated by only small differences. These are important observations, confirming both the limitations of the scoring system and the nature of the results to be expected. The use of scoring can give the exercise a spurious objectivity and it is important not to get lost in games with numbers; the scoring of the individual criteria is a matter of judgement and the difference between a score of 2 or 3 results in a

Ind	Type	Surv	Pot	Div	Amen	Doc	GrA	GrC	Total
A	1	3	2	3	2	3	1	1	37
A		1	2	3	3	3	1	1	34
S	1a	3	2	2	3	1	1	1	29
S	1	3	2	1	2	3	1	1	29
A	1	3	2	2	3	1	1	1	29
A	4	2	3	1	3	2	1	1	29
A	1	3	2	2	1	3	1	1	29
A	1	3	3	1	1	2	2	1	29
A	4	3	2	3	1	1	1	1	26
S	1	3	3	2	1	1	1	1	26
S	1	3	3	2	1	1	1	1	26
S	1	3	3	2	1	1	1	1	26
S	1	3	2	1	1	3	1	1	26
A	4	3	3	2	1	1	1	1	26
S	3	2	2	2	3	1	1	1	24
S	1a	2	2	1	3	2	1	1	24
S	1	3	2	2	1	2	1	1	24
–	1	3	2	2	1	2	1	1	24
A	1	2	2	2	1	3	1	1	24
–	1	3	2	2	1	1	2	1	24
A	5	3	3	1	1	1	1	1	23
–	1a	2	2	2	1	2	2	1	22
A	2	2	1	2	3	1	1	1	21
–	1	2	2	3	1	1	1	1	21
–	1	3	2	1	1	2	1	1	21
S	4	3	2	2	1	1	1	1	21
A	2	3	2	2	1	1	1	1	21
A	1	3	2	1	1	2	1	1	21
A	1	3	2	1	1	2	1	1	21
A	1	2	2	1	2	2	1	1	19
–	1b	2	2	2	1	2	1	1	19
–	4	2	2	2	1	1	2	1	19
A	1	2	2	1	2	2	1	1	19
–		2	2	2	1	2	1	1	19
–	1	2	1	3	1	1	1	1	18
–	1	3	1	1	1	2	1	1	18
–	1	3	2	1	1	1	1	1	18
–	1	3	2	1	1	1	1	1	18
S	1	3	2	1	1	1	1	1	18
estimated threshold									
S	1a	2	2	1	2	1	1	1	16
A	3	2	2	1	1	2	1	1	16
A	1a	2	2	1	1	2	1	1	16
–	1	2	2	1	1	2	1	1	16
–	6	2	2	1	1	1	2	1	16
–	1	2	2	2	1	1	1	1	16
E	3	2	1	2	1	2	1	1	16
E	3	2	2	1	1	1	1	2	16
–	1	2	2	2	1	1	1	1	16
–	1	2	1	1	2	2	1	1	16
E	3	2	2	1	1	2	1	1	16
–	1	2	2	2	1	1	1	1	16
–	1c	2	2	2	1	1	1	1	16
–	1	2	1	2	1	2	1	1	16
–	1	2	2	2	1	1	1	1	16
–	6	2	2	1	1	2	1	1	16
A	1	2	2	1	1	2	1	1	16
E	1a	2	2	1	1	1	1	2	16

Table 17.1. Ranking of moated sites.

5-point difference in the total score. However, this is not to undermine the results; experience would suggest that the division of examples of a monument class into groups of 'clearly nationally important', 'clearly not nationally important', and 'around the threshold' is a reasonable reflection of reality, with a small proportion of sites among those classified as nationally important appearing as outstanding to a greater or lesser degree. Many nationally important sites are likely to be described as good examples of their class rather than in terms of superlatives. The extent to which the size of the borderline group can be minimized depends greatly on the extent of our understanding of the monument class. Similarly, we could subdivide the sites below the threshold to identify groups of sites that, while not being of national importance, are still of regional or local importance (all nationally important sites are, of course, of regional and local importance as well).

The scoring also takes a restricted view of the criteria, with no weighting being given to any particular criterion. Individual monuments may be moved up and down the ranking as a result of more specific considerations, such as membership of an important group or wider complex of remains or the particular suitability of a monument for use as an educational resource. In addition, it is important to ensure that the selection mirrors the diversity of the resource, both in including examples of all types and in reflecting regional and/or topographical variation, rather than treating all the examples as though they are alike.

The use of scoring can be clearly seen, therefore, to be an aid to judgement, not a replacement for it. It is, however, a powerful aid, organizing the judgement process, enabling the presentation of initial results and their further analysis, allowing the retrospective analysis of previous judgements ('past policy capture'), and providing the mechanism for the feedback that is an essential part of the formation of consensus.

There also appears to be a broad consensus over which sites are of 'national importance'. This can be expressed as 'all those sites scoring 3 for "survival" and all other sites of equivalent importance when all of the criteria are taken into account'; while this sounds reasonable, the issues involved are more complex and involve examination of 'class characterization'.

Similar assessments of moated sites have been carried out elsewhere in England. A selection based on the expression of the consensus in the last paragraph would lead to sample sizes varying from 10 % in counties where survival is poor to more than 50 % where survival is generally good. This analysis by county is actually an over-crude representation of the variability of survival of archaeological sites in terms of zones defined by topography and land use; sites tend to survive least well in the more intensively settled and farmed zones and best in the more marginal areas, which are less representative of past human activity. In practice, therefore, not only does the scored analysis require adjustment to reflect regional and topographical diversity but the threshold must be adjusted to ensure that a sufficiently representative sample is identified, including poorly preserved examples from areas where survival is generally poor. Retrospective analysis of previous assessments in areas of poor survival demonstrates a recognition of this need but not, in general, a systematic and consistent response to it: while some poorly preserved sites have been identified as important, where there are few well-preserved examples this has only occurred on an ad hoc basis.

For each monument class, a different proportion of the surviving resource may be identified as of national importance. For rare monument classes particularly representative of their period, such as Neolithic long barrows, all surviving examples, irrespective of their state of preservation, are considered to be nationally important. For moated sites, which are relatively numerous and only one of a number of monument classes representing the medieval period, some 30–40 % may be of national importance. For Bronze Age round barrows, also numerous but highly representative of their period and exhibiting great diversity, the figure may be some 60 %. The percentages attached to these examples are only meant to illustrate the point, not to confirm guidelines applicable to all situations: for example, all surviving round barrows in the area around Avebury, a World Heritage Site, are likely to be considered nationally important.

Identifying the different proportions of each monument class that may be identified as being of national importance establishes a broad framework for comparison between the monument classes, in effect identifying monuments considered to be of national importance irrespective of their class. In general, the proportions are identified with reference to the 'class characterization' criteria described above. An attempt has also been made to score these criteria (Darvill 1988) but only with limited success; it is therefore not described here. The three main reasons why this attempt was not successful are, however, worth noting.

Firstly, classification does not necessarily split different parts of the resource into similar sorts of groupings, and those groupings that are identified may overlap. For example, monument classes include moated sites and medieval villages but moated sites can be a component of the latter. Similarly, a Bronze Age barrow can occur in isolation or as an element of a cemetery. Such questions of scale will be examined further below.

Secondly, the diversity of the archaeological resource is such that each site has the potential to hold unique information that will be lost if that site is destroyed. Accordingly, and irrespective of 'representativeness' or the harder-edged decisions that may be required if a site is threatened, almost all well-preserved sites can be considered to be of importance. The qualifier 'almost' is included because some kinds of remains are so extensive and repetitive (e.g. certain kinds of field systems) that a selection must be made and more recent archaeological sites may survive in such numbers and be sufficiently well understood that extensive preservation is neither merited nor practicable; in short, the potential for gaining information from these sites does not justify all well-preserved examples being identified as being of national importance.

Thirdly, certain classes of monument are valued for reasons other than those covered by the identified criteria. For example, castles and abbeys lend themselves more readily to educational and recreational use than sites consisting of slight earthworks and are more evocative of major historical events, such as the Norman Conquest or the Dissolution. The application of such considerations can be seen in practice in the additional criteria adopted by English Heritage for the review of the properties in its current portfolio (English Heritage 1992).

Assessment of an individual site

There is no absolute scale of values that can be applied to archaeological sites. Some sites can be described in terms of superlatives, for example, 'one of the three best examples in the region'; very few sites, by definition, can qualify as 'the best'. In more general terms, sites can be divided into groups along the lines of 'nationally important', 'regionally important', and 'locally important', with the essential caveat that all assessment is on the basis of existing knowledge and any site can reveal hitherto hidden remains of national importance when covering layers are stripped away.

Archaeological resource managers will not routinely have time to go through a systematic national or regional analysis of the type described above. Indeed, with a few notable exceptions (Groube 1978; Groube and Bowden 1982; SPTAAWP 1986), the basis for such systematic analyses had not been laid down before the work of the MPP. For sites of exceptional quality, this has not mattered to a great extent. For those sites that are nationally important by virtue of the more obvious criteria, such as 'survival' or 'rarity', reasonable assessments can be made using intuitive and limited peer-aided judgement strategies (e.g. taking advice from a topic expert). For sites that are important for less obvious combinations of qualities, or where conflicts of interest demand a higher standard of assessment (e.g. in evidence to public inquiries), more thought is required.

The scored analysis above provides a useful basis for higher standards of assessment, leading to statements such as: 'the site is one of the 30 per cent of all known examples that have been identified as being of national importance'. For sites like the one that is thirteenth in Table 17.1, this statement can be extended by pointing out that it exhibits above average survival and has good documentation. For sites like the one ranked fifteenth in Table 17.1, it can be noted that although its survival is not outstanding it is of an unusual type and has a high amenity value. It is difficult to take such value judgements much further for most sites and, for the reasons pointed out above, it is important to avoid the intellectually and philosophically redundant exercise of quoting total scores.

Harder-edged judgements

The sample of sites identified for long-term preservation has to be sufficiently large and representative that it can reasonably be thought to provide the resource for future research questions, not just those that can currently be identified, and to provide a range of opportunities for asking the same question; it is seldom that one archaeological site can provide a complete and certain answer to a given question. Where a specific site is threatened, however, the emphasis shifts to a more intensive focus on the immediately known potential of the site, backed up by further evaluation of the survival of the deposits (e.g. by trial excavation), where necessary. This harder-edged judgement is made by the same process as the more general assessments but is necessarily more severe and, since the conservation options are likely to have financial implications, it will be more selective in terms of both what can be preserved for the future and perhaps recorded in the present.

Consensus

Given the complexity of the judgements and the range of factors that have to be taken into account, the identification of a consensus of opinion plays an important part in the assessment of field remains; it is, in any case, necessary for an individual to persuade others that a view he or she holds can be regarded widely as valid.

For the monument classes that are better known and understood, as demonstrated above, a substantial consensus has grown up through time. More generally, recognition of the importance of archaeological remains can be seen to have developed since Victorian times. The first Ancient Monuments legislation in 1882 identified for protection a small number of monuments, all prehistoric and all clearly 'monumental' (e.g. Stonehenge). By the time this legislation was consolidated in 1913 the importance of visible Roman and medieval monuments, such as castles, abbeys and town walls, was clearly recognized. Nowadays, the word 'monument' (AMAA Act 1979: Section 61) can be used to define for protection buried remains with no obvious above-ground component, the changes through time illustrating a developing appreciation of academic value. Consensus has evolved through a process of decision and feedback.

Of course, a consensus cannot necessarily be identified either for the less well-known monument classes or with respect to the less tangible criteria and values. For example, the explosion of archaeological data from aerial photography has left a legacy of unclassified sites that are not sufficiently well understood to allow assessments to be made in anything but the most general terms. There is therefore a continuing process of archaeological study and assessment, each cycle involving the establishment of a consensus for that cycle by making the judgement process reasonably ordered and explicit and thus informing others and enabling feedback. Feedback, whether in acrimonious dispute, through ordered committee meetings, by formal and informal consultation, or through time as opinions 'settle', is a key mechanism. System-aided judgement strategies aid that mechanism.

Consensus is not always easy to establish and within the archaeological profession different interest groups may argue for the greater or lesser importance of the sites with which they are especially concerned. For the great majority of sites the extent of disagreement is unexceptional and few problems are encountered at the more general levels of assessment. However, there is an important point to be made. For much of the time, the world at large accepts the assessments of professional advisors concerning the importance of archaeological sites and disagreements within the profession are largely invisible. This apparent unanimity within the profession begins to break down with harder-edged judgements. It is important to recognize that the final level of assessment may be that of the public inquiry, where arguments between professionals may be aired and the final decision will not be left to the profession. This, in effect, sets the standard for professional judgement; the ability to argue persuasively, on the basis of a well-marshalled consideration of the data, is an essential skill of the archaeological resource manager. Importantly, this observation identifies the necessary relationship between the views of the profession and those of the world at large.

This relationship, and the recognition that the individual archaeologist will also have views as a member of the wider world, have a bearing on the particular problems experienced in establishing a consensus on the importance of monuments from the more recent past. Twentieth-century industrial remains may be seen as important historical sites by some but as no more than scarred and contaminated land by others (e.g. china-clay workings in Cornwall). The cruise missile hangers at Greenham, Berkshire, are certainly a part of our history, but should they be preserved as monuments? Should the recently burnt part of Windsor Castle be rebuilt as it was before the fire or should the opportunity be taken to contribute a modern statement to this historic monument? Even more controversial, the recently discovered Nazi bunker in Berlin (Meyer 1992) brings the archaeologist face to face with modern society and both the positive and negative symbolic values it holds. For these more recent remains consensus may not have had time to form and, indeed, differing perceptions of why archaeological remains are important may be exposed. As G.J. Wainwright (1992) has recently noted, these range from the, perhaps dangerous, 'sense of national identity' (used in PPG 16 – DoE 1990a) to the 'source for the European collective memory' (European Convention on the Protection of the Archaeological Heritage 1992).

ASSESSMENT AND THE ARCHAEOLOGICAL RESOURCE

The discussion of assessment in this chapter has been framed in terms of the individual monument or archaeological site of a recognized type. This simplification has been deliberate in order to demonstrate the basic principles; but reality is more complicated. In practice, we also have to undertake the assessment of sequences of overlapping monuments, urban areas, and various forms of landscape (Darvill et al. 1987; Darvill 1992b) and to consider strategies in relation to those parts of the archaeological resource that are poorly known or understood (e.g. lithic scatter sites).

Some groups of monuments, such as barrow cemeteries, may be treated generally as single monuments. In practice, this means that there will be two levels of assessment: of the overall site in comparison to other similar sites and of its component parts (i.e. individual barrows) in their own right, including their contribution to the overall site. These two assessments will then need to be combined to give a final assessment of the value of the remains; thus, for example, a poorly preserved barrow may not be considered to be nationally important in its own right but may qualify as a component of a nationally important cemetery.

As the scale at which the resource is examined expands to include groups or complexes of monuments, multi-period settlements and the wider landscape, so the professional judgements become more difficult. The major historic towns have experienced continuity of occupation, with shifts in the density or focus of settlement, over very substantial periods of time: the buried archaeological remains that have formed and the historic buildings and structures that survive together represent the largest and most complex archaeological sites in the country (Startin 1991). Classification of the remains into different urban forms (e.g. Roman small town) and component monuments (e.g. castle) or areas is required to delineate data sets for initial assessment. Final assessment of a given site in a town will require these various assessments to be combined (Darvill 1991a).

In general assessments of the archaeological resource, three levels can be recognized. Firstly, individual settlements may be judged as a whole and, of course, the major historic towns are recognized as being of national importance. Secondly, identified monuments (e.g. castles) or component areas will be judged individually in their own right. Thirdly, specific sites will be subjected to harder-edged judgements as developments are proposed. The nature of these has been illustrated recently in the study of York (Arup 1991), although it is important to recognize that this study, with its emphasis of current research questions, does not represent a long-term conservation strategy. Historic towns are, of course, not only assessed for their academic value. Town walls, street patterns, individual monuments, and groups of monuments and buildings contribute to the overall townscape. Similar considerations will obviously influence the assessment of historic landscapes, but the study of these is in its infancy (Darvill 1992b). In practice, many recognized landscapes, such as that represented by the essentially Bronze Age archaeology of Dartmoor, albeit overlain by later industrial remains, are more or less unique in survival terms and have a recognized importance that transcends that of their component parts. As with towns, the three different levels of assessment can be identified.

In general, that which we do not understand (i.e. classify) will be difficult to assess. This seemingly obvious statement packs a hidden punch – anything we do not understand is important enough to justify further study and this is itself a form of assessment.

CONCLUSION

The assessment of field remains is difficult. It is, however, not impossible. There should be no embarrassment in accepting that the required professional judgements involve a degree of subjectivity and that the values established cannot be translated into economic terms. The aim of this chapter has been to confirm that the task of making such assessments can be organized and explained. The ability to argue persuasively, on the basis of a well-marshalled consideration of the data, is identified as an essential skill for the archaeological resource manager.

CHAPTER 18

DEVELOPMENT OF REMOTE SENSING

Part 1: Aerial photography for archaeology

Robert H. Bewley

INTRODUCTION

This part of Chapter 18 describes the process of aerial photography for archaeology. It includes a brief history of the subject, a short description of the technical aspects of aerial photography, and an explanation of the organization and funding of aerial photographers and libraries in Britain. The way in which the information from aerial photographs is mapped and future developments in the subject of aerial archaeology are also covered.

Aerial photographs contain information of enormous importance for modern archaeology that is basic to evaluation work (Palmer and Cox 1993). They are an underutilized resource and are often misused. They can provide information on early prehistoric sites through to the modern period, including recent and dramatic changes to our industrial heritage. One common misconception is that aerial photographs are synonymous with crop and soil marks; although crop marks play an important role in any archaeological study they are only one part.

For the non-specialist the formation of crop and soil marks has to be briefly explained. Whenever the subsoil or bedrock has been cut into or altered there is the possibility of crop or soil marks being formed. For example, a ditch cut into any rock will fill up with material of different characteristics to the surrounding bedrock. This difference can manifest itself when the land above the ditch has been ploughed and sown with a crop; the ditch is likely to retain more water and more nutrients than the bedrock through which it has been cut. In dryer years, the crops above the ditch grow taller because their roots can obtain more water and nutrients for stronger growth. As they are growing longer and taller they ripen later than the surrounding crop and are darker for longer. This colour (and height) difference is clearly visible from the air (see Fig. 18.1).

With soil marks the main difference is one of colour; soil marks are normally seen during the autumn and winter months. When the fields are being ploughed the difference in colour between a ditch that has been filled up with organic matter and the bare soil is clearly visible. A full explanation of the formation of crop marks and soil marks, as well as the pitfalls of interpreting these marks, has been well covered by Wilson (1982).

Author's note: this part of Chapter 18 has been written as a personal view and is in no way a reflection of policy of any one organization. Most of what follows is based on experience gained from aerial photography in England; where possible the differences between England and other parts of the UK have been explained.

Figure 18.1. Standlake, Oxfordshire. Phases of destruction are displayed as one moves from the modern village, bottom left, to the top right. Earthworks of the shrunken medieval village give way to crop marks of the prehistoric and Romano-British periods. Gravel quarries, some filled with water, represent the final destruction of a past landscape. RCHME, Crown Copyright.

TECHNIQUES

There is not space here to cover the techniques of archaeological aerial photography; the subject has been covered by Riley (1987: 17–40) and Wilson (1982). There are two basic types of aerial photography: vertical and oblique.

Vertical photographs are used by practitioners in a variety of disciplines, including archaeologists, geographers, soil scientists, planners, engineers and solicitors. Taking vertical photographs is, however, a highly specialised and relatively expensive technique carried out by military institutions or commercial companies, utilizing expensive cameras and specially adapted aircraft.

Oblique photography, using hand-held cameras, from high-wing aircraft, such as a

Cessna 150/152 (two-seater) or 172 (four-seater) is much more accessible to the archaeologist. This type, taken through an open window with medium-format cameras (using 120, 220 or 70mm films) or 35mm SLR cameras, makes up most photography used in archaeology. Traditionally, photography has been on black-and-white film (using Ilford FP4 and FP3 (70mm), Kodak Tri-X, TMAX and Technopan), but more colour shots (using slide film, and some colour-print films) are now being taken. A small amount of false-colour, infra-red film is used but the difficulties in handling it outweigh the information gained. Oblique photography forms part of the annual aerial archaeological surveys throughout the UK (and indeed much of Europe); it has been estimated that over 500 hours of flying is carried out in the UK alone each year. On average this can yield approximately 1,500–2,000 new sites or additional information on known sites each year.

UNDERTAKING ARCHAEOLOGICAL AERIAL SURVEYS

Before embarking on any aerial survey there are a number of legal and practical points that have to be observed. The legality of using a particular aircraft and pilot has to be established. The aircraft to be used must have a Certificate of Airworthiness up to the Public Transport (Passenger) Category. Every pilot has to have a licence, three categories of which concern us here: a Private Pilot's Licence (PPL), a Basic Commercial Pilot's Licence (BCPL) and a Commercial Pilot's Licence (CPL). Currently the majority of pilots who are engaged in aerial photography for archaeology have a BCPL or CPL. Fully commercial operations, which charge more for their services, have an Air Operator's Certificate (AOC). The Civil Aviation Authority (CAA) have agreed to issue exemptions from the Air Navigation Order (1989) to allow pilots with either a BCPL or a CPL to fly passengers for archaeological aerial photography without an AOC. These exemptions are only valid for flights sponsored by one of the three Royal Commissions, and are issued annually.

THE DEVELOPMENT OF AERIAL PHOTOGRAPHY

The history of aerial photography has been covered more extensively than space allows here (Crawford 1954; Daniel 1975; Deuel 1969; Hampton 1989; Riley 1987; St Joseph 1951; Whimster 1983; Wilson 1982).

The earliest aerial photographs were taken from balloons (Deuel 1969: 13). Not surprisingly, one of the first aerial photographs for archaeology was of Stonehenge, taken from a balloon (Capper 1907; Wilson 1982: 11). The development of flying, aircraft and photography during and after the First World War provided the platform from which aerial survey for archaeology could be launched. Without the foresight and understanding of one man, O.G.S. Crawford, the subject would not have taken off so successfully. His early papers (Crawford 1923, 1924) paved the way for the seminal work *Wessex from the Air* (Crawford and Keiller 1928) and his professional papers *Air Survey and Archaeology* (Crawford 1928) and *Air Photography for Archaeologists* (Crawford 1929) are standard texts.

During the decade leading up to the Second World War, Crawford and a number of colleagues (Major Allen, Sqn Ldr Insall and R.G. Collingwood) developed the technique of aerial photography and combined it with fieldwork. The results were published in the quarterly archaeological journal *Antiquity*, whose founder and editor was Crawford himself. The war provided the impetus for the development of photography and aviation that would be of immense benefit, and not just for archaeology.

Until 1945 aerial photography in Britain was carried out by a few pioneers, such as Major Allen, Derrick Riley, Jim Pickering, and Arnold Baker to name but a few. In 1949 the Cambridge University Committee for Aerial Photography (CUCAP) began aerial survey in Britain for a variety of purposes, one of which was archaeology (St Joseph 1966). Crop-mark landscapes were recorded in the gravel areas and with the massive rebuilding and new town expansions in the late 1940s and through the 1950s, the gravels, rich in archaeological sites, were also under great threat. This threat was recognized in the 1960 Royal Commission publication *A Matter of Time*, which had a considerable effect on the way in which archaeology in England was carried out, even if it took ten years before the formation of Rescue (Jones 1984; Rahtz 1974b). Moreover, aerial photography also allowed for the discovery of new types of site, often as earthworks, and the new discipline of medieval archaeology grew alongside aerial photography (Beresford 1950; Beresford and St Joseph 1977).

After the Second World War the development of aerial photography for archaeology to the present day can be divided into three parts. Each part helped the other to exist; there is not space here to do more than list these major events. Firstly, in 1949 the CUCAP was created, a year after the Curatorship in Aerial Photography had been established (St Joseph 1996: 5); some reconnaissance had taken place since 1945 from Cambridge. The Committee is still active in aerial survey, especially vertical surveys, and holds a collection of over 400,000 prints.

Secondly, in 1965 the Air Photographs Library within the Royal Commission on the Historical Monuments of England (RCHME) was established (Hampton 1989). The RCHME started the Air Photographs Library (now the National Library of Aerial Photographs, NLAP) 'to implement the Commission's resolution to . . . "use air photography to build up rapidly a record of field monuments throughout England"'(Hampton 1989: 17). Initially this was a collection of the regional and locally based aerial photographers' work but soon came to include the results of the RCHME's own work; this collection now holds between 500,000 and 750,000 prints. It also holds the collection of vertical photographs that resulted from the postwar survey by the RAF, which was formerly the Department of the Environment's collection (over a million prints); the RCHME was given responsibility for these in 1984 and since then has computerized the original flight traces. The collection also holds verticals from other sources. For any given area of interest the relevant photographs can be listed and made available for consultation.

The Scottish and Welsh Commissions also carry out their own programmes of aerial reconnaissance and have done so for the past decade in Scotland and more recently in Wales. The results of their work are archived in the National Monuments Records for Scotland (NMRS) and the NMR for Wales.

The RCHME embarked upon its programme of flying in 1967 to support its own terrestrial surveys, including buildings and urban areas (Hampton 1989). Since then the Air Photography Unit (APU), which includes the NLAP, has been carrying out over 200 hours of aerial survey per year; the photographs from each survey are accessioned in to NLAP annually. The APU now has two offices, one in Swindon and one in York, to enable it to carry out aerial surveys over most of England. This objective would not, of course, be possible without the third element in the organization of aerial photography in Britain.

The regionally based aerial photographers, often referred to as the 'regional flyers', received government funds for the first time in 1976 (in England the initial grant was for a total £10,000) and this has continued to the present day. By 1992/93 the funding had increased in England to £25,000, in Scotland to around £4,500, and in Wales to £14,000. Until 1975 all the costs of flying were borne by the flyers themselves; the dry summers of 1975 and 1976 ushered in a new era. The Council for British Archaeology (CBA) formed an Aerial Archaeology Research Committee that pressed for funds to be made available for aerial photography. The Department of the Environment, through its Inspectorate for Ancient Monuments (later English Heritage) started funding to the tune of £10,000; this was increased to £20,000 by 1985. In 1986/87 responsibility was transferred from English Heritage to the RCHME for grants to regional flyers. These grants are primarily for the flying costs and are seen as joint projects with the local institutions and organizations, which augment them in a number of ways (Griffith 1990).

A similar situation pertains in Wales and Scotland. The Royal Commission on the Ancient and Historical Monuments of Wales (RCAHMW) now has responsibility for co-ordinating aerial survey in Wales. In 1993/94, Cadw (Welsh Historic Monuments) will vire £14,000 for monitoring its Scheduled Ancient Monuments from the air. This programme has been under way for a number of years and is proving a very cost-effective method of managing a diverse archaeological resource. RCAHMW has a similar sum for its own aerial reconnaissance.

In Scotland the Royal Commission on the Ancient and Historical Monuments of Scotland (RCAHMS) allocated around £4,500 in 1992/93 to their regional flyers. As in Wales, the archaeologists are organized on a regional basis and by the nature of the landscapes have to cover larger areas than in England. The Scottish Commission has its own flying programme, which has been continuing over the past ten years; results have recently been published by Gordon Maxwell (1992).

The RCHME acknowledged that funds should also be made available for 'post-reconnaissance work'. This work involves cataloguing the information about the aerial photographs; usually through the local Sites and Monuments Record (SMR), but it also includes having all the information relating to the photographs (film numbers and national grid references) incorporated into the NLAP database. The annual English budget for this in 1991/92 was £35,000; in 1992/93 this was increased to £140,000 to assist in the enhancement of the SMRs. Further funding may also become available specifically for mapping from aerial photographs according to the National Mapping Programme standards (see below).

AERIAL PHOTOGRAPHIC LIBRARIES

There are three main sources of aerial photographs for archaeology in Britain. These three hide a multitude of sources and a huge variety of type of library. Fortunately, the National Association of Aerial Photographic Libraries (NAPLIB) has recently produced a *Directory* of over 360 libraries or sources of aerial photographs; the address is listed at the end of this chapter.

National (specialist) collections

CUCAP and NLAP are the main sources for England, although there are others (see *NAPLIB Directory*). There is a Central Register of Air Photography for Wales, at the Welsh Office, Cathays Park, Cardiff. Also the RCAHMW collections of verticals and obliques are in the NMRW in Aberystwyth. The RCAHMS holds obliques taken by itself, the regional flyers and CUCAP. The vertical collection is under negotiation for transfer to RCAHMS but is currently held as part of the Scottish Office's Air Photography Unit in Edinburgh. (There are national collections of vertical and oblique photographs taken by commercial companies or by the Ordnance Survey for mapping; these are listed in the *NAPLIB Directory*.)

Local or regional collections

Where county councils have been instrumental in commissioning vertical surveys (for census figures for example) collections are often available for archaeological study. There are also the collections that have built up with the grant-aid from the Royal Commissions and are often combined with historic aerial photographs; Norfolk is a good case in point which has a publicly accessible archive. Further information about the collections in each county or region can be obtained from the *NAPLIB Directory*.

Private collections

There are a number of private collections throughout the country and by consultation with the appropriate 'curator' or owner of the collection, access may be granted.

THE PURPOSE OF AERIAL SURVEY

Taking and curating aerial photographs is only one part of the process of aerial survey. Aerial photography for archaeology is only part of archaeological survey; aerial photography's contribution to these other complementary techniques is its cost-effectiveness and its comprehensive approach.

It is important to understand that it is an interpretative process by which the information from an aerial photograph is made into an archaeological record. The creation of archaeological record maps has been going on since the Ordnance Survey (OS) began its work, especially with the creation of the Archaeology Division within the OS in the 1920s. The OS transferred responsibility for this work to the three Royal Commissions in 1983 and this in turn led to the creation of National Archaeological Records. During the 1980s these developed as a combination of map-based information and computerized databases. Similarly the growth of county-based SMRs led to much discussion on how all types of information should be used at both national and local level.

Riley (1987) describes the mapping techniques available for the air-photo interpreter. These fall into two categories: manual and computerized methods, the aim being to remove the distortion of the oblique view to the plan view. Large-scale detailed plans can be made from aerial photographs using desktop computers as well more expensive photogrammetric machines; this type of mapping is very important for the management and protection of archaeological sites and landscapes. Decisions as to which site or area is to be mapped or needs protection are dependent on having knowledge of the archaeology of the whole country. To achieve a national level of mapping a manual method, 'sketch plotting', has normally been used, although combining this method with computer approaches is becoming feasible. The 1:10,000 scale map is now becoming the standard scale in England and sites are mapped onto a translucent film overlay. Most county SMRs have a map-base at this scale with varying degrees of aerial photographic information plotted on them. At the time of writing, these maps are an inconsistent record (in England), not only as graphical representations of the archaeology, but also in the descriptions of the archaeological sites. Terms such as 'crop mark', 'enclosure', and 'native site' are now not sufficient to cope with the everyday demands being made of county archaeologists and SMR officers under the Department of the Environment's Planning Policy Guidelines (PPG 16), especially in cases of detailed evaluation.

In England, the RCHME has begun working towards a National Mapping Programme, the aim of which is to produce a 1:10,000 archaeological map of England, taking information from available aerial photography, to be accompanied by a computerized database. Pilot programmes for this are now coming to an end and include surveys in Kent, Hertfordshire, the

Thames Valley and the Yorkshire Dales National Park. These were all jointly funded by English Heritage and the RCHME. Other surveys undertaken by RCHME, which has also been instrumental in designing the National Mapping Programme, are the area of the chalk Wolds of Eastern Yorkshire, Dartmoor, Bodmin Moor and Cheviot.

The National Mapping Programme (England) is currently being developed within the APU's Swindon and York offices, with some of the work being externally funded by the RCHME (RCHME 1992). The methods employed by the RCHME have been developed over the last decade to make the best use of the available resources. Mapping techniques have developed in a technological way, with the aid of computers. The biggest change, however, has been in the way in which records are created from the information on aerial photographs. As mentioned above, it used to be sufficient to use catch-all labels such as 'crop-mark' or 'native site'. With the requirements of PPG 16 and English Heritage's Monuments Protection Programme (MPP), there was a need for a systematic descriptive process for labelling crop-marks. Deliberations of the Aerial Archaeology Research Group (AARG) on classification in the 1980s, and work done by Whimster (1989) funded by RCHME, English Heritage (EH) and CUCAP, led to further discussions between RCHME and EH. In 1988 computerized classification was designed (Edis *et al.* 1989). This is a computerized system for crop-mark classification (known as MORPH) that aims to standardize terminology. The use of the system cannot be described fully here, and it has developed considerably since Edis and colleagues' article was published. Originally it was designed for crop-mark areas but a survey of the Yorkshire Dales National Park, partly funded by the RCHME and EH, provided the framework for developing the system for earthwork and stonework sites, including large industrial sites.

In MORPH the basic distinctions are of shape and size, with other morphological and topographical aspects being taken into consideration. A site that might have been labelled 'enclosure' or 'native site' could now be described depending on its shape and size. The descriptions in the database are created using a menu-driven screen; there are validity and reliability ratings for each description and interpretation.

CONCLUSIONS

There can be no doubt as to the cost-effective nature of aerial photography and the subsequent mapping and record creation. The nature of the work is such that skilled air-photo interpreters with a good archaeological knowledge are required. The low priority currently given to aerial photography in university training courses means that the employing bodies have to train staff. This limits the efficiency with which national programmes can be operated. There are further limitations in the use of aerial photographs; archaeological features recorded by aerial photography represent only one method of survey. As the other section of this chapter will show, there is a whole range of techniques that can also record archaeological sites. Combining the results of the various techniques is an essential component of evaluation work.

It has been known for many years that sites recorded from aerial photography are in fact a small percentage of what is actually under the surface. The results of this technique should not be used in isolation; follow-up fieldwork and excavation are vital if we are to understand and record the full extent of prehistoric and historic Britain. Before this follow-up work can provide fruitful results the initial primary-level mapping has to take place; otherwise sites will be chosen for excavation or destruction, or even preservation, without their context being known. In English Heritage's plan for the next decade (English Heritage 1991a: 43) the case is argued for a crop-mark survey in which a number of sites, especially sites that are representative of a group or class of site, should be test excavated. If this plan is acted upon it will be a major step forward.

The next major step for aerial archaeology has to be the introduction of Geographical Information Systems (GIS) as part of working practices. From the moment the photographs have been taken to the point at which they are interpreted, mapped and a record created, there is a role for GIS. In the aircraft it is now possible to have a portable Global Positioning System (GPS) that can record where you are and when you take a photograph; this information can then be linked to the databases that hold the information on the existing photographic coverage for that area. This means that the aerial surveyor can be much more interactive with what has gone on before so that future programmes of aerial survey can be targeted with greater effect.

Once on the ground the air-photo interpreter should be able to use GIS for assistance in mapping and recording the information on the aerial photograph. There should never be any substitute for the interpretation phase, which is the one aspect of the work that has to be done by trained staff. GIS in aerial survey would pay dividends in terms of information retrieval alone. The linkage between photograph, interpreted map or plan and the textual database would increase the speed and flow of information. Any enquirer would then be able to see the mapped and textual information in one medium at any relevant scale. The technology is available now, but the initial costs of setting up such systems, especially if the photographs are to be stored electronically, are very high and a careful cost-benefit analysis would have to be done. Many county authorities and national bodies are currently exploring the possibilities.

CONTACT ADDRESSES

Aerial Archaeology Research Group (AARG). This group meets annually to discuss the techniques, discoveries, and all matters concerning aerial photography for archaeology. It has no permanent address, since its officers rotate; for further information write to one of the addresses below.

Air Photo Services (APS). 7, Edward St, Cambridge CB1 2LS. Independent aerial archaeologists who undertake aerial survey and mapping projects.

Cambridge University Committee for Aerial Photography (CUCAP). The Mond Building, Free School Lane, Cambridge CB2 3RF. Tel: 0223 334578, fax: 0223 334400. The Collection may be visited by members of the public during normal office hours. Photographs cannot be borrowed but prints can be purchased; orders ordinarily take about a month. Prices depend on print size. Copyright is retained by the University or the Crown.

National Association of Aerial Photographic Libraries (NAPLIB). C/o The Curator, CUCAP.

National Library of Air Photographs (NLAP). RCHME, Alexander House, 19 Fleming Way, Swindon SN1 2NG. Tel: 0793 414100. This is a branch of the National Monuments Record for England. Photographs can be consulted by prior arrangement. An express service can be provided for urgent requests (costs and details from the above address).

The Royal Commission on the Historical Monuments of England (RCMHE). Fortress House, 23 Savile Row, London W1X 2JQ. The national body for survey and record in England (see also NLAP above).

The Royal Commission on the Ancient and Historical Monuments of Wales (RCAHMW). Crown Buildings, Plas Crug, Aberystwyth. Dyfed SY23 2HP. The national body of survey and record for Wales.

The Royal Commission on the Ancient and Historical Monuments of Scotland (RCAHMS). John Sinclair House, 16 Bernard Terrace, Edinburgh EH8 9NX. The national body of survey and record for Scotland.

CHAPTER 18

DEVELOPMENT OF REMOTE SENSING

Part 2: Practice and method in the application of geophysical techniques in archaeology

Chris Gaffney and John Gater

This section charts the application of geophysical techniques in modern archaeology as practised in Britain. In a recent article (Gaffney *et al.* 1991) the authors discussed the potential of specific techniques and their role in archaeological evaluation. While there is inevitably some overlap between these two works, this part of the chapter will consider the wider role of geophysics in archaeological fieldwork. In particular, discussion covers the range of techniques and differing methodologies available to answer a variety of archaeological problems. This is not strictly a review of geophysical applications in archaeology; the reader is advised to consult the following references for such information: Aitken 1974; Aspinall 1992; Carr 1982; Clark 1975, 1990; Heron and Gaffney 1987; Scollar *et al.* 1990; Tite 1972a, 1972b; Wynn 1986. However, for those readers who are unfamiliar with the background to the involvement of geophysical techniques in archaeology, a summary of the major trends is included.

A BRIEF HISTORY OF GEOPHYSICAL TECHNIQUES IN BRITISH ARCHAEOLOGY

Historically, geophysical techniques have been used to 'flesh out' the excavations of individual sites once features had been identified. For geophysicists, this seemed to be a last resort, an appendage to be used only if time and funding would permit. While this approach had its successes, the input of geophysical data into mature archaeological strategies was rare. Indeed, although the outlets for archaeological publication increased dramatically during the 1960s and 1970s the provision for the dissemination of geophysical results in this period actually decreased with the virtual demise of the specialist journal *Prospezioni Archeologiche*. Some observers regarded this as a potential new era: the lack of a specialist journal might entail results being reported in mainstream archaeological journals. However, this was a false dawn, the reasons for which are not obvious. One may suppose that the initial slow speed and uncertainty of data collection may have had an effect as would the limited display options available at the time. What is evident, however, is that despite the lack of publications, geophysical techniques have become part of the British archaeologist's toolkit (Spoerry 1992b).

This acceptance may be described as a product of the inevitable trickle-down of new technology into archaeological applications: during the 1980s dedicated and reliable Earth resistance, and more importantly fluxgate gradiometer, instruments were marketed in Britain. These instruments included data loggers, thus allowing the automatic recording of digital readings into the rapidly expanding world of computerized data analysis. However, to accept this as a main cause of the acceptance of geophysics would be an oversimplification of the recent foundation of geophysical techniques in British archaeology. The major reason why geophysics has been so successful in the late 1980s and early 1990s has less to do with technology, and more to do with the nature of the information required by archaeologists. In short, the ever-increasing needs of archaeologists in the rapid evaluation of large tracts of land has provided the *raison d'être* for geophysical techniques in archaeology. In those instances where traditional archaeological techniques have been found wanting, geophysical applications have become the norm.

The strengths of geophysical techniques can be contrasted with traditional archaeological techniques: where information from fieldwalking data can be general, geophysical data is often specific and where trenching is expensive, geophysical investigation is cheap. The additional information provided by the methodologies used by archaeogeophysicists is greatest in the precise mapping of potential remains. This allows developers to understand their obligation to the study of the area that their work is threatening to destroy. The alternative is excavation resulting in the discovery of a plethora of archaeological features within a trench, a situation in which the archaeologist can merely guess the representative nature of the findings, never mind their extent.

Of course there are disadvantages: for example, there is rarely any dating evidence from geophysical techniques; interpretation can also be difficult. Neither of these facts, however, negates the use of the techniques themselves. The former merely illustrates the contention that geophysical techniques should be meshed within a battery of other techniques, provided they are tried and tested. The latter is more critical in that a thorough knowledge of geology and site conditions is often required to assess the likely success of a technique and hence indicate accurately levels of confidence.

WHAT TYPE OF TECHNIQUES ARE SUITABLE?

At the outset it is necessary to make distinctions between what may be termed evaluation work and investigations that form part of a research project. The list of techniques used in evaluations is limited compared with those used for research interests. This is primarily because an archaeological evaluation requires that the methods used should be rapid, and the results quick to process and relatively easy to interpret and display. As a consequence, the techniques most often used in evaluations are soil resistivity, magnetometry (fluxgate gradiometry), and occasionally soil magnetic susceptibility. As the major objective is to map the archaeological potential of an area, and not to estimate depth or stratigraphic relationships, these three techniques are normally ideally suited to the task.

The principles of the two main geophysical techniques (resistivity and magnetometry) depend upon the contrast between the physical properties of a feature and those of the surrounding deposits (for a more detailed discussion see Aitken 1974; Tite 1972). Resistivity surveying involves the insertion of electrical currents into the ground and measurement of their resistance in relation to differing buried features. Walls will normally result in high resistance responses and waterlogged ditches will have a low resistance. Magnetic techniques involve the detection of small localized changes in the intensity of the earth's magnetic field associated with buried features. A pottery kiln, for example, will give a very strong magnetic anomaly because of the fired clay/brick structure; a ditch or pit will also produce a measurable anomaly if there is a magnetic contrast between the fill and the strata into which the feature is cut. The contrast is partly dependent upon the magnetic susceptibility of the soil/subsoil and measurement of this phenomenon can form a prospecting technique in its own right. This is because human occupation tends to result in an enhancement of the susceptibility of the soil (Le Borgne 1955, 1960; Tite 1972). For example, sites that survive in the topsoil can be detected even if all the features have been 'lost'.

The major advantage of the two common techniques of soil resistivity and magneto-metry is the simplicity of method, which has been demonstrated in countless surveys. This requires the site to be gridded into 20m or 30m blocks with detailed measurements taken within each grid. The sample interval is usually 1m or less and the spacing between traverses 1m. In this way, where conditions are favourable, extremely accurate and detailed maps of buried archaeological features can be obtained. However, the archaeo-logical picture is not complete unless consideration is given to areas of past 'activity'.

Activity is used here as a broad category of information that considers man's influence on his environment. This manifests itself as modifications in the physical and/or chemical properties of the topsoil. These may be far-reaching and lie well beyond the traditional definition of a site. Two techniques that are used in this way are soil phosphorus and mag-netic susceptibility analysis, although other soil attributes, such as trace element levels, have also been successfully mapped and interpreted as archaeologically significant (see Bintliff *et al.* 1992). In recent years the measurement of topsoil magnetic susceptibility has become the most important of these indicators.

To simplify the use of magnetic susceptibility, it is possible to identify three intensities of topsoil sampling: coarse, medium or fine. The coarse sampling interval is more appro-priate to identifying potential archaeological areas within a landscape. In such work, sam-ple intervals will be in the order of one measurement every linear 10–50m depending upon the size of the project. This degree of sampling intensity will provide background information with regard to the suitability of an area for more detailed magnetic work as well as indicating the potential of large archaeological sites in the area (see e.g. Clark 1991: fig. 105). Normally any areas of anomalously high susceptibility will be assessed by gradiometer. The second sampling intensity (medium density) requires a sample interval of 10m or less in order to define activity areas (Gaffney *et al.* 1992; Gurney *et al.* 1992). For producing specific information about activity within small sites, a fine sampling inter-val in the order of every metre will be necessary (see e.g. Allen 1990). However, it is questionable as to whether such a level of work is appropriate to many archaeological problems, especially in topsoil studies where the plough redistributes the soil.

The phenomena measured in geophysical investigations (contrasts of moisture and magnetic properties), represent bulk changes. Therefore, the methods that are traditionally used give information on what is there rather than how much and at what depth. However, the latter questions are increasingly frequently asked of geophysicists. It must be realized that this is not an attempt to wrestle the spade from the archaeologist's grasp, but another refinement on the information to be assessed before costly excavation. For those people used to geophysical prospecting within the mineral-extraction industry an analogy may be useful: the traditional magnetic and resistance tools are used in the location of a scarce resource (archaeology), while the newer questions relate to an estimation of the quantity of that scarce resource that exists and its extraction depth.

Although it is convenient to differentiate the work undertaken in response to the two questions asked by archaeologists, it is an uneasy divide in that resistance and gradiometer data both contain information that can provide rough estimates of depth. Also, by varying the methods, a good approximation of depth can be realized. For example, geological geo-physicists have long used 'expanding' resistivity arrays to assess the depths of deposits, while a variation on this also allows vertical 'pseudo-sections' to be constructed (e.g. Edwards 1977). The latter approach has been successfully applied archaeologically because archaeologists are accustomed to viewing data as sections through the earth (e.g. Imai *et al.* 1987; Nishimura and Kamai 1991; Stephens *et al.* forthcoming). A promising alternative also utilizing resistive changes is that of tomography, which is a technique borrowed from medical imagery (e.g. Noel and Walker 1991; Noel and Xu 1991). Both of these are useful appendages in the non-invasive armoury, especially when used in conjunction with an area survey.

Other techniques that have been touted for the collection of vertical section information include seismic methods (e.g. Goulty *et al.* 1990) and radar (e.g. Stove and Addyman 1989). The latter requires electromagnetic energy pulses to be transmitted through the ground and measures reflected signals that have been produced by interfaces between materials of differing electrical properties. Seismic investigation requires an artificially generated seismic wave to be reflected or refracted at interfaces between materials of contrasting reflection coefficients. Unfortunately, some claims for the success of the techniques, in particular for radar, have been overstated and these have provoked considerable attention from specialists within civil engineering and archaeology (e.g. Atkin and Milligan 1992). A recent review article noted that 'Radar survey techniques currently in use are reminiscent of early days of more conventional geophysical surveys with a noticeable lack of mutual appreciation of the problem of surveyor and archaeologist' (Aspinall 1992: 240). Without wishing to delve too deeply into the problems associated with radar, it is certain that considerable research is required into the resolution of exact depth and individual feature interpretation at the archaeological level. At present none of the data acquired by any of the depth-determining techniques described above can be readily interpreted at the scale required by the archaeologist. However, gross changes can be identified, and that is the limit of the resolution demanded in civil engineering applications.

It can be concluded from the above discussion that two avenues are often explored by geophysicists: area survey (mapping of anomalous data after a background has been established) and depth detection of layers and features. It is perhaps useful to summarize the use of geophysical techniques in archaeological geophysics, by thinking of three levels of work (Figs 18.2–18.4). The first two (Levels I and II) are most widely used in projects associated with planning applications, whereas Level III surveys are more appropriate to archaeological research work and unusual planning problems.

SAMPLING IN AN ARCHAEOLOGICAL CONTEXT

General sampling strategies have been discussed elsewhere (Gaffney *et al.* 1991), and although they are mainly applicable to evaluation work, the criteria for adopting such strategies can apply equally well in research projects that involve, for example, investigating landscapes. Various strategies are outlined here and reference is made to a few case studies. These case studies serve to demonstrate the way sampling strategies can be designed to answer particular archaeological questions.

The scale of some developments can be extremely large, for example, mineral-extraction sites and housing developments; while others are linear in shape, such as pipeline and road schemes. Under such circumstances it is often not possible, nor desirable, to survey the whole of the threatened area, particularly within planning timescales. In deciding upon an appropriate sampling strategy, the nature of the expected archaeology, the ground cover, the topography and the local geology will all affect the way each site is investigated.

A desktop evaluation will usually identify known archaeological sites and these may be targeted for detailed geophysical work. The initial aims of the geophysics may be to define features visible on aerial photographs, investigate the extent of anomalies associated with artefact scatters, evaluate the nature of earthworks, and carry out prospecting in areas

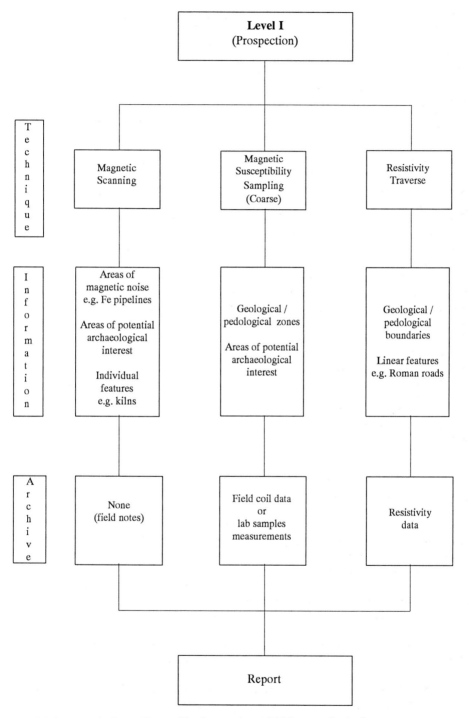

Figure 18.2. Some standard strategies considered appropriate to initial prospection work.

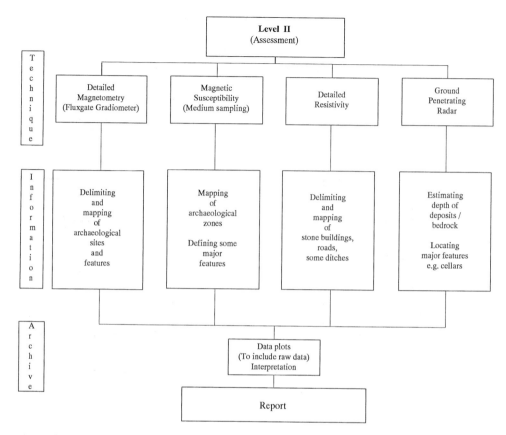

Figure 18.3. Common techniques used in archaeological assessment and evaluation.

adjacent to sensitive and protected sites. Detailed work over predefined areas, with contingency allowances for expansion where necessary, will be appropriate in such instances. It is often required that geophysical techniques will also be used in the investigation of areas of varying archaeological potential within the proposed development. In such instances, a combination of magnetic scanning, magnetic susceptibility sampling and a modified sampling strategy is usually appropriate. As a general guide it is recommended that the sample blocks for gradiometry should not be less than 40 x 40m, unless other conditions (e.g. easement restrictions) dictate otherwise. This is because a background has to be defined before areas of anomalous readings can be identified. A suitable percentage survey sample usually will be dependent upon the archaeological sensitivity of the area under threat.

The following theoretical (and actual) case studies are examples of the way areas can be evaluated using geophysical techniques.

Projects affecting areas of less than 1ha: Level II and III Surveys

It is debatable as to whether areas affecting less than 1ha should be sampled. Sampling may be appropriate where resistivity work is required, but for magnetometry full coverage is desirable. This will provide a far better assessment of a site and diminish the possibility of misinterpretation of the results.

210

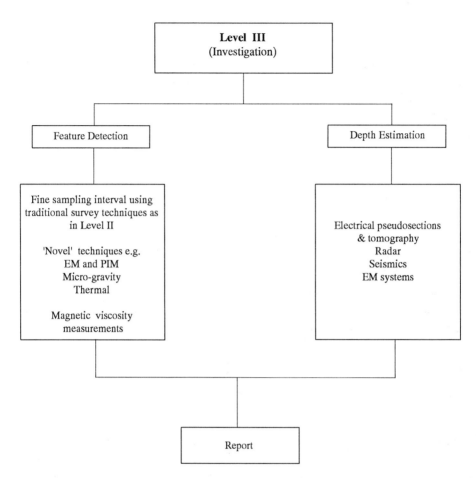

Figure 18.4. Some possible techniques used to investigate exact feature location and depth determination.

Housing development, mineral extraction or other projects, affecting areas greater than 1 ha: Level I and II Surveys

In areas where there are no archaeological or topographic determinants, then a modified systematic sampling strategy is appropriate. Survey blocks or transects are positioned within each field based on existing boundaries, unless there is an overriding reason for using the National Grid. Use of the latter can make survey very difficult and does not necessarily allow for expansion of the survey samples. By using a grid system based on existing boundaries, blocks can be investigated in a semi-random way or at predefined intervals in order to maximize coverage.

At Shepton Mallet, Somerset, a series of small investigations were carried out for differing developers in different areas on the outskirts of the existing town. While each component survey provided specific information about each field, it was only when viewed in a wider context that the true archaeological importance could be assessed; it became possible to predict confidently the previously unknown limits of the Romano-British settlement based upon geophysical sampling and selected excavation by the

Birmingham University Field Archaeology Unit. This information will be of great help in the future planning of the present town, and is an example of how seemingly piecemeal evaluations can contribute to archaeological knowledge.

A major pipeline or new road: Level I and II Surveys

For example, a recent pipeline project passing through the archaeologically rich chalk wolds of North Humberside was deemed to warrant a 100 % detailed geophysical investigation. By contrast, geophysical work in advance of construction of another major pipeline from Grangemouth to Cheshire was confined to known areas of interest. In a third case, when a pipeline was planned from Humberside to Hertfordshire, a 10 % sampling strategy was adopted, in addition to investigating known sensitive areas. In the last case, the exploratory geophysical work identified at least three new major archaeological sites. Used in this mode of operation, geophysical techniques are a powerful addition to an archaeological investigation, complementing artefact recovery and aerial photography.

WHAT IS TO BE EXPECTED IN A GEOPHYSICAL REPORT?

At present there are no guidelines available for those setting geophysical briefs as part of an archaeological evaluation. As a result, the standard of reports varies considerably across the country and this absence of even basic conformity leads to a wide variation in the quality of surveys and reports.

Inevitably there must be some variation as to the content of a specialized geophysical report. It is obvious that, for example, the style and display of information will be different when reporting resistance or radar data. However, the reports should still be comprehensible on the same level, namely that any geophysical fieldwork should be followed by a clearly reasoned technical report. There must be sufficient information within the report to allow a specialist reader to understand what instrumentation was used, how the data were collected, what processing has been undertaken on the data and how the data have been displayed. This will allow the specialist to understand the logic behind the interpretation of the data and the limits of confidence that should be placed upon that interpretation.

Specifically the report should contain information on location, topography, geology, soils and the known archaeology of the site. There must be recognition of instances when information on these subjects is not known, as this may affect the certainty of the interpretation.

Data processing and the style of display are the most individual elements of a report. While it is the responsibility of the geophysicist to display the data in a format that illustrates his or her final interpretation it is also true that the effects of each process step should be documented and displayed. That is, displays of the raw data should be provided after every smoothing or filtering algorithm. This allows an estimation of the quality of the data and a check for any 'artefacts' produced by the processing that may have been mistaken for anomalies produced by archaeological features. In general, as little processing as possible should be undertaken.

It is difficult to apply any rigid rules with regards to the display of geophysical data. The experience of the geophysical operator will decide what is the most appropriate method depending upon the nature of the results. However, whatever form is chosen – dot density, X–Y traces, grey-scale images, contours, three-dimensional terrains (Fig. 18.5) – it is vital that a clear interpretation diagram is included. Additionally, in order for a geophysicist to make an independent assessment of the results, at least one plot of the raw data should be included. An X–Y trace or grey-scale image is most appropriate for this; both are capable of showing the full range of the data.

The report should also include a non-technical summary with sufficient information to allow

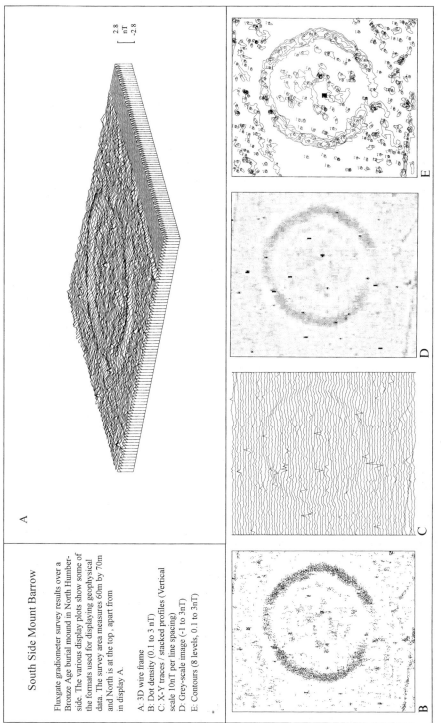

South Side Mount Barrow

Fluxgate gradiometer survey results over a Bronze Age burial mound in North Humberside. The various display plots show some of the formats used for displaying geophysical data. The survey area measures 60m by 70m and North is at the top, apart from in display A.

A: 3D wire frame
B: Dot density (0.1 to 3 nT)
C: X-Y traces / stacked profiles (Vertical scale 10nT per line spacing)
D: Grey-scale image (-1 to 3nT)
E: Contours (8 levels, 0.1 to 3nT)

Figure 18.5. Displaying geophysical data.

the interested reader to gain an idea of the scope of the work and the general success, or otherwise, of locating archaeological remains. All diagrams should be produced at reasonable scales. By this it is suggested that both the data and separate interpretation diagrams should be reproduced at a scale from which exact measurements can be taken, allowing the efficient positioning of trenches. Summary plots of data and interpretation can be included at a scale allowing an overview of the survey. An appropriate scale for the former might be 1:500 and the latter at the scale at which other information is being summarized (usually 1:1250 or 1:2500). It is not adequate to provide data at only the smaller scale as its quality cannot be assessed at that level. Similarly, it is generally regarded as inappropriate to produce interpretations drawn on top of data diagrams. Interpretative diagrams should be clear, separate diagrams that can be understood by a non-technical client. Those reporting the results should be aware that the interpretation is the bottom line for many of the individuals or groups that commission a survey.

Naturally it would be useful in all cases for the geophysical report to amalgamate known archaeological information from the proposed development area. However, as geophysical techniques are non-invasive, they are often now used as a primary technique and, accordingly, reports are often required to be submitted before other information can be assimilated. Therefore, those who commission geophysical reports should not be surprised when interpretations are tentative, especially when information such as geological context or expected type of archaeological remains are lacking.

WHAT SHOULD HAPPEN TO THE REPORT AND DATA?

The geophysical report may be a stand-alone piece of work or part of an integrated approach to a proposed development area. As a result, it is expected that the written report will be submitted to the sites and monuments record for the region concerned. However, the computerized data must also be maintained for future interrogation and all competent groups will have some form of data archive that they will attempt to maintain in perpetuity. Although there is no central archiving store for geophysical data in Britain, it is hoped that all practitioners will eventually participate in such a scheme.

LEGISLATIVE ISSUES

Legislative considerations are often overlooked by clients commissioning geophysical surveys. This fact probably arises because most remote-sensing techniques are by their nature non-invasive. However, although a site will not be physically disturbed by a survey, written permission is still a prerequisite to carrying out work on a Scheduled Ancient Monument. No differentiation is made between surveys carried out as part of a planning evaluation and those that are research oriented. Persons working to strict deadlines, therefore, should be aware that geophysical contractors have to adhere to legal frameworks.

English Heritage will issue a Section 42 Licence on behalf of the Secretary of State for sites in England granting permission to carry out surveys; Cadw (Wales), Historic Scotland and the Historic Monuments and Buildings Branch (Northern Ireland) will act in similar capacities in their respective countries.

ACKNOWLEDGEMENTS

The authors would like to thank Dr Carl Heron (University of Bradford) for commenting on an earlier draft of this chapter. Thanks are also due to members of staff at Geophysical Surveys of Bradford who have helped in the preparation of this chapter. The survey at South Side Mount was carried out with the Humberside Archaeological Unit whose help we gratefully acknowledge.

CHAPTER 19

THE DISSEMINATION OF INFORMATION

Catherine Hills

It is no longer as easy to write a 'cookbook' account of how to disseminate archaeological information as it was in 1966 when Grinsell, Rahtz and Warhurst's *The Preparation of Archaeological Reports* was published. This chapter is perhaps less descriptive than might be expected, and is as much concerned with the problems of publication as with the character of publication. This is not necessarily a bad thing: only dead things can be dissected in a detached and uninvolved manner. Archaeology, and its publication, is not dead, even if much of its subject matter is. There is a great deal of archaeological information and there have been many successful attempts to communicate it. There are also undeniable problems that need to be confronted and solved.

Since the mid-1980s there have been two separate debates on the writing of archaeology. There is the establishment view, expressed in two reports known by the names of the professors (Frere and Cunliffe) who chaired the committees that produced them (DoE 1975a; Cunliffe 1982), in a discussion paper (Society of Antiquaries 1992), and in the policy documents on the management of archaeological reports produced by English Heritage (English Heritage 1989 and 1991b; MAP 1 and MAP 2, respectively). These deal with the preservation by record of the vast accumulation of archaeological data produced by excavations over the past forty years, and the dissemination of that record.

Another debate, conducted by theoretical archaeologists influenced by anthropology, linguistics and philosophy, represents not one but many different views concerning the possibility, or rather impossibility of knowing the past. It identifies the artificiality of all forms of communication, and assesses the degree to which any piece of archaeological writing can claim to be an objective view of a real past rather than an exercise in propaganda or personal opinion (e.g. Shanks and Tilley 1987b; Baker and Thomas 1990; Bapty and Yates 1991; Chapter 2).

Both debates address real problems, but at times it seems that they exist in different worlds, neither of them inhabited by anyone else. Neither speaks directly to the public at large. The official view involves storage of information in data banks or archives, accessible only to those who know how to get into them. Most people will have to take the brief published summaries at their face value, and the committee production suggested for reports is likely to produce works too boring to read unless one has to. The theoretical literature is often couched in terms too obscure for most other archaeologists to understand, and some of it, if taken to logical conclusions, denies the possibility of knowledge or its communication. Fortunately, most archaeological literature falls somewhere between these two extremes.

The most important audience to be addressed in terms that make clear both the interest and the importance of what we are saying is the wider public. This is not an uncouth monster, to whom a few carefully filleted pieces of information can occasionally be fed, done up in a pretty package. The public is in fact everyone. Archaeologists themselves, whether practical or academic, can only claim detailed knowledge of very small parts of the subject: most of the time they are in the same position as the interested layman. The real divide is between those who are already interested in the subject, and willing to take some trouble to find out more, and those who know nothing about it, and care less. The second audience is the real challenge.

COMMUNICATION CHANNELS

What means are available for communication? There is of course the traditional bedrock of archaeology, the excavation report, and, arising from it, academic synthesis and discussion of all kinds, published in monographs and learned journals, filtering down to textbooks and more general works. Despite the acknowledged problem of non-publication, there is now an enormous and multifarious literature on all aspects of archaeology. From the groaning bookstalls of recent conferences it might seem our problem is overpublication: too many books, for which none of us can afford either the time or the money. If you spend all your time reading, you will never write anything yourself. On the other hand, if you don't know what others have already said, you may repeat them and will not know of research relevant to your own. Here the answer must be greater emphasis on bibliographies or abstracts, like the excellent and underused Council for British Archaeology abstract series, now being replaced by *British Archaeological Bibliography*. Reviews and review articles also serve a vital function, although if done properly they demand significant amounts of potential research time from the reviewer. Both bibliographies and reviews are tools, means to an end and not ends in themselves: they are essential guides to the literature, not substitutes for it.

Most archaeologists get their up-to-date information from visiting each other's excavations, looking at material in stores and museums, and talking to each other (see Chapters 20 and 21). They also attend conferences. These are not always such valuable sources of new information as one might expect. Small, well-structured seminars where all the participants contribute and are familiar with the material and its problems can be extremely productive. Large archaeological conferences, however, serve political and social functions as much as intellectual ones. And the lecture is not such an easy format for communication as it seems. The written word is not the same as the spoken, and the ways we absorb information from the written page and through eyes and ears are different. Just reading a paper aloud is often a waste of time: better to photocopy it and hand it round. Alternatively, a lecture can all too often lapse into incoherent and disconnected rambling or a series of jokes. But when it works, speaking to an audience communicates more, and better, than reading to them. This is less of a problem when the paper consists of a presentation of a recent excavation or finds where pictures break up the text, which may be fairly straightforward, than for more synthetic or abstract topics. Most people, of course, reckon that the argument they had in the pub after the lecture was a lot more useful than the lecture itself, and they are probably right.

A more formal channel of communication is newspapers and periodicals; archaeology is often well reported in local newspapers, but of the nationals only *The Times* and the *Independent* think it worth regular coverage. There are also several good archaeological magazines, such as *Current Archaeology, Interim: Archaeology in York* and the *London Archaeologist*, all of which present recent discoveries and research in a lively accessible way to a non-specialist audience while still being very useful to archaeologists.

Schools are crucial, since most people get their introduction to the range of subjects our society thinks are worthwhile there. If children start with the idea, however vague, that archaeology is a legitimate subject about which they do know something, they are more likely to take it seriously in the future. The emphasis on sources for history has allowed archaeology a foothold, and Anglo-Saxon England at least has a place in the primary school curriculum in England. There are now good resource packs for teachers put out by English Heritage or other organizations, like the West Stow Anglo-Saxon village, some presenting up-to-date ideas in an imaginative format.

There are also less direct channels of communication. Prehistoric people and archaeologists appear in novels, films, and plays. How many of us first became interested in the past by reading the novels of Rosemary Sutcliffe (see Evans 1989 for discussion of archaeological novels)? Even in *The Archers* archaeology occasionally appears, though usually not as we would like it, and an episode of the TV series *Lovejoy* recently centred on an archaeological excavation. Mosaics and Egyptian mummies have appeared in cigarette advertisements and artists like Richard Long use ancient monuments as inspiration for their own works. These kinds of communication are less a direct message from archaeologists than a reflection of how the subject is perceived by others, and of attitudes to the past and its remains. It is not just fun, but very important to study them if we want to find out how to get our own version across. Do people really think Indiana Jones is a typical archaeologist and does it matter if they do? Are we all, and should we be seen as, mostly either hairy young men with mud on our boots or bald-headed boffins (also male)? Perhaps familiarity with more of the less colourful or eccentric members of the profession would make it seem less odd and freakish – terms dangerously close to 'marginal and irrelevant'.

The rest of this chapter concentrates on what could be seen as the opposite extremes of archaeological communication: the archaeological report and television programmes. These can and should be more directly connected than is always the case. The dissemination of archaeological information, through whatever media to whatever audience, involves in principle the same method. Specific evidence is described, analysed and fitted into a wider context. The difficulty and the challenge lies in the balance between evidence and story. We should always be ready to see how the essentials of our latest work could be made into an interesting fifteen-minute talk, film or popular article. But those essentials should be the result of careful distillation of all the evidence we have to hand, not a restatement of what we thought before we began.

THE ARCHAEOLOGICAL REPORT

The traditional archaeological report is a printed volume containing an introduction to the site, a summary and discussion of the excavated evidence, conclusions as to its meaning and, at the back, all the evidence: for example, plans, sections and finds catalogues. During the 1960s, publication became the problem it has remained ever since because of the explosion of material, an explosion that resulted from a simultaneous increase in the scale of excavation and in the detail and range of types of information that could be extracted from what was dug up. Ever since, we have been quietly drowning in our own data while complaining vociferously about the non-appearance of everyone else's.

In 1975 the Frere Committee (DoE 1975a) tackled the problem of unpublished excavations in an era of rising print costs. It was suggested that four levels of records existed, of which only Level IV – 'synthesised descriptions with supporting data and selected finds and specialist reports relevant to synthesis' – really needed to be published. What had previously been the bulk of an archaeological report (Level III) – 'full illustration and description of all structural and stratigraphic relationships' – together with classified finds lists and drawings and specialist analyses might simply be made available 'as required': as duplicates, fiche, microfilm or computer printout. At first this seemed a sensible solution to an intractable problem, especially since most readers use the introductory sections of reports far more than the supporting data. However it met resistance, partly from those who felt that only real printed pages constituted publication, but also as the drawbacks of fiche became apparent. Although in the past only occasional use may have been made of the detailed report, it was always there and without too much effort anyone doubting the conclusions could refer to the supporting evidence. Now it became more difficult.

There was continued disagreement as to the dividing line between Levels III and IV and a suspicion that those with sufficient influence could still publish 'properly'; only ordinary mortals would see their work consigned to the wastebasket of fiche, or still worse, archive. Also, none of this had solved the problem of the time and expense still involved in post-excavation, even if the results barely saw the light of day. Increased funding of post-excavation also reduced the funds available for excavation. People become archaeologists because they like the outdoor life, the immediacy of discovery, the feel of the past, and the experience of working in a team solving practical problems. Directing an excavation means running a fairly complex enterprise, often involving large numbers of people and using many different skills. This does not always equip one well for spending years alone indoors chewing it all over. It is not surprising that some have gone on digging instead of writing up.

The Cunliffe Report (Cunliffe 1982) introduced the emphasis on selectivity that has been the keynote of all such discussion in the past decade. It stated 'the temptation to excavate more than can reasonably be processed . . . should be stringently controlled' (1982: 3). This runs counter to the psychological instincts encouraged by rescue archaeology, especially as it was seen in the 1960s and 1970s (Rahtz 1974b) – dig it today because tomorrow it will have been destroyed – which of course partly caused the publication problem. But it is of course true that the rate of destruction continues to be such that excavation cannot hope to keep pace. In seeking a solution subsequent policy documents by English Heritage have developed the idea of the research design. Priorities should be established and selective excavations only allowed in order to pursue the design's objectives. While most would agree with this in principle, the precision of prediction and monitoring at all stages laid down in MAP 2 (English Heritage 1991b) could threaten to inhibit research.

In order to produce a research design to the required MAP 2 standards it might seem that one needs to have dug the site already; funding for publication requires 'a chapter by chapter breakdown of the report, giving the contents of each' (English Heritage 1991b: 35). Since the analysis of the data will not have been carried out before post-excavation funding is agreed, the framework for that analysis can only be based on the immediately apparent results of the excavation – in other words, the interim report and/or the concluding site tour. The possibility that more detailed analysis might throw up completely new facets of information, or even prompt a rethink of the whole site, is all but denied in a format of this type. This is production-line archaeology, going from evaluation to excavation, to record and on to archive and, perhaps, partial publication.

This is a practical way of dealing with the kind of digging arising now from developer funding, involving the rapid processing of numerous small excavations by many different people within severe constraints of time and money. It may also work on larger, open sites of the kind picked up as crop marks in aerial photographs, where a combination of survey and trial excavation may allow fairly accurate prediction of results and resources needed. But confining the excavation and analysis of complex sites, especially urban ones, to a straitjacket of predetermined committee-based research is unlikely to add much to our understanding of such sites. Teasing out the significance of all the fragmentary layers and redeposited finds from an urban site is a frustrating and time-consuming task for which there are no short cuts.

If, for example, you suddenly think part of the site might have been a clothworking establishment or a church, not only will that involve pursuit of relevant comparative evidence, but it will also require re-examination of previously inexplicable fragments of stratigraphy or artefacts. Only the explanation that accounts for most of the evidence, and is not contradicted by any of it, can be allowed to stand. Going halfway, as in the end most people have to, may produce, metaphorically, a half-built house with all the floors in the wrong place and the wrong inhabitants assigned to each. If the analysis is not done by the excavator, who has at least some of the record in his or her head, it will be far more difficult for a future researcher. The idea that archaeological evidence is somehow neutral and that it can be completely and objectively recorded for analysis by anyone at a future date has been discredited both in theory and in practice. And yet that is the principle of the archive: a vast accumulation of data for future reference.

The Society of Antiquaries paper introduced a new emphasis. As its authors pointed out, twenty years of confronting the problem of non-publication have not made it go away. 'The backlog of unpublished reports is very large and growing rapidly . . . it is impossible to find out what is happening' (Society of Antiquaries 1992: 5). The priority now is somehow to let people know what has been excavated, what records exist and how they can be found, rather than pressing for a published report of every small dig. The paper suggests the publication of an annual compendium, a list of all archaeological work that has taken place in the previous year plus summary reports. This, if it can be achieved, will be extremely valuable: in Scotland, *Discovery & Excavation* has fulfilled this role since the 1950s. At present it is almost impossible to find out systematically for England what has been done and by whom. At least a list would suggest where further reference might be made.

All of these official documents have one fundamental flaw. They all encourage the publication of conclusions ('synthesis') without evidence or with only selected evidence. In the Frere Report (DoE 1975a) it was 'supporting data' and reports 'relevant to synthesis' while MAP 2 does at least allow for alternative interpretations (English Heritage 1991b: 39). In fact they are no longer concerned with the dissemination of information directly from the record of the excavation: they are concerned with the creation and maintenance of an archive, from which subsequent researchers may be able to quarry information. Therefore it is crucial not only that the 'compendium' or something like it should be created, but that a different attitude towards the whole problem should develop.

At present, the evidence is increasingly separated from the conclusions. Eventually much of it will be neither bound in printed pages nor even in fiche or computer printout – media in themselves still very offputting to many readers. It will be in archive, often in a museum, not always easy of access. The Society of Antiquaries paper (1992) recognizes the difficulties facing museums involved in maintaining archives and suggests setting up new repositories. Even if this can be done, it will simply continue the consolidation and official sanction of a situation where most academic interpretation, let alone popular communication, operates at one or more removes from the original data. Even the synthesis is all too often a tidied-up version of the interim report, which has not really taken account of all the details. This is a tendency to be resisted: we must still go back to the basic evidence.

Electronic information systems may make this more possible in future, as long as they do not drive further wedges between the computer-literate and non-literate. Desktop publishing may increasingly provide part of the answer for publication. Given that readerships can often be counted in hundreds, it is not impractical for authors to think of producing their own reports. The problem is limited circulation and publicity, but use of an agency like Oxbow Books may solve that. The gains in terms of speed of production could be enormous.

The official policy of preservation by record in an archive, however necessary and practical it may be, plays directly into the hands of critical theorists. Even where there is a curated archive, as in London, 'practically no use has been made of it by students' (Cunliffe 1990: 671). The reader takes the easy way out and reads only the synthesis, believing it, or not, if they already trust the author. On this basis it is quite legitimate to dismiss all archaeological writing as an exercise in power politics, a form of 'domination and control' (Shanks and Tilley 1987b: 207). 'It doesn't matter what you say as long as you say it in the right way' (Shanks and Tilley 1987b: 23). If you are an established name in archaeology people will believe your synthesis. If you aren't, they won't. Constant critique may seem negative, but it is necessary if unthinking perpetuation of existing views is to be avoided.

After all this, what is actually being published? It is impossible here to look at more than a small and unfair sample. For example, the series *East Anglian Archaeological Reports* now has more than fifty titles published and many more in the pipeline. Overall, this is a successful series that has produced comprehensive reports on excavation and survey, both recent and dating back many years, including work by amateurs as well as professionals. Sites are published as a whole, either alone or grouped with other similar ones (except for the first few volumes which adopted a more magazine-like format). Finds and specialist reports are included as text or fiche. There are few volumes of free-standing finds or environmental reports, and where they exist, there are usually excavation reports as well: the West Stow Anglo-Saxon village was published in 1985, the animal husbandry from the same site a few years later (West 1985; Crabtree 1990). Towns, notably Norwich, also figure but this is to a large extent a rural-based series. A more superficial look at publications from the Oxford Unit and the Wessex Trust suggests a similar policy of publication by site or group of sites, through the relevant county journal, the monograph series attached to those journals, or through the *CBA Research Report* series.

Urban units have a more difficult task and have tried more varied solutions. At Winchester, Martin Biddle, the trail-blazer of urban archaeology in the 1960s, adopted the traditional style of publication in large hardback printed books emanating from an established academic press. Publication was envisaged within a historical framework: volumes would appear on Roman, Saxon and medieval Winchester. So far substantial historical volumes and a massive finds report have appeared (Biddle 1976; Keene 1985; Biddle 1990). No site reports, except for the cemetery at Lankhills, and no period volumes are yet to hand. Why not? It is of course true that such an undertaking is not lightly carried through to completion. The scale and complexity of Winchester, and some of its successors, may have come near to defeating their excavators, who may not have appreciated until too late just how frustrating and time-consuming their tasks would be. Part of the answer also lies in the means of publication, here shown up at its slow and expensive worst.

The historical framework, however, has probably made things even more difficult than they already were. Volumes dealing with different periods of Winchester's history could well seem the logical end result of the massive excavations that took place in the 1960s and again more recently. But this may not be the best format for the publication of basic excavation data. Before any volume can be completed, all the individual site reports need to be finished and then definitively filleted to allocate the Roman layers to the Roman volume, the Saxon to the Saxon and so on. Thus nothing can be completed before everything is finished. Also, it leaves little room for ambiguity and may render it impossible for a reader to assess how reliably any part of the stratigraphy and finds have been assigned to one of the periods rather than another, in other words, to check conclusions against evidence.

Winchester was a pioneer, with all the problems that entailed. Other units have learnt from Winchester's experience and have tried other formulae. The York Archaeological Trust uses fascicules, the publication of sections of what are envisaged ultimately as a series of some twenty volumes. Some of these volumes are defined by period: Anglian York, post-medieval York. These pose the same problem for the reader as Winchester. Once any site has been dismantled into phases, and those phases published separately in different volumes, how can the whole exercise be checked? Sites that fall completely, or nearly completely, into one period are not a problem, nor are those where the different periods are separated, for example, by abandonment. But others may pose considerable difficulties.

It is noticeable that the list of published fascicules is biased towards what in earlier days might have been seen as subsidiary specialist reports on, for example, pottery, finds or environmental evidence, rather than accounts of the excavations. The reason for this is partly that it is less difficult to take a specific group of material, to catalogue, describe and discuss it, and perhaps to put it down and come back to it at a later date without losing half the previous effort, than it is to disentangle structures and stratigraphy. Specialists also often actually earn their living by writing reports on their chosen subject, and so they get the work done. Excavators may have moved on to dig another site, or they may have posts in universities, units or museums where administrative and academic functions may occupy most of their time and energy.

Does it matter if finds are published without their context? The York Coppergate site is now almost fully published – except for the site itself. A summary of the site stratigraphy is given in each fascicule, and there are pages of lists of correlations between finds numbers and context numbers. In theory it should be possible to use the eventual site report with the other volumes. So far we can read about bones, textiles, pottery and metalwork from the site in a series of excellent volumes (e.g. Bayley 1992; Walton 1989), but not about the structures, the stratigraphy and the matrix that holds all the rest together and gives it meaning. Will the final report provide that matrix, or will it be another free-standing volume?

The tendency to separate 'the site' from 'the finds' is followed elsewhere, for example in London, where the publication problems are especially complex (Cunliffe 1990), and where recent publications on Saxo-Norman London include a slim volume on buildings and streets (Horsman et al. 1990), and a massive tome on finds and environmental evidence (Vince 1992). The Ancient Monuments laboratory now publishes a list, and will provide individual copies, of unpublished specialist reports. This is useful, and must go some way to alleviating the justifiable frustration of specialists who complete their reports on time only to see them languish for years while the rest of the report is unwritten or unpublished. But there are dangers in this disintegration. There is a tendency for specialists to explain everything in their own terms, and to give priority to their own evidence. Contradictions between stratigraphy and typology may not be apparent if detailed reference is not made from one to the other, and may be resolved by each author in favour of their own type of information.

This separation is to some extent a legacy of the time when archaeologists thought the past could be taken apart like clockwork and reassembled at will. The reintroduction of humanism under the guise of some aspects of post-processualism has reminded us what a muddle human life is and was, and also how interconnected everything is. Somehow we have to find ways of looking at all the evidence as an interconnected whole and then, somehow, extract a story that fits as much of the evidence as possible. Some people have suggested new imaginative ways of writing reports including the use of videos, interactive video-discs, computer graphics and even writing a report as historical fiction (Spector

1991). Some of these experiments may turn out to work better than conventional methods. Nevertheless, somehow, somewhere an awful lot of basic boring information has to be both on record and properly digested to produce a clearly argued and fully supported story.

POPULARIZATION

The report may be the repository of the basic excavated data, but it is not really a convenient means of communication to anyone but specialists. Synthesis, discussion and popularization are all necessary as well. The crucial point is to maintain the link between data and discussion. Some authors take the trouble to go back to the evidence and to sift the facts from the 'factoids', as Millett has called them (1990: xvi). But all too often what is written is a repackaging of existing material under pressure to produce results quickly. This is a more serious problem in the field of popular communication than in academic writing. Academics after all are trained to be critical and should be able to work out for themselves what is new and what is rehash. But commercial publishers and radio or television producers looking for a way into a subject find it harder to discriminate. There is still a two-way barrier between academics and professionals and 'the media'; this in turn forms a barrier between archaeologists and the wider public. There is a general perception of academics and professionals as being too boring to be able to communicate properly to a wider audience. Professional writers, journalists and media experts are expected to transmit the material. This is fine when they take account of recent work but not when they do a 'scissors and paste' from old books and ideas they took from school thirty years earlier.

On the other hand, although in Britain we have a tradition of scholarly popularization envied by other countries, the idea that 'popular' writing is easy and unimportant is still prevalent. Scholars hesitate to spend time on work that seems to add nothing of 'significance' to their lists of publications and to be a 'waste' of scarce research time. This is the kind of attitude that leads to accusations of ivory-tower irrelevance. In a democracy, for reasons of self-interest alone, archaeologists cannot afford not to engage enough of the public's interest for politicians to believe there could be votes in the subject, and therefore a need to fund it. In a less cynical vein, knowledge is of very little use if it is not made public: the mentality of the collector who gloats in his study over the gem of wisdom known only to himself is not unknown to archaeology: but it is an evolutionary dead-end. Many archaeologists believe, and try to convince others, that archaeology has something to say, that it is fun, useful, interesting, even essential. These days the way to do that is through pictures, not words.

For many people visual images are more accessible, and more powerful than words, whether written or spoken. Television is the most powerful medium of communication in the late 20th century, and if we want people to know about archaeology we must use it. The difficulty lies both in deciding what message to convey, and how, in a medium more like a distorting glass than a mirror, and also in persuading anyone to give us airtime in the first place.

Archaeology fared better in television's early days than ever since. In the 1950s the archaeological quiz *Animal Vegetable Mineral* achieved great popularity among those who then owned television sets. Mortimer Wheeler and Glyn Daniel became successively television personality of the year. The successful formula of a quiz involving eccentric personalities and equally peculiar objects remains at the back of the minds of television executives, together with the other ingredients identified by Bruce Norman, last producer of the BBC series *Chronicle*: treasure, exotic locations and dead bodies (Norman 1983). Any attempt to put over serious ideas about archaeology on television has to take account of the prevalence of this limited conception of the subject, and also of the vulnerable position of all minority subjects, which will never produce mass audiences for advertisers. Success in getting on air often comes down to the commitment of a few key individuals, both on the creative side, and in the hierarchy of television, who are willing to stick their necks out on behalf of a subject that many of their colleagues do not take very seriously.

The first producer of *Chronicle*, Paul Johnson, was one of the first of such figures. The programmes created for that series, now sadly discontinued, were often models of what can be done within the documentary format. This is ideal for communicating the outlines of an archaeological topic. Film, graphics, commentary and interviews with archaeologists can all combine to produce what is in essence a more elaborate lecture, or a more vivid book. It is true that *Chronicle* had its fair share of faraway places, treasure and bodies – with and without flesh – and that in audience-ratings terms the most successful pro- grammes were those on Lindow Man (ancient dead body) and the *Mary Rose* (an under- water 'Pompeii' with royal interest). But they also showed that it is possible to go straight from original research, not just excavation results but ideas, to the screen. Twenty years on, the programme on the implications of radiocarbon dating with Magnus Magnusson and Colin Renfrew is still a very good exposition of the subject. When first shown it would have been new to many archaeologists, as well as everyone else. More recently, a programme on Cranborne Chase in the *Down to Earth* series was a presentation of the bones of a substantial body of research by the three archaeologists who had just published two large, complex books on the subject.

Documentaries tend to preach to the converted or at least the mildly interested. Audience surveys show middle-aged, middle-class profiles. Much of the message is car- ried in words as well as pictures and some parts are rather slow-moving. Younger audi- ences are less attuned to words, having been brought up on advertisements and pop videos with quick, zappy visual images. They are thought to be turned off by – and to turn off – the traditional documentary. This is probably why the television hierarchy has turned them off as well, to our great loss. Archaeology sometimes still appears in the guise of 'nature', as for example when David Attenborough turns from more attractive species to consider man. But since the end of *Chronicle* and the Sutton Hoo project there does not seem to be a reliable slot for archaeological documentaries.

Archaeology does still figure in children's television, mostly but not exclusively in schools programmes: *Now Then* on BBC 2 with Tony Gregory and Francis Pryor was not a school programme. Reconstruction, and re-enactment, of past lives bulks large in these, which means that they can vary from excellent and imaginative evocations to rather feeble dressing-up exercises. Videos of all kinds, some very good, are now widely used in museums and at ancient monuments. Like documentary films, these are really a modern substitute for the lecture or the site tour and are only likely to be seen by those who have already taken the trouble to get to the museum or site, or have been brought there by their teacher.

Another format tried recently was that of the magazine programme, the Channel 4 series *Down to Earth* presented by this contributor. Instead of a half hour or forty minutes devoted to one subject, several topics were squeezed into half an hour. There were complaints of oversimplification and scrappiness from those who wanted meaty documen- taries. In fact, many subjects can be dealt with in ten or fifteen minutes as well as they can in forty. Comparison of the *Down to Earth* item on the prehistoric man found preserved by ice in the Alps and the full-length *Horizon* programme on the same subject showed that, except for information on date and detail of the artefacts not available during the filming, the former covered nearly as much ground.

The lesson drawn from our experience was that the interest of archaeology lies in a combination of the immediate contact with a specific bit of the past, and the way in which that small part contributes to a wider picture. People arguing with each other should be used sparingly, and the politics of archaeology are not usually gripping to the rest of the world. Things like scientific wizardry, the glamour of golden treasure and the creepiness of skeletons can be used to attract people's attention. But the real point is the story they help to tell about some aspect of how people lived, and what they did, in the past and also in what that tells us about how we are today.

Perhaps it is really more important to get archaeology on the news than on its own, clearly defined separate programmes. An extended archaeological news item, like those that sometimes appear on *Channel 4 News*, is likely to reach more of the people not already interested in the subject than is a specifically designated archaeology programme. It may persuade them that it is a subject worth taking seriously if it is counted as 'news'. Such pieces are an encouraging sign that archaeology is taken seriously, and is seen as a genuine concern of a significant part of the population, which is a prerequisite for the dissemination of any further detailed archaeological information by whatever means.

CHAPTER 20

VISITORS WELCOME

Mike Parker Pearson

Archaeology is now recognized as a legitimate consideration in planning control. Private organizations are funding large amounts of work. Publicity about archaeological discoveries is copious. And yet there is a crisis looming over archaeology's survival, not simply from cuts in public spending but also from loss of committed public support. Professionalization has forced out the grass-roots participants just when volunteers in nature conservation are growing in numbers. Developers may become warier of paying for archaeology when their expectations of discoveries are not matched by the meagre nature of finds. Archaeology in Britain runs the risk of becoming boring, bureaucratic and inconsequential.

Instead of welcoming 'visitors', we should be encouraging 'participants'. To carry the public with us requires more than glossy brochures and shop-window consumerism. We require a sea change in professional attitudes to truly involve as many people as possible and to reach the parts we've never reached. But where does the funding come from? What we would like to do and what we end up doing are often two different things, because of pressures of time and limits of funds. Education, publicity and 'outreach' are some of the first items to be cut from budgets hard-pressed even to ensure that salaries are paid. County archaeologists are often too busy and archaeological education officers are a rare breed indeed. English Heritage includes funding for presentation in its rescue project grants but local authorities have not yet taken up the proposal that it may be reasonable and justified to ask private developers to include a presentational element in their support of archaeology. Perhaps we could be thinking about presentational and educational aspects being included in the archaeological briefs provided by local authorities.

Against this background of meagre funds and limited resources, archaeologists have been pretty good at advertising themselves, their institutions, their sponsors and patrons, and their achievements. Archaeologists are periodically exhorted to do still more to involve the public in their work, and yet, in Britain, no archaeological organization has failed to strengthen its public profile in the last ten years. There are newsheets, newspapers, brochures, teaching packs, site guides, regional tour operators, open days, education officers, resource centres, popular books and multi-media presentations. The use of increasingly sophisticated and expensive means for bringing in visitors has been extensive. Most professional archaeologists no longer need to be apprised of the technical innovations and organization, as put together so well in *Visitors Welcome* (Binks *et al.* 1988). But perhaps we have concentrated too much on the medium at the expense of the message. The form of presentations may be arresting, intriguing and eye-catching but what about the content?

Everyone has an opinion on what is good for archaeology's public. The differences of opinion can be great. The providers of heritage centres and re-enactments are vilified for their exploitative and cynical marketing of the past. Those who raise political issues in archaeology are castigated for their political bias and for rocking the boat. Some organizations have formulated codes of conduct. For example, the 'Campaign for Real Heritage' at Flag Fen is guided by three rules: the past must not be mystified; the past must not be cheapened or trivialized; every interpretation is capable of reinterpretation (Pryor 1989).

There is a substantial and continuous flow of literature addressing these philosophical issues (Lowenthal and Binney 1981; McBryde 1985; Schadla-Hall 1985; Wright 1985; Hewison 1987; Uzzell 1989a, 1989b; Layton 1989a, 1989b; Gathercole and Lowenthal 1990; Mackenzie and Stone 1990; Fowler 1991; Hooper-Greenhill 1991; Walsh 1992).

Archaeology is, of course, a social phenomenon. Its practice and practitioners are products of the economic and class relationships of contemporary society. Surveys of attitudes towards archaeology (Merriman 1991; Hodder *et al.* 1985) indicate that it still retains a high-brow image and that it means little to most people from working-class backgrounds. It is part of a plethora of tastes and activities by which dominant cultural groups define themselves as refined, knowledgeable, and discerning (see e.g. Bourdieu's 1984 study of class life styles). Nearly all archaeologists are propagandists for their subject, often with a passion, and few would wish to restrict its appeal to a narrow class niche. So how well have we done in taking archaeology to the people? If only one in four people buy books, then the medium of the written word may be relatively limited. Exhibitions and displays that use pictorial or three-dimensional representations and spoken words are probably more successful than text-explained exhibits. Archaeology is regularly reported in the quality papers but almost never in the rest. Bestsellers about the past are either romantic novels or veer towards the mystical. Even the popular television series *Down to Earth* attracts a relatively small Channel 4 audience.

Yet the growth of archaeology's appeal is noticeable. Merriman's 1991 survey indicated that interest in archaeology and the past was not class-restricted among the younger generations. Although archaeology and prehistory receive short shrift in the National Curriculum, there are many teaching resources, support co-ordinators (education officers in English Heritage, the Council for British Archaeology and local authorities) and enthusiastic teachers who are instilling an interest at an early age (see e.g. Corbishley 1992; Halkon *et al.* 1992).

Archaeologists have expanded their passive audience, but their active grass-roots support has declined drastically. The role of the amateur has been marginalized with the necessary professionalization of the discipline, and opportunities for people to participate in the process are increasingly few and far between. As archaeology has joined the consumer culture, the public must pay for their voyeuristic experiences. Archaeological 'shopping' involves purchases from archaeological dreamsellers of authentic experiences of the past, but misses out sadly on the involvement in discovery and interpretation behind the shop window. You can look, you can even touch, but it's getting harder to join in. Of course, many people are interested yet never want to be involved. Looking through the glass is as close as they want to come. Yet we should surely be encouraging active participation as widely as possible. The comparison with wildlife interests, where many amateurs are acknowledged specialists and experts, is becoming less and less sustainable.

The motives that draw people to archaeology are undoubtedly complex and varied. Escapism, fantasy, curiosity, amusement, and reassurance may be some of the more readily articulated (Lowenthal 1985). In our culture, leisure is positively loaded as a moral value. People may use their leisure time to play, develop their creativity, and improve their psychological wellbeing (Goodale and Witt 1985). Archaeology may offer some amusement, a sideshow of escapist distractions, but what more does it involve? Social engineering concepts of instruction and moral betterment, expressed in the 19th century by Pitt Rivers among others (Bowden 1991: 141–2), are now viewed as patronizing, unsophisticated and deeply conservative. But many archaeologists are concerned that mere amusement, 'the happiness of those who cannot think' (Alexander Pope, cited in Goodale and Witt 1985: 3), is not enough.

According to David Uzzell (1989a: 10), the signs are not promising: 'Despite the use of a profusion of technologies to enhance visitor understanding and enable learning, it would seem from research on the effectiveness of exhibitions that visitors to museums actually do not learn very much.' Similar concerns have been voiced about the popular and successful Jorvik Viking Centre in York (Schadla-Hall 1985), though the reviewer suggested that this was the fault of the presentation rather than the visitor. We may complain that many people simply lack a developed sense of curiosity, but perhaps they are not being sufficiently challenged. A few years ago I was surprised to hear from a senior Soviet archaeologist, V.I. Masson, that he considered archaeology to be psychology: we must prevent people from becoming Neanderthals living in centrally heated flats! No senior figures in British archaeology had, at that time, expressed such strong sentiments about the purpose of the subject. A few years on, such views are common currency among archaeologists and heritage managers. Interpretation is about encouraging people to think for themselves (Aldridge 1989). It is not instruction but provocation (Tilden 1977: 9).

The primary object of interpretation is to create a sense of discovery and a sense of wonder (Stevens 1989). It is also to provide food for thought; to attempt to shake people out of their 'Neanderthal' docility. In the words of the French historian Fernand Braudel (1980), we visit the past in order to understand better the present. Through archaeology we visit different times and different cultures, with some aspects similar to our own lives and others very different. In this exploration of sameness/difference we may come to see just how arbitrary and historically rooted are our own 'universal truths'. In the same way that Francis Fukuyama has proclaimed 'the end of history', archaeologists perhaps unwittingly promulgate the notion that the past is dead, that we are close to the top rung of the ladder of progress. In such ways we reinforce our feelings of superiority to the societies of the past, and teach people to be contemptuous of those 'primitive' peoples from long ago. Through this contempt for the people of the past we are liable to instil contempt for the millions who live in pre- or non-industrial societies (Stone and MacKenzie 1990).

'What's history if you can't bend it a bit?' was the reply to criticisms of deliberate distortion of the past for financial gain during the 1988 Armada celebrations (Hewison 1989). The potential misrepresentation of past events for purposes of modern spectacle has been viewed with alarm by archaeologists. The staging of a battle between French and British troops of the Napoleonic period in a Palmerstonian fort has been compared to the hypothetical re-enactment of the Battle of Waterloo in the Tower of London between the Ermine Street Guard and the Sealed Knot (Fowler 1989)! Perhaps a more apt example is the annual gathering of Druids at (or near) Stonehenge. The point still stands, however. But there is a more difficult problem that this opposition between bent history and objective accuracy fails to accommodate. We are all aware of the distortions of prehistory to justify racist and territorial aims under the Nazis (Arnold 1992). Even without such gross misreadings of the evidence, all reconstructions of the past are in some sense constructs of the present. Our categorization of past times into eras (Roman, Neolithic, etc.) carries implicit meanings and interpretations that guide our thoughts about what happened, and how, in the past. We may strive to maintain an objective and minimalist stance in interpretation, but such an approach is likely to be misleading as well as boring. Cautious interpretations are likely to invoke a pragmatic utilitarianism in explaining the evidence. Employing our 20th-century notions of common sense, we are destined to imprint forever the present onto the past. As a result, we learn nothing other than that past cultures were dirtier, technologically less sophisticated versions of ourselves.

This does not mean that anything goes; that we can make up whatever we like regardless of the evidence. Instead we have to come to terms with realizing that the distinction between myth and reality in the past is not as clear-cut as some of us might wish. While we balance a concern for accurate reporting with the need to avoid a 'dead' archaeology of lifeless and meaningless artefacts, we are still constructing creation myths (albeit with a strong component of hard evidence). For example, archaeology in Britain may be used to portray the rise of the nation state, the establishment of democracy, or even the rise of capitalism. Other myths (the insignificance of Britain in world politics until the last 1,000 years; the long history of English individualism, for example) may be ignored or used in other circumstances. All interpretive frameworks are, one way or another, mythic stories that are re-enacted, retold and presented as truth. This relativization should not make us fearful of how to decide which version of the past is true. Instead we should relish the possibilities for multiple interpretations and the primacy that this puts on the act of interpretation. The most popular myths of the prehistoric past are 'fringe' beliefs in a golden age of harmony, earth forces and mysticism. The adherents of fringe archaeology are put off by the smug, exclusive, know-it-all condescension of the professionals (Williamson and Bellamy 1983a). Through various rhetorical devices (Gero 1989) they cultivate an image of unfairly treated underdog: they know the real truth but are derided by the blinkered establishment. Such alternative myths are psychological props and legitimations, beyond dispute, to New Age Travellers, among others. Such closed minds, on both sides, are hindrances to tolerance and understanding. As we develop a more critical archaeology, able to debunk and evaluate competing mythic claims on the past, so we may come to understand better the past in the present rather than simply for its own sake.

The development of the heritage industry in recent years has had a profound impact on archaeology and its presentation to the public. The past and the present are interactive: what happened in history is a question that is answered according to the worries and obsessions of the late 20th century. What is happening today is a question that drives us all to examine our history for guidance. The force of the public's interests and enthusiasms moulds the heritage industry's presentations. Archaeologists can feed that force, or struggle against it: in either case, our role as mediator between past and present can be directive but our actions within that role are inherently reflexive.

Since the Department of the Environment stated that heritage would give a feeling of continuity and a sense of security to face the difficult years ahead (DoE 1975b), there has been an undercurrent of concern for the ways in which heritage differs from history. Within a climate of industrial decline, some observers view the heritage industry as a bolstering of nationalist sentiment, a thinly disguised presentation of right-wing interests, a sanitization of some rather dubious past events, and a cloying and nostalgic sentimentality for an 'olde and merrie England' that never existed (Hewison 1987; Ascherson 1987, 1988; Wright 1985). If history is a critical and liberating method of re-evaluating our lives and our society then heritage is a suffocating embrace of cultural chauvinism (Hewison 1989). With English Heritage initially prepared to sell off a number of the nation's monuments, the past has been packaged for consumption in every form (see also Chapter 1).

There is no doubt that archaeologists have clung gratefully to the skirts of the heritage boom. The houses and gardens of past aristocracies are very much at the heart of this boom but archaeologists have found ways of using the stimulus and opportunities to good effect. The increasing interest in recording standing buildings and industrial monuments, and in reconstructing historic gardens, has moved the techniques of archaeology into the limelight of more recent history. Archaeology has become not simply the study of the ancient past but also the investigation of material culture right up to the present. Yet for many practitioners, as well as onlookers, it may seem no more than a method; a motiveless yet systematic sifting through the physical rubbish of history. Do we simply provide the evidence and let the purveyors of dreams market the myths and stories that they wish to tell?

If heritage is a distortion of history in terms of accuracy and critical interpretation, it may also purvey a past that is pastiched and collaged. According to Hewison (1989), this 'pick 'n' mix' approach weakens our knowledge and understanding of history. There are very obvious implications for archaeology. Nearly all archaeological presentations are site-specific. Equally our own specialisms are chronologically narrow. Our stories are of fragmented and isolated times and places that rarely relate explicitly to the epic narrative of how the world has changed in the long term. It is possible to use the concept of place to powerful effect; to develop interest in local history and archaeology. Yet perhaps what is achieved is a local pride (another 'historic market town') rather than a key to understanding a wider past.

There may be a conflict of interest between 'giving the public what they want' (the consumer is always right in the ideology of the marketplace) and 'instructing the populace in what's good for them' (patronizing Victorian-style philanthropism). It can be argued that most people want escapism rather than having to think about the world's problems, and prefer breathtaking spectacle to academic education. For some, the way forward has been a middle ground. The market does not entirely dictate the content, the message, but it does have a considerable impact on the medium. So what are archaeology's messages?

1. Archaeology is interesting! You don't have to be an expert to do it. Neither do you have to be white or middle class. There is very little take-up of archaeology by ethnic minorities. Organizations that archaeologists work for may have equal opportunity policies, but there is virtually no attempt to encourage positively these minorities. A recent project by the Countryside Commission has explored the reasons why members of ethnic minorities fear the white-dominated countryside. It is a hostile landscape of jealously guarded private property and unfriendly natives. The Countryside Commission has set up a scheme with leaders of Asian communities in northern English towns to take coach parties on days out into the country, so that they might overcome their misgivings and feel confident that the countryside is theirs too. Active involvement of interested amateurs in fieldwork and post-excavation has fallen as professionalism has risen. We must encourage a greater sense of participation if public support is not to be alienated. Archaeological remains are a limited resource and, as such, particularly susceptible to control and exclusion. Self-important power play by professionals is to be avoided wherever possible.

2. Archaeology is not just about white culture. While members of ethnic minorities are British citizens, they are often not considered to be English (or Scottish, Welsh or Irish). Such tags have a racial rather than political connotation and have the effect of excluding rather than integrating. We often ignore the multiracial composition of prehistoric and historic Britain (to be the subject of a Museum of London exhibition). There were black soldiers in Britain during the Roman period and people of all creeds and colours in the historic period. Equally, considerations of the late medieval and post-medieval periods rarely place Britain in the context of the world system and explain the origins and development of commercial links with different parts of the world. Recent work in the eastern USA and in Britain has involved local black communities and focused on the identification of black material culture and historical figures rather than on the standard images of enslavement and powerlessness (Paynter 1989; Garrison 1990; Belgrave 1990). Such approaches may need lengthy negotiations with community leaders.

3. Look after the archaeological remains of the past. In some cases, such as the Rose Theatre, the public seem to be more vigilant and vociferous than the professionals. The conservation ethic has wide support and many people understand and are in sympathy with the basic concepts, as imported from nature conservation. We like to think that this ethic contributes to environmental awareness yet it can be easily perverted for nationalist and racist ends. For example, the Nazis stressed the value of preservation as a national project to secure the remains of their supposed Germanic ancestors (Arnold 1992).

229

4. See how we've been wrecking our environment for millennia, not just the last century. Upland moors are still viewed by many as natural wildernesses. Archaeology can contribute to the green issue (Macinnes and Wickham-Jones 1992; see also Chapter 22) and is a good way of providing time depth and social context. Greenpeace already employs such imagery, using the timespans of the earth's existence and of human prehistory, to show how suddenly and relatively recently the scale of global pollution has rocketed.

5. How do we interpret the past? Recent ventures, such as the Archaeology Resource Centre (ARC) in York, help to demystify the archaeologist's task of discovering society and people from bones and stones. The past becomes open, accessible and reinterpretable rather than closed and known. An unidentified iron object in Scunthorpe Museum, labelled 'We don't know what it is either', is not an admission of failure but an invitation to participate. If the public are invited to contribute and to learn about the difficulties of interpretation, they will share an involvement rather than remain excluded and passive onlookers.

6. To be or not to be? There's a British hypersensitivity to dressing up in costume (Waterson 1989) though it does seem to be successful with children. Perhaps it is problematic, since it contradicts the premise above, presenting the past as if it is known and fully reconstructible. It demands no mental effort to interpret the past, but it does have the advantage of ethnographic enquiry. The strangeness and difference of past ways of life can be appreciated if done well. It requires more than dressing up the diggers around the trench or enacting a mock battle. If the point is to be made, it requires a formal theatrical setting and structure.

7. Have you found any gold? Everyone loves a good find and it's no surprise that the treasure hunt, the quest for the thing in itself, is still top of the public's agenda. Authentic artefacts are the stuff of the fine-art trade and relationships with users of metal detectors still have a lot of ground to make up. The problem of looting and illegal dealing around the world is also likely to get worse rather than better. If popular pressure groups can appear to stop certain sites being destroyed then perhaps more thought should go into mobilizing public opinion on dealing in stolen antiquities (see Chapter 6).

8. Archaeology, roots, and the local community. There have been relatively successful initiatives in community archaeology. Even so, local history, oral tradition and genealogy are considerably more popular. No doubt this is because they can touch the human element more deeply and more immediately. Yet archaeology can be integrated into local studies and is a valuable tool for seeing changes in the physical landscape and built environment. It's instructive to note just how often those most interested in local history are the relatively recent incomers into a community; perhaps the real locals don't need to worship their roots.

9. The present past. The archaeological past is faceless, nameless and remote, cut off from the present by a conceptual rift. Many aspects of history prior to the Industrial Revolution are deemed unimportant for today. Yet we should be using archaeological concepts imaginatively, for the recent past and the present. A recent TV series on interior decor in the modern house (*Signs of the Times*) was described to me as a great piece of archaeology. Rather than simply using modern contexts to explain archaeological methods (demonstrating stratigraphy through the filling of a dustbin, for example), we should also be doing an 'archaeology of us' based on material culture studies (Rathje 1974; Gould and Schiffer 1981; Shanks and Tilley 1987a).

10. Early man and early woman – engendering the past. Stereotypes in the portrayal of men's and women's activities in the past are more likely to be extrapolated from existing roles rather than the archaeological evidence. We should be exploring multiple interpretations and challenging people to re-evaluate the present. Otherwise our models of the past

in our own image simply reinforce existing prejudices and 'universal truths' that are, in fact, culturally specific practices. Beware of presenting women in reconstruction drawings as passive background.

11. Club-wielding cavepersons. The primitivization of the past leads to racist attitudes towards non-industrialized nations. Over 20,000 years ago the man buried at Sunghir (CIS) was wearing a very flashy costume, not a crude hearth rug. Why do prehistoric Britons get portrayed as long-haired, badly dressed hippies/New Agers (or perhaps it's the other way round)? This is completely contrary to the evidence from well-preserved burials of the Danish Bronze Age and from the finds of prehistoric razors, tweezers etc. And why do Romans get presented as clean and tidy ringers for chartered accountants? The Roman period still exercises a powerful hold on the public imagination – perhaps its apparent degree of civilization, role model for empire, and 'sameness' to our own times need debunking.

12. Hot interpretation. This phrase was coined by David Uzzell (1989c) to bring a more powerful, and truthful, impact to interpretation. The past should shock us. One of his examples is the massacre of the Jews at Clifford's Tower in York. He points out that today's interpretive displays at the monument have avoided the grisly details of this sordid episode. We tend to glorify past wars and annexations. Perhaps the row over Columbus represents the beginning of a new attitude.

13. Skeletons. It seems that the Home Office has been blissfully unaware of the quantities of human remains exhumed without licences by archaeologists, and their display to a fascinated public when legally they should be curtained behind screens. Respect for the dead is a big and difficult issue (Layton 1989a; Rahtz 1985: 42–7). Providing that the necessary measures are taken to avoid outrage (in Britain, remains from after, say, 1850 or those claimed by disaffected minority groups), we should be engaging people's curiosity even more, rather than sanctimoniously recommending reburial. Our attitude towards death is already bizarre enough in the way that it is hidden and secret in our culture. It is worse to take away the one opportunity that most people have to see dead bodies in one form or another. The lid is coming off this taboo in Britain but notions of decency in hiding away the dead still lead to racist judgements of other societies' more up-front ways of death.

14. Banging the drum. Armada celebrations, battle re-enactments, and royal pageantry are ceremonial invocations by which the nation state is given substance and legitimated. We like to think that we do not promote a jingoistic and chauvinist notion of nationhood, and undoubtedly other nations have reached greater excesses (Trigger 1984; Gathercole and Lowenthal 1990). However, we frame much of our research and presentation in national terms, without widening the issues to the world society.

This discussion may seem to some to be an exercise in political correctness, rather than in useful and achievable goals for archaeologists committed to their public. Many of these proposals might appear out of reach to the hard-pressed unit manager or fieldworker. Even if we can't implement such schemes and approaches immediately, I hope that they will provide food for thought. It is not that we should be writing a past where we speak of Neolithic 'persons' as 'vertically challenged', among other forms of politically correct jargon. Rather, we must develop a greater consciousness about our own power as archaeologists and seize the initiative more readily. Otherwise we will just drift along behind the commercial operations, adopting and adapting the cobbled-together ethos and morals of the marketplace.

CHAPTER 21

MUSEUM ARCHAEOLOGY
Susan Pearce

Museums and their archaeological collections have come into being piecemeal over the past two centuries or so, and both the institutions and the nature of the collections show a corresponding diversity. Institutionally, museums range from the great national bodies, through the major regional museum services, which are in many ways the backbone of archaeological curatorship, to small or specialized museums, such as the one at Fishbourne, that may hold particular material of great interest. The collections these museums hold are themselves part of the intellectual history of modern times, beginning with the 17th-century 'cabinets of curiosities', running through the romantic notions of the later 18th- and 19th-century barrow diggers, reflecting and encouraging the development of typological accumulations and studies through the 19th and 20th centuries, and witnessing the steady growth of excavation to what would now be recognized as 'professional' standards.

The archaeological museums and their collections need to be understood in terms of their contribution to our understanding of the past, and especially in the light of the developing quality of material culture theory. They need to be understood also as social and intellectual documents in their own right that have contributed, in terms of who collected the material and why, to the creation of ethnic values, gender values and value judgements and so to the construction of social practice.

An important element in this construction is the body of issues that revolves around present-day problems of acquisition and disposal. The level of recent excavation activity has meant an enormous accumulation of finds. In London the work of the units and societies has generated some 1,000 cubic metres of finds, with the same quantity again expected in the next 20 years, and the experience is much the same across the country. Although the rate of excavation may be slowing a little, the practice of competitive tendering runs the risk of disrupting good working relationships between units and museums built up over a number of years. The proper care of such huge collections would absorb an absurd level of resource, and demands for such resource would be perceived as luxuriously excessive. On the other hand, although collections can be rationalized by various arrangements between museums, the outright disposal or destruction of archaeological material is very difficult because there is no way of knowing what the future knowledge yields of any body of material may be. The best solutions are likely to lie with a cull of some bulk material before museum acquisition, coupled with a mixture of high principle and good professional management within the museum. In this, the Codes of Practice prepared by the Museums Association, and those under consideration by the Society of Museum Archaeologists are very helpful.

Within this broad social and cultural framework, the archaeological museum has three principle areas of responsibility: the management of the archaeological material; the presentation of this material in a wide range of display and interpretative projects; and the practice of research into both the 'archaeological' dimension of the material as this has been traditionally understood, and into its cultural nature as one of the agents that has helped to create our present views about the past. The first two of these responsibilities will be considered in the two main sections that follow, and the third is addressed in the final section. All three are large areas, which can only be touched on here, and the interested reader is referred to recently published further treatment with extensive references (Pearce 1990). The *Standards in the Museum Care of Archaeological Collections* published by the Museums and Galleries Commission (MGC 1992) is essential reading in the area.

MANAGING COLLECTIONS

The archaeological museum archive

The management of the museum archaeological archive is at the heart of the museum operation, for without collections there would be no broader issues of context and interpretation. 'The archive' was a term brought into prominence by its use in the Frere Report (DoE 1975a), where it meant the whole product of excavation organized in an accessible form, which rendered it capable of critical re-examination. The archive was seen as the prime information source, and the form of final publication correspondingly less significant. The background to the archive concept lay in the enormous increase in excavation that the rescue movement had stimulated, linked with a general refining of recording systems that enabled a much more detailed and precise record of an excavated site to be developed by the early 1970s, and the development in information yield from environmental sampling procedures. With this ran an acute awareness that excavation is essentially a destructive exercise, so that a former site now exists only in its preserved archive. The archive concept can be usefully extended to cover the entirety of archaeological collections.

The implications of this archive for curatorship are obviously enormous, but the curatorial role is an active, not a passive, one. The curator's relationship with his archive is a steady process of interaction in which the existing and incoming collections, the management of museum policies, and the exercise of judgment, are woven together in the explicit actions and decisions that make up every working day.

Collection management policies

The nature of the archive as a whole, both existing and potential, is not simple, but embraces a cross-cutting range of identities, depending upon whether it is seen from a physical, museological, archaeological or historical view. Successful collection management demands recognition of these complexities, and an ability to organize and effect strategies that take all interplay into account. Collection management embraces acquisition and disposal policy, with special emphasis on issues such as collecting-area policies, policies that relate to the type and period of material to be collected, loans, purchases and donations, legal matters such as title and insurance, and collection methods. A collection management policy should relate all these matters to the care needs of the collections in terms of access, documentation, storage and conservation, and each museum will evolve a particular policy that brings the broader issues in line with its specific history and character.

Issues in storage and conservation

The archive embraces not only the archaeological material itself, but also a considerable volume of written, printed, pictorial, film, and computer disk material. This has to be housed according to organizational and care standards that guarantee its accessibility, security and safety from deterioration. In practice, these principles result in conflicting needs, in the resolution of which curatorial judgment needs to be exercised.

233

Accessibility and security, as in all institutions, can be difficult to combine and, more particularly, the principle of accessibility means that decisions have to be made about the parts of the collections that are used most, how this should influence the way in which the material is arranged, and how best use can be made of the available space. It would, in the light of this, be relatively easy to devise a use of space that put much-used material in areas equipped as joint store and work rooms, less-used material in the next most accessible stores, possibly linked with the displays and offered as visible storage (Ames 1977), and seldom-used material in more remote stores, perhaps in a separate building if the rest of the collections are held in the museum itself.

There is, however, a major difficulty. For good museological reasons of accession and documentation, there is a strong instinct to keep together the material from a specific excavation or collection and therefore to divide the whole into the three classes on a collections basis; but much research and some display is carried out on a period basis or an artefact-type basis that cuts across collections. Equally, the class-three material is unlikely to comprise complete collections, but rather to involve, for example, the animal bones or undecorated body sherds from excavations whose other material may be frequently consulted. It can, of course, also from an environmental and security point of view, often make good sense to store groups of small finds like coins, Roman brooches or Bronze Age metalwork together, but most curators would hesitate before picking all the worked flint, for example, out of a range of collections and storing these in a single place.

It is very difficult to devise a theoretical system that can take account of these conflicting needs (Watkins 1986), and any such system will prove to be very fragile when it is applied to actual museum situations. In practice, it is usually best to admit that neither hard organizational structures nor ideals of purity are helpful, and to treat the various potential groupings on their own merits, bearing in mind their particular requirements.

There is a large literature on the maintenance of collections in store, which covers this complex subject in detail from all angles. No attempt will be made to summarize it here, and the interested reader should consult Thompson (1978), Leigh (1982) and the *Environmental Standards for the Permanent Storage of Excavated Material from Archaeological Sites* (1984) issued by the Archaeology Section of the United Kingdom Institute for Conservation (UKIC) as basic texts.

However, one area of mutual concern to curators and conservators must be mentioned. In 1983 UKIC issued to its members their *Guidance for Conservation Practice*, which defined the responsibilities of conservators in relation to the care and treatment of objects (see Ashley-Smith 1982; printed in Shell and Robinson 1988: 259–60). It makes clear statements on the need to preserve evidence rather than removing it during the conservation process, and on the desirability of undertaking only treatment that can be reversed. It defines conservation as, 'the means by which the true nature of the object is preserved', and uses the term 'true nature' to include evidence about the origin, construction and materials of the piece. It stresses, also, how important it is that both conservators and curators should accept this ethical attitude.

However, in the case of archaeological objects a number of difficulties arise. The object as it emerges from the ground is an encapsulation of its history up to that moment; but the unravelling of that history by the modern investigative techniques of the conservator inevitably involves the destruction of evidence as much as the preservation of a version of the artefact. As Corfield puts it: 'while many general statements have been made about the importance of reversibility in conservation processes, the whole concept has been the subject of scrutiny as it has become more and more apparent that few conservation processes can be considered really reversible' (Corfield 1988: 261).

In a nutshell, the emphasis is now on finding out about a piece, rather than on cleaning it, because the information embedded in the various accretions or products of corrosion may be as diagnostic as the bare object itself. The object that emerges at the end of this process is not, and never again can be, the object that came out of the ground, and therefore a full documentary and photographic record is an essential part of the conservation process (Keene 1980). A most important element in the conservator's responsibility is, therefore, a judgment of the correct balance between, on the one hand, the recovery of evidence and, on the other, the preservation of evidence through minimum intervention and as close an approximation as possible to the ideal of irreversibility.

Investigation in depth requires the closest co-operation between conservator and archaeologist (Cronyn 1980). Detailed work is very time-consuming, and so the choice of objects to be examined in depth is difficult, and must be made on both archaeological and physical grounds, so that the yield in information is as great as possible. The conservators need to know as precisely as possible what questions require answers, and they prefer exact questions put to them about specific objects or groups of objects. Similarly, conservators need information about the context of the find and the structural interpretation the archaeologist puts on it, the approximate date or period of the artefact, and who will undertake its study. The framework for this kind of work is best developed jointly as part of the overall strategy for the excavation site, but it must be very flexible because it is the unexpected that will usually occur.

Documentation

The considerable resources required to store and conserve archaeological archives, and indeed to produce them by excavation or collection in the first place, can only be justified if the archives are genuinely available for use: this cardinal principle means that the material itself, and all related information that pertains to it and is embodied in it, should be accessible, and in turn implies that the information is held on an organized documentation system.

Good documentation also ensures that collection handling and recording is monitored and controlled, and gives clear proof of the ownership of the collection. It helps to establish a sensible acquisitions policy that takes account of existing holdings and monitors the adherence to that policy, it offers satisfactory accounting to interested parties like auditors and insurers, and it provides the information needed by museum staff for exhibition, education, conservation and research, and by outside researchers and the general public.

The problems to be faced in creating a modern and serviceable documentation system are complex, embracing the considerable labour resource involved, the difficulties of system choice (particularly in the modern computer market), and the problems implicit in old collections, frequently poorly recorded, and existing record systems of varying degrees of complexity and incompatibility. To this must be added the difficulties in creating systems that can bring together the needs of excavators and the longer-term requirements of a museum service.

Again, all these issues are being discussed at great length and degree of detail. The reader is advised to consult the specialized journals and groups like *Computer Applications in Archaeology*, *Archaeological Computing Newsletter*, the Museums Computer Group, and the extensive services and literature offered by the Museum Documentation Association.

The archive: some conclusions

It is clear that the range of the archaeological archive, as it has come to be understood over the last decade, will require a more informed and more complex documentation system than the traditional approaches could offer. 'The well-tempered archive', to borrow Stewart's phrase (Stewart 1980: 22) would encompass the actual transference of finds and documents to the museum numbering systems, the application of satisfactory documentation and data standards, and the provision of well-organized storage, all expressed in an archival policy. Such a policy would aim to translate into physical premises and working practices all the aspects of collection management that have just been discussed. This must be operated in a climate of genuine co-operation between curators and excavators, and between the curators of different museum services. A few museums, like some of the English county services, are putting an integrated approach to archaeological collections into practice. Such systems, no doubt, represent the ideal rather than the present reality for many museums, but it is the ideal to be aimed at, so that collections are not just held, but truly managed.

MUSEUMS, THE PUBLIC AND THE PAST

Museums and our public

The term 'public' here is used in the simplest and most colourless sense, and means all those people who do not consider themselves to be professional (or quasi-professional) curators or archaeologists. This group, the huge majority of the population, can be divided into three fairly clear sectors. The greater proportion of the adults are those who have no real interest in understanding the past, in the sense that professionals would use that phrase. The smaller section of the adults are those who do take an informed interest in the past. Apart from these, there are the children, whose interests are not yet fixed.

Let us concentrate first on the adults. A number of surveys (Merriman 1991) have made it abundantly clear that, unsurprisingly, the dividing line between the interested adults and the others follows that which separates the better-off and the well-educated from the rest. In this, museums in Britain mirror Bourdieu's perceptive analysis of cultural 'habitus' and 'cultural capital', closely linked to other kinds of economic capital, where possession of the code enables the owner to enjoy what a museum offers, while lack of it means that museum material seems meaningless and rapidly becomes boring (see also Chapter 20). Those who are excluded now question the value of what has no importance for them, and develop an argument that asks why relatively large sums of money should be expended on maintaining institutions for which they see little use, and to whose cultural and intellectual values they do not subscribe. This is the stance of many ley-line enthusiasts, Stonehenge cult-makers and treasure hunters whose 'alternative' archaeology has been described as 'a kind of popular repossession of the past' (Williamson and Bellamy 1983b: 57). At the end of the day, these difficulties cannot be met by argument, but only by a prolonged and sympathetic endeavour to teach the cultural code.

Talk of difficulties must be balanced by a further consideration: we have a great deal to build on. Merriman's survey (1991) showed that some 90 % of museum visitors and 65 % of non-visitors thought that the past was worth knowing about – a large and encouraging proportion. The principal heritage locations like Stonehenge, Jorvik and Bath all attract approaching a million visitors yearly. The survey, however, also shows that what the majority of people find most rewarding are objects in their own setting, either out of doors or perhaps in reconstructions, an element of self-discovery, and ideally some kind of link to their own family or neighbourhood. Museums have a particular responsibility towards mediating the past to the public, and it is to the ways in which this is discharged that we must now turn.

Enquiry services and treasure hunters

Enquiry services (taken here to mean the identification of objects brought in by members of the public) is one area of museum activity that genuinely involves all kinds of people; and their willingness to penetrate the formalities of entrance hall, attendant staff and enquiry forms is a true index of the power of this curiosity about the past. The critical literature about archaeological enquiry services is very sparse, and very few museums seem to have a policy on enquiries that covers areas like the depth to which they should be researched and the time that the curator should spend talking personally to the enquirer. Enquiries have traditionally had a lower priority than most other museum activities. This clearly reflects the traditional cleavage between the curator, for whom archaeology and its artefacts are to do with the nature of past societies and the process of change, and the enquirer, whose interest concentrates upon how old the object is, what it is at the crudest level, and how much it is worth, all in the context of personal possession sometimes expressed in unattractive terms.

It is true that the gulf of interest between curator and public is frequently deep and genuine, that much of the material brought in is of little interest from any informed point of view, and that any substantial extension of the enquiry service that might give the layperson more contact with the curator would have a major impact upon time and resources. It is, however, also true that the act of making the enquiry is often more important than the enquiry itself, and that an improved enquiry service would be one important way of making the museum service more accountable and more responsive to the needs of the public. One suggestion is the provision of an 'enquiries room', which would have a range of reference books of the more accessible type, maps, and perhaps handling specimens of all the more common kinds of enquiry, backed up by free fact-sheets and similar information. The enquirers could be encouraged to discover more about their objects here, although they would probably need curatorial assistance, and perhaps they could help the curator to complete the records that are needed for the museum, the Sites and Monuments Register, and so on. This could be a valuable extension of the enquiry relationship, and indeed often happens informally in the curator's office; but its formal implementation would undoubtedly be very demanding.

If enquiry services are one of the most important interfaces between the wider public and museums, one of the most difficult areas here is the whole broad question of treasure-hunting, which often surfaces in the most direct fashion across an object brought in for identification. Treasure-hunting as a phenomenon has been discussed in some depth in the archaeological press, with an increasing degree of sympathy in some quarters in recent years (Gregory 1983). Gregory, for example, speaks of the problem as being 'an ethical and social one'. He discusses the middle-class, serious, polite and university-educated style of archaeology and describes 'the inevitable result' as 'the evolution of alternative, working-class archaeology born of a coalition of the detector-manufacturers, collectors and detector-users revolving around the collection of material . . . with an emphasis on its monetary value depending on the individual involved' (Gregory 1986: 25–6). The treasure-hunters see themselves as pursuing a legitimate hobby, motivated not primarily by financial gain but by a desire to find out about the past and to come into tangible contact with it, which makes them equal and equivalent to other kinds of archaeologists.

Two fundamentally contrasting attitudes have emerged in archaeological circles, one which prizes archaeological purity above all else and will have no connections with the hunters, and the other, which seeks a working relationship. These attitudes are essentially unreconcilable, but there seems to be a growing sense that no stricter legislation is likely to be forthcoming, and that, as Crowther puts it, 'polemic is no substitute for dialogue' (Crowther 1983: 19). Useful co-operation between museums and other archaeologists with the treasure-hunter clubs seems to be a possibility, and offers the chance that known archaeological sites will be respected and finds properly recorded. The clubs, of course, house the 'respectable' hunters, who are willing to abide by their codes. Beyond and outside are the 'rogue' hunters, primarily concerned with profit and with the looting of known sites. Indeed, a distinction is beginning to develop among archaeologists between 'metal-detector users', meaning those with whom it may be proper to associate, and 'treasure-hunters', who are beyond the pale. The rogue hunters are recognized almost everywhere for what they are but as they can only be stopped by the force of public opinion, and as the responsible hunters make up an important part of that opinion, it would be foolish to let the best be the enemy of the good.

Education

It is now time to turn to formal school-based education. Moves by central government are now making individual schools responsible for deciding how much advantage they take of the education services museums offer, both for school visits to museums and use of specimen loan material. There is a fear that, given financial constraints, museum education services will be squeezed out of the school timetable. A balance to these worries may be provided by the National Curriculum's emphasis on hands-on experience and the ability to infer general principles from specific evidence: museum archaeology is obviously ideally placed to provide scope for this kind of teaching (Corbishley 1992).

More general tensions underlie the contemporary problems and politics of resource use. Hill (1987: 144) has shown that archaeology sees education as a commodity, as a way in which archaeologists can communicate what they regard as the important results of their work to the public, and so justify the public money spent on archaeology in a highlyvisible and obviously responsible way. Teachers, similarly, see archaeology as a commodity, making some use of the scope for skills learning and for projects that it offers, but failing to understand the nature of the discipline. Hill (1987: 144) found that

> the overwhelming majority of teachers have little understanding of modern archaeology so the result of their use of the discipline is largely misrepresentative, perpetuating dubious stereotypes of what archaeology is and what it can be. The stress placed on teaching the right methods is often at the cost of fact. Several teachers have suggested to the author that it does not matter if the facts are completely wrong, so long as the children learn to use their historical skills correctly.

As a result, neither teachers nor archaeologists understand what the other is trying to achieve, and the product is potentially both bad archaeology and bad education.

These differences in intention play their part in how children see the past. An interesting survey undertaken by the Southampton Archaeology in Education team covered 117 children aged 10–12 years from a variety of backgrounds in Southampton, in an effort to understand how children conceive of the past and its people (Emmott 1987). The findings of the survey showed that the children were only just beginning to understand time as an abstract concept, and that they tended to think of history as about kings and queens. Nevertheless, 80 % of the replies said that the past was important. The children tended to see past people as less clever than us because they lacked our technology, and they seemed to take a similar view of non-Western cultures. These images of the past 'originate in the content of school curriculum, children's books and television programmes' that generate a 'distorted, ethnocentric and sexist view of the past, which forms a lasting impression and impinges on [children's] images of the present' (Emmott 1987: 139).

These interlinked debates have stimulated a stream of publications and projects, and there is at least general agreement that archaeology should be taken much further in schools than is usually done at present. At primary level a museum archaeology programme must be carefully planned, so that sources like handling material (either used in the museum or as part of a loans service) are integrated with exhibition visits, and backed up by appropriate work and activity sheets, like the *Asterix at the British Museum: Ancient Britons and Gauls Children's Trail* issued by the British Museum Education Service, or the useful activity sheets put out by the Cleveland Archaeology Service on *The Norton Saxons*, with their information and puzzles on the dig and cemetery. Secondary-level teaching will involve the development of a close relationship with the demands of the National Curriculum, and of archaeology-based studies in relation to it.

The potential implications for curatorship are obviously considerable, in both the primary and secondary spheres. A better understanding of the nature of archaeology, and of the way in which archaeologists think about the past, needs to be given to teachers, while archaeologists need to understand more about the aims of contemporary education. A nation-wide forum to think out the needs and resource implications, perhaps building on the work of the Council for British Archaeology, may be the answer here. All archaeological institutions, but perhaps particularly museums, should be involved, and the archaeologists should recognize that, in the simplest sense at least, archaeology has most at stake.

Exhibiting archaeology

Putting 'archaeology', that is the past in its material aspect, on display is a complex business. Exhibitions in their morphological juxtaposition of plan, selected objects and graphics (in the broadest sense) create their own kinds of knowledge, and may therefore be analysed in such epistemological terms. All human history exhibitions are representational, and so provoke questions about the nature of their relationship to 'a past reality' and to historical change. Archaeological exhibitions are intended to interpret material culture or perhaps to demonstrate how material culture can be interpreted, and therefore face familiar problems surrounding the study of artefacts; and further difficulties revolve around the transmission of all these messages to a viewing public.

Our improving notions of exhibition morphology shows that different exhibition layouts stimulate different kinds of understanding. Displays with strong axial structures, small spaces between display units, and the intention of moving a visitor along a predetermined route, present knowledge as if it were the map of a well-known terrain where all the relationships are well understood, while exhibitions with looser structures and a variety of circulation routes show knowledge as a proposition, stimulating further, or different, propositions. The ground plans of two exhibitions at the British Museum (Figs 21.1 and 21.2) show the kinds of contrasts involved.

All exhibitions are either didactic or intended to evoke feelings, and most hope to be both. The ethical basis of the didactic exhibit is grounded in the belief that knowledge is morally good, partly in an absolute sense and partly because it helps to develop socially responsible citizens who identify constructively with their community and its traditions; it looks back to Victorian ideas about self-betterment, tainted though these are with much political and social hypocrisy. The didactic approach contrasts with the emotive or mood-making exhibition, grounded in the rather different conviction that an experience of the ancient, the exotic and the beautiful is good because it enables us to share in the common scope of human experience, to live more interestingly and to accept more easily the essential precariousness of life.

What then, for the visitor constitutes a good experience in an archaeology gallery?

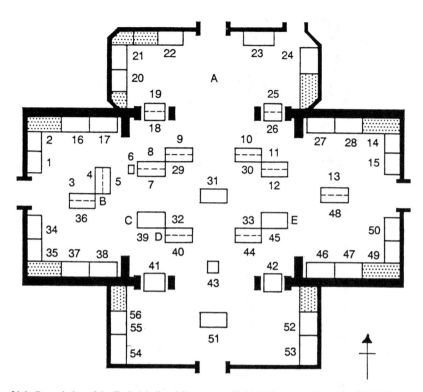

Figure 21.1. Ground plan of the Early Medieval Room at the British Museum as it was in 1991. The sequence of 45 cases includes a series on the migration and post-migration tribes *c*. AD 400–1100 (cases 1–15), a series on the Late Antique and Byzantine World (cases 16–28), a sequence on the Germans, Anglo-Saxons, Celts and Vikings, with a strong British emphasis (cases 29–50) and a separate section on the Sutton Hoo ship burial (cases 51–56). The lattice work plan offers a loose structure and a variety of circulation routes.

What makes an archaeology exhibition successful? There is a broad level of agreement about the ways in which the effectiveness of exhibitions generally can be assessed and the success of exhibitions evaluated (Miles *et al.* 1988; Stansfield 1981), and these involve detailed procedures of observation and feedback linked to very specific recommendations of gallery layout and design. Processes like critical appraisal and market research leading to front-end evaluation and the statement of exhibition objectives, formative evaluation as part of development and production, and summational evaluation undertaken after the exhibition is open, provide a framework through which the operation of the exhibition can be monitored.

In broader terms, which are admittedly difficult to monitor, a successful archaeology display, like a good television programme or book, has to be one that keeps the visitor attracted until the show is finished; if the visitor is carried along with his interest caught, then he will go away with some enlargement of knowledge or sympathy, and that is success.

SOME CONCLUSIONS

The management of archaeological museum collections, as of all archaeology, ultimately justifies itself in terms of the increase in knowledge and understanding it offers, and the

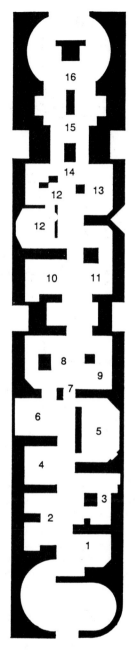

1 Use of Natural Resources
8000–5000 BC

2 A Way of Life Preserved
4000–1200 BC

3 Life, Ceremony and Death
4000–2000 BC

4 Settlement and Defence
1000 BC–AD 43

5 Landscapes Through Time
3200 BC–AD 1100

6 A Way of Death
300–200 BC

7 Master Craftsmen
100 BC–AD 50

8 Soldiers and the Army
AD 43–410

9 Pagans and Christians
50 BC–AD 410

10 Cemeteries and Society
AD 400–1100

11 Church and Monastery
AD 650–1650

12 The Medieval Countryside
AD 600–1650

13 Castles and Norman Lords
AD 1066–1200

14 Developing Technology
AD 800–1600

15 The Growth of Medieval Towns
AD 900–1600

16 Lindow Man

Figure 21.2. Ground plan of the temporary exhibition Archaeology in Britain held at the British Museum in 1987. The exhibition has strong axials in a linear structure and expects the visitor to move in a predetermined route (after British Museum Teaching Material 1987).

enrichment of all our everyday lives it makes possible. Ultimately, all this, in its turn, depends upon research work carried out upon the material, work that is designed to enhance our understanding of what material culture from the past can tell us.

Research is often seen as difficult work in museum circles, and this, I believe, is the result of accumulated misunderstandings rather than the outcome of any genuine problems. It is the curator's task to carry out the management of archives, and this, as we have seen, is an active rather than a passive process, which contributes its own positive influence to the research process. The curator must also, it goes without saying, make collections and information available to all bona fide students. It is an equally true but often underestimated fact that the professional management of, for example, the petrological analysis of early lithic material across a collection, contributes directly to our research base. Similarly, understanding of the history and development of collections adds to our understanding of the developing sense of the past and its nature. Intimately intertwined with all this, and to a large extent its product, will be what is sometimes called 'pure' research: that is, the academic study of an aspect of the past. Future research lies in a better understanding of how this can be carried out, and what the outcomes of any piece of work are likely to be. Museums should – as many do – think in terms of the development of research strategies that bring all the different pieces together.

This brings us back to our starting point. Museums and their collections are very different, and, like all long-term institutions, embody a variety of strengths and characters. This chapter has discussed some common concerns and, perhaps, suggested some future directions.

CHAPTER 22

ARCHAEOLOGY AS LAND USE

Lesley Macinnes

INTRODUCTION

The recognition of archaeology as a major element in the landscape is not new, though its perception as a legitimate management concern in the modern landscape has only seriously developed in recent years.

Early discussions of archaeological management tended to concentrate on conservation of masonry structures and in particular on monuments in state care (e.g. Thompson 1981). Management of field monuments, where archaeology coincides with different land uses, has only been a subject of detailed consideration relatively recently, though there have been discussions of the general need for monument protection (e.g. Baker 1983). Nevertheless, a few publications (e.g. Lambrick 1985; Hughes and Rowley 1986; Darvill 1986: 79–85; Darvill 1987) have identified the growing recognition of archaeology in a wider land-management context, especially the developing connection between archaeology and nature conservation. Since Lambrick's publication in particular, there have been major advances on the ground, and the relationship between different working practices is now gradually becoming built into legislation, national policy and working practices (e.g. Macinnes and Wickham-Jones 1992).

Archaeological management requires specific action: there is no such thing as 'benign neglect' in this context (Morgan Evans 1986: 9; Barclay 1992a). This chapter reviews the areas where archaeology is related to modern land management, and assesses the problems, benefits and opportunities that arise.

ARCHAEOLOGY AND LAND USE

Agriculture

Agriculture is a major land use in the British countryside, as indeed it has been since the Neolithic period. Throughout the UK agricultural practices offer the paradox of being the major factor responsible for the good preservation of archaeological sites in upland areas, and the major agent of destruction in lowland areas, at least since the Second World War. There have been numerous studies of crop-mark archaeology, through which the adverse effects of intensive agricultural cultivation on archaeology are well documented, even if not always specifically examined (e.g. Fulford and Nichols 1992). Some studies have been conducted because of the vulnerability to land improvement of sites lying in marginal land, such as those by the Royal Commission on the Ancient and Historical Monuments of Scotland in the 1950s; by contrast, few surveys of sites in upland locations have been linked explicitly to agricultural practices (as opposed to forestry). Agricultural policy for the UK and the European Community is now undergoing a dramatic alteration and current deliberations about changes in the aims of agriculture and its support mechanisms have focused attention on the association between agriculture and conservation. As a result, the benefits, and problems, of the relationship between archaeology and agriculture need closer consideration (see English Heritage/MAFF n.d.; and Historic Scotland's guideline leaflet *Managing Scotland's Archaeological Heritage*).

In upland areas throughout the UK archaeological sites have survived as visible field monuments in a generally good state of preservation, in heather moorland and unimproved grassland, whether managed for sheep or sport (grouse- and deer-shooting). The management needed to maintain such areas for these uses is essentially benign to archaeology, if it is carried out well: sheep-grazing has been established as the principal form of management in both grassland and moorland since the Victorian period, with regular burning undertaken in moorland areas. On the other hand, these practices can be damaging to archaeology if carried out badly, such as through erosion caused by over-grazing or uncontrolled burning. If these traditional forms of management are favourable for archaeology, however, their withdrawal is not, leading in particular to bracken, scrub and woodland regeneration that both obscures currently visible features and damages hitherto well-preserved archaeological deposits. The continued preservation of archaeological features in the uplands, therefore, requires the continuation of farming in those areas on a scale comparable to that of the present.

Within this general framework, however, the specific issues are not simple, and the interests of archaeology and upland farming do not always precisely coincide. For instance, the spread of bracken threatens archaeological sites and is at least in part due to a recent preference for sheep- rather than cattle-grazing as a result of agricultural subsidies; it can also be exacerbated by a reduction in the level of grazing. Both sheep and cattle can, however, cause localized problems of erosion. Woodland shelter belts can also damage and obscure archaeological features, while fencing, tracks, drains, etc. can all cause problems if insensitively located from an archaeological point of view. Similarly, the well-preserved archaeological and palaeoenvironmental evidence that survives within peatland is threatened by peat extraction at a variety of scales. Yet all of these can be minimized, avoided or improved with specific management actions.

In marginal land archaeological sites tend to survive as upstanding features in grazed improved grassland: often the sites have been damaged by ploughing in episodes of land improvement in the recent past. Sometimes they may be drained, enclosed or bisected by fencing; used for quarrying, dumping, storage or feeding stock; affected by vehicle access; or covered in scrub where they have been left unimproved, but not managed for their own sake. Gorse, whin and bracken are frequent problems on sites in such locations; equally, drying out of wetland sites through agricultural drainage can occur. Current grant schemes do not support land improvement or drainage to the same extent as previously, and sites in marginal land can now more often be left undisturbed under more beneficial stock-grazing regimes. Where such land is grazed and improved by non-intensive means such as liming, archaeological sites will generally benefit, though they will still be subject to localized problems of stock-related erosion; but where land is left to revert to an untended or ungrazed state, there may in the longer term be problems of scrub coverage of archaeological features, or fire-risk from rank grasses. For archaeological purposes, therefore, maintenance of such grassland in reasonable condition is preferable, with avoidance of both overstocking and wholesale stock removal.

Moreover, on such grassland, readily visible sites are often accessible, and afford opportunities for recreation and diversification from farming activities. In this respect, archaeological preservation requires that farming continues in marginal land; but it can also form an alternative land-management objective in farm-diversification schemes as the scale and intensity of farming on this land reduces with changes in agricultural policy.

It is in the lowlands that the biggest conflict between farming and archaeology arises, though ironically the recognition of sites that have been reduced to crop marks in the past largely depends on continued arable cultivation. Arable cultivation damages archaeological features in every way imaginable, but notably in the reduction of earthworks and gradual removal of below-ground deposits, especially if deep drainage or subsoiling is carried out. Even where sites survive as visible features in 'islands' within arable fields, there are erosion problems caused by continual encroachment by the plough, by the growth of trees, scrub or rank vegetation, and by colonization by rabbits, as such areas are seldom managed actively or in an archaeologically beneficial manner. There have been instances, too, of farmers removing or bulldozing well-preserved sites because of the nuisance of ploughing around them.

Even where ploughing continues, measures can be taken to minimize further damage to archaeological features, while at the same time offering benefits to problems like soil erosion: for example, by reducing the depth or frequency of ploughing; avoiding pan-busting or subsoiling; leaving a buffer zone around surviving archaeological features; or allowing access. However, in the current climate, which seeks to reduce arable land in the UK, archaeological sites may stand to gain by being left fallow or put into Set Aside, provided that appropriate management is undertaken (though others could continue to suffer at an increased rate if intensity of use is enhanced on a smaller acreage of land). Moreover, with the trend towards greater diversification within the British lowland landscape, archaeological sites can offer an attractive alternative land use, as the farm trails that are becoming more and more common demonstrate. Here archaeology can also combine with nature conservation to offer complementary, and mutually advantageous, benefits to farmers, while at the same time enhancing the conservation, recreational and amenity value of previously intensively farmed land.

Various grant schemes now work to the potential benefit of archaeological sites within farm land. Principally, Set Aside presents opportunities to take sites out of regular arable cultivation. At the European level, however, Set Aside is seen as a measure to control food production, not to enhance the conservation of the countryside, and land is set aside on a rotational and thus temporary basis. The drawback of this scheme for both conservation generally and archaeology in particular, therefore, is that the selection of eligible land depends on its cultivation history rather than its conservation value. As a result, archaeological features may not be included in Set Aside land, and where they are they win only a temporary reprieve from cultivation; the needs of archaeological management and the aims of Set Aside do not always work together. There have, nevertheless, been successes that show the potential of the scheme, a potential that will be considerably enhanced if the longer term Set Aside currently being considered within reforms in the Common Agricultural Policy (CAP) is encouraged by future agricultural support schemes.

Perhaps the best model of archaeological needs being integrated into farm-management schemes, however, is the Environmentally Sensitive Areas (ESA) scheme (see also Chapter 5). This has several objectives, all connected to encouraging environmentally friendly and conservation-oriented farming practices, based on a whole-farm conservation plan. These aims include nature conservation, landscape and archaeological objectives and show clearly not only how archaeological management relates to agricultural management, but also how different conservation objectives can interrelate. At its basic level of protection, this scheme provides the opportunity to prevent incidental damage to archaeological features through ignorance or unsympathetic farming practices. In its most recently revised form, it also offers the potential to undertake active management of archaeological features, such as removal of trees, scrub and rabbits, introduction of appropriate grazing regimes and repair of erosion scars. An important element of the ESA scheme is the preparation of whole-farm conservation plans in which different elements of conservation value are identified and balanced in a single management plan. Archaeological management is, however, optional for the farmer, while some other conservation aims are compulsory. Despite this fact, these provisions allow archaeological management to be undertaken as an integral part of general agricultural management, rather than as a separate and unrelated activity. This connection should help to make the farming community more aware of archaeological features and their management needs, and should gradually improve the perception of archaeology as an integral part of the modern landscape.

To some extent, therefore, current agricultural support schemes recognize archaeology as part of modern land management, and are beginning to incorporate the conservation considerations enshrined in Section 17 of the Agriculture Act 1986. This situation could be improved by imminent reforms of the CAP, if archaeological considerations are built into the accompanying 'agri-environmental' programme. In stressing stewardship of the land as a management aim, rather than simply food production, these reforms may allow archaeological management to be carried out under mainstream agricultural grant systems to a greater extent, and thereby establish it as a legitimate objective of modern land management. While such a reorientation could be overturned by a return in agricultural policy to an emphasis on food production, it would, nonetheless, link archaeological management more firmly with conservation of the environment; this seems unlikely to disappear entirely from consideration in any agricultural reform in the foreseeable future.

For the future, therefore, it is possible to envisage a situation where traditional land management on an upland farm is maintained in preference to, for example, permitting woodland regeneration because of its archaeological significance; or where the selection of land for semi-permanent Set Aside is made for its archaeological value. Furthermore, such a scenario need not diminish other conservation objectives since their interests can often be served at least to some extent by management sympathetic to archaeological features. This ideal is, however, still a long way off.

Archaeology is also a good option for farmers wishing to diversify into recreational interests under agricultural grant schemes as it provides attractions for visitors and can be well displayed with minimal cost. This primarily requires the creation of access to monuments within farmland, together with low-key interpretation, either of the archaeological aspect alone or linked to other interests on the farm. This can benefit archaeology by identifying sites as positive features in the landscape. Although there is a danger of potential exploitation of the features of interest, this risk can be avoided by careful management and monitoring procedures. It might also help raise the profile of archaeology both within the farming community and among the public since visitor access is usually a prime aim of farm-diversification schemes. So far, however, grants under this scheme have seldom been applied to archaeological features.

Forestry

The damaging effects of commercial forestry on archaeology have been well-aired in recent years (Proudfoot 1989; Barclay 1992b). Ground preparation, particularly ploughing, can cause archaeological damage, as can planting and the growth cycle, through root disturbance and obscuration of features. Felling processes can also be destructive, through vehicle damage and the removal and uprooting of trees. Even hand-planted and naturally regenerated scrub or woodland will disturb and obscure archaeological features, though the damage is likely to be reduced in these circumstances. Until recently, most forestry has been carried out in upland areas of Britain, affecting extensive areas of well-preserved archaeological remains principally in Scotland, northern England and Wales, but the recent trend to afforest the better farmland of the British lowlands, as agricultural production is reduced, now also threatens rich crop-mark complexes throughout eastern Britain.

Nevertheless, forestry and woodland have also led to some archaeological benefits: tree coverage has prevented the destruction of archaeological sites by other agencies, for example, agricultural practices or commercial development. Moreover, woodland has its own archaeological value, since its management has always been important for domestic and industrial activities. The management of woodland itself can, therefore, be archaeologically important; for instance, maintaining traditional coppicing practices and areas of ancient woodland will allow the retention of a historically important element of the landscape. Here the needs of archaeological sites coincide with those of forest management and can enhance nature conservation at the same time.

Provisions to protect and manage archaeological sites within areas supported by forestry grant schemes are now in place in some parts of the country, putting archaeology in a much stronger position in relation to forestry than other conservation interests (see also Chapter 5; and the Forestry Commission's guideline leaflet on *Forests and Archaeology*). These cover most forestry in Britain, since relatively little planting now occurs without grant aid, and includes both Forestry Commission planting schemes and private enterprises. These provisions allow identified archaeological features of importance to be protected, either by their exclusion from a forestry scheme or by adaptations within the scheme. In the former case archaeological features cease to be a forestry management issue, but in the latter they should become an integral part of forest management. For instance, archaeological features can be incorporated into forest plantations as open spaces for fire breaks or deer lawns, and should be accessible from forest rides for ease of management (though not positioned on the rides themselves as they are open to vehicular pressure). In this way archaeological management can be harmonized with other forest management needs. In addition, damage to sites already under forest and woodland cover can be ameliorated by removal of trees, with appropriate care, and protection from replanting. Such protection is a basic principle of archaeological management in woodland, together with the avoidance of planted areas close to archaeological features to prevent self-seeding regeneration, and appropriate management to keep features clear of trees, scrub and bracken. Although these needs may appear to sit uncomfortably with the aims of commercial forest interests, archaeological sites can become the focus of conservation interest, by helping to provide variety within a woodland habitat, as well as by offering a valuable recreational attraction in multi-purpose forests. These principles should be recognized in the concept that is developing within the forest industry of 'living' or 'community' forests, where the close integration of woodland with other aspects of land use and human activity is envisaged.

In addition to forest plantations, archaeological management is required in relation to the natural regeneration of woodland, which grant schemes increasingly seek to encourage. No ploughing is needed, though there may be some scarification of the ground surface and limited planting. Archaeological features in these areas require conscious management and necessitate the inclusion of more open spaces within the woodland than the management of naturally regenerated woodland itself might need. Protection and management of archaeological features must, therefore, be specifically provided within areas identified for regeneration schemes, as these are set up under appropriate grant regulations.

Multi-use forestry incorporates archaeology as one of its objectives, particularly on the recreational side. Archaeological elements are now commonly included within forest trails on Forestry Commission land, for instance. In this respect at least, forestry succeeds in integrating different conservation needs with forest management itself to enhance the forest environment as a whole and make it a focus for popular interest instead of an inaccessible zone of timber production. While it has to be admitted that, in the eyes of many, commercial forestry has transformed the landscape in an unsympathetic way that has not respected other interests, this is changing with Forestry Commission landscaping policies and practice. Recent shifts in forestry policy have demonstrated how a primary land use can at least begin to adapt to accommodate competing needs in the landscape.

Nature conservation

More has been written recently on archaeological management in relation to nature conservation than any other land use (Lambrick 1985; Macinnes and Wickham-Jones 1992). The management needs and objectives of both subjects can be both complementary and conflicting and this leads to a complicated, but close, relationship. Archaeological management can encourage nature conservation on sites, while protection of land for nature conservation value can enhance archaeological management and conserve the setting of monuments. Conflicts do, however, arise, where, for example, the interests of nature conservation are inimical to good archaeological management and vice versa. In specific instances one interest may have paramount importance, though in most cases mutually beneficial compromises can be reached, for example, removing trees from archaeological sites gradually rather than in one fell swoop.

As repositories of nature conservation interest, archaeological sites can be important (e.g. Berry 1992). Unploughed sites within arable land may be the only focus for conservation diversity in an area, though the vegetation itself might be archaeologically damaging. Similarly, in marginal land 'unimproved' archaeological sites may have interesting conservation value, such as showing old woodland or meadow species. In upland areas there is also often a coincidence of interest, for example, peatlands and wetlands have both nature conservation and archaeological value. One of the difficulties in both retaining this common value and avoiding conflict is recognizing where there is overlap and where management requirements differ. This can only be achieved through regular contact, consultation and mutual understanding and awareness, and designated areas provide the easiest focus for developing such procedures. They also provide an opportunity to explore the interrelationship between the two interests and to establish complementary management procedures and techniques that can be applied more widely. Such opportunities have been explored most successfully to date in specific areas that contain both nature conservation designations and features of archaeological interest, such as National Parks or large estates, or under the local planning system where responsibility for both interests often lies together (Smith 1992; Iles 1992). Since landowners or land managers cannot always distinguish between the needs of archaeology and those of nature conservation, it is to the benefit of all, as well as the environment as a whole, if a mutually acceptable approach to land management can be developed through regular consultation.

Some recent schemes seek to improve the condition and conservation value of particular areas of land: the Countryside Stewardship Scheme in England and the Tir Cymen Scheme in Wales (see below). Both incorporate archaeological protection, and the Countryside Stewardship scheme additionally provides opportunities for the positive management of archaeological features. Paradoxically, however, the interrelationship between archaeology and nature conservation is often more fully addressed in the management of agriculture and forestry, since the conservation value of land under these primary land uses can be enhanced if different conservation interests coincide on a single piece of land, such as the presence of wild flowers on an archaeological site. This factor also facilitates properly integrated approaches to land management.

Landscape management

The link between archaeology, other land uses and conservation interests is also to be found in matters relating to the wider landscape. This is recognized in the consideration of archaeology within Areas of Outstanding Natural Beauty and National Scenic Areas, as well as by the increasing acceptance of the importance of the setting of archaeological sites in the landscape enshrined in Planning Policy Guidance Note 16 (PPG 16) and its equivalents (see Chapter 5). In general considerations of landscape it is crucial that the fundamental unity of the different interests in the land be recognized, at least to the extent that they all affect the development of, and changes to, the modern landscape.

Archaeology is a vital component in understanding the landscape and in recognizing the implications of, and managing, change, since past human activity has played a major part in the way the British landscape looks today. Indeed, it is now widely accepted that the British landscape is fundamentally a historic landscape. Yet, archaeological management also needs to consider its impact on the wider landscape: for example, removing trees from an archaeological site, or removing historically important field boundaries, may have considerable implications for the appearance of the landscape and its subsequent management. Similarly maintaining the setting of archaeological sites can have an affect on a very wide area of land. From both viewpoints, therefore, archaeological considerations should be built into landscape assessments as a factor in all decisions affecting landscape management and change (Morgan Evans 1985; Lambrick 1992).

The urban environment

Although archaeology is most often perceived as a concern of rural land management, it is in fact also of concern in urban situations. Not only do earlier sites sometimes survive in urban locations, but towns and cities also have their own considerable archaeological heritage, epitomized by the wealth of the remains found under our major towns and cities, such as Perth, York or London. In this context archaeological considerations have to be built into the planning process and catered for within urban developments, a relationship that has been fully considered elsewhere (Baker 1983; Chapter 5). In the context of archaeology as land use, however, there are relevant points to consider. The reclamation of industrial land in particular has major implications for Britain's rich industrial archaeological heritage (Clark 1992), while the preservation of these sites carries implications for the appearance and future development of urban areas. As in rural areas, archaeology has specific needs that must be considered in relation to other uses of the land, and balanced to provide an acceptable overall land-use strategy wherever possible. Industrial monuments, for example, might be re-used rather than removed, as at New Lanark; or archaeological interests might be incorporated into open green spaces around towns and cities or within urban developments, which not only protects the features, but also offers an additional recreational interest. Archaeological features also provide an important element of the conservation and recreational interest of the countryside around British towns, and can form a significant element in conservation areas.

Recreation and access

Issues of access and recreation lead to both pressures and opportunities for archaeology. With diversification of interests within the British landscape, a general extension of leisure time and increasing economic reliance on tourism, there is now considerable pressure to allow access to features of archaeological interest. This carries an increased risk of erosion pressure on monuments as a result of higher visitor numbers, as can be clearly seen at some monuments open to the public. There can be no doubt, however, that this trend also provides opportunities for interpretation and public education leading to a potentially improved understanding of the past and the features that survive from it. Archaeological features can, therefore, provide a focus for alternative uses of the modern landscape that enhances the public's understanding of its development on the one hand and their perception of the range, significance and needs of archaeological sites on the other: this potential is recognized within areas like National Parks (below), and within the tourist industry. Moreover, archaeology and nature conservation have an important complementary value in the interpretation of the landscape that has been recognized for some time in particular areas, such as Heritage Coasts (see Chapter 7). Yet schemes linking the two for the benefit of the landscape as a whole are still not developed as a matter of routine.

Common considerations

The above examples raise common problems: most fundamentally the identification of archaeological features; the extent of the area of archaeological sensitivity; and management requirements, which vary from site to site. Solutions to these problems differ around the country and depend to a large extent on the quality of the local database, held in Sites and Monuments Records (SMRs), the availability of archaeological advice, and the execution of field inspections, whether on a strategic or response basis. There is also a basic problem of lack of awareness among other land users and managers of the nature, significance and needs of the archaeological heritage in the British landscape: these aspects need to be addressed before archaeology can be more widely incorporated into management plans relating to primary land uses.

One way of extending such appreciation is to demonstrate the value of archaeology in research and education. Archaeological research and investigation can inform our understanding of the development of the modern landscape and different land-management practices, including agriculture and forestry. It also aids the interpretation of such aspects of the land, and environmental education generally, by providing a link with people, who are generally interested in their ancestors and their interaction with the environment. Similarly, archaeology can benefit from the researches carried out for other disciplines, enhancing our understanding of the human past by providing information on the development and management of the natural environment in which people once lived. In this sense different aspects of modern land use can be demonstrated to be closely related and have mutually enhancing links that can feed back into modern management strategies and can be of considerable value in environmental education.

ARCHAEOLOGY AND INTEGRATED LAND MANAGEMENT

Archaeology, then, has its specific needs, but it must also be considered in relation to competing demands on the land. The overall aim must be to maximize the benefits and minimize the conflicts, while avoiding too much compromise on the principles of best archaeological management. Indeed this is the real challenge of modern land management: to achieve a strategy that recognizes and accommodates these various legitimate interests in the land. There are now a number of frameworks that may allow this aim to be achieved. The principal examples are described below.

National Parks

National Parks, which have been designated in England and Wales under the National Parks and Access to the Countryside Act 1949, provide a good opportunity for integrated land management, since responsibility for different types of land use is invested in a single management unit (see Smith 1992: 127–31). The stated purpose of National Parks is to preserve and enhance the natural beauty of the areas and promote public enjoyment of them. Although the protection of cultural heritage is not specifically included in their aims, most National Parks have in practice recognized the importance of this aspect of their areas, and the recent review of the National Parks has recommended that this dimension be formally included in a new purpose statement (Edwards 1991: 11). National Parks have the potential to protect archaeological sites from inimical activities through specific management agreements and a co-ordinated approach to land use. They can also enhance the landscape through integrating different conservation aims and through diversification in land-management objectives. Achievement of this potential is facilitated by composite management plans and appropriate management payments. This potential may not always be realized in practice, but the review has identified ways in which consideration of archaeological interests can be improved: the compilation of adequate databases; the inclusion of archaeology within farm plans, and within access, management and interpretation agreements; the provision of appropriate expertise; and stronger archaeological legislation, together with delegation of responsibility to National Park Authorities (Edwards 1991: 24). Adoption of such recommendations should ensure that archaeology is more frequently and satisfactorily incorporated into management within the Parks.

At a more local level, Regional and Country Parks provide comparable opportunities for integrating archaeological objectives with other management and recreational aims. These are generally recognized as particularly sensitive areas by local planning authorities.

National Heritage Areas

There are no National Parks in Scotland. Recently, however, a new framework for integrating conservation objectives with competing land uses on a voluntary basis has been defined: National Heritage Areas (NHAs). It is the responsibility of Scottish Natural Heritage (SNH) to recommend such areas to the Secretary of State for Scotland, and in doing so the organization is expected to consult widely with other land-use, landowning and local interest groups. Designated areas would be managed through management boards, comprising representatives of the principal planning, land-use and interest groups, which would seek to co-ordinate the different management objectives for the area. In principle, NHAs should take the need for archaeological management into account in defining both the areas themselves and their appropriate management, particularly in view of SNH's responsibility under the Natural Heritage (Scotland) Act 1991 to take account of archaeology (see Chapter 5). No NHAs have as yet been designated, however, and it therefore remains to be seen how this will work in practice.

The National Trust

The National Trust for England and Wales (NT) and National Trust for Scotland (NTS) are charitable bodies concerned with the preservation of land and buildings of historic or natural interest. Since the Trusts have large landholdings and have a remit for conservation and interpretation, they have, like National Parks, the potential for a co-ordinated and integrated approach to land management. The NT has recognized the existence and value of archaeological features for some time now and incorporated them into databases and estate-management plans (Thackray and Hearn 1985: 51–7). The NTS is actively increasing the incorporation of this aspect of the landscape into its work and has already undertaken archaeological surveys of several of its estates. Perhaps more than any other body, the Trusts have the potential to manage and interpret their estates within the context of the full time-depth of the landscape. In practice, however, the components tend to be managed individually and the interpretation concentrates on single dimensions, most notably at the traditional NT properties. Nevertheless, these components are brought together, and to an extent interpreted, as a wider whole in heritage trails, particularly coastal walks.

Environmentally Sensitive Areas

Environmentally Sensitive Areas (ESAs) are designated under the Agriculture Act 1986 and provide a good model for integrated land management because they recognize different conservation objectives and relate them to agricultural activity. This is achieved through the preparation of whole-farm conservation plans, which integrate all activities on an individual farm. The protection of archaeological features is one of the basic requirements that farmers must observe on joining the scheme, though the onus is firmly on the farmer to identify the features. The value of the scheme is consequently limited by the known archaeology and the capabilities of, or advice provided to, individual farmers (see Smith 1992: 131–2). Nevertheless, where identified, archaeological features are included in an integrated approach to land use and are protected from inadvertently unsympathetic farming practices. ESA schemes have been in existence since 1987, but there have been recent improvements to these early schemes, and those newly designated, which allow the potential for greater integration of archaeological features in positive management by their inclusion in a conservation action plan. Within these plans, positive works may be undertaken to improve the condition of archaeological sites, in the same way as for nature conservation features, and both are balanced within an overall management plan. The benefits of these schemes for archaeology is that they bring the concept of archaeological management into the world of the ordinary farmer; they increase the level of funds potentially available for archaeological management beyond those available from archaeological bodies alone; and, most importantly, they tie archaeological management directly to more routine land uses and establish a co-ordinated approach to land management. As a result, this integrated approach might gradually become more fully appreciated outwith ESAs themselves and be adopted in other farming schemes under the general conservation provisions of the Agriculture Act 1986.

Countryside Stewardship and Tir Cymen

The Countryside Stewardship (CS) scheme, administered by the Countryside Commission for England, has been set up to demonstrate that public enjoyment of, and access to, the countryside can be combined with commercial farming and other land management interests (Countryside Commission 1991b). The scheme seeks to combine landscape, wildlife, historic and access interests, and specifically includes consideration of archaeological and historic features by identifying historic landscapes as one of the seven landscape types eligible for management agreements. In identifying eligible historic features and their management requirements, farmers are recommended to obtain appropriate advice, and in assessing applications the Countryside Commission seeks appropriate archaeological advice, normally from the local authority. English Heritage may additionally provide funds for survey to identify eligible historic features. Eligible features include both natural and man-made elements of the landscape, such as parkland, woodland or earthworks, and payments are made at two levels: simple management actions, and more complex plans or restoration work. The historic landscape aspect of this scheme has only been introduced recently, though archaeological advice has already been actively sought, but the potential of the scheme to link the management of archaeology with other land uses is clearly very high (see Smith 1992: 132–3).

The Tir Cymen scheme, administered by the Countryside Council for Wales, similarly seeks to develop the skills of farmers in the management of wildlife, landscape, archaeo-logy and geology, together with provisions for public access (Countryside Council for Wales 1992). Unlike the CS scheme, however, provisions for archaeological features relate to protection rather than positive management, except in the case of historically important field boundaries.

There are no similar schemes in Northern Ireland and Scotland at present.

Sites of Special Scientific Interest

There is considerable scope for improving the management of archaeological sites within Sites of Special Scientific Interest (SSSIs). Designated under the Wildlife and Countryside Acts of 1981 and 1985, and administered by English Nature, Scottish Natural Heritage and the Countryside Council for Wales, these areas are notified for particular nature con-servation interest and a list of potentially damaging operations (PDOs) identified. The landowner is required to notify the appropriate body of any intent to carry out any of these operations, and that organization can seek to negotiate a management agreement to avoid them. The conservation value of some SSSIs might conflict with the best management of archaeological sites within them, for example, maintaining woodland interest, while some of the PDOs may also be damaging to archaeology. Archaeological interest is not normally a consideration in either designation or management agreements. Yet management of archaeological features within an SSSI can lead to a reduction in the nature conservation value of the feature if carried out as an entirely separate exercise. Nevertheless, with appropriate mechanisms for consultation, it should be possible in most cases to reach an agreed management plan for an archaeological site within an SSSI, since the former is usually only a small proportion of the latter; however, procedures are not normally in place to achieve an integrated approach to the management of these different conservation interests. Failure to achieve this can be due to a combination of factors: a lack of aware-ness that there is another conservation interest on a piece of land; a lack of understanding of what the management requirements for each interest are; and a lack of resources to pur-sue the site meetings and modified management prescriptions that are necessary for the two interests to be successfully combined. Nevertheless, the situation has improved markedly in recent years and discussions between archaeological and nature conservation bodies at both national and local level will undoubtedly lead to further progress.

National Nature Reserves are areas of nationally important nature conservation value, managed by, or under agreement with, the national nature conservation agencies. As with SSSIs, the management of archaeological features could be better integrated with that of the natural heritage.

Archaeological management agreements

The AMAA Act 1979 makes provision for grants for management work on archaeological sites: such payments are for the active management of archaeological or historic features and can take the form of one-off grants or longer-term management agreements. In some cases the aims or needs of other conservation interests are considered in management pre-scriptions, but usually only if the site has some specific known value. The relationship between management for archaeological purposes and that for nature conservation value is gradually being recognized, and there is considerable potential to carry out the manage-ment of archaeological features in a way that enhances rather than diminishes their nature conservation interest (Darvill 1987; Wainwright 1989: 168). The problems in achieving this are identical to those identified above for SSSIs, though again progress is being made.

Monuments in the care of the state (Chapter 5) are in many ways the equivalent of national nature reserves, since the national archaeological bodies are directly involved in their management. Some progress has recently been made in incorporating the manage-ment of nature conservation within that of monuments in care.

The Ministry of Defence

The Ministry of Defence (MOD) has made tremendous strides in recent years to widen the land-use base of at least its less sensitive landholdings, and to incorporate conservation considerations in its land management. This is exemplified by its regular magazine *Sanctuary*, which covers a wide range of conservation subjects related to defence land-holdings and MOD activities. This work is guided by an MOD conservation officer, and several conservation groups on which relevant conservation interests are represented. The potential of this more open approach is emphasized by the success of the Salisbury Plain project, where English Heritage in particular has worked with the MOD to produce a management plan for an area of land highly important both archaeologically and for defence purposes (Morgan Evans 1992). This management plan identifies areas of extreme archaeological sensitivity that will be preserved in all cases (except a national emergency), and areas where sites are sensitively managed within areas used for other land uses or defence activities.

Other areas

A variety of other opportunities exist to pursue the management of archaeological features in relation to other land-management interests. Examples include the work of the John Muir Trust in Scotland, where archaeological survey and management have been built into recent estate-management plans; large private estates where the management of all features falls under the responsibility of a single owner or manager, such as the Duchy of Cornwall in Avon, the Weld Estate in Dorset (see Iles 1992) and water company land in England or Wales; and through local organizations where natural and cultural heritage interests are often both represented. These opportunities are likely to expand as archaeo-logy is linked with other interests in the various ways outlined above, particularly if national policy becomes more integrated, and progress is aided by the considerable degree of communication that now exists between archaeological, conservation and land-manage-ment groups at national and local level throughout the country.

Summary

Overall, then, there is considerable potential for integrated land management where the value of the whole can be enhanced by the considered management of the component parts. There is of necessity compromise involved, but this is not at an unacceptable level in the vast majority of cases. Resources can, however, be a real problem in achieving both the time to prepare integrated management plans, since more time and personnel are involved, and the funds needed to achieve the management objectives, which will tend to be more complex. The way is spearheaded by the designated areas and large management bodies, but there are also opportunities to apply the principle more widely throughout the British landscape.

THE FUTURE

The only way to recognize the unity of the landscape is to aim towards a form of land management that fully integrates different land uses and objectives (see Miles 1992). This would mean that archaeological considerations could stand alongside nature conservation, and even agriculture and forestry, as one possible objective of modern land management and as one of several criteria to be considered in decision-making. The management choices made for any piece of land would recognize the variety of factors of interest and value in the modern landscape and would seek a solution that balanced as many of those interests as possible, or, in particular circumstances, recognized one as paramount. For example, an important archaeological landscape might be maintained under a traditional (though improved) management regime rather than given over to woodland regeneration; or, conversely, established woodland might be retained on a monument because of particularly important wildlife or botanical interests. This important objective will, however, only be realized when financial support recognizes the legitimacy of different interests in the land, and can offer comparable levels of support to them all, together with appropriate mechanisms to achieve them.

ACKNOWLEDGEMENTS

I would like to thank Gordon Barclay, David Breeze, Bill Hanson, Dai Morgan Evans and Ian Ralston for their helpful comments.

BIBLIOGRAPHY

ABRC (Advisory Board for Redundant Churches) 1991 *Annual Report*. London: ABRC.

AMBS (Ancient Monuments Board for Scotland) 1983 *Ancient Monuments Board for Scotland, Thirtieth Annual Report 1983*. Edinburgh: HMSO.

AMBS 1986 *Ancient Monuments Board for Scotland, Thirty-third Annual Report 1986*. Edinburgh: HMSO.

AMBS 1988 *Ancient Monuments Board for Scotland, Thirty-fifth Annual Report 1988*. Edinburgh: HMSO.

AMBS 1991 *Ancient Monuments Board for Scotland, Thirty-eighth Annual Report 1991*. Edinburgh: HMSO.

Aberg F. A. & Leech R. H. 1992 'The National Archaeological Record for England: Past, Present and Future', in Larsen, 157–69.

Addyman P. V. 1974 'York: The Anatomy of a Crisis in Urban Archaeology', in Rahtz 1974b, 153–62.

Addyman P. V. & Morris R. K. eds 1976 *The Archaeological Study of Churches*. (Council for British Archaeology Research Report 13.) London: CBA.

d'Agostino B. 1984 'Italy', in Cleere, 73–81.

Aitken M. J. 1974 *Physics in Archaeology*. Oxford: Clarendon Press. 2nd edn.

Aldridge D. 1989 'How the Ship of Interpretation was Blown Off Course in the Tempest: Some Philosophical Thoughts', in Uzzell 1989a, 64–87.

Allen J. L. & Holt A. St J. 1986 *Health and Safety in Field Archaeology*. London: Standing Conference of Archaeological Unit Managers (with later updates).

Allen J. R. L. & Fulford M. G. 1990 'Romano-British Wetland Reclamations at Longney, Gloucestershire, and Evidence for the Early Settlement of the Inner Severn Estuary', *Antiq J* 70, 288–326.

Allen M. J. 1990 'Magnetic Susceptibility', in Bell M. *Bream Down Excavations 1983–1987*, 197–202. (English Heritage Report 15.) London: HBMC.

Ames M. 1977 'Visible Storage and Public Documentation', *Curator* 20, 65–79.

Anon 1986 *Preservation by Record: The Work of the Central Excavation Unit 1975–85*. London: HBMCE.

Anon 1989 'Archaeology and Development: Report of a One-day Conference', *Property Journal, the Journal of the British Property Federation* 14 3, 16–21.

Apted M. R. *et al.* 1977 *Ancient Monuments and Their Interpretation. Essays Presented to A. J. Taylor*. London and Chichester: Phillimore.

Arnold B. 1992 'The Past as Propaganda', *Archaeology* 45 4, 30–7.

Arup (Ove Arup & Parters and the Department of Archaeology, University of York in association with B. Thorpe) 1991 *York Archaeology and Development Study*. Manchester: Ove Arup. (Ove Arup & Dept Archaeol Univ York for York City Council & English Heritage.)

Ascherson N. 1987 'Why "Heritage" is Right-wing', *The Observer*, 8 November 1987, 9.

Ascherson N. 1988 'Leaving Our Old Curiosity Shop', *The Observer*, 17 January 1988, 7.

Ashley-Smith J. 1982 'The Ethics of Conservation', *The Conservator* 6, 1–5.

Aspinall A. 1992 'New Developments in Geophysical Prospection', *Proc Brit Acad* 77, 233–44.

Aspinwall & Company 1991 *Planning Application and Environmental Statement for the Disposal of Controlled Wastes by Landfilling at Risley, Cheshire*. Manchester: Aspinwall and Company. 3 vols.

Atkin M. & Milligan R. 1992 'Ground-probing Radar in Archaeology – Practicalities and Problems', *Fld Archaeol* 16, 288–91.

Austin D. 1987 'The Future of Archaeology in British Universities', *Antiquity* 61, 227–38.

BADLG (British Archaeologists and Developers Liaison Group) 1989 *Model Agreement Between Developer/Client and the Appropriate Archaeological Body*. London: British Property Federation for BADLG (shorter version also available).

BADLG 1991 *The British Archaeologists and Developers Liaison Group Code of Practice*. London: BADLG (Joint British Property Federation and Standing Committee of Archaeological Unit Managers publication). 3rd edn (first published 1986).

BAN (*British Archaeological News*) Editorial 1988 'Rescue on the Cheap', *Brit Archaeol News* 3: 2, 13.

BAN Editorial 1989 'The Lessons of York', *Brit Archaeol News* 4: 2, 13.

BAN Editorial 1990 'Archaeology and the Private Sector', *British Archaeol News* 5: 4, 42.

Baker D. B. 1977 'Survey and the Historic Environment', in Rowley T. & Breakall M. eds *Planning and the Historic Environment*, vol. II, 1–23. Oxford: University Dept of External Stud.

Baker D. B. 1983 *Living With the Past: The Historic Environment*. Bedfordshire.

Baker D. B. 1987 'Editorial – Getting the Act Together', *Fld Archaeol* 7, 86–7.

Baker F. & Thomas J. eds 1990 *Writing the Past in the Present*. Lampeter: St David's University College.

Bapty I. & Yates T. eds 1990 *Archaeology After Structuralism: Post-structuralism and the Practice of Archaeology*. London: Routledge.

Barclay G. J. 1992a 'Vegetation Management on Ancient Monuments in Forestry and Other Areas', *Aspects of Applied Biology* 29, 105–11.

Barclay G. J. 1992b 'Forestry and Archaeology in Scotland', *Scottish Forestry* 46, 27–47.

Barclay G. J. 1992c 'The Scottish Gravels: A Neglected Resource?', in Fulford & Nichols, 106–24.

Barker P. 1974 'The Origins and Development of RESCUE', in Rahtz 1974b, 280–85.

Barker P. 1982 *Techniques of Archaeological Excavation*. London: Batsford.

Barker P. 1987 'Not Drowning, Just Treading Water', *CBA Annual Report* 37, 70–6.

Barrett J. 1987 'Contextual Archaeology', *Antiquity* 61, 468–73.

Barrett J., Bradley R. & Green M. 1991 *Landscape, Monuments and Society*. Cambridge: Cambridge University Press.

Barrett J. & Kinnes I. eds 1988 *The Archaeology of Context in the Neolithic and Bronze Age: Recent Trends*. Sheffield: Department of Archaeology and Prehistory, University of Sheffield.

Bayley J. 1992 *Non-Ferrous Metalworking from Coppergate* (The Archaeology of York 17/7.) London: Counc Brit Archaeol for York Archaeol Trust.

Belgrave R. 1990 'Black People and Museums: The Caribbean Heritage Project in Southampton', in Gathercole & Lowenthal, 63–73.

Beresford M. W. 1950 'Maps and the Medieval Landscape', *Antiquity* 24, 114–18.

Beresford M. & St Joseph J. K. S. 1977 *Medieval England. An Aerial Survey*. Cambridge: Cambridge University Press.

Beresford Dew R. 1977 'Rescue Archaeology: Finance 1976–1977', *Rescue News* 13, 4–6.

Berry A. Q. 1992 'Integrating Archaeology and the Countryside: Clwyd County Council's Approach to Archaeological Site Management', in Macinnes & Wickham-Jones, 155–60.

Bersu G. 1940a 'King Arthur's Round Table', *Trans Cumberland Westmorland Antiq Archaeol Soc* 40, 169–206.

Bersu G 1940b 'Excavations at Little Woodbury', *Proc Prehist Soc* 6, 30–111.

Biddle M. 1974 'The Future of the Urban Past', in Rahtz 1974b, 95–112.

Biddle M. ed. 1976 *Winchester in the Early Middle Ages. An Edition and Discussion of the Winton Domesday* (Winchester Studies 1). Oxford: Clarendon Press.

Biddle M. ed. 1990 *Object and Economy in Medieval Winchester*. (Winchester Studies 7: ii.) Oxford: Clarendon Press.

Biddle M. & Hudson D. 1973 *The Future of London's Past*. Worcester: Rescue Publications.

Binks G., Dyke J. & Dagnell P. 1988 *Visitors Welcome: A Manual on the Presentation and Interpretation of Archaeological Excavations*. London: HMSO.

Binney M. & Burman P. 1977a *Churches and Chapels: Who Cares?* London: British Tourist Authority.

Binney M & Burman P eds 1977b *Change and Decay: The Future of Our Churches*. London: Macmillan.

Binns G. & Gardiner J. (comp) 1990 *Guide to Undergraduate University Courses in Archaeology, with a Note on Non-University Courses*. London: CBA. 3rd edn.

Bintliff J., Davies B., Gaffney C., Snodgrass A. & Waters A. 1992 'Trace Metal Accumulation in Soils on and around Ancient Settlements in Greece', in Spoerry 1992b, 9–24.

Birk A. (Parliamentary Under-Secretary of State) 1977 *Opening Address at the Oxford Conference 1976*, JPEL Occ Papers.

Boniface P. & Fowler P. J. 1993 *Heritage and Tourism in 'the Global Village'*. London: Routledge.

Boulting N. 1976 'The Law's Delays: Conservationist Legislation in the British Isles', in Fawcett, 9–33.

Bourdieu P. 1984 *Distinction: A Social Critique of the Judgement of Taste*. London: Routledge Kegan Paul.

Bowden M. 1991 *Pitt Rivers: The Life and Archaeological Work of Lieutenant-General Augustus Henry Lane Fox Pitt Rivers, DCL, FRS, FSA*. Cambridge: Cambridge University Press.

Bowler P. J. 1989 *The Invention of Progress. The Victorians and the Past.* Oxford: Blackwell.

Boyne R. & Rattansi A. eds 1990 *Postmodernism and Society.* London: Macmillan.

Bradley R. 1984 *The Social Foundations of Prehistoric Britain.* London: Longman.

Bradley R. & Fulford M. 1980 'Sherd Size in the Analysis of Occupation Debris', *Univ London Inst Archaeol Bull* 17, 85–94.

Brand C. M. & Cant R. G. 1980 *Modern Legislation for the Protection of History: The Ancient Monuments and Archaeological Areas Act 1979.* (Scot Planning Law & Practice Occas Pap 2.) Glasgow.

Braudel F. 1980 *On History.* Chicago: University of Chicago Press.

Breeze D. J. 1988 'Planning and Archaeology: The Legislative Framework', in Selman, 1–4.

British Standard 5750 – Quality Systems. Part 1 (1987 as amended): *Specification for Design/Development, Production, Installation and Servicing.* Parts 1/2 (1987 as amended): *Quality Manual Appraisal for Service Industries.* Part 8 (1991): *Guide to Quality Management and Quality Systems Elements for Services.* Doc. No. E000146 (1991): *Guidance Notes for Application to Education and Training.* Milton Keynes: British Standards Institution.

Brönner W. 1982 *Deutsche Denkmalschutzgesetze.* Bonn: Deutsches Nationalkomittee für Denkmalschutz.

Burnham B. 1974 *The Protection of Cultural Property: Handbook of National Legislations.* Paris: International Council of Museums.

Burrow I. 1984a 'The History of the Sites and Monuments Records System', in Burrow 1984b, 6–15.

Burrow I. ed. 1984b *County Archaeological Records: Progress and Potential.* Taunton: Association of County Archaeological Officers.

Burrow I. & Hunter R. 1990 'Contracting Archaeology? Cultural Resource Management in New Jersey, USA', *Fld Archaeol* 12, 194–200.

CASG (Contract Archaeology Study Group, IFA) 1988 'Report of the Contract Archaeology Study Group', *Fld Archaeol* 8, 115–17.

CAWP (Contract Archaeology Working Party) 1988 *Professional and Public Archaeology – Contract Archaeology Session.* Birmingham: polycopied papers circulated by the IFA Contract Archaeology Working Party at the 1988 Archaeology in Britain Conference.

CBA (Council for British Archaeology) 1974 *Archaeology and Government. Report of a Working Party of the CBA and RESCUE.* London: CBA.

CBA 1982 *Guidelines for the Preparation of Contracts for Archaeological Excavations.* London: CBA.

CBA 1988a (CBA Committee for Nautical Archaeology *et al.*) 1988 'A National Policy for Nautical Archaeology', *Brit Archaeol News* 3, 31.

CBA 1988b (CBA Countryside Committee) 1988 'A Policy for the Countryside', *Brit Archaeol News*, 3, 57–60.

CBA Wales 1988 *Policy and Recommendations for Rescue Archaeology in Wales.* Abermule, Montgomery: CBA Wales.

CBI (Confederation of British Industry) 1991 *Archaeological Investigation – Code of Practice for Minerals Operators.* London: CBI (first published 1982).

CCC (Council for the Care of Churches) 1988 *Archaeology and the Church of England, A Report by the Council for the Care of Churches and the Cathedrals Advisory Commission.* London: Council for the Care of Churches.

CDC (Clydebank District Council) 1992 *Clydebank Local Plan, Finalised Draft.* Clydebank: Clydebank District Council.

CoE (Council of Europe) 1979 *Monument Protection in Europe.* Deventer: Kluwer.

CoE 1992 *European Convention on the Protection of the Archaeological Heritage.* (European Treaty Series 143.) Strasbourg: Council of Europe.

CRC (Central Regional Council) 1992 *Central 2000: Central Regional Council Structure Plan.* Stirling: Central Reg Counc Development & Planning Dept.

Capper J. C. 1907 'Photographs of Stonehenge as Seen From a War Balloon', *Archaeologia* 60, 571.

Carnett C. 1991 *Legal Background of Archaeological Resources Protection* (US Dept of the Interior, National Park Service, Technical Brief, 11).

Carr C. 1982 *Handbook on Soil Resistivity Surveying.* Evanston, Illinois: Center for American Archaeology Press.

Chadwick P. 1991 'Appendix 2 – A Model Specification on which to Base a Project Design', in Swain, 55–6.

Champion T. C. 1991 'Theoretical Archaeology in Britain', in Hodder I. ed. *Archaeological Theory in Europe: The Last Three Decades.* London: Routledge.

Champion T. C. ed. 1989 *Centre and Periphery: Comparative Studies in Archaeology.* London: Unwin Hyman.

Chapman R., Kinnes I. & Randsborg K. eds 1981 *The Archaeology of Death*. Cambridge: Cambridge University Press.

Chapman W. 1989 'The Organisational Context in the History of Archaeology: Pitt Rivers and Other British Archaeologists in the 1860s', *Antiq J* 69, 23–42.

Cherry J. F., Gamble C. S. & Shennan S. J. eds 1978 *Sampling in Contemporary British Archaeology*. (British Archaeological Report 50.) Oxford: BAR.

Childe V. G. 1925 *The Dawn of European Civilisation*. London: Kegan Paul.

Childe V. G. 1949 *Social Worlds of Knowledge*. Oxford: Oxford University Press.

Chippindale C. 1991 'Editorial', *Antiquity* 65, 5–6.

Chippindale C., Devereux P., Fowler P. J., Jones R. & Sebastian T. 1990 *Who Owns Stonehenge?* London: Batsford.

Chippindale C. & Gibbins D. eds 1990 'Heritage at Sea: Proposals for the Better Protection of British Archaeological Sites Underwater', *Antiquity* 64, 390–400.

Church in Wales, 1992 *Interim Report on the Commission on Faculties*. Penarth: Church in Wales Publications.

Church of Scotland 1983 *Care for Your Church*. Edinburgh: The St Andrew Press.

Churchill R. & Lowe A. 1988 *The Law of the Sea*. Manchester: Manchester University Press.

Clark A. J. 1975 'Archaeological Prospecting: a Progress Report', *Journ Archaeol Sci* 2, 297–314.

Clark A. J. 1990 *Seeing Beneath the Soil*. London: Batsford.

Clark C. 1992 'The Brown Debate: Archaeology; Ecology; and Derelict Land', in Macinnes & Wickham-Jones, 146–51.

Clark J. G. D. 1934 'Archaeology and the State', *Antiquity* 8, 414–28.

Clark J. G. D. 1952 *Prehistoric Europe: The Economic Basis*. London: Methuen.

Clark J. G. D. 1968 *Archaeology and Society*. London: Methuen.

Clarke D. L. 1973 'Archaeology: The Loss of Innocence', *Antiquity* 47, 6–18.

Clarke D. V., Cowie T. G. & Foxon A. 1985 *Symbols of Power at the Time of Stonehenge*. Edinburgh: HMSO.

Cleere H. F. 1991 'Archaeology in the National Parks', *Brit Archaeol News* 6, 29.

Cleere H. F. ed. 1984 *Approaches to the Archaeological Heritage*. Cambridge: Cambridge University Press.

Cleere H. F. ed. 1989 *Archaeological Heritage Management in the Modern World*. (One World Archaeology 9.) London: Unwin Hyman.

Coker A. 1992 'The Potential Environmental Gains and Losses from Coast Protection and Sea Defence Works', in Penning-Rowsell E. C. ed. *et al.*, *The Economics of Coastal Management*, 118–45. London: Belhaven Press.

Collcutt S. N. 1991 'Access to Sites and Monuments Records – A User's Pointed View', *Fld Archaeol* 14, 256–7.

Collingwood R. G. 1938 'King Arthur's Round Table', *Trans Cumberland Westmorland Antiq Archaeol Soc* 38, 1–31.

Collingwood R. G. 1939 *An Autobiography*. Oxford: Oxford University Press.

Collingwood R. G. 1946 *The Idea of History*. Oxford: Oxford University Press.

Condori C. M. 1989 'History and Prehistory in Bolivia: What About the Indians?', in Layton 1989a, 46–59.

Cookson N. 1991 'All that Glitters', *New Law Journal* 141, 1255–7.

Corbishley M. ed. 1992 *Archaeology in the National Curriculum*. London: CBA & English Heritage.

Corfield M. 1988 'The Re-shaping of Metal Objects', *Antiquity* 62, 261–5.

Countryside Commission 1991a *Heritage Coasts: Policies and Priorities 1991*. Cheltenham: Countryside Commission.

Countryside Commission 1991b *Application Packs for Countryside Stewardship*. Cheltenham.

Countryside Council for Wales 1992 *Tir Cymen: A Farm Stewardship Scheme*. Bangor.

Crabtree P. 1990 *West Stow: The Animal Husbandry*. (East Anglian Archaeol Rep 47.)

Crawford O. G. S. 1923 'Air Survey and Archaeology', *Geographical Journ*, May 1923, 324–66.

Crawford O. G. S. 1924 'The Stonehenge Avenue', *Antiquaries J* 4, 57–9.

Crawford O. G. S. 1928 *Air Survey and Archaeology*. (Ordnance Survey Professional Papers, new ser 7.) Southampton.

Crawford O. G. S. 1929 *Air Photography for Archaeologists*. (Ordnance Survey Professional Papers, new ser 12.) Southampton.

Crawford O. G. S. 1954 'A Century of Air Photography', *Antiquity* 28, 206–10.

Crawford O. G. S. & Keiller A. 1928 *Wessex from the Air*. Oxford.

259

Cronyn J. 1980 'The Potential of Conservation', in Keene, 8–9.

Crowther D. 1983 'Swords to Ploughshares: A Nationwide Survey of Archaeologists and Treasure Hunting Clubs', *Archaeological Review from Cambridge* 2: 1, 9–20.

Cunliffe B. W. 1982 *The Report of a Joint Working Party of the Council for British Archaeology and the Department of the Environment.* London: DoE.

Cunliffe B. W. 1990 'Publishing in the City', *Antiquity* 64, 667–71.

DoE (Department of the Environment) 1975a *Principles of Publication in Rescue Archaeology.* Report by a Working Party of the Ancient Monuments Board for England, Committee for Rescue Archaeology. London: DoE.

DoE 1975b *What is Our Heritage? United Kingdom Achievements for European Architectural Heritage Year 1975.* London: HMSO.

DoE 1978 *The Scientific Treatment of Material from Rescue Excavations. A Report by a Working Party of the Committee for Rescue Archaeology of the Ancient Monuments Board for England.* London: DoE.

DoE 1983 *Criteria for the Selection of Ancient Monuments.* (Press Notice 523.) London: DoE.

DoE 1985 *Guidance Notes to Those Concerned in the Survey for Listing.*

DoE 1987a *How to Appeal Against Listing*, September 1987.

DoE 1987b *Historic Buildings and Conservation Areas – Policy and Procedure.* (DoE *Circular 8/87.*) London: HMSO.

DoE 1988 *Schedule of Ancient Monuments.* London: English Heritage. 46 vols.

DoE 1989a *Environmental Assessment: A Guide to the Procedures.* London: HMSO.

DoE 1989b *The Water Act 1989: Code of Practice on Conservation, Access and Recreation.* London: Department of the Environment, Ministry of Agriculture, Fisheries and Food and the Welsh Office.

DoE 1990a *Planning Policy Guidance Note 16: Archaeology and Planning.* (PPG 16) London: HMSO.

DoE 1990b *This Common Inheritance.* London: HMSO.

DoE 1990c *The Government's Response to Heritage at Sea.* (Announced 20 December 1990.) London: DNH.

DoE 1991 *News Release No 256.* 25 April.

DoE & Department of National Heritage 1992a *Responsibilities for Conservation Policy and Casework.* (DoE Circular 20/92 & DNH Circular 1/92.) London: DoE.

DoE 1992b *Coastal Zone Protection and Planning: The Government's Response to the Second Report from the House of Commons Select Committee on the Environment.* Cmd 2011.

DoE & Welsh Office 1992c *Planning Policy Guidance Note 20: Coastal Planning.* (PPG 20) London: HMSO.

DoE 1992d *This Common Inheritance: The Second Year Report.* London: HMSO.

DoE 1992e *Ecclesiastical Exemption from Listed Building Control.* Consultation Paper by the Directorate of Heritage and Royal Estate (DoE). London: DoE.

DoE (NI) (Department of the Environment (Northern Ireland)) 1990 *Finding and Minding 1986–89: A Report on the Archaeological Work of the Department of the Environment for Northern Ireland.* Belfast: DoE (NI).

Dalwood H. 1987 'What is Professional Archaeology?', *Fld Archaeol* 7, 104–5.

Daniel G. E. 1975 *A Hundred and Fifty Years of Archaeology.* London: Duckworth.

Darvill T. 1986 *The Archaeology of the Uplands: A Rapid Assessment of Archaeological Knowledge and Practice.* London: CBA.

Darvill T. 1987 *Ancient Monuments in the Countryside: An Archaeological Management Review.* London: HBMC.

Darvill T. 1988 *Monuments Protection Programme: Monument Evaluation Manual, Parts I and II.* London: English Heritage.

Darvill T. 1991a *Monuments Protection Programme: Monument Evaluation Manual, Part IV.* London: English Heritage.

Darvill T. 1991b 'Chairman's Notes', *Fld Archaeol* 15, 263–4.

Darvill T. 1992a *Valuing Britain's Archaeological Resource.* Bournemouth University (Inaugural Lecture).

Darvill T. 1992b *Monuments Protection Programme: Monument Evaluation Manual, Part III.* London: English Heritage.

Darvill T. & Atkins M. 1991 *Regulating Archaeological Work by Contract.* (Inst Fld Archaeol Tech Pap 8.) Birmingham: Institute of Field Archaeologists.

Darvill T. & Gerrard C. 1992 'Evaluating Archaeological Sites: The Cotswold Archaeological Trust Approach', in Darvill T. & Holbrook N. eds *Cotswold Archaeological Trust Annual Review* 2 (for 1990), 10–14. Cirencester: CAT.

Darvill T. C., Parker Pearson M., Smith R. & Thomas R. eds 1978 *New Approaches to our Past*. Southampton: Southampton Univ Archaeol Soc.

Darvill T., Saunders A. & Startin B. 1987 'A Question of National Importance: Approaches to the Evaluation of Ancient Monuments for the Monuments Protection Programme in England', *Antiquity* 61, 393–408.

Davidson, J.L. 1986 'The Collection of Antiquarian Information for the Early Ordnance Survey Maps of Scotland', *Proc Soc Antiq Scot* 116, 11–16.

Davidson J. L. & Henshall A. S. 1989 *The Chambered Cairns of Orkney*. Edinburgh: Edinburgh University Press.

Davies D. R. 1985 'The Management of Guardianship Monuments', *Ass Stud Conserv Hist Build/Trans* 10, 49–53.

Davies E. J. 1991 'Striking the Balance Between Economic Forces and Environmental Constraints', *Journ Planning & Environment Law Occas Pap* 18, 43–66. London: Sweet & Maxwell.

Deuel L. 1969 *Flights into Yesterday*. New York.

Devereux P. 1991 *Earth Memory. The Holistic Earth Mysteries Approach to Decoding Ancient Sacred Sites*. London: Quantum.

Dobinson C. & Gilchrist R. eds 1986 *Archaeology: Politics and the Public*. Papers given to the Young Archaeologists Conference in York 1984. York: York Univ Archaeol Publ 5.

Doran J. E. & Hodson F. R. 1975 *Mathematics and Computers in Archaeology*. Edinburgh: Edinburgh University Press.

Drake J. C. & Fahy A. M. 1987 *Guide to Archaeology on Community Programme*. (Inst Fld Archaeol Occas Pap 2.) Birmingham: IFA.

Drewett P. L. 1987 'The Institute of Archaeology and Field Archaeology', *Univ London Inst Archaeol Bull* 24, 127–39.

Dromgoole S. 1989 'Protection of Historic Wreck: The UK Approach. Part I: The Present Legal Framework', *Int J of Estuarine and Coastal Law* 4: 1, 26–51.

Dromgoole S. 1992 'Transfer of Administrative Responsibility for Historic Wrecks', *Int J of Estuarine and Coastal Law* 7: 1, 68–74.

EHM (Hanna M.) 1986 *English Heritage Monitor 1986: A Yearly Analysis of Trends Affecting England's Architectural Heritage*. London: English Tourist Board.

Edis J., Macleod D. & Bewley R. 1989 'An Archaeologist's Guide to Classification of Cropmarks and Soilmarks', *Antiquity* 63, 112–26.

Edwards C. 1989 'The Responsible Developer – What Should He Do?' (Published on a facsimile of the official notepaper of Prudential Portfolio Managers Limited.) In: *Pre-Conference Papers: Archaeological Remains and Development 27th November 1989*, 41–6. London: Henry Stewart Conference Studies.

Edwards L. S. 1977 'A Modified Pseudosection for Resistivity and I.P.', *Geophysics* 42, 1020–36.

Edwards R. 1991 *Fit for the Future: Report of the National Parks Review Panel*. Cheltenham.

Ellison A. B. 1981 *A Policy for Archaeological Investigation in Wessex: 1980–85*. Salisbury: Trust for Wessex Archaeology.

Emmott K. 1987 'A Child's Eye View of the Past', *Archaeological Review from Cambridge* 6: 2, 129–42.

English Heritage, 1986, *Rescue Archaeology Funding: A Policy Statement*. London: English Heritage.

English Heritage 1989 *The Management of Archaeology Projects*. London: HBMC.

English Heritage 1990 'Competitive Tendering for Archaeology Projects', *Fld Archaeol* 13, 216.

English Heritage 1991a *Exploring Our Past: Strategies for the Archaeology of England*. London: HBMC.

English Heritage 1991b *The Management of Archaeological Projects*. London: HBMC. 2nd edn.

English Heritage 1991c 'Rescue Archaeology Funding: A Policy Statement', *Engl Heritage Conserv Bull* 14, 7–9.

English Heritage 1991d 'English Heritage Corporate Plan 1991–95', *Engl Heritage Conserv Bull* 15 (suppl).

English Heritage 1991e *Archaeology Review 1990–91*. London: HBMC.

English Heritage 1992a *Managing England's Heritage: Setting Our Priorities for the 1990s*. London: English Heritage (pamphlet circulated to members).

English Heritage 1992b *New Work in Historic Churches*. London: HBMC.

English Heritage 1992c *Development Plan Policies for Archaeology: Advice Note for Local Planning Authorities*. London: HBMC.

English Heritage n. d. *An Analysis of Central Government (DAMHB) Support in 1982/83 for the Recording of Archaeological Sites and Landscapes in Advance of Their Destruction*. London: HBMC.

English Heritage/MAFF (Ministry of Agriculture, Fisheries & Food) n. d. *Farming Historic Landscapes and People*. London: English Heritage and Ministry of Agriculture, Farming and Fisheries.

261

Evans C. 1989 'Digging with the Pen: Novel Archaeologies and Literary Traditions', *Archaeological Review from Cambridge* 8: 2, 185–211.

FJC (Faculty Jurisdiction Commission) Report 1984 *The Continuing Care of Churches and Cathedrals; the Report of the Faculty Jurisdiction Commission.* London: Church Information Office.

FRC (Fife Regional Council) 1992 *A List of Archaeological Sites of Regional Importance.* Glenrothes: Fife Reg Counc Econ Development Planning Dept.

Fawcett J. ed. 1976 *The Future of the Past.* London: Thames & Hudson.

Featherstone M. ed. 1990 *Global Culture. Nationalism, Globalization and Modernity.* London: Sage Publications.

Firth A. & Ferrari B. 1992 'Archaeology and Marine Protected Areas', *Int J Nautical Archaeol* 21: 1, 67–9.

Fisher A. R. 1985 'Winklebury Hillfort: A Study of Artifact Distribution from Subsoil Features', *Proc Prehist Soc* 51, 167–80.

Fisher P. M. 1980 'Applications of Technical Devices in Archaeology: The Use of X-rays, Microscope, Electrical and Electromagnetic Devices and Subsurface Interface Radar', *Studies in Mediterranean Archaeology* 63, 1–64.

'Fitzpatrick L.' (pseudonym) 1991 'Developer Column', *Fld Archaeol* 15, 266.

'Fitzpatrick L.' (pseudonym) 1992 'Developer Column', *Fld Archaeol* 16, 292.

Fleming A. 1988 *The Dartmoor Reaves. Investigating Prehistoric Land Divisions.* London: Batsford.

Flinder A. & McGrail S. 1990 'The United Kingdom Advisory Committee on Historic Wreck Sites', *Int J Nautical Archaeol* 19: 2, 93–102.

Forestry Commission 1991 *Grants and Procedures.* Edinburgh: Forestry Commission.

Fowler P. J. 1974 'Motorways and Archaeology', in Rahtz 1974b, 113–29.

Fowler P. J. 1987 'What Price the Man-made Heritage?', *Antiquity* 61, 409–23.

Fowler P. J. 1989 'Heritage: A Post-Modernist Perspective', in Uzzell 1989a, 57–63.

Fowler P. J. 1992 *The Past in Contemporary Society. Then, Now.* London: Routledge.

Fraser D. 1984 'Sites and Monuments Records: The State of the Art', in Burrow, 47–55.

Fraser D. 1986 'The Role of Archaeological Record Systems in the Management of Monuments', in Hughes & Rowley, 17–26.

Frayling C. 1992 *The Face of Tutankhamun.* London: Faber & Faber.

Frere S. S. 1988 'Roman Britain since Haverfield and Richmond', *History and Archaeology Review* 3, Spring 1988, 31–6. Gloucester: Alan Sutton.

Friedman J. & Rowlands M. 1977 *The Evolution of Social Systems.* London: Duckworth.

Friell J. G. P. 1991 'Archaeology and the Trunk Roads Programme', *Engl Heritage Conserv Bull* 13, 8.

Fulford M. G. & Huddleston K. 1991 *The Current State of Romano-British Pottery Studies: A Review for English Heritage.* (English Heritage Occas Pap 1.) London: HBMC.

Fulford M. G. & Nichols E. eds 1992 *Developing Landscapes of Lowland Britain. The Archaeology of the British Gravels: A Review.* (Soc Antiq Lond Occas Pap 14.) London.

Gaffney C. F., Gater J. A. & Ovenden S. M. 1991 *The Use of Geophysical Techniques in Archaeological Evaluations.* (IFA Techn Pap 9.) Birmingham: IFA.

García Fernández J. 1987 *Legislación sobre Patrimonio Histórico.* Madrid: Editorial Tecnos.

García Fernández J. 1989 'The New Spanish Heritage Legislation', in Cleere, 182–94.

Garrett-Frost S. 1992 *The Law and Burial Archaeology.* (Inst Fld Archaeol Tech Pap 11.) Birmingham: IFA.

Garrison L. 1990 'The Black Historical Past in British Education', in Stone & MacKenzie, 231–44.

Gater J. 1990 'Professional Standards in Archaeological Geophysics', *Fld Archaeol* 13, 217.

Gathercole P. & Lowenthal D. eds 1990 *The Politics of the Past.* London: Unwin Hyman.

Gero J. 1989 'Producing Prehistory, Controlling the Past: The Case of New England Beehives', in Pinsky V. & Wylie A. eds *Critical Traditions in Contemporary Archaeology: Essays in the Philosophy, History and Socio-politics of Archaeology*, 96–103. Cambridge: Cambridge University Press.

Gero J. & Conkey M. 1991 *Engendering Archaeology.* Oxford: Blackwell.

Gibbs L. 1987 'Identifying Gender Representation in the Archaeological Record: A Contextual Study', in Hodder, 79–89.

'Gildas' 1988 'Le déclin et la chute de l'archéologie britannique', *Nouvelles archéol* 31, 40–2.

Goodale T.L. & Witt P.A. eds 1985 *Recreation and Leisure: Issues in an Era of Change.* State College, Pennsylvania: Venture.

Gould R.A. & Schiffer M.B. eds 1981 *Modern Material Culture: The Archaeology of Us*. New York: Academic Press.

Goulty N. R., Gibson J. P. C., Moore J. G. & Welfare H. 1990 'Delineation of the Vallum at Vindolanda, Hadrian's Wall, by Shear-wave Seismic Refraction Survey', *Archaeometry* 32, 71–82.

Goyder J. 1992 'Treaties and EC Matters. European Community Free Movement of Cultural Goods and European Community Law', *International Journal of Cultural Property* 1: 1, 219–25.

Green E. L. ed. 1984 *Ethics and Values in Archaeology*. New York: The Free Press (Macmillan).

Gregory T. 1983 'The Impact of Metal Detecting on Archaeology and the Public', *Archaeological Review from Cambridge* 2: 1, 5–8.

Gregory T. 1986 'Whose Fault is Treasure-hunting?', in Dobinson & Gilchrist, 25–7.

Griffith F. M. 1990 'Aerial Reconnaissance in Mainland Britain in the Summer of 1989', *Antiquity* 64, 14–33.

Griffiths M. 1991 'Past Perfect? The DoE Planning Policy Guidance on Archaeology and Planning', *Mineral Planning* 46, 9–12.

Grimes W. F. 1960 *Excavation on Defence Sites 1939–1945*. London: HMSO.

Grimes W. F. 1968 *The Excavation of Roman and Medieval London*. London: Routledge & Kegan Paul.

Grinsell L., Rahtz P. & Warhurst A. 1966 *The Preparation of Archaeological Reports*, London. (2nd edn, 1974, by Grinsell, Rahtz & Price-Williams, D.)

Groube L. M. 1978 'Priorities and Problems in Dorset Archaeology', in Darvill *et al.*, 29–52.

Groube L. M. & Bowden M. 1982 *The Archaeology of Rural Dorset: Past, Present and Future*. (Dorset Nat Hist & Archaeol Soc Monogr 4.) Dorchester.

Gurney D. 1992 'Phosphate and Magnetic Susceptibility Surveys of the Ploughsoil and Determinations from Features', in Gregory A. K. *Excavations in Thetford 1980–1982: Fison Way*, 181–7.

HBMC (Historic Buildings and Monuments Commission for England) 1989 *English Heritage Report and Accounts 1988–1989*. London: HBMC.

HMSO 1987 *House of Commons. First Report from the Environment Committee, Session 1986–87, Historic Buildings and Ancient Monuments* (Sir Hugh Rossi, Chairman). 3 vols. London: HMSO.

HSE (Health and Safety Executive) 1990 *Diving Operations at Work: Guidance on Regulations*. London: HMSO.

Halkon P., Corbishley M. & Binns G. eds 1992 *The Archaeology Resource Book 1992*. London: CBA & English Heritage.

Hamlin A. 1989 'Government Archaeology in Northern Ireland', in Cleere, 171–81.

Hamlin A. & Lynn C. eds 1988 *Pieces of the Past: Archaeological Excavations by DoE (NI) 1970–1986*. Belfast: HMSO.

Hampton J. N. 1989 'The Air Photography Unit of the Royal Commission on the Historical Monuments of England 1965–85', in Kennedy 1989, 13–28.

Hart M. 1987 'The SERC Experiment in Science-based Archaeology', *Proc Brit Academy* 73, 1–22.

Harvey D. 1989 *The Condition of Postmodernity. An Enquiry Into the Origins of Cultural Change*. Oxford: Blackwell.

Hawkes C. F. C. 1954 'Archaeological Theory and Method: Some Suggestions From the Old World', *American Anthropologist* 56, 155–68.

Heaton M. 1988 'Contract Archaeology (Review of Proceedings at the 1988 Archaeology in Britain Conference)', *Fld Archaeol* 9, 132.

Heaton M. 1991 Letter to the Editor, *Fld Archaeol* 14, 259.

Heighway C. M. ed. 1972 *The Erosion of History: Archaeology and Planning in Towns*. London: CBA.

Heron C. P. & Gaffney C. F. 1987 'Archaeogeophysics and the Site: Ohm Sweet Ohm?', in Gaffney C. F. & Gaffney V. L. eds *Pragmatic Archaeology: Theory in Crisis?*, 71–81.(Brit Archaeol Rep Brit Ser 167.) Oxford: BAR.

Herrmann J. ed. 1981 *Gesetze, Verordnungen und Bestimmungen der DDR: Archäologische Denkmale und Umweltgestaltung*, 233–55. Berlin: Akademie-Verlag.

Hewison R. 1987 *The Heritage Industry: Britain in a Climate of Decline*. London: Methuen.

Hewison R. 1989 'Heritage: An Interpretation', in Uzzell 1989a, 15–23.

Higgs E. S. ed. 1972 *Papers in Economic Prehistory*. Cambridge: Cambridge University Press.

Hildred A. & Oxley I. 1992 'Maritima Revisited', *Fld Archaeol* 17, 335–6.

Hill Sir George 1936 *Treasure Trove in Law and Practice from the Earliest Time to the Present Day*. Oxford: Clarendon Press.

Hill J. 1987 'Confessions of an Archaeologist Who Dug in School: or, is Archaeology in Schools a Good or Desirable Thing?', *Archaeological Review from Cambridge* 6: 2, 143–56.

Hill J. D. 1989 'Re-thinking the Iron Age', *Scott Archaeol Rev* 6, 16–24.

Hinchliffe J. 1986 *Preservation by Record: The Work of the Central Archaeological Unit 1975–85*. London: HBMC.

Hingst H. 1964 *Denkmalschutz und Denkmalpflege in Deutschland*. (Badische Fundberichte, Sonderheft 7.)

Hingst H. & Lipowschek A. eds 1975 *Europäische Denkmalschutzgesetze in deutscher Übersetzung*. Neumünster: Karl Wachholtz.

Hinton D. A. 1992 'Confidentiality and PPG 16', *British Archaeological News* 7: 6, 74.

Historic Scotland 1991 *Corporate Plan 1991–94*. Edinburgh: HS.

Hoare R. Colt 1812 *The Ancient History of Wiltshire*. London: Miller.

Hobley, B. 1987 'Rescue Archaeology and Planning', *J Roy Town Planning Inst (The Planner)* 73: 5, May, 25–7.

Hodder I. 1982 *Symbols in Action*. Cambridge: Cambridge University Press.

Hodder I. 1986 *Reading the Past*. Cambridge: Cambridge University Press.

Hodder I. 1989 'Writing Archaeology: Site Reports in Context', *Antiquity* 63, 268–74.

Hodder I. 1992 *Theory and Practice in Archaeology*. London: Routledge.

Hodder I. ed. 1987 *The Archaeology of Contextual Meanings*. Cambridge: Cambridge University Press.

Hodder I. ed. 1989 *The Meaning of Things. Material Culture and Symbolic Expression*. London: Unwin Hyman.

Hodder I., Parker Pearson M., Peck N. & Stone P. 1985 'Archaeology, Knowledge and Society: Surveys in Britain'. Cambridge. (Typescript.)

Hodson F. R., Sneath P. & Doran J. 1966 'Some Experiments in the Numerical Analysis of Archaeological Data', *Biometrika* 53, 311–24.

Hooper-Greenhill E. 1991 *Museum and Gallery Education*. Leicester: Leicester University Press.

Horne D. 1984 *The Great Museum: The Re-presentation of History*. London: Pluto.

Horsman V., Milne C. & Milne G. 1990 *Aspects of Saxo-Norman London I: Building and Street Development*. (London and Middlesex Archaeological Society, Special Papers.)

Howarth W. 1992 *Wisdom's Law of Watercourses*. Crayford, Kent: Shaw and Sons Ltd. 5th edn.

Hughes M. & Rowley L. eds 1986 *The Management and Presentation of Field Monuments*. Oxford: University Dept of External Stud.

Hunter J. R. 1992 *Your Church and Its Archaeology*. Bradford: Diocese of Bradford.

IAM (Inspectorate of Ancient Monuments) 1984 *England's Archaeological Resource: A Rapid Quantification of the National Archaeological Resource and a Comparison with the Schedule of Ancient Monuments*. London: IAM.

ICAHM (International Committee on Archaeological Heritage Management) 1989 *Archaeology and Society: Large Scale Rescue Operations – Their Possibilities and Problems*. (ICAHM Report 1.) Stockholm: ICAHM.

ICAHM 1990 *Charter for the Protection and Management of the Archaeological Heritage*. Paris: ICOMOS.

ICOMOS (International Council on Monuments and Sites) 1990 *Directory of Archaeological Heritage Management*. Oslo: ICOMOS.

IFA (Institute of Field Archaeologists) 1987 *The Institute of Field Archaeologists: Memorandum and Articles of Association*. Birmingham : IFA (as amended).

IFA 1988a *By-Laws of the Institute of Field Archaeologists: Code of Conduct*. Birmingham: IFA (as amended).

IFA 1988b 'Report of the Interim Procurement Regulation Steering Committee', in *IFA Annual Report* 5. Birmingham: IFA.

IFA 1989 *Directory of Members 1988–1989*. Birmingham: IFA.

IFA 1990 *By-Laws of the Institute of Field Archaeologists: Code of Approved Practice for the Regulation of Contractual Arrangements in Field Archaeology*. Birmingham: IFA.

IFA 1992 *Directory of Educational Opportunities in Archaeology*. Birmingham: IFA.

IFA n.d. Pamphlet on Membership. IFA: Birmingham (also 1992 edition).

IFA Council 1987 'Notes from Council – Directory of Consultants', *Fld Archaeol* 7, 89.

Iles R. 1992 'Integrated Conservation Management on Private Estates', in Macinnes & Wickham-Jones, 134–9.

Imai T., Sakayama T. & Kaiomori T. 1987 'Use of Ground Probing Radar and Resistivity Surveys for Archaeological Investigations', *Geophysics* 52, 137–50.

Inland Revenue 1986 *Capital Taxation and the National Heritage*. London: HMSO.

JNAPC (Joint Nautical Archaeology Policy Committee) 1989 *Heritage at Sea: Proposals for the Better Protection of Archaeological Sites Underwater*. London: National Maritime Museum.

Jaworski T. 1981 *Legal Foundations of the Protections of Cultural Property in Poland*. Warsaw: Ministry of Culture and Arts.

Jesson M. 1973 *The Archaeology of Churches*. London: CBA.

Jobey G. 1990 'The Society of Antiquaries of Newcastle-upon-Tyne', *Archaeol Aeliana* 5 ser. 18, 197–216.

Jones G. D. B. 1984 *Past Imperfect. The Story of Rescue Archaeology*. London: Heinemann.

Joyce S., Newbury, M. & Stone P. eds 1987 *Degree, Digging, Dole: Our Future? Papers Presented at YAC '85 Southampton*. Southampton: YAC '85 Organising Committee for Southampton Univ Archaeol Soc.

Keene D. 1985 *Survey of Medieval Winchester* (Winchester Studies, 2). Oxford: Clarendon Press.

Keene S. ed. 1980 *Conservation, Archaeology and Museums*. (Occas Pap, 1, UK Institute for Conservation.)

Keller G. V. & Frischknecht F. C. 1966 *Electrical Methods in Geophysical Prospecting*. London: Pergamon Press.

Kennedy D. ed. 1989 *Into the Sun. Essays in Air Photography in Archaeology in Honour of Derrick Riley*. Sheffield: University Dept of Prehist & Archaeol.

Kennet W. 1972 *Preservation*. London: Temple Smith.

King T. F., Hickman P. P. & Berg G. 1977 *Anthropology in Historic Preservation; Caring for Culture's Clutter*. New York: Academic Press.

Kolb D. 1990 *Postmodern Sophistications. Philosophy, Architecture and Tradition*. Chicago and London: University of Chicago Press.

Kristiansen, K. 1984 'Denmark', in Cleere, 21–36.

LUC (Land Use Consultants) 1992 *Conservation Issues in Strategic Plans*. Rugby, Warwickshire: LUC. (Consultation draft prepared on behalf of the Countryside Commission, English Heritage and English Nature.)

Lamb R. G. 1982 *The Archaeological Sites and Monuments of Scotland, 16: Rousay, Egilsay and Wyre, Orkney Islands Area*. Edinburgh: RCAHMS.

Lambrick G. 1991 'Competitive Tendering and Archaeological Research: The Development of a CBA View', in Swain, 21–31.

Lambrick G. 1992 'The Importance of the Cultural Heritage in a Green World: Towards the Development of Landscape Integrity Assessment', in Macinnes & Wickham-Jones, 105–26.

Lambrick G. ed. 1985 *Archaeology and Nature Conservation*. Oxford: University Dept of External Stud.

Lang N. A. R. 1992 'Sites and Monuments Records in Great Britain', in Larsen, 171–83.

Larsen C. U. ed. 1992 *Sites and Monuments: National Archaeological Records*. Copenhagen: National Museum of Denmark.

Latham R. & Matthews W. eds 1974 *The Diary of Samuel Pepys*, vol. 8 (for 1667). London: G. Bell & Sons.

Lawrence E. 1989 'The Costs of An Interesting Find'. In: *Pre-Conference Papers: Archaeological Remains and Development 27th November 1989*, 47–56. London: Henry Stewart Conference Studies.

Lawson A. J. 1987 'Research Strategies in Wessex', in Mytum & Waugh, 79–85.

Lawson A. J. ed. 1989 'Draft Approved Practice in Contracting Archaeology and Competitive Tendering', *Fld Archaeol* 11, 179.

Layton R. ed. 1989a *Conflict in the Archaeology of Living Traditions* (One World Archaeology, 8). London: Unwin Hyman.

Layton R. ed. 1989b *Who Needs the Past? Indigenous Values and Archaeology* (One World Archaeology, 5). London: Unwin Hyman.

Le Borgne E. 1955 'Susceptibilité Magnétique Anormale du Sol Superficiel', *Annales de Géophysique* 11, 399–419.

Le Borgne E. 1960 'Influences du Feu sur les Propriétés Magnétiques du Sol et du Granit', *Annales de Géophysique* 16, 159–95.

Le Patourel H. E. J. 1972 *The Moated Sites of Yorkshire*. (Soc for Medieval Archaeol Monogr 5.) London.

Leigh D. 1982 'The Selection, Conservation and Storage of Archaeological Finds', *Mus J* 82: 2, 115–16.

Lewis G. 1989 *For Instruction and Recreation: A Centenary History of the Museums Association*. London: Quiller Press.

Lock D. 1988 'Project Management', in Lock D. & Farrow N. eds *The Gower Handbook of Management*, 599–630. London: Gower Publishing Co.

Longworth I. H. 1992 'Snettisham Revisited', *International Journal of Cultural Property* 1: 2, 333–41.

Lorenzo J. L. 1984 'Mexico', in Cleere, 89–100.

Lowenthal D. 1985 *The Past is a Foreign Country*. Cambridge: Cambridge University Press.

Lowenthal D. 1989 'Heritage Revisited: A Concluding Address', in Uzzell 1989b, 212–16.

Lowenthal D. & Binney M. eds 1981 *Our Past Before Us. Why Do We Save It?* London: Temple Smith.

MAP 1: see English Heritage 1989.

MAP 2: see English Heritage 1991b.

MGC (Museums and Galleries Commission) 1992 *Standards in the Museum Care of Archaeological Collections*. London: Museums and Galleries Commission.

MoF (Ministry of Finance, Northern Ireland) 1966 *An Archaeological Survey of County Down*. Belfast: HMSO.

McBryde I. ed. 1985 *Who Owns the Past?* Oxford: Oxford University Press.

McGimsey III C. R., & Davies H. A. 1984 'United States of America', in Cleere, 116–24.

Macinnes L. 1990 'Ancient Monuments in the Scottish Countryside: Their Protection and Management', *Scott Archaeol Rev* 7, 131-8.

Macinnes L. 1991 'Preserving the Past for the Future', in Hanson W. S. & Slater E. A. eds *Scottish Archaeology: New Perceptions*, 196–217. Aberdeen: Aberdeen University Press.

Macinnes L. & Wickham-Jones C.R. eds 1992 *All Natural Things: Archaeology and the Green Debate*. (Oxbow Monogr 21.) Oxford: Oxbow.

MacIvor I. & Fawcett R. 1983 'Planks from the Shipwreck of Time: An Account of Ancient Monumentry, Then and Now', in Magnusson M. ed. *Echoes in Stone*, 9–27. Edinburgh: Scottish Development Department.

Malim T. 1990 *Archaeology on the Cambridgeshire County Farms Estate: A Review of Archaeological Management on the Estate*. Cambridge: Cambridgeshire County Council & English Heritage.

Manley J. 1987 'Archaeology and Planning: A Welsh Perspective', *J Plann Envir Law*, 466–84, 552–63.

Marine Conservation Society 1991 *The Challenge of Marine Protected Areas*. Ross on Wye: Marine Conservation Society.

Marine Directorate, Department of Transport 1984 *Proposals for Legislation on Marine Wreck: A Consultative Document*. London: DoT.

Marine Directorate, Department of Transport 1986 *Historic Wrecks. Guidance Note*. London: DoT.

Marvell A. 1990 'Evaluating Archaeological Sites – Methods and Techniques: ABC 1990', *Fld Archaeol* 13, 230.

Maxwell G. S. 1992 'Aerial Survey in South-East Perth', *Current Archaeol* 131, 451–4.

Maxwell G. S. ed. 1983 *The Impact of Aerial Reconnaissance on Archaeology*. (Res Rep Counc Brit Archaeol 49.) London: CBA.

Mellor D. 1992 'Face to Face with the Facts of Strife', *The Guardian* 2, 4 Dec.

Mellor J. 1986 'A Community Archaeology Project in Leicestershire', *Rescue News* 40, 3.

Mellor J. 1988 'MSC – What Next? The Adult Training Initiative and the Role of Archaeological Bodies', *Rescue News* 45, 3.

Merriman N. 1991 *Beyond the Glass Case: The Past, Heritage and the Public*. Leicester: Leicester University Press.

Meyer K. E. 1992 'Digging Berlin's Chamber of Horrors', *Archaeology* 45: 4, 24–9.

Miles J. 1992 'Environmental Conservation and Archaeology: Is There a Need for Integrated Designations?', in Macinnes & Wickham-Jones, 97–104.

Miles R., Alt M., Gosling D., Lewis B. & Tout A. eds 1988 *The Design of Educational Exhibits*. London: Unwin Hyman.

Miller D., Rowlands M. & Larsen M.T. eds 1989 *Domination and Resistance*. London: Unwin Hyman.

Miller D. & Tilley C. eds 1984 *Ideology, Power and Prehistory*. Cambridge: Cambridge University Press.

Millett M. 1990 *The Romanisation of Britain: An Essay in Archaeological Interpretation*. Cambridge: Cambridge University Press.

Morgan Evans D. 1985 'The Management of Historic Landscapes', in Lambrick, 89–94.

Morgan Evans D. 1986 'The Management of Archaeological Sites', in Hughes & Rowley, 9–16.

Morgan Evans D. 1992 'The Paradox of Salisbury Plain', in Macinnes & Wickham-Jones, 176–80.

Morris R. K. 1989 *Churches in the Landscape*. London: Dent.

Murray D. M. 1992 'Towards Harmony: A View of the Scottish Archaeological Database', in Larsen, 209–16.

Museums Association 1989 'Museums – a National Resource, a National Responsibility', *Mus J* 89: 8, 36–7.

Mynors C. 1989 *Listed Buildings and Conservation Areas*. London: Longman.

Mytum H. & Waugh K. eds 1987 *Rescue Archaeology – What's Next?* (Univ York Dept Archaeol Monogr 6.) York.

NDC (Newbury District Council) 1990 *Newbury Local Plan*. Newbury: Newbury District Council.

NPPG 1992: see SOEnD 1992a.

NRA (National Rivers Authority) 1991 *The Water Environment: Our Cultural Heritage*. Solihull: NRA (Severn-Trent Region.)

Newsom G. H. 1988 *Faculty Jurisdiction of the Church of England*. London: Sweet & Maxwell.

Nishimura Y. & Kamai H. 1991 'A Study on the Application of Geophysical Prospection', in Pernicka & Wagner, 757–63.

Noel M. & Walker R. 1991 'Development of a Resistivity Tomography System for Imaging Archaeological Structures', in Pernicka & Wagner, 767–76.

Noel M. & Xu B. 1991 'Archaeological Investigation by Electrical Resistivity Tomography: A Preliminary Study', *Geophys J Int* 107, 95–102.

Norfolk County Council 1988, *Norfolk Countryside Strategy: 6, Historic Landscapes and Archaeology*. Draft Consultative Report, June 1988. Norwich: NCC.

Norman B. 1983, 'Archaeology and Television', *Archaeological Review from Cambridge* 2: 1, 27–32.

O'Keefe P.J. & Prott L.V. 1984 *Law and the Cultural Heritage*. Vol. 1: *Discovery and Excavation*. Abingdon: Professional Books.

Olivier A. 1989 *Safety in Archaeological Fieldwork*. (CBA Practical Handbooks in Archaeology 6). London: CBA.

Open University 1988 *Professional Judgement*. Milton Keynes: Open University. D 321.

Owen-John H. 1986 *Rescue Archaeology in Wales*. Swansea: University College (Mainwairing-Hughes Award Ser 3).

Owen-John H. 1992 'Who Needs Archaeology?', in Macinnes & Wickham-Jones, 89–96.

PAN 1992: see SOEnD, 1992b.

PPG 16 1990: see DoE 1990a.

PPG 16 (Wales) 1991: see Welsh Office 1991.

Pagoda Projects 1992 *An Evaluation of the Impact of PPG 16 on Archaeology & Planning*. London: public report (dated 31 January 1992) commissioned by English Heritage.

Palmer N. E. 1981 'Treasure Trove and the Protection of Antiquities', *Modern Law Review* 44, 178–87.

Palmer R. & Cox C. 1993 *Uses of Aerial Photography in Archaeological Evaluations*. (IFA Techn Pap 12.) Birmingham: IFA.

Parsons D. 1989 *Churches and Chapels: Investigating Places of Worship* (Counc Brit Archaeol Practical Handbook, 8). London: CBA.

Paynter R. 1990 'Afro-Americans in the Massachusetts Historical Landscape', in Gathercole & Lowenthal, 49–62.

Pearce S. 1990 *Archaeological Curatorship*. Leicester: Leicester University Press.

Pernicka E. & Wagner G. A. eds 1991, *Archaeometry '90*. Basel: Birkhäuser Verlag.

Philp B. 1974 'Kent, Dover, and the CIB Corps', in Rahtz 1974b, 73–8

Pitt Rivers A. H. L. F. 1874 'Principles of Classification', reprinted in Pitt Rivers, *The Evolution of Culture*, 1906, Oxford: Oxford University Press.

Pitt Rivers A. H. L. F. 1887–98 *Excavations in Cranborne Chase*. London: 4 vols.

Pollard A. M. 1989 'The Funding of Archaeological Science', *Fld Archaeol* 11, 173–5.

Pollard A. M. 1990 *Report of the Co-ordinator for Science-Based Archaeology 1987–1990*. Swindon: Science & Engineering Research Council.

Powell K. & de la Hey C. 1987 *Churches: A Question of Conversion*. London: SAVE Britain's Heritage.

Prehistoric Society 1988 *Saving our Prehistoric Heritage. Landscapes under Threat*. London: The Prehistoric Society.

Princ M. 1984 'Czechoslovakia', in Cleere, 12–20.

Prott L. V. & O'Keefe P. J. 1989 *Law and the Cultural Heritage*. Volume 3: *Movement*. London: Butterworths.

Proudfoot E. V. W. 1986 'Commentary – the First Forty Years', *Scott Archaeol Gazette* 12, 2–5.

Proudfoot E. V. W. ed. 1989 *Our Vanishing Heritage: Forestry and Archaeology* (Counc Scott Archaeol Occas Pap 2). Edinburgh: CSA.

Pryor F. 1985 *The Fenland Project Report No. 1: Archaeology and Environment in the Lower Welland Valley* (East Anglian Archaeol Rep 27). Cambridge: Cambridgeshire Archaeological Committee.

Pryor F. 1989 ' "Look What We've Found" – A Case Study in Public Archaeology', *Antiquity* 63, 51–61.

RCAHMS (Royal Commission on the Ancient and Historical Monuments of Scotland) 1990 *North-East Perth: An Archaeological Landscape*. Edinburgh: HMSO.

RCAHMS 1992 *Inventory of Argyll 7*. Edinburgh: HMSO.

RCHME (Royal Commission on the Historical Monuments of England) 1960 *A Matter of Time*. London: HMSO.

RCHME 1968 *An Inventory of Historical Monuments in the County of Cambridgeshire 1: West Cambridgeshire*. London: HMSO.

RCHME 1978 *Royal Commission on the Historical Monuments of England. A Survey of Surveys*. London: RCHME.

RCHME 1991 *The Archaeology of Bokerley Dyke*. London: HMSO.

RCHME 1992a *Annual Report 1991/92*. London: RCHME.

RCHME 1992b *Yorkshire Textile Mills: The Buildings of the Yorkshire Textile Industry 1770–1930*. London: HMSO.

RCHME 1993 *Recording England's Past: A Review of National and Local Sites and Monuments Records in England*. London. (Forthcoming.)

RCHME & English Heritage 1992 *Thesaurus of Archaeological Site Types*. London: RCHME & EH.

Raemaekers J. 1992 'Green Plans and Local Government: An Integrated Approach to the Environment?', in Macinnes & Wickham-Jones, 140–5.

Rahtz P.A. 1985 *Invitation to Archaeology*. Oxford: Blackwell.

Rahtz P. A. 1974a 'Rescue Digging Past and Present', in Rahtz 1974b, 53–72.

Rahtz P. A. ed. 1974b *Rescue Archaeology*. Penguin: Harmondsworth.

Ralston I. & Thomas R. eds 1993 *Archaeology and Environmental Assessment*. (Inst Fld Archaeol Occas Pap 5.) Birmingham: IFA.

Rathje W. 1974 'The Garbage Project: A New Way of Looking at the Problems of Archaeology', *Archaeology* 27, 236–41.

Redman M. 1990 'Archaeology and Development', *J of Planning & Environment Law*, February, 87–98.

Redundant Churches Fund 1990 *Churches in Retirement*. London: HMSO.

Reichstein J. 1984 'Federal Republic of Germany', in Cleere, 37–47.

Renfrew C. 1973 'Monuments, Mobilisation and Social Organisation in Neolithic Wessex', in Renfrew C. ed. *The Explanation of Culture Change*, 539–58. London: Duckworth.

Renfrew C. & Bahn P. 1991 *Archaeology. Theories, Methods, and Practice*. London: Thames & Hudson.

Renfrew C. & Shennan S. J. eds 1982 *Ranking, Resource and Exchange*. Cambridge: Cambridge University Press.

Rhind A. H. 1858 *The Law of Treasure Trove: How Can it be Best Adapted to Subserve the Interests of Archaeology?* Edinburgh: Thomas Constable.

Richards C. & Thomas J. 1984 'Ritual Activity and Structured Deposition in Later Neolithic Wessex', in Bradley R. & Gardiner J. eds *Neolithic Studies*, 189–218 (Brit Archaeol Rep, 133). Oxford: BAR.

Riley D. N. 1987 *Air Photography and Archaeology*. London: Duckworth.

Rodwell W. J. 1987 'Rescue and Research in Churches and Cathedrals', in Mytum & Waugh, 93–8.

Rodwell W. J. 1989 *English Heritage Book of Church Archaeology*. London: Batsford.

Rodwell W. J. & Rodwell K. 1977 *Historic Churches – a Wasting Asset* (Counc Brit Archaeol Res Rep 19). London: CBA.

Ross M. 1991 *Planning and the Heritage*. London: E. & F.N. Spon.

Rowlands M. 1980 'Kinship, Alliance and Exchange in the European Bronze Age', in Barrett J. & Bradley R. eds *Settlement and Society in the British Later Bronze Age*, 15–55. (British Archaeol Rep 83.) Oxford: BAR.

Rowlands M., Kristiansen K. & Larsen M. eds 1987 *Centre and Periphery in the Ancient World*. Cambridge: Cambridge University Press.

Roy Waller Associates Ltd 1991 *Environmental Effects of Surface Mineral Workings*. (Department of the Environment Research Report.) London: HMSO.

SAS (Society of Antiquaries of Scotland) 1974 *Archaeology and Local Government*. Edinburgh: SAS.

SDD (Scottish Development Department) 1989 *List of Ancient Monuments in Scotland*. Edinburgh: HMSO.

SERC (Science & Engineering Research Council) 1985 *SERC Report: The Funding of Research in Science-based Archaeology in Universities and Polytechnics*. Swindon: SERC.

SIBA 1992 *Standards in British Archaeology: Archaeological Desk-Based Studies*. Birmingham. (Draft Standard issued for membership consultation in August 1992 by the Standards in British Archaeology Working Party of the IFA.)

SO (Scottish Office) 1992 *The Structure of Local Government in Scotland: Shaping the New Councils*. Edinburgh: HMSO.

SOEnD (Scottish Office Environment Department) 1992a *National Planning Policy Guideline: Archaeology and Planning* (draft version). Edinburgh: SOEnD.

SOEnD 1992b *Planning Advice Note: Archaeology and Planning* (draft version). Edinburgh: SOEnD.

SPTAAWP (Salisbury Plain Training Area Archaeological Working Party) 1986 *Report 1984–5*. Bristol: Property Services Agency.

St Joseph J. K. S. 1951 'A Survey of Pioneering in Air-photography Past and Future', in Grimes, W. F. ed. *Aspects of Archaeology in Britain and Beyond: Essays Presented to O. G. S. Crawford,* 303–15. London: H.W. Edwards.

St Joseph J. K. S. ed. 1966 *The Uses of Air Photography.* London: A. & C. Black (2nd edn, 1977, London: John Baker).

Saville A. 1990 'Public Inquiry Problems – a Note from the Conservation Co-ordinator', *PAST* (Newsletter of the Prehistoric Society) 4, 11–12.

Schadla-Hall R. T. 1984 'Slightly Looted: A Review of the Jorvik Viking Centre', *Mus J* 84: 2, 62–4.

Schiffer M. 1976 *Behavioural Archaeology.* New York: Academic Press.

Schild R. 1993 'Polish Archaeology in Transition', *Antiquity* 67, 146–50.

Scole Committee, The, 1973 *The Problems and Future of East Anglian Archaeology.*

Scollar I., Tabbagh A., Hesse A. & Herzog, I. 1990 *Archaeological Geophysics and Remote Sensing.* Cambridge: Cambridge University Press.

Scrase T. 1991 'Archaeology and Planning – a Case for Full Integration', *Journ Planning & Environment Law,* December 1991.

Selkirk A. 1988 'What's in a Name?', *Brit Archaeol News* 3: 1, 3.

Selkirk A. 1990 'The Current Archaeology Down to Earth Guide to British Archaeology', *Curr Archaeol* 11, suppl i–xxii.

Selman P. ed. 1988 *Archaeology and Planning.* Stirling: Stirling Univ Environmental Conservation Unit.

Shanks M. & Tilley C. 1987a *Reconstructing Archaeology: Theory and Practice.* Cambridge: Cambridge University Press.

Shanks M. & Tilley C. 1987b *Social Theory and Archaeology.* Oxford: Polity Press.

Shell C. & Robinson P. 1988 'The Recent Reconstruction of the Bush Barrow Lozenge Plate', *Antiquity* 62, 248–60.

Shennan S. J. ed. 1989 *Archaeological Approaches to Cultural Identity.* London: Unwin Hyman.

Shepherd I. A. G. 1986 *Exploring Scotland's Heritage: Grampian.* Edinburgh: HMSO.

Shepherd I. A. G. 1988 'Archaeology in Environmental Conservation in Grampian', in Selman, 27–35.

Shepherd I. A. G. 1989 'Archaeology, Forestry and Planning: A Planner's Problem', in Proudfoot, 31–3.

Shepherd I. A. G. 1992 'The Friendly Forester? Archaeology, Forestry and the Green Movement', in Macinnes & Wickham-Jones, 161–8.

Sheridan A. 1991 'What's Mine is Her Majesty's: The Law in Scotland', in Southworth E. ed. *What's Mine is Yours! – Museum Collecting Policies,* 35–40 (The Museum Archaeologist, 16). London: Society of Museum Archaeologists.

Siehr K. 1992 'Preliminary Draft Unidroit Convention on Stolen or Illegally Exported Cultural Objects (Approved by the Unidroit Study Group on the International Protection of Cultural Property at its Third Session on 26 January 1990)', *International Journal of Cultural Property* 1: 1, 252–5.

Silverstone R. 1989 'Heritage as Media: Some Implications for Research', in Uzzell 1989b, 138–48.

Smith G. S. & Ehrenhard J. E. 1991 *Protecting the Past.* Boca Raton: CRC Press.

Smith K. 1992 'Protected Landscapes: Integrated Approaches to Conservation Management', in Macinnes & Wickham-Jones, 127–33.

Smith L. 1986 'The National Trust Archaeological Survey in the East Midlands', *E Midlands Archaeol* 2, 23–6.

Society of Antiquaries of London 1992 *Archaeological Publication, Archives and Collections: Towards a National Policy.* London. (Typescript draft.)

Sparrow C. 1982 'Treasure Trove: A Lawyer's View', *Antiquity* 56, 199–201.

Spector J. 1991 'What This Awl Means: Toward a Feminist Archaeology', in Gero & Conkey, 386–406.

Spoerry P. 1992a *The Structure and Funding of British Archaeology: The RESCUE Questionnaire 1990–1.* Hertford: Rescue Publications.

Spoerry P. ed. 1992b *Geoprospection in the Archaeological Landscape.* Oxford: Oxbow Books.

Staffordshire County Council 1991 Call for Approved List of Tenderers. *Fld Archaeol* 14, 254.

Stansfield G. 1981 *Effective Interpretative Exhibitions.* Cheltenham: Countryside Commission.

269

Startin B. 1991 'Protecting the Archaeology of our Historic Towns', *Conserv Bull* 13, 14–15.

Stephens C., Aspinall A. & Pocock J. (forthcoming) 'Resistivity Pseudosections, Theoretical Model Field Observations'.

Stevens T. 1989 'The Visitor – Who Cares? Interpretation and Consumer Relations', in Uzzell 1989b, 103–7.

Stewart J. 1980 'Integrated Excavation and Museum Recording Systems: Methods, Theories and Problems', *Museum Archaeologist* 5, 11–27.

Stone P. & MacKenzie R. 1989 'Is There an 'Excluded Past' in Education?', in Uzzell 1989a, 113–20.

Stone P. & MacKenzie R. eds 1990 *The Excluded Past: Archaeology in Education*. London: Unwin Hyman.

Stove G. C. & Addyman P. V. 1989 'Ground Probing Impulse Radar: An Experiment in Archaeological Remote Sensing at York', *Antiquity* 63, 337–42.

Strickland T. J. 1992a Letter to the Editor, *Fld Archaeol* 16, 307.

Strickland T. J. 1992b Letter to the Editor, *Fld Archaeol* 17, 338.

Suddards R. W. with Hicken D. & Hardman P. 1988 *Listed Buildings: The Law and Practice of Historic Buildings, Ancient Monuments and Conservation Areas*. London: Sweet & Maxwell. 2nd edn.

Swain H. ed. 1991 *Competitive Tendering in Archaeology*. Hertford: Rescue Publications/SCAUM.

Tabata R. S. *et al.* eds 1992 *Joining Hands for Quality Tourism. Interpretation, Preservation and the Travel Industry*. (Procs of the Heritage Interpretation International Third Global Congress, 3–8 November 1991.) Honolulu: University of Hawaii.

Tanaka M. 1984 'Japan', in Cleere, 82–8.

Tatton-Brown T. 1989 *Great Cathedrals of Britain*. London: BBC Publications.

Tesch M. 1984 *Antikengesetze zwischen Denkmalschutz und Forschung: eine vergleichende Untersuchung*. Frankfurt-am-Main: Peter Lang Verlag.

Thackray D. W. R. & Hearn K. A. 1985 'Archaeology and Nature Conservation: The Responsibility of the National Trust', in Lambrick, 51–7.

Thapar B. K. 1984 'India', in Cleere, 63–72.

Thomas C. 1974 'Archaeology in Britain 1973', in Rahtz 1974b, 3–15.

Thomas J. 1990 'Monuments From the Inside: The Case of the Irish Megalithic Tombs', *World Archaeol* 22, 168–78.

Thompson G. 1978 *The Museum Environment*. London: Butterworths.

Thompson M. W. 1977 *General Pitt-Rivers: Evolution and Archaeology in the Nineteenth Century*. Bradford-on-Avon: Moonraker Press.

Thompson M. W. 1981 *Ruins: Their Preservation and Display*. London: British Mus Publ.

Thompson M. W. 1983 *Ruins: Their Preservation and Display*. Scarborough.

Tilden F. 1977 *Interpreting Our Heritage*. Chapel Hill: University of North Carolina Press.

Tilley C. 1989 'Discourse and Power', in Miller, Rowlands & Tilley, 41–62.

Tilley C. 1990 *Reading Material Culture*. Oxford: Blackwell.

Tindall, A. & McDonnell, G. 1979 'Universities and Archaeology – a New RESCUE Survey', *Rescue News* 19, 1–3.

Tite M. S. 1972a *Methods of Physical Examination in Archaeology*. London: Seminar Press.

Tite M. S. 1972b 'The Influence of Geology on the Magnetic Susceptibility of Soils on Archaeological Sites', *Archaeometry* 14, 229–36.

Trigger B. 1984 'Alternative Archaeologies: Nationalist, Colonialist, Imperialist', *Man* n.s. 19, 355–70.

UGC (University Grants Committee) 1989 *Report of the Working Party for Archaeology*. London: UGC.

UNESCO (United Nations Educational Scientific and Cultural Organisation) 1985 *Conventions and Recommendations of UNESCO Concerning the Protection of the Cultural Heritage*. Paris: UNESCO.

UNESCO 1985 onward *The Protection of Movable Cultural Property*. (1 volume per state; over 40 published to date.) Paris: UNESCO.

Ucko P. 1987 *Academic Freedom and Apartheid*. London: Duckworth.

Uzzell D. L. ed. 1989a *Heritage Interpretation*. Vol. 1: *The Natural and Built Environment*. London: Belhaven.

Uzzell D.L. ed. 1989b *Heritage Interpretation*. Vol. 2: *The Visitor Experience*. London: Belhaven.

Uzzell D.L. 1989c 'The Hot Interpretation of War and Conflict', in Uzzell 1989a, 33–47.

Vince A. ed. 1992 *Aspects of Saxo-Norman London II: Finds and Environmental Evidence*. (London and Middlesex Archaeological Society, Special Papers.)

Wainwrigh, G. J. 1978 'Theory and Practice in Field Archaeology', in Darvill *et al.*, 11–27.

Wainwright G. J. 1984 'The Pressure of the Past', *Proc Prehist Soc* 50, 1–22.

Wainwright G. J. 1989 'The Management of the English Landscape', in Cleere, 164–70.

Wainwright G. J. 1991 *Archaeological Review 1990–1*. London: English Heritage.

Wainwright G. J. 1992 *Exploring Our Past*. Inaugural lecture, Southampton University.

Wainwright M. 1992 'Bumps and Daisies', *The Guardian* 2, 20 November, 22–3.

Walsh D. (chairman) 1969 *Report of the Committee of Enquiry into the Arrangements for the Protection of Field Monuments 1966–8*. London: HMSO.

Walsh K. 1992 *Representation of the Past: Museums and Heritage in the Post-modern World*. London: Routledge.

Walton P. 1989 *Textiles, Cordage and Raw Fibre from 16–22 Coppergate*. (The Archaeology of York17/5.) London: CBA for York Archaeol Trust.

Waterson M. 1989 'Opening Doors on the Past', in Uzzell 1989a, 48–56.

Watkins M. 1986 'Order or Chaos', in *Dust to Dust: Field Archaeology and Museums*, 54–9 (Society of Museum Archaeologists Conference Procs, Vol. 2).

Watson I. 1991 *Lullingstone Roman Villa: A Handbook for Teachers*. London: English Heritage.

Watson J. 1990 Letter to the Editor, *Fld Archaeol* 13, 235.

Weaver J. 1992 *Exploring England's Heritage: Cumbria to Northumberland*. London: HMSO.

Welsby P. A. 1985 *How the Church of England Works*. London: Church Information Office Publishing.

Welsh Office 1991: *Planning Policy Guidance Note 16: Archaeology and Planning*. Welsh Office: Cardiff.

West S. 1985 *West Stow, The Anglo-Saxon Village*. (East Anglian Archaeol Rep 24.)

West Sussex County Council 1988 Call for a Selected List of Tenderers. *Fld Archaeol* 8, 123.

Whimster R. P. 1983 'Aerial Reconnaissance from Cambridge: a Retrospective View 1945–80', in Maxwell, 92–105.

Whimster R.P. 1989 *The Emerging Past*. London: RCHME.

White R. F. & Iles R. 1991 *Archaeology in National Parks*. Leyburn: National Parks Association.

Wildlife Division, Department of the Environment & Welsh Office 1992a *Marine Consultation Areas: A Consultation Paper*. Draft Circular issued 26 February 1992. Bristol: Directorate of Rural Affairs.

Wildlife Division, Department of the Environment 1992b *Marine Consultation Areas: A Description*. Draft issued February 1992. Bristol: Directorate of Rural Affairs.

Williamson T. & Bellamy L. 1983a *Ley Lines in Question*. Kingswood: World's Work.

Williamson T. & Bellamy L. 1983b 'Ley-lines; Sense and Nonsense on the Fringe', *Archaeological Review from Cambridge* 2: 1, 51–8.

Wilson D. R. 1982 *Air Photo Interpretation for Archaeologists*. London: Batsford.

Wright P 1985 *On Living in an Old Country: The National Past in Contemporary Britain*. London: Verso.

Wynn J. C. 1986 'Archaeological Prospection: An Introduction to the Special Issue', *Geophysics* 51, 533–7.

YCC (York City Council) 1992 *Conservation Policies for York: Archaeology*. York: YCC.

Zhuang Min 1989 'The Administration of China's Archaeological Heritage', in Cleere, 102–8.

INDEX

9, 253; ecclesiastical buildings 89, 97; EH policy 32; ESAs 52; forestry 246; Heritage Coasts 74; Historic Buildings Council for 52; listed buildings 77, 81; local authority archaeologists 34; monuments under Guardianship 49; National Parks 251; NMR 24; planning policy 53; portable antiquities 56–9, 60, 61; PPG 16 (Wales) 45–6, 47, 53, 165; *PPG 20* 73; regional cover 11; Rescue Archaeology Group in 34; scheduled monuments 21, 44, 45, 46; SMRs 25, 103; Tir Cymen scheme 248, 253; underwater sites and wrecks 66, 67; water company land 254; *see also* Cadw; Royal Commission on Ancient and Historical Monuments in Wales

water companies 40, 48, 53, 109, 182, 254; *see also* National Rivers Authority
Water Resources Act (1991) 53
Wessex 36, 150, 155, 220
Wildlife and Countryside Acts 76, 253
Winchester 14, 36, 149, 220–1
Windsor Castle fire 2–5, 195
women 16, 17, 230–1
World Heritage Convention (1972) 123

York 34, 36, 49, 107, 145, 149, 221, 230; Jorvik Centre 227, 236
York Archaeology and Development Study 127, 129, 131, 196